Body-States, Petrucelli's compendium o[f] of eating disorders, is a major contributio[n] and clinically recalcitrant of syndromes nicians, represent mostly an extended interpersonal viewpoint; namely, that the symptoms of eating disorders represent an embodied metaphor for experience with others in a sociocultural matrix. The individual articles are lively, varied, and by no means doctrinaire. This book will be of great interest and value to a wide spectrum of readers.

> —**Edgar A. Levenson**, MD, Fellow Emeritus, Training, Supervising Analyst, and Faculty at the William Alanson White Institute; Author of *Fallacy of Understanding: The Ambiguity of Change* and *The Purloined Self*

While it is usually true that one should not judge a book by its cover, this book may be an exception to that rule. The cover art well captures the disorganized, dissociated, and fragmented minds, bodies, and psychological worlds of many eating-disordered and traumatized people. In *Body-States*, Jean Petrucelli has produced much more than one would expect from even a first-rate anthology of readings; indeed, this book pushes the envelope of current theory and practice. Drawing on recent developments in interpersonal and relational psychoanalysis, this book provides a model for an interdisciplinary and yet theoretically coherent approach to a complex clinical syndrome. While of obvious value to those who treat patients struggling with eating disorders, this book also serves as a basis for examination of such contemporary clinical ideas as enactment, multiple self-states, trauma, dissociation, body-states, and non-verbal communications.

> —**Lewis Aron**, PhD, Director, New York University Postdoctoral Program in Psychotherapy & Psychoanalysis

Nourishment is where we start from, but what happens when food, quite literally, becomes the only real home we have? And what kind of home can food be once it becomes a refuge from relationships, from freer exchanges? Once it becomes a home from home? In *Body-States* we have a book that renews our appetite for these fundamental contemporary questions. With a remarkable range of wit and sympathy, of generosity and intelligence, *Body-States* frees us to think differently about these elemental things. Eating disorders, like all the other so-called disorders, lead us to believe that somewhere there can be an appropriate order. The essays in *Body-States*, in their range and their engagement, show us how we might talk about eating now without telling people how they should live.

> —**Adam Phillips**, psychoanalyst and writer

Open this volume and prepare for an educational feast! The editor, Jean Petrucelli, has once again assembled a superb collection of innovative contributions on the psychodynamic treatment of eating disorders. Impressive in scope, depth, and understanding, this text is filled with papers that are at once wise, practical, theoretically sophisticated, yet highly readable. The essays will appeal to all thoughtful clinicians who seek to integrate contemporary relational approaches with other treatment modalities and cultural considerations into their practice. Specialists in the field of eating disorders will find it an essential reference, laced with examples that offer refreshing insight, hope, and savvy clinical guidance.

—**Kathryn J. Zerbe**, MD, FAED, Training and Supervising Analyst, Oregon Psychoanalytic Center; Author of *The Body Betrayed: Women, Eating Disorders, and Treatment* and *Integrated Treatment of Eating Disorders: Beyond the Body Betrayed*

BODY-STATES: INTERPERSONAL AND RELATIONAL PERSPECTIVES ON THE TREATMENT OF EATING DISORDERS

In this edited volume, Jean Petrucelli brings together the work of talented clinicians and researchers steeped in working with patients with eating disorders for the past 10 to 35 years. Eating disorders are about body-states and their relational meanings. The split of *mindbody* functioning is enacted in many arenas in the eating-disordered patient's life. Concretely, a patient believes that disciplining or controlling his or her body is a means to psychic equilibrium and interpersonal effectiveness. The collected chapters in *Body-States: Interpersonal and Relational Perspectives on the Treatment of Eating Disorders* elaborate the essential role of linking symptoms with their emotional and interpersonal meanings in the context of the therapy relationship so that eating-disordered patients can find their way out and survive the unbearable.

The contributors bridge the gaps in varied protocols for recovery, illustrating that, at its core, trust in the reliability of the humanness of the other is necessary for patients to develop, regain, or have—for the first time—a stable body. They illustrate how embodied experience must be cultivated in the patient/therapist relationship as a felt experience so patients can experience their bodies as their own, to be lived in and enjoyed, rather than as an "other" to be managed.

In this collection, Petrucelli convincingly demonstrates how interpersonal and relational treatments address eating problems, body image, and "problems in living." *Body-States: Interpersonal and Relational Perspectives on the Treatment of Eating Disorders* will be essential reading for psychoanalysts, psychotherapists, psychologists, psychiatrists, social workers, and a wide range of professionals and lay readers who are interested in the topic and treatment of eating disorders.

Jean Petrucelli is director and co-founder of the Eating Disorders, Compulsions & Addictions Service; supervising analyst, teaching faculty, at the William Alanson White Institute, New York City; adjunct clinical professor of psychology at New York University's postdoctoral program; and editor of several books. She specializes in the interpersonal treatment of eating disorders and addictions, lectures widely throughout the United States, and is in private practice in Manhattan.

PSYCHOANALYSIS IN A NEW KEY BOOK SERIES

DONNEL STERN
Series Editor

When music is played in a new key, the melody does not change, but the notes that make up the composition do: change in the context of continuity, continuity that perseveres through change. Psychoanalysis in a New Key publishes books that share the aims psychoanalysts have always had but that approach them differently. The books in the series are not expected to advance any particular theoretical agenda, although to this date most have been written by analysts from the interpersonal and relational orientations.

The most important contribution of a psychoanalytic book is the communication of something that nudges the reader's grasp of clinical theory and practice in an unexpected direction. Psychoanalysis in a New Key creates a deliberate focus on innovative and unsettling clinical thinking. Because that kind of thinking is encouraged by exploration of the sometimes surprising contributions to psychoanalysis of ideas and findings from other fields, Psychoanalysis in a New Key particularly encourages interdisciplinary studies. Books in the series have married psychoanalysis with dissociation, trauma theory, sociology, and criminology. The series is open to the consideration of studies examining the relationship between psychoanalysis and any other field—for instance, biology, literary and art criticism, philosophy, systems theory, anthropology, and political theory.

But innovation also takes place within the boundaries of psychoanalysis, and Psychoanalysis in a New Key therefore also presents work that reformulates thought and practice without leaving the precincts of the field. Books in the series focus, for example, on the significance of personal values in psychoanalytic practice, on the complex interrelationship between the analyst's clinical work and personal life, on the consequences for the clinical situation when patient and analyst are from different cultures, and on the need for psychoanalysts to accept the degree to which they knowingly satisfy their own wishes during treatment hours, often to the patient's detriment.

BODY-STATES: INTERPERSONAL AND RELATIONAL PERSPECTIVES ON THE TREATMENT OF EATING DISORDERS

Edited by Jean Petrucelli

Routledge
Taylor & Francis Group

NEW YORK AND LONDON

First published 2015
by Routledge
711 Third Avenue, New York, NY 10017

and by Routledge
27 Church Road, Hove, East Sussex, BN3 2FA

Routledge is an imprint of the Taylor & Francis Group, an informa business

© 2015 Taylor & Francis

Library of Congress Cataloging-in-Publication Data
Body-states : interpersonal and relational perspectives on the treatment of
    eating disorders / edited by Jean Petrucelli.
      p. ; cm. — (Psychoanalysis in a new key book series ; vol. 22)
    Includes bibliographical references.
    [DNLM: 1. Eating Disorders—psychology.   2. Eating Disorders—
therapy. WM 175]
    RC552.E18
    616.85′26—dc23
    2014007274

ISBN: 978-0-415-62956-0 (hbk)
ISBN: 978-0-415-62957-7 (pbk)
ISBN: 978-1-315-75817-6 (ebk)

Typeset in Times New Roman
by Apex CoVantage, LLC

TO MY SIBLINGS,
JOANNE, MICHAEL, JOSEPH, TERESA
AND STEVEN
AND THEIR COUNTERPARTS . . . AND
TO OUR
MOM FOR INSPIRING IT ALL.

CONTENTS

CONTENTS

CONTENTS

CONTENTS

ABOUT THE EDITOR

Jean Petrucelli, PhD, is a clinical psychologist and a psychoanalyst, director and co-founder of the Eating Disorders, Compulsions & Addictions Service (EDCAS); fellow; supervising analyst; teaching faculty; conference advisory board chair, and founding director of the Eating, Disorders, Compulsions & Addictions 1-year educational certificate program at the William Alanson White Institute for Psychotherapy and Psychoanalysis. She is an adjunct clinical professor of psychology at the New York University postdoctoral program in psychotherapy and psychoanalysis; associate editor for *Contemporary Psychoanalysis;* and member of the BODI Group, conducting research on the intergenerational transmission of body image and embodiment.

Dr. Petrucelli is editor of the books *Knowing, Not-Knowing & Sort-of-Knowing: Psychoanalysis and the Experience of Uncertainty* (Karnac Books, 2010); and *Longing: Psychoanalytic Musings on Desire* (Karnac Books, 2006); co-editor of the book *Hungers and Compulsions: The Psychodynamic Treatment of Eating Disorders and Addictions* (Rowan & Littlefield/Jason Aronson Inc., 2009, 2001). She specializes in the interpersonal treatment of eating disorders and addictions and lectures at colleges, universities, institutes, psychoanalytic societies, and treatment facilities. She is in private practice in New York City.

CONTRIBUTORS

Iris Ackerman, PhD, is a clinical social worker who received her doctorate from New York University. She completed her postdoctoral training in psychoanalysis and psychotherapy at Adelphi University/Derner Institute of Advanced Psychological Studies and completed a 1-year educational program in Eating Disorders, Compulsions and Addictions at the William Alanson White Institute, NYC. She maintains a full-time private practice in East Rockaway, Long Island, working with adolescents, young adults, and adults in individual, marital, and group therapy.

Catherine Baker-Pitts, PhD, LCSW, is a lecturer at NYU and a faculty member and co-director of the training program for psychotherapists at the Women's Therapy Centre Institute, specializing in eating and body-image problems. She is a founding member of the National Eating Disorders Association as well as a current member of NEDA's Clinical Advisory Council; journal editor of *Eating Disorders* and author of numerous booklets and papers on the intersection of media culture, gender, technology, and the body. She is a member of the BODI Group. In her private practice, she treats people with a range of body-based difficulties and consults with patients pre- and postelective cosmetic surgeries.

Judith Brisman, PhD, is the founding director of the Eating Disorder Resource Center in NYC. She is co-author of *Surviving an Eating Disorder: Strategies for Family and Friends* (3rd edition, 2009) and she is on the editorial board of *Eating Disorders: The Journal of Treatment and Prevention.* Dr. Brisman is an associate editor for the journal *Contemporary Psychoanalysis* and is a supervisor of psychotherapy and EDCAS teaching faculty at the William Alanson White Institute. She has published and lectured extensively regarding the interpersonal treatment of eating disorders and is well known for her expertise in running training seminars and presentations.

Philip M. Bromberg, PhD, is a training and supervising analyst of the William Alanson White Institute, and adjunct clinical professor of psychology at the New York University postdoctoral program in psychoanalysis and psychotherapy. He is emeritus co-editor-in-chief of *Contemporary Psycho-analysis* and an editorial board member of *Psychoanalytic Dialogues and Psychoanalytic Inquiry*. Dr. Bromberg is most widely recognized as author of *Standing in the Spaces: Essays on Clinical Process, Trauma, and Dissociation* (Analytic Press, 1998); *Awakening the Dreamer: Clinical Journeys* (Analytic Press, 2006); and *The Shadow of the Tsunami: And the Growth of the Relational Mind* (Routledge, 2011).

Sandra Buechler, PhD, is a training and supervising analyst at the William Alanson White Institute and faculty for EDCAS. She is a supervisor at Columbia Presbyterian Hospital's internship and postdoctoral programs and at the Institute for Contemporary Psychotherapy. A graduate of the William Alanson White Institute, Dr. Buechler has written extensively on emotions in psychoanalysis, including papers on hope, joy, loneliness, and mourning in the analyst and patient. Her books include *Clinical Values: Emotions that Guide Psychoanalytic Treatment* (Analytic Press, 2004); *Making a Difference in Patients' Lives: Emotional Experience in the Therapeutic Setting* (Routledge, 2008); and *Still Practicing: The Heartaches and Joys of a Clinical Career* (Routledge, 2012).

Dana L. Charatan, PhD, received her doctorate in clinical psychology from the Chicago School of Professional Psychology. She maintains a private practice in Boulder, Colorado, where she works with individuals with various eating, body, and exercise related disorders. Dr. Charatan is a faculty member and clinical supervisor at the Boulder Institute for Psychotherapy and Research, where she teaches and sits on the training committee for their pre- and post-doctoral psychology and master's internship programs. She is a member of the Early Career Committee for APA's Division 39.

A. Mittsi Crossman, MD, received her BA from Yale while working with research teams at the Yale Child Study Center and Conduct Clinic. She attended University of South Florida College of Medicine and completed her residency at Bellevue Hospital in NYC in adult psychiatry at NYU School of Medicine, as well as a fellowship in addiction psychiatry. Dr. Crossman worked as unit chief of the Dual Diagnosis Inpatient Unit in Bellevue Hospital. She is a diplomat for the American Board of Psychiatry and Neurology and in General Psychiatry and Addiction Psychiatry; has an academic appointment with NYU; and has been intensively trained in DBT. Her interests lie in trauma, addictions, eating disorders, and personality disorders and she maintains a private practice in NYC.

Jacqueline Ferraro, DMH, is a fellow, supervisor of psychotherapy, faculty, steering committee member and supervisor of EDCAS; member of executive committee, faculty and supervisor of Child and Adolescent Psychotherapy Training Program; and associate director of Parent Center at the William Alanson White Institute. She is in private practice in NYC treating children, adolescents, and adults.

Carrie D. Gottlieb, PhD, is a clinical psychologist, currently in full-time private practice in Manhattan, specializing in the treatment of adults and adolescents with eating disorders and substance abuse issues, and is a steering committee member and faculty of the EDCAS program at the William Alanson White Institute. She has received training in cognitive behavioral, interpersonal, relapse prevention, and DBT therapies. She participated in post graduate training at the NY State Psychiatric Institute at Columbia Presbyterian Hospital in the division of substance abuse and a 1-year educational program at the William Alanson White Institute in Eating Disorders, Compulsions, and Addictions. In addition, she served as director of the day treatment program at the Renfrew Center of NY.

Caryn Gorden, PsyD, is a clinical psychologist and psychoanalyst in private practice in NYC. She is a graduate of the NYU Postdoctoral Program in Psychotherapy and Psychoanalysis and a Faculty member of the EDCAS program at the William Alanson White Institute and the Stephen Mitchell Center. She presents and writes about the intergenerational transmission of trauma and regularly works with members of the Orthodox Jewish population.

Elizabeth Halsted, PhD, is a supervisor of psychotherapy at WAWI; teaching faculty and steering committee member of EDCAS at the William Alanson White Institute. She is a chapter author of "A Shoe Is Rarely Just a Shoe: Women's Accessories and Their Psyches," in *Longing, Psychoanalytic Musings on Desire,* edited by J. Petrucelli, published by Karnac Books, 2006. She is in private practice in NYC and is a consultant to the Rudolph Steiner School in Manhattan.

Andrea Hamilton, PhD, received her PhD in clinical psychology from Northwestern University and developed specializations in providing psychological consultation to the medically ill and in the treatment of eating disorders and obesity. She participated in a postdoctoral fellowship in consultation-liaison psychiatry at Memorial Sloan-Kettering Cancer Center. She joined the faculty of Memorial Sloan-Kettering and established the Psychosocial Services Division of the Department of Gynecological Oncology where she served as director, providing psychological services and sexual health consultation to those affected by gynecological cancer and its treatments. She has published in the area of psycho-oncology and sexual health. Dr. Hamilton is currently a psychoanalytic candidate in the NYU postdoctoral program in psychotherapy and psychoanalysis, where she has received the Benjamin Wolstein and Harris Fellowships. She currently has a private practice in NYC.

Jill C. Howard, PhD, is a supervisor of psychotherapy, teaching faculty; steering committee member of EDCAS at the William Alanson White Institute. She is an adjunct full professor at Long Island University. She has published numerous papers on infidelity and the use of money in relationships. She is in private practice in NYC.

Sharon Kofman, PhD, MPH, is a training and supervising psychoanalyst, director of the Low-Cost Psychotherapy Supervision Service; faculty member in the Psychoanalytic Training Program, the EDCAS training program, and the Child and Adolescent Training Program at the William Alanson White Institute. She is a member of the faculty at the Parent-Infant Program at the Columbia Psychoanalytic Center and an adjunct lecturer of psychology at the Payne Whitney Woman's program at Weill-Cornell Hospital. She has a private practice in New York City.

Sue Kolod, PhD, is a supervising and training analyst, steering committee and faculty member of EDCAS and former chair of the COF at the William Alanson White Institute. She is co-editor of the blog *Contemporary Psychoanalysis in Action.* Dr. Kolod has written numerous chapters and articles about the impact of hormones on the psyche. Her work also focuses on the impact of hormones on sexuality. She maintains a fulltime private practice in Brooklyn and Manhattan.

Emily A. Kuriloff, PsyD, is a training and supervising analyst, faculty, and member of the EDCAS faculty at the William Alanson White Institute; editor for *Special Issues* and former book review editor for the journal *Contemporary Psychoanalysis;* author of the book *Contemporary Psychoanalysis and the Legacy of the Third Reich: History, Memory and Tradition* (Routledge, 2013).

Zev Labins, MD, is a clinical asst. professor of psychiatry at Columbia University College of Physicians & Surgeons, is certified by the American Board of Psychiatry & Neurology in the specialty of psychiatry and the subspecialty of addiction psychiatry and certified in psychoanalysis by the American Academy of Psychoanalysis and Dynamic Psychiatry. He is a distinguished fellow of the American Psychiatric Association and the American Academy of Psychoanalysis and Dynamic Psychiatry.

Anne F. Malavé, PhD, is a clinical psychologist and psychoanalyst, faculty, supervisor of psychotherapy, and member of the steering committee and faculty of EDCAS at the William Alanson White Institute. She maintains a private practice with offices in Manhattan, New York City, and in Dutchess County, upstate New York.

Pat Ogden, PhD, is a pioneer in somatic psychology and the founder/director of the Sensorimotor Psychotherapy Institute, an internationally recognized school specializing in somatic–cognitive approaches for the treatment of posttraumatic stress disorder and attachment disturbances. She is a clinician, consultant, international lecturer and trainer, and first author of *Trauma and the Body: A Sensorimotor Approach to Psychotherapy* (W.W. Norton and Co., 2006).

Barbara Pearlman, PhD, is a clinical psychologist and group analyst specializing in the treatment of eating disorders for over 28 years. She runs the Finchley Clinic for Eating Disorders—a private out-patient facility in North London.

Previously she supervised an out-patient clinic at Watford General, an NHS hospital, and created and supervised an in-patient, day-patient and out-patient eating disorder clinic at the North London Priory. She was also consultant supervisor to a regional eating disorder service in North East Essex. Dr. Pearlman is a founding member and Associate Director of the Independent Psychology Service (IPS)—a network of private clinical psychologists, psychiatrists, and therapists in North London. The IPS provides assessment and treatment for individuals, couples, and families.

Sarah Schoen, PhD, is on the faculty and steering committee of EDCAS at the William Alanson White Institute. She is also a supervisor of psychotherapy at the White Institute and a former supervising psychologist at the Bellevue/NYU Program for Survivors of Torture. She is in private practice in New York City.

The BODI Group

Catherine Baker-Pitts, PhD, LCSW—The Women's Therapy Centre Institute, NYC

Carol Bloom, LCSW—The Women's Therapy Centre Institute, NYC

Luise Eichenbaum, LCSW—The Women's Therapy Centre Institute, NYC

Linda Garofallou, MS—Children's Hospital of NJ at Newark Beth Israel Medical Center

Susie Orbach, PhD—The Women's Therapy Centre Institute, London & NYC

Jean Petrucelli, PhD—The William Alanson White Institute, NYC; NYU Postdoc

Victoria Sliva—The New School for Social Research, NYC

Suzi Tortora, EdD, BC-DMT—New School for Continuing Studies; Pratt Institute, Brooklyn, NY

Janet Tintner, PsyD, is Division 1 faculty and supervisor of psychotherapy; steering committee member, supervisor and faculty member of EDCAS at the William Alanson White Institute, NYC. She also runs a stroke support group at St. Lukes Hospital, NY. Dr. Tintner writes and teaches extensively on obesity and is in full time private practice in NYC.

FOREWORD

The Body as Self-State

Several years ago, in a conversation with Jean Petrucelli about her (2010a) 'tennis' paper, "Serve, Smash, and Self-States," we discussed its central emphasis on self-states and affect regulation—especially the development of her view that the body has a mind of its own and that what the body 'knows' is being transmitted from the body to the mind as organized by the central nervous system. It was an idea whose 'rightness' I could feel as well as understand. It also struck me, even back then, that her insight was achieved not through linear thinking but required a mind so creative that she could arrive at this groundbreaking insight only by releasing herself from the time-honored frame that limits our view of what the body knows as information coming from the central nervous system. Her mind was able to move her in a new direction because she was able to move in the opposite direction from how this is usually conceived.

I had not until then thought about the body as a self-state, but the more we talked the more accurate it felt. If the body's mind speaks its own language, and it is an affective language, then the more you learn to listen to it affectively, without trying to think about it, the more fluent it becomes in letting you know what you need to know.

It then became easy for me to imagine why, if the body is indeed a self-state, it will function most reliably if its own mind can, as needed, simultaneously interface with the mind's (left-brain) capacity for cognition without interfering with the functioning of the (right-brain's) affective knowing (which is what we call 'body memory'). I could see the role of normal dissociation in this adaptive fluidity—a powerful new example of what Petrucelli (2010b) has called 'sort-of-knowing.' So many questions for further exploration then opened up. If the body as self-state is indeed an adaptive use of normal dissociation, can this help to account for why the language of the body (affect) depends on the mind of the body to hold its language as a *regulatable* experience? I could already feel myself in even greater awe of our capacity to bypass cognition and enter a state that we call being in a 'zone' or 'on a roll' or 'in a groove.'

René Magritte challenged both convention and the definition of *reality* by placing the words "This is Not a Pipe" within his iconic painting. What the viewer looks at in the painting is indeed not a pipe but the *image* of a pipe. Jean Petrucelli might easily have titled what is between these covers "This is Not a Book of Edited Papers." Do not be fooled by the format. It is the groundbreaking perspective of Dr. Petrucelli that inspires each chapter, and my use of the word *groundbreaking* should not be taken lightly.

—Philip M. Bromberg, PhD

References

Petrucelli, J. (2010a). Serve, smash and self-states: Tennis on the couch and courting Steve Mitchell. *Contemporary Psychoanalysis, 46,* 578–588.

Petrucelli, J. (2010b). *Knowing, not-knowing & sort-of-knowing: Psychoanalysis and the experience of uncertainty.* London, England: Karnac.

ACKNOWLEDGMENTS

We live in an era of having to fight the constant pressure to conform or pretend; we work tirelessly, we create, we dream, and we play. What seemed like a simple, manageable plan, that of bringing together colleagues doing groundbreaking work in the treatment of eating disorders to create an anthology to share their thoughts and experiences, is not an endeavor that one should attempt to entertain in their spare time. The mammoth undertaking that editing such a compilation becomes could not have been accomplished without the generosity of time, hard work, efforts, sympathetic ears, and compassion of those swept up in the maelstrom of this project . . . —and there were many.

To begin, the members of my Eating Disorders, Compulsions & Addictions (EDCAS) steering committee: Jacqueline Ferraro, Carrie D. Gottlieb, Elizabeth Halsted, Jill C. Howard, Sue Kolod, Anne F. Malavé, Sarah Schoen, and Janet Tintner, and EDCAS faculty members at the William Alanson White Institute, brought their own singular approaches and areas of expertise that highlight these chapters. In particular, I want to acknowledge Sarah Schoen, Jill C. Howard, and Janet Tintner for always going above and beyond in their ability to help and feed me just the right amount of inspirational nourishment. I feel blessed by the genuine curiosity and intellectual heft of all my contributing authors whose ideas flow through these chapters and I am thankful for their generosity in sharing their theoretical and clinical knowledge. I would also like to acknowledge the work of the BODI group members, who faced the daunting task of working across universes and creating a new clinical assessment tool that was many years in the making.

The theoretical underpinnings of this book could have only come to fruition because of the work of several, starting with Philip M. Bromberg, whose seminal ideas on self-states has influenced a generation of analysts. On a personal note, Philip has continued to provide immeasurable support and inspiration for every project that I undertake, and I am incredibly moved by the Foreword he authored for this anthology. I could not have done this without him. My other heroes/ mentors include Edgar A. Levenson, Donnel Stern, Steve Mitchell, Lew Aron, and Susie Orbach, whose accepted wisdom has greatly influenced my thinking and has allowed me to apply psychoanalytic wisdom to clinical treatment for patients with eating disorders. Donnel Stern has also graciously provided a home for this anthology in his Psychoanalysis in a New Key Book series, for which I am deeply grateful and humbled.

The painstaking editing of this book could not have been accomplished without the cherished help of a few colleagues and friends that have read various parts of this book and offered detailed critiques and commentaries: Philip M. Bromberg, Joseph Canarelli, Jill C. Howard, Ruth Livingston, Nick Samstag, Sarah Schoen, Donnel Stern, and members of my writing group led by Sue Kolod, whose comments and feedback were enormously providential. I feel immense gratitude to Ruth Livingston, who persevered in the face of time constraints and shared her pearls of wisdom with constructive edits along the way. I would like to thank Annelisa Pederson for her expertise and skillfulness in copy editing, ensuring all my *i*s were dotted and my *t*s were crossed. Additionally, thanks goes out to Kristopher Spring, who offered me the initial opportunity to become part of the Routledge family, and to Kate Hawes and her crew, including Kirsten Buchanan, for their infinite patience in shepherding this book to publication.

Once more, I want to express my love and appreciation to my family: my devoted mom, a world-class Scrabble player; my late dad, with his infinite wisdom, who still watches over me and sometimes lets me know that; my siblings and all their parts; my cherished, remarkable, and playful daughters Juliette and Jade, who, as legend has it, and just for the record, as they have told me, never once cried when they were babies; and my love and soul mate, Steve, who affably endures.

Lastly, I am forever indebted to my patients, for their multitude of gifts: their humanity, courage, and willingness to go beyond and let themselves be known and seen, in ways that permeate and transform us together, over lifetimes.

INTRODUCTION

'With a Little Help from My Friends'

Jean Petrucelli

No one quite experienced the pure vulnerability and fractured quality of body-states like poor Humpty Dumpty, whose epiphany, unfortunately, was short-lived. He was sitting on a wall, believing he was in control, when, suddenly, all was shattered. Alas, he couldn't be repaired.

If one thinks about this in terms of body-states, Humpty's experience is an interesting metaphor for the role of body-states in our patients with eating disorders or disordered eating. How do we put our patients—many of whom thought they were 'in control' with their eating rituals—back together again? My interpersonal colleagues and I have attempted to deconstruct the essential role of understanding body-states in the treatment of eating disorders. We hope that our exploration will have a longer shelf life and better outcome than the ill-fated Humpty Dumpty.

When I reflect on my 29 years of work with patients with eating disorders, it now seems to me that the "heartbeat of the therapeutic dance" may be the body representation of self-states and the body-to-body dialogue between them. I just didn't know it—then. A number of prominent clinicians and thinkers in the interpersonal and relational field (i.e., Bromberg, 1998, 2006, 2011; Stern, 1997, 2010; Levenson, 1979, 1983, 1991; Aron & Anderson, 1998; Mitchell, 1988, to name a few) have offered psychoanalytic ideas such as multiple states theory, dissociation, unformulated experience, mutuality and intersubjectivity. This has catalyzed my own thinking and has led me to 'collage' and apply these innovative touchstones of interpersonal and relational theory to patients with eating disorders. Stern's clear and incisive writings on understanding experience that one has not yet been reflected on or not yet put into words lies at the heart of our work with patients with eating disorders (i.e., what is unformulated in words often gets enacted through the body and bodily actions). In addition, our understanding of eating disorders and bodies includes acknowledging other trailblazers (Orbach, 1978, 2009; McDougall, 1989; Goodsitt, 1983; Zerbe, 1993; Sands, 1991; Davis, 1991; Brisman, 1992, 1995; Barth, 1988). I am especially grateful to the work of Bromberg, whose eloquent writing defines and illuminates our understanding of self-states with the idea of experience being lived 'between the spaces.'

1

Bromberg's ideas have propelled my own thinking—to realize that the body, too, has its place in space.

At base, eating disorders are about the understanding of various body-states and their relational meanings, creating and 'allowing' these states existence. The split of mindbody or bodymind functioning is always being enacted in many arenas in the eating-disordered patient's life. Concretely, a patient believes that disciplining or controlling his or her body is a means to psychic equilibrium and interpersonal effectiveness. One might conceive of an eating disorder as an attempt at self-cure, which ultimately fails and leads to further isolation, chaos, and helplessness. It is through the linking of symptoms, with these symptoms emotional and interpersonal meanings, in the context of the therapy relationship, that patients with eating disorders can find their way out. The work allows them to identify, formulate, and eventually create a bridge to understand the sequestered body-states that they inhabit in their attempts to survive the unbearable.

When one is in the throes of an eating disorder, one is trapped in the prison of his or her own bodymind. One cannot imagine freedom because one cannot imagine what it is like to change. Finding freedom is not effortless, and only those deprived of it have the barest inkling of what it is. Interpersonal and relational treatment provides our patients with eating disorders with an opportunity to find—in the words of Harry Stack Sullivan, one of the founders of interpersonal psychoanalysis—solutions to eating problems, body image, and 'problems in living.'

This anthology is a collection of papers that encompass the work of many talented clinicians and researchers steeped in working with patients with eating disorders for the past 10 to 35 years. As with most anthologies, this is not a volume meant to be read in one sitting. Rather, take your time, enjoy and savor the subtle delicacies of taste as you pick and choose what your heart, mind, and body wish to digest. The overarching topics include how we build a bridge over the bodymind divide; clinical applications and techniques; eating disorders as disorders of desire; the interface of self and affect regulation with neurobiology and attachment; bodies in interaction; family complexities; religion; body image and the reflexive mind; the role of the body in anticipation of the future; appetite; agency and gender; gift-giving; hormones and the body narrative; understanding body-states from the multiplicity of a self-states model; preadolescence to adolescence complications and the body; the treatment of obesity and binge eating; the role of culture and history; blending CBT/DBT and interpersonal theory; the role of psychopharmacology; internal language enhancement and eating disorders; intergenerational transmission of embodiment; and sustainability in recovery: A wide menu, for sure.

The lyrical expressions of our chapter titles are meant to remind us of necessary cultural, creative, and playful aspects of our work that are essential to hold in the treatment of patients with eating disorders—so "we built this [book] on rock and roll." We hope to capture inner rhythms as a portal to deeply felt experiences that sometimes defy verbal expression but may be manifested in the body.

The book is divided into 5 parts. Part I, "Finding Beauty in the Beast: Interpersonal Perspectives and Treatment of Eating Disorders," includes two chapters by Petrucelli. In the first chapter, "Mermaids, Mistresses, and Medusa: Getting 'Inside Out and Outside In' the Relational Montage of an Eating Disorder," Petrucelli delineates a template to consider eating disorders by taking biology, individual psychology, culture, social norms, and biases into account. Setting up a foundation for treatment from a biopsychosocial perspective involves utilizing a multidisciplinary outpatient team—that is, a nutritionist, psychiatrist, internist, and others—as well as action-oriented techniques, such as the use of the detailed inquiry, contracting, journal writing, and food logs. With an interpersonal perspective, clinically examining 'what happens' as these techniques are used becomes the gateway to understanding the unspoken bargains each patient makes in the service of protecting the self. Creating tolerable 'unsafety' occurs in clinical moments when the body and the self-reflexive function of the mind meet in treatment on 'safe but not too safe' ground, as Bromberg (1998, 2006, 2011) has illustrated.

Chapter 2 is titled, " 'My Body Is a Cage': Interfacing Interpersonal Neurobiology, Attachment, Affect Regulation, Self-Regulation, and the Regulation of Relatedness in Treatment With Eating-Disordered Patients." Petrucelli explores how we can mindfully integrate the neurobiological workings of the brain, the psychological experience of self and self-as-embodied, and the interpersonal context of relationships. She considers the mutual impact of the mind and the body on patient and analyst as part of the clinical treatment process as together they jointly process, experience, and reflect, on the 'bodily goings on' as a clinical mindbody–bodymind conundrum.

Part II includes six chapters on the topic of "The Mindbody and the Bodymind: Reflections Inside and Outside Reality and Subjectivity." The section opens with Chapter 3, by Schoen, titled " 'You're the One That I Want': Appetite, Agency, and the Gendered Self" and explores the complex relationship between eating problems and gendered identity, as eating troubles are deeply entwined with gendered subjectivities. Painful tensions between separation and connection, dependency and autonomy, and being the subject or the object of desire—tensions that are often at the heart of eating problems—derive in part from the binaries implicated in the cultural construction of gendered categories. Drawing on the relevant feminist and psychoanalytic literature, Schoen illustrates how interpersonal or relational psychoanalytic approaches are uniquely suited to helping patients with eating problems live more comfortably in their gendered skins by exploring the interplay of cultural context and psychological forces as they emerge in therapy.

In Chapter 4, " 'Stretched to the Limit': Body Image in the Reflexive Mind," Halsted considers how body image is the psychic boundary between internal and external body fantasies fluctuating within each self-state and experience. She integrates the concept of reflexive functioning into a developmental theory of body image, illuminating how integrative failures result in body-image disturbances and distortions. Halsted explores complex theoretical aspects as they are applied to an array of tools and intervention strategies with a particular focus on clinical listening, detailed inquiry, and the awareness of both the therapists' and patients' bodies.

In Chapter 5, "'I Can See Clearly Now the Rain Has Gone': The Role of the Body in Forecasting the Future," Ogden, shares her work with the unconscious processes and body to body communications that take place beneath the words during the therapy hour. She maintains that these communications relationally convey and sustain implicit, unconscious beliefs, and affects that have anticipatory and predictive functions, often based in the past. These implicit processes, visibly reflected in gesture, posture, prosody, facial expressions, eye gaze, movement habits, and unconscious affect, reflect the 'implicit self,' which might be relatively unified or comprise several dissociative parts of the self. Ogden highlights 'embodied' mentalizing and the centrality of body experience as a primary source of therapeutic action to foster adaptive affect regulation, challenge maladaptive predictions, and integrate dissociative parts.

Chapter 6, "'Look At Me. . . . What Am I Supposed To Be?': Women, Culture, and Cosmetic Splitting," by Baker-Pitts, explores how many women choose cosmetic surgery to both identify and cut out parts of the maternal figure in an effort to separate from her, and that these women need to surgically 'fix' what has felt unacceptable in the (m)other's eyes. She observes how women who do not know their own mind through an affective mirror or their bodies through affectionate contact tend to view their body in terms of 'parts,' a view that is sadly supported by cultural ideas. Cosmetic surgery is then offered up and undertaken to mend splits between mind and body and to reposition the objectified female as a subject with agency. Baker-Pitts critically examines dyadic relationships that do not enable knowing oneself, but instead require splitting off parts of the body-self and addresses the multiple self and body states that emerge in different relational configurations.

Charatan, in Chapter 7, "'I Won't Grow Up, Not Me': Anorexia Nervosa and Maturity Fears Revisited," examines anorexia nervosa from a feminist gender-development viewpoint, shedding light on why it may be understandable that some women choose starvation as a means of psychic survival. Charatan reconceptualizes the construct of maturity fears through a gender development/relational lens to explicate why these women have come to fear growing up, thus embodying a culturally-prescribed gender role long associated with weakness, passivity, and a lack of agency.

The last chapter in this section, Chapter 8, "'Spitting Out the Demons': The Perils of Giving and Receiving for the Anorexic Patient" is by Howard. Howard explores the giving and receiving of gifts, both in the consulting room and out, as a manifestation of the forbidden desire that is central to the inner life of the anorexic patient. She highlights how the need to stave off disappointment and despair in relationships as well as the fear of being engulfed, or engulfing the other, creates distortions in the capacity to give, both literally and figuratively. Howard views how gifts may either be given excessively or, conversely, as objects that may be hoarded, to manage the intolerable buildup of anxiety around the experience of emptiness, or power and control. Enactments that we see in treatment reflect difficulties with self-regulation around desire and make gift-giving a rich external arena in which to explore the patient's impoverished inner world.

The next section, Part III, "Treating the Family, the Young, the Hormonal, and the Religious: Developmental, Familial, and Cultural Contexts," begins with Chapter 9, "'What's Going On, What's Going On?': An Interpersonal Approach to Family Therapy With the Eating-Disordered Patient," by Brisman, and explores how and why the engagement of the family, an essential part of treatment when working with a child or adolescent with an eating disorder, is highly controversial. She discusses polarized views that range from guiding the family toward direct refeeding and food monitoring, to urging complete parental disengagement from the issues with food. Brisman addresses how to assess what is most effective in each individual family, taking into account an appreciation of the family dynamics from an interpersonal perspective and discusses how family systems theory and an interpersonal approach can dramatically collide.

In Chapter 10, "'Bridge Over Troubled Waters': Girl's Growing Bodies, Growing Minds, Growing Complications," Ferraro focuses on puberty in girls and the ways in which developmental and interpersonal perspectives can enlighten and inform clinical work. Puberty is a remarkable time of transition when girls come to inhabit many 'new bodies' as they experience a multiplicity of self-states in the process. During puberty, physiological and cognitive changes, of preadolescent and adolescent girls, intermingle with changing psychological, familial, social patterns, and needs. Ferraro focuses on how awareness of these processes and their potential to contribute to the development of eating disorders, disordered eating, and self-harmful behaviors is critical to clinical understanding and treatment.

In Chapter 11, "'The Circle (Cycle) Game': Ovarian Hormones, Self-States, and Appetites," Kolod looks at the hormonal body and its interaction with the psyche. She asks, "How many psychotherapists actual know the menstrual histories of their patients, eating-disordered or not, or have asked anything about their patients' hormonal experience?" Rather than focusing on mindbody, she explores bodymind as she delves into how women's experience of hormonal shifts can be understood and used in the service of furthering change. She demonstrates how the avoidance of this line of inquiry has been based on sexism and concern over the ways in which the hormonal body has been used to support a negative view of women. Kolod reveals the impact of ovarian hormones on mood, identity, sense of self, and appetite, as women experience different self-states during the course of their menstrual cycle.

Chapter 12, "'Body and Soul': Eating Disorders in the Orthodox Jewish Population," jointly authored by Gorden and Kofman, presents a psychoanalytic perspective on the psychodynamics and incidence of eating disorders in the Orthodox Jewish population. The authors consider the role of intergenerational transmission of persecution and trauma on the subsequent generations of Holocaust survivors by exploring the factors contributing to how and why these experiences get communicated and enacted through eating-disorder symptoms, treatment dilemmas, and management issues that may be unique to this population.

The next section Part IV, centers on "Appetite Regulation in an Interpersonal and Cultural Context." Tintner opens this section, Chapter 13, with "'These Boots *Aren't* Made for Walking, but That's Just What They'll Do': The Use of the Detailed Inquiry in the Treatment of Obesity." She playfully explores the use of interpersonal techniques, primarily, the detailed inquiry, in the treatment of obesity. Tintner discusses some of the difficulties in treating obesity and shares a clinical case that involves the use of detailed but obvious—if taboo—questions that helped a patient become aware of how 'out of shape' or, rather, 'out of her body' she was. Tintner is mindful that feelings of shame and despair about the inability to control appetite as well as facing the physical limitations in being morbidly obese are painful to access, and argues that it is precisely the awareness of these shameful feelings that may help the patient face the problem. It is the question, not the interpretation, that is central to awareness of what is physically and experientially obvious but unfaceable.

Chapter 14, "'No Self Control': Working in the Binge-Eating Spectrum," by Malavé, describes an interpersonal psychoanalytic approach to the treatment of people with binge-eating problems. Using case material to illustrate clinical points, Malavé pays close attention to the moment-by-moment fluctuations, rhythms, and shifting tides as the bingeing enters the consulting room and is engaged within the transference-countertransference field. Through her case illustration, she shows us how bingeing behavior is an experience that is not only personal and private but also fundamentally interpersonal: That is, not only is the binge about food, but it is also a lived experience between people.

Chapter 15, by Hamilton, is titled "'Sweet Thing': Racially Charged Transferences and Desire in the Interpersonal Treatment of a Black American Woman With Binge-Eating Disorder—Who Needs Chocolate Cake When You Can Have Chocolate Men?" Hamilton discusses a case of an African American woman with binge-eating disorder and obesity, and focuses on trauma induced, longstanding patterns of dysregulated emotional states that disrupt feeding and interfere with the recognition and satisfaction of desire and need. She highlights some of the unique factors associated with eating disorders, sexuality, and body image in African American women as well as exploring how symptoms of unsatisfying relational experiences—including sexual ones—often follow similar patterns of dysregulation alongside the presenting eating-disorder symptoms.

Chapter 16, "'Bewitched, Bothered, and Bewildered': Boundaries Shared and Denied," by Ackerman, is about the analyst's disclosure of a dream to a 23-year-old patient with bulimia and the clinical material that ensued as a result. Ackerman explores a theme centered on 'bothering,' 'being a bother,' and 'mutual bothering' that becomes a pervasive part of the fabric and texture of her patient's analytic treatment. In discussing the co-constructed dynamics of this shared dream event, new and creative territory became available that allowed them to explore boundaries, need, desire, hope, and the denial of all.

This section ends with a distinctive chapter (Chapter 17), "'Hooked on a Feeling': Emotions That Facilitate the Movement From Compulsion to Choice—Three Bodies. . . . Patient, Analyst, and Supervisor," by Buechler. She writes from the point of view of being a supervisor to a therapist working with a patient with severe binge eating, with a particular focus on the emotional exchanges between all the participants. Buechler focuses on the feelings that get stirred in her as a supervisor with the idea that all emotions exist in a system—the intensity of any one emotion modulates the intensity of all others. Buechler asks, "What brings about the 'tipping point' in a treatment, when it really takes hold? What are the feelings that facilitate significant change in the treatment, and in the supervision? And, how does someone who is 'hooked' on the highs of a binge get attached to more healthful joys?"

Part V: "Beyond the Interpersonal and Across the Universe: History, Clinical, and Assessment Tools Across Modalities" includes five chapters; two discuss the incorporation of adjunct treatments in interpersonal treatment: CBT/DBT and psychopharmacology, two involve the creation and use of innovative assessment clinical tools, and one explores anorexia from a historical context. In Chapter 18, Gottlieb examines the similarities and differences between cognitive behavioral and dialectical behavior therapies and interpersonal psychotherapy. With a brief introduction to CBT and DBT in terms of affect regulation strategies, Gottlieb explores the blending of these approaches to create a rich and full treatment approach.

Chapter 19, co-authored by A. Mittsi Crossman and Zev Labins, is titled, "'One Pill Makes You Larger, and One Pill Makes You Small' . . . and the Ones that Doctor Gives You May or May Not Do Anything at All: A Brief Summary of Pharmacological Approaches in the Treatment of Eating Disorders." They present a brief overview of the psychopharmacology of eating disorders within the comprehensive context of physiological, psychological, and cultural factors.

In Chapter 20, Pearlman introduces the ILE, Internal Language Enhancement, a novel treatment for eating disorders based on research into the neuroscience of emotional processing. Pearlman argues that by discovering the trigger emotion and resymbolizing the concrete thought and language with the patient in a non-threatening environment, treatment can help the patient strengthen the symbolic pathway and weaken the overused concrete/body pathway in the brain.

In Chapter 21, The BODI Group, a multidisciplinary team composed of psychoanalysts, body and movement therapists, and clinical researchers investigate through the creation of a new clinical tool, the BODI (Body Observational Diagnostic Interview), the intergenerational transmission of embodiment. A basic premise of their research is that the body is shaped relationally: It is relationally emergent, mutually influenced, and regulated. Regarding transmission, they describe body states as having their own line of development distinct from mental processes and propose that a mother's recognition and experience of her daughter's body as differentiated from her own will enable the daughter to develop the potential for indwelling.

Chapter 22, by Kuriloff, " 'Across the Universe': Christians, Patients, Women With Anorexia Nervosa, Then and Now," explores past and present innovations within the interpersonal tradition in the clinical treatment of eating disorders. She begins with pioneer Hilde Bruch (1972), associated with Harry Stack Sullivan and the William Alanson White Institute, who recognized that the qualities of relationships within and beyond the family were often at the heart of the problem. Today clinicians of all stripes consider the interpersonal realm of the patient as part of every assessment and intervention. However, as Kuriloff notes, this was, at one time, outside the norm and remains only sometimes considered within the context of medical and behavioral treatments.

We have reached an era where worlds are now colliding: I am referring to the realm of eating disorders and that of interpersonal/relational thinking. In 1995, when we started the Eating Disorders, Compulsions & Addictions Service at the William Alanson White Institute, it was like tilting at windmills to convince psychoanalysts that one's relationship to food could be understood interpersonally; that trauma might often be a component in the work; that eating-disordered patients could learn to think symbolically rather than just concretely; and that analytic work could occur slowly over time.

With over 50 years of research in the field of understanding eating disorders, many questions still remain, and no one consistent or comprehensive definition of 'recovery' exists. Clinicians and researchers continue to grapple with the quest to bridge the gaps in defining a protocol for recovery, knowing that, at its core, trust in the reliability of the humanness of the other is a necessary ingredient to help one develop, regain, or have—for the first time—a stable body. Embodied experience must be cultivated and demonstrated in the patient/therapist relationship as a felt experience in its mutuality so patients can learn to have a body that is lived in rather than experiencing it as an "other" to be managed.

Interpersonal therapy helps build the bridge that allows patients to use words as an expression of who they are. It is a way of reaching these patients through an analytic perspective never before articulated this clearly. The interpersonal approach to eating disorders involves respecting and inviting the symptom into the treatment while, at the same time, recognizing symptomatology as a means of understanding something that cannot, at first, be communicated directly with words. As anyone who has ever treated a patient with an eating disorder knows, there is no way one can avoid getting pulled into a patient's dynamics: Ultimately, you must become a part of it. You cannot treat this group from the outside. Interpersonal psychoanalysis has always taken this as foundational to treating anyone.

When working with our eating-disordered patients and coming face to face with feelings of helplessness—theirs and ours—we are often tempted to think that if we just do more, we will feel more secure, less anxious or worried. This leads to despair as it is easy to lose sight, in the clinical conundrums we encounter, of the importance of helping our patients to remember or regain the value of who they are—*as is*. Real recovery takes a long time.

Our eating-disordered patients want to be happy: They have lived in fear of emotions that feel intolerable or unbearable with maladaptive solutions. Living without these emotions is not the question at hand—learning how to live better with them is. Our co-created attempts to render a patient 'whole' again are hopefully 'lost' and 'found' in the heart, soul and body of these chapters.

References

Aron, L., & Anderson, F. (1998). *Relational perspectives on the body.* Hillsdale, NJ: Analytic Press.

Barth, D. (1988). The treatment of bulimia from a self-psychological perspective. *Clinical Social Work Journal, 16*(3), 270–281.

Brisman, J. (1992). Bulimia in the late adolescent: An analytic perspective to a behavioral problem. In J. O'Brien, D. Pilowsky, & O. Lewis (Eds.), *Psychotherapies with children: Adapting the dynamic process.* Washington, D.C.: American Psychiatric Press.

Brisman, J. (1995). Psychodynamic psychotherapy and action-oriented technique: An integrated approach. In I. Yalom & J. Werne (Eds.), *Treating eating disorders* (pp. 311–370). San Francisco, CA: Jossey-Bass.

Bromberg, P. (1998). *Standing in the spaces: Essays on clinical process, trauma, and dissociation.* Hillsdale, NJ: Analytic Press.

Bromberg, P. (2006). *Awakening the dreamer: Clinical journeys.* Hillsdale, NJ: Analytic Press.

Bromberg, P. (2011). *The shadow of the tsunami and the growth of the relational mind.* New York: Routledge.

Bruch, H. (1972). *Eating disorders: Obesity, anorexia nervosa and the person within.* New York: Basic Books.

Davis, W. (1991). *Reflections on boundaries in the psychotherapeutic relationship in psychodynamic treatment of anorexia and bulimia* (pp. 68–85). New York: Guilford Press.

Goodsitt, A. (1983). Self-regulatory disturbances in eating disorders. *International Journal of Eating Disorders, 2,* 51–60.

Levenson, E. A. (1979). *The fallacy of understanding.* New York: Basic Books.

Levenson, E. A. (1983). *The ambiguity of change.* New York: Basic Books.

Levenson, E. A. (1991). *The purloined self.* New York: Contemporary Psychoanalysis Books.

McDougall, J. (1989). *Theaters of the body.* New York: Norton & Co.

Mitchell, S. A. (1988). *Relational concepts in psychoanalysis: An integration.* New York: Harvard University Press.

Orbach, S. (1978). *Fat is a feminist issue: The anti-diet guide to permanent weight loss.* New York: Paddington Press.

Orbach, S. (2009). *Bodies.* London: Picador.

Sands, S. (1991). Bulimia, dissociation and empathy: A self-psychological view. In C. Johnson (Ed.), *Psychodynamic treatment of anorexia and bulimia* (pp. 354–372). New York: Guilford Press.

Stern, D. (1997). *Unformulated experience: From dissociation to imagination in psychoanalysis.* Hillsdale, NJ: Analytic Press.

Stern, D. (2010). *Partners in thought: Working with unformulated experience, dissociation, and enactment.* New York: Routledge.

Zerbe, K. (1993). *The body betrayed: A deeper understanding of women, eating disorders, and treatment.* Carlsbad, CA: Gurze Books.

Part I

FINDING BEAUTY IN THE BEAST

Interpersonal Perspectives and
Treatment of Eating Disorders

1

MERMAIDS, MISTRESSES, AND MEDUSA

Getting 'Inside Out and Outside In' the Relational Montage of an Eating Disorder

Jean Petrucelli

> Yesterday, I thought that because 'I'm fat,' eating was a bad habit. You want me to associate to the word 'Curves'? . . . OK . . . Marilyn Monroe, child bearing hips, fat, sexual prey, shaped like your mother, large breasted, fat, hour glass, made fun of, puberty, sexy, overweight, the opposite of a model, get stared at, not like my friends growing up, not petite, fat. Fat, fat, fat . . . I know it is time to sink or swim but it's a big ocean and I don't know where to go. Even if I were a mermaid, the current I follow seems to always lead me into the shark's den. I feel helpless. Yesterday, I wanted to flee where the pain would not follow me. Yesterday, I would not have believed that you or anyone would have any interest in my self-hatred, understand my starvation, or feel my hunger to not live. Today, I sort-of-know differently. But tomorrow, I want to not just know but *feel* things that will help my life never be the same.
>
> (Anonymous voices)

Familiar words, but many voices evoke the haunting chill of living on the precipice of life and in the emotional abyss of an eating disorder. Past, present, and future collapse for patients with eating disorders: The insidious negative self-talk is too loud, and/or the aftermath of trauma too pervasive and/or the affects are too overwhelming.

What might have been a full life becomes reduced to the myopic world of a 'single bagel.' Certainly culture, with its many offerings of visual objectification, provides eating-disordered patients much opportunity to feel scrutinized, objectified, and cut off from their bodies. And, when bodies are experienced as 'mere aesthetic wrappers of the self' (see Chapter 6), while simultaneously being thought of as central signifiers of one's identity, one is more vulnerable to expressing pain via an eating disorder. Yet cultural influences on the development of eating disorders are only one part of a much larger mystery.

13

Eating disorder symptoms, for all their painful behavioral constrictions, hold complex, personal stories of the sufferer's relationship, not only to food and her body but to the caretakers who fed and didn't feed them—to the relational context in which needs were met or dismissed, and in which life came to feel as if it could or could not hold the potential for satisfaction, possibilities, and meaning. At their core, eating disorders are disorders of desire in which wanting, longing, hunger, and the vulnerability of reaching with one's appetite towards the 'world of others' has been subverted. Like mermaids in search of a sea, mistresses in search of a Madame, or Medusa in search of a man, eating-disordered patients remain mythically haunted and psychically alone. They live between two worlds: the world of food and the world of people. In this chapter, I will discuss how an interpersonal/relational psychoanalytic approach to working with eating disorders clarifies the links between symptom and meaning, action and words, isolation and relatedness.

Working psychoanalytically with the treatment of eating disordered individuals requires the necessary integration of behavioral change and behavioral techniques. Harry Stack Sullivan, one of the founders of interpersonal theory, had a behavioral sensibility. He was not a behaviorist in the strict sense of the term but was fascinated by what actually goes on between people in the real world. As Steve Mitchell (1999, p. 90) recognized, "The roots of this sensibility for Sullivan were in the philosophical pragmatism that dominated the American social science of his day. There is no use talking about what you can't see or measure operationally, Sullivan believed. In trying to understand 'human difficulties in living,' it is much more conceptually economical to study what people actually do with one another." With an eating-disordered patient, food often takes the place of 'an Other.' Therefore, we understand our patient's relationships to food and others and their day to day lived experience as being relevant information, as important as what we wish to understand about an inner fantasy life. Our work, as analysts, involves actively intervening. In particular, I will focus on the ways in which the direct, concrete engagement with eating disorder behaviors can build bridges to elaborating personal and interpersonal meanings trapped in these actions.

Eating disorders require integrative thinking. They are complex illnesses that are multidetermined and require a multidisciplinary approach. They must be thought about and treated in a sociocultural context, while taking into account the individual's biology, genetic predisposition and vulnerability, as well as a host of psychological determinants. A person's underlying genetic structure shapes his or her vulnerability and resilience, which affects how she perceives, organizes, and responds to experiences (Maine, 2010).

Eating disorders interfere with a normal ability to hold the conflicting tensions of hunger and satiety: Therefore, one must also consider the effects of early developmental feeding and issues of attachment. Alongside attachment issues, we must also take into account how self and affect regulation difficulties play a role in understanding how eating is felt and symbolized: "If affects are the metaphorical juice of life—the aliveness that on some level everyone yearns for" (Glennon, 2012) then to be fully engaged in life, one must have access to a broad range of emotional experiences. For an eating-disordered patient, symptoms truncate emotional experience, serving both expressive and defensive functions. These behavioral enactments often demonstrate something that is not yet articulated about the patient's subjective state, in which the body is used in the service of the mind (Stolorow & Atwood, 1991). When patients' affects are split off by an unconscious fear that their experience will be unbearable, they end up living a marginal existence. Our eating-disordered patients struggle with their underlying terror of interpersonal relatedness, which is often obscured by their symptoms.

Unlike classical psychoanalytic approaches, which are sometimes less receptive to alternative treatment models, interpersonal and relational treatment offers models flexible enough to integrate other modes of thinking and working. Confronting some of the challenges of working with patients with anorexia, bulimia, bulimarexia, and binge eating, we, as psychoanalysts, are forced to clarify and expand our thinking and practice.

Contemporary understanding of successful treatment for these eating-disordered patients demands an integrated and profound appreciation for how genetic vulnerability, attachment, family history, affect regulation, and cultural context mesh in the clinical picture. More and more, we realize we need to fine-tune our interpersonal and relational thinking about therapeutic action—both our successes and failures with eating-disordered patients—and recognize that treatment often requires creativity to step outside of the proverbial box.

An interpersonal/relational perspective values the unique fit between patient and therapist by offering an opportunity for a mutually regulating system. There is a link between a patient's self-regulation with food and the way in which the patient regulates relatedness with the therapist. The relational dyad between patient and choice of food (as part of the symptom) is highly textured. Why do some patients binge on sugar, some on salt or a combination of both, while still others only on healthy foods? Does it have to do with someone's capacity to recognize the after effects of ingesting salt versus sugar, for example, as they affect the individual differently? Thinking clinically then, to what 'flavor' is our patient intuitively responding in our personality that allows this patient to feel comfortable enough to begin this work? And how do we, as therapists, stay empathetic to a human condition that, at times, seems alien, destructive, and unbearable? How do we begin to see the interpersonal meanings and unique ways our patients choose to take us in or spit us out?

An interpersonal/relational approach takes as a starting point the idea that an eating disorder symptom is not something to simply get rid of, but rather something that holds dissociated parts of oneself and one's relational history. A patient with an eating disorder may feel like the symptoms have 'minds of their own' as they find voice through the body. Our work requires helping these patients learn how to have a different relationship to their self-states, body-states and their bodies—a relationship that allows them to "feel generative and animated as well as alive to ordinary discontents and longings" (Orbach, 2009, p. 76). This is a tall order.

Symptoms, Self-States, and Body-States

Throughout this work, as we discover the disowned or dissociated parts of a person, we experience and witness various self-states and body-states that accompany eating disorders. We observe the adaptive function of dissociation processes as patients attempt to maintain "self-continuity and self-organization" (Bromberg, 1998, p. 206) with the use of symptoms, such as starving, bingeing, and purging. Since eating-disordered patients communicate through these dramatic bodily actions, they comprise a population where alexithymia (Barth, 2001; Krueger, 2001) and unformulated experience (Stern, 1997) rule.

Not only do these patients have difficulty identifying their emotions, but they often also have difficulty distinguishing and appreciating the emotions of others. And for those who *do* have a sense of what they feel, spoken words may not be enough to completely express their experience. The fear of not being understood and the shame they bear dampens curiosity that is required for self-exploration. Not knowing what they feel can be unbearable in and of itself. Eating disorders speak to a loss of faith in the reliability of human relatedness. Words fail these patients and their trust in the reliability of the other is broken.

In the eating-disordered patient, symptoms are "used" to compensate for a lack of a capacity to reflect and deal with conflict, or to counteract difficulty in mentalizing. Unable to reflectively experience a part of oneself or another, this patient has difficulty experiencing having a mind of one's own. Meanwhile, self-development is sadly derailed. On a gut level, eating-disordered patients do not feel that others can imagine what they feel on the inside. They never feel like they are 'good enough.' For these patients, self-states—ways of being and expressing that allow a certain representation or part of the self to emerge—might be defined as the experience of what they can and/or cannot be curious about, relative to the self-state they are in. Sometimes, what is needed is for the patient to experience that we can know her experience, and feel it viscerally in *our* bodies (Sands, 1997), creating an uncanny, 'shared' body-state. Patients can experience relating to the analyst—another body in the room sometimes—by projecting his or her disowned parts onto the analyst and by relating to the analyst as an embodied other. In turn, processing this mutual experience allows the patient to experience body-states relationally and to reflect upon this experience. A body-state has to do with embodiment: how one lives in the body, at a given moment, relative to the felt experience. This can be internally accepted as a part of oneself—or not. By definition, body-states are nonverbal experiences and may not be known through the mind with words. The body 'articulates' the unspoken.

Interpersonal/relational perspectives recognize that the therapist, engaging with the patient's disowned/dissociated self- and body-states, will inevitably be pulled into the relational dynamics implicated in the patient's symptoms. You cannot treat this group from the outside; you have got to get your hands dirty and dig in the dirt. Interpersonal and relational psychoanalysis has always taken this as foundational to treating anyone.

Digging in the Dirt

How can we understand a patient's relationship to food—what he or she does with it and how he or she thinks of it—in relational terms? Entering treatment, a person's relationship with food is often the single-most significant relationship in his or her life. The symptoms have lost connection to the problems and vulnerabilities that stimulated their onset and have a life of their own: They are now ingrained habits, with their own rhythms and expressions. For example, food may begin as a "valued friend/secret companion that helps" lessen anxiety or soothe unbearable feelings. Over time, however, food may become a "strict taskmaster or abusive tyrant that harshly punishes transgressions" (Davis, 2009, p. 37). The therapist is often pulled into this relational configuration, first idealized and valued, and then feared as the rule maker.

With the eating-disordered patient, the analyst lives in the interplay between attending directly to the food and disengaging from the pull to do so, compulsive patterns that have roots in relational interactions. When we feel the tug to attend or disengage, we are simultaneously sensing patients shifting from one part of them to another—in other words, shifting in self- or body-states. Let's say you are talking with an actively symptomatic patient and you realize you have spent an entire session talking about things other than the symptom (i.e., no discussion of the patient's relationship to food and eating). Most likely you have been pulled into a dissociative process, alerting you that the eating-disordered part of the patient is no longer in the room.

It is crucial to create a safe and reliable relationship with a patient with an eating disorder, but it is also very difficult. It means finding traction and a way to intervene between the patient's relationships to food. The next section addresses this difficulty.

Finding Traction, Getting Gritty, Coming Clean

A central feature of working in an interpersonal or relational way involves focusing on the uniqueness of each patient, each analyst, and, therefore, each analytic dyad. If a crucial ingredient in therapeutic action involves being known by one's analyst, then the question becomes this: How is the patient's uniqueness best revealed or uncovered (Glennon, 2012)? How do we obtain a historical narrative and enter into an eating-disordered patient's ritual-obsessed private world of food? For starters, we must try to understand the reasons that food and body image issues may have been important in the family of origin. Food is a central issue in most people's lives. We all have memories of and feelings about family mealtime, family food behaviors, cultural and family messages around image, appearance and success. Food is also, of course, a particularly compelling substitute for what Kohut (1972) called an internalized "self-object function"—the aspect of a parent/child relationship that provides the first medium for the transmission of soothing and comfort. By turning to food, the person attempts to circumvent the need for

17

human self-object responsiveness in order to avoid further disappointment and shame. Food is trustworthy. How do we, as therapists, become 'trustworthy,' and help legitimize our patients' needs and yearnings, sometimes giving these feelings words before the patient can?

We live in an era of uncertainty, where sort-of-knowing (Petrucelli, 2010) predominates. Although the eating-disordered population wants immediate results, recovery involves a long-term therapeutic process. Therapists who work with multiple eating-disordered patients often report an accumulation of tension in themselves. Some of this tension arises from their patients' *urgent* need to gain immediate control over their lives. Thus, the delayed gratification of a psychoanalytically oriented psychotherapy poses a particular challenge for the therapist who then may, countertransferentially, feel a patient's sense of urgency.

Further complicating matters, social trends are at odds with participating in meaning-centered long-term treatment. Through texting, tweeting, twittering, swiping, and Skyping, the concepts and experiences of 'sitting with feelings,' 'holding thoughts,' and 'delaying gratification' are challenged as obsolete modes of being, doing, or operating in the world. This adds an additional layer to an already complex problem with patients with eating disorders because of their difficulties with discriminating, holding, and choosing. Their tendency toward emotional anesthetization via bingeing/binge and purge cycle, or deprivation/starvation leads to a numbing thinking and feeling, of restricting knowing what one knows. The irony is that these patients urgently wish to control their lives, and, paradoxically, in order to fully be in control, one must learn to relinquish control and find a way to tolerate life's ambiguities.

Eating disorders are disorders of desire, and for desire to stay on the agenda, it must stay on the analytic menu. Perhaps oddly, a patient with anorexia refuses food in order to keep her desire alive—because, by refusing food, she privileges desire and keeps a space for her desire to live. If she says she eats nothing, then *nothing* is the object that holds her desire and keeps her feeling something (Fink, 2004). Witnessing patients who eat garbage, or patients who eat raw, coarse vegetables in order to have violent bloody purges, or patients who maim, brand, or cut their bodies, we are also exploring behavioral attempts to feel or subvert desire. Being mindful of the textured and problematic influences that culture and technology add to issues around desire, we struggle to find the key—a way to come between our patients' relationship with food. For patients to explore the significance of pleasure, desire, emotional intimacy, and safety, they must ultimately talk about things other than eating, weight, shape, and food.

But we will get nowhere unless we begin with direct symptom-focused approaches around the food and food behaviors and feelings—this, to establish the stability (physiologically, medically, and psychologically), which we hope will allow for the normalization of eating. Thus, we respect and invite the symptom into the treatment, while recognizing the symptom(s) as avenues for understanding something that cannot be communicated directly with words. To me, symptom relief is actually the easiest part of this work. The more challenging part is the long-term, structural, behavioral, and personality change that requires creating 'new neural templates.' Long-term recovery requires something more subjective than simply symptom relief. Bromberg (2011, pp. 98–100) refers to this as a more flexible community of neural networks in the brain that will support the mind's ability to allow greater interconnection between self-state networks with more flexible self-state networks.

Patients don't care how much you know, until they know how much you care. Treatment must convey empathic acceptance while simultaneously pushing for things to be different. We need an integration that simultaneously sustains a collaborative alliance and an explicit push for change (Maine, 2010). Bromberg (2011) wrote, "What most nourishes the soil of therapeutic growth—is a patient's capacity to change while remaining the same—it is the foundation of development because it is the foundation of hope" (p. 93). When our patients can feel that being with them as they are brings us genuine pleasure from who they are in spite of their struggles and symptoms, they can see glimmers of hope even if we must hold their hope until they can. Holding the hope often necessitates another kind of integration, one requiring the use of adjunct resources in a team approach.

The Team: A Modern Relational Family

In utilizing a team approach, the growth of new relational foundations can concurrently be addressed alongside the patient's psychological issues. We might want to think of this as the patient and analyst in a mother–infant dyad held within the network of an extended family. Treatment may be thought of as multidimensional, combining individual, group, and family/marital work as well as psychopharmacology, nutritional counseling, dental, gynecological (sometimes), and medical consultation. As we integrate data points from additional adjunct resources in utilizing a team approach, we gain insight into a larger picture of the patient's life. We see how our patients can navigate systems, how they advocate for themselves, how they manage to survive in the material world in spite of their very real difficulties.

Learning the Language of Food and Body-Speak

In interpersonal/relational theory, we learn to speak the patient's language, and the use of analytically informed active techniques often results in highlighting previously unrecognized aspects of the transference. Nowhere is this more important than with patients with eating disorders: We need to learn to speak *their* language, a language of food and bodily concerns (Brisman, 1994). At the same time we must introduce a language of mindfulness, self-care, groundedness, and the possibilities for human contact and a life. Our first job is to discover all the patient's body selves or parts, and then form relationships with each of them. Why? Because each part holds its own truth, its own reality, and its own agenda, and all must be taken seriously. In reference to understanding unformulated experience, sometimes it requires "having to find what you don't know how to look for" (Stern, 2008, p. 398). How do we engage severely eating-disordered patients, opening a window to awareness and insight into dissociated areas? Sometimes it happens, intentionally or not.

The Starving Soul of Lucy

Lucy struggled with severe anorexia. She had a relationship to food and eating that read like a clandestine taboo love affair—anticipation fueling excitement, intimacy enveloped in secrecy, and disappointment and emptiness when it was over. She allowed herself only to want *one thing*. Our unraveling of the language and mysteries of her 'romance,' finding a way to come between her relationships to food, occurred unexpectedly in a single moment, a moment in which our mutual enactment became an important source of information. It was a difficult consult: I had to tell her many things she did not want to hear, relating to the severity of her anorexia. When she stood at the door to leave, her hand on the knob, she suddenly decided to linger and ask a question. I had said this was not a 'typical' consult. It was the word *typical* that grabbed her. What did I mean?

That moment—her lingering, an 'almost' ending, anticipating a transition, a loss, a switch—helped me understand a key dynamic that was also mirrored in her relationship with food. Lucy's relationship to her bagel was her one and only secret love affair. She began and ended each day with different pieces of a single bagel. She described how she would cut her bagel into 12 pieces—to use her words, "skin off the top, skin off the bottom," and then eat the "flesh in the middle." Between top, bottom, and middle, inside-outside, skin and flesh, her unintegrated aspects of self and body experience were enacted with her bagel. She would take over an hour to eat each piece in this ritualistic way. Terrified of the food ending, which represented the terror of the 'black hole' and 'nothingness' of time, she became fixated on the saving process and would hold off on eating until she was beyond exhaustion. She told me, "I can't just finish something and go on. . . . When I'm done with my bagel, I become totally unfocused. . . . I save the last bites to help me transition. I call it 'ramping up.' If I don't have the food to use as an organizing principle, I don't feel like I'm a functioning human being. That's why the first thing I purchase in the morning is the last thing I must eat at night" (Petrucelli, 2004, p. 337).

Her doorknob question had to do with my comment that ours was not a 'typical' consult. It was the word *typical* that made her curious, that spurred her to ask me how the consult was not typical. Her question, and how and when she asked it, had both content and process significance. Her 'action of lingering' illuminated an aspect of her self-experience regarding her difficulty with transition: She was letting me know I had engaged perhaps an ounce of curiosity and the possibility of hope that even if she were to change, she would never be 'typical.' I needed to respect and invite Lucy's relationship to her bagel and the severity of her fears into the room. For many months, all we talked about was her bagel. For Lucy, her relationship with her bagel was her life.

Getting Data Through Techniques Linking Acts and Words

In the initial phase of treatment we must gather data. For instance, what is Lucy's 'bagel'? The techniques we can use to understand this analytically may include playing with food metaphors, a detailed inquiry, contracting, and food journaling. These techniques help us understand how, when, and what went wrong, and also what worked. We gain access to much of the nonverbal communication through the use of techniques that link acts to words, informed by interpersonal thinking. An interpersonal approach to treatment is clinically more oriented to acts and experiences than to theories and interpretations. We try to get facts—or at least get patients to talk about what they subjectively experience as facts—so that we can have something concrete to work with. In Sullivan's (1953, 1954) view, such immediacy and direct connection to patient's real-life situations were highly effective. He paid careful attention to specifics. Sullivan's willingness to use language that sounded acceptable to the patient was an example of his eagerness to learn from the patient. Obtaining specifics about a patient's eating disorder involves the use of techniques that link words and actions. Doing so, we discover the patient's capacity to self-soothe, self-regulate, tolerate emotional experience, and manage appetite and desire. These techniques help us to *name* the emotions the patient is experiencing, rather than leaving the patient to be overwhelmed by them. It is not the specific techniques but rather the relational interactions around them that create meaning. These interactions become part of the attachment and affect regulation process. Often the worsening of symptoms is the patient's way of upping the ante—'speaking louder' so the therapist can hear the patient's unformulated communication. By using action-oriented tools, patients begin to differentiate between, and move from, the self-limiting statements of "I am . . ." to "I feel . . . ." The "I feel" statements begin the process of recognition, identification, and acknowledgment of a feeling without being consumed by it (Kuriloff, 2004). The co-construction of meaning allows us as therapists to help patients reshape and redirect their inner experiences so they may have more freedom of choice, and a greater sense of agency to become the author of their own story. How they tell their story is through the use of actual food as metaphor, the use of food metaphors, and food as a concretized sense of identity. For some patients, the notion of 'you-are-what-you-eat' becomes a reality. What remains undifferentiated is the distinction between the patient as a person and food, in and of itself. Eating changes the patient's need for relationships, as food becomes the substitute for this need. For example, a patient wrote the following:

> *Food becomes a metaphor for me. I notice food. I am preoccupied with it—getting it, avoiding it, analyzing it. What you can do with it, how you can cure with it; how you can vary its taste. It fascinates me. When I'm lost in thinking about what to eat and how much to eat, there is no room for anyone else. I don't have to be alone—I'm in the company of my food*

thoughts. Yet, somehow the food is never right. It needs to change. The amount is never right. Some way or another there is always something wrong.

These words speak to their relationship to food and the psychic retreat that patients enter which is part of the disorder itself.

Food Metaphors and Metaphor as Food

Using food metaphors is one way of speaking an eating-disordered patient's language. As we shift the focus from food and weight toward an interpersonal exchange, talking about the therapeutic relationship via food metaphors is an effective way to build a symbolic bridge, enabling a patient with an eating disorder to link various aspects of his or her self-experience. For example, consider the regulation of relatedness between patient and analyst. There is the analyst's potential of listening, waiting, and reverie, and there is the patient's potential of digesting how much of the analyst's words can be taken in before the patient feels overwhelmed, 'too full,' or 'stuffed'—dissociating or 'purging' the other. There is a kind of unknowing that is necessary for analytic work, but we also have to help patients 'savor' new ideas by letting them 'percolate,' or 'brew,' analogous to tolerating ambiguity or holding conflicted thoughts. We sometimes experience the impulsive expulsion—the metaphorical spitting out—of words and feelings as a 'purge,' or their punishing silence as a way to 'starve' themselves of an 'other.' We help our patients' articulate experience with words, identify the nameless but powerful emotions that are unattended to, and together decide how we might tolerate the ambiguity of a moment. If you ask a patient, "What are you really hungry for?" they might answer that dark and lurking in the ebony of night, they can sneak a morsel or maybe just a bite. It might not be a binge, as they are not hungry for food, but looking for things that will 'fill' them, heal them from being broken and bruised. They are hungry for compassion, protection, faith, love, family, and, in a sense, they are starving to know recovery and to break free of these chains that bind them.

Nonetheless, linking behaviors to specific feelings can feel like a familiar menu of criticism, engendering feelings of shame that may be more than they can digest. It is helpful to use straightforward direct questions, but in tiny morsels, offered in espresso spoons. Perhaps these can help the patient identify and manage feelings without our necessarily expecting symptoms to disappear or diminish.

Do Ask, Do Tell: The Detailed Inquiry as Tasting Menu

The detailed inquiry can promote a sense of safety that enables the patient to reveal information, including the disclosure of an eating disorder, sometimes for the first time. As you explore the patient's food and bodily obsessions, you may help the patient build skills that regulate affect (see Barth, 2001, 2008; Brisman, 1995, 1998; Davis, 1991; Kuriloff, 2004; Petrucelli, 2004, 2010). Using Sullivan's

(1953,1954) detailed inquiry and Levenson's (1988) pursuit of the particular, I try to be curious, searching for meaning in interactions or behaviors, while keeping an eye on shifts in feeling states. I start by asking directly, but sometimes data occurs in unexpected clinical moments. Either way, we discover previously veiled information that emerges as we look to decode meaning through an analytic lens.

In this beginning phase of treatment, taking a detailed history involves an intricate description of specific moments around eating, the symptomatic behaviors of starving, bingeing, purging, or bodily obsession, and the affective states that accompany these actions. The history includes tiny details of a patient's daily life that account for significant parts of his or her experience. It is in these details that we may discover perplexing gaps in the patient's understanding of emotions and behavioral patterns, which might otherwise have been overlooked. Sometimes therapists have difficulty asking questions such as, "Exactly how many chocolate cakes did you have?" "Which garbage can did you pull the food out of?" "How do you get yourself to purge—fingers or forks?" or "Do you brush your teeth after a purge?" With these questions, we, as analysts, are trying to determine if dissociation is at play or if the patient lacks the capacity of mindfulness. Perhaps it has never occurred to this patient that the disordered behavior leaves a trail of clues and crumbs. Perhaps this is the relational point. The goal is to join our patients in an exploration of what, when, and where, so we can begin to understand how to help them develop the capacity to process, modulate, and manage overwhelming affects that have never been verbalized.

A detailed inquiry is a valuable tool for inquiring about the self-care necessary for being centered and grounded in one's life. Self-care includes understanding patterns and behaviors regarding food, sleep, and what one does for fun. I try to learn not only what patients eat, but when, how, and what they do and feel while they are eating; I ask how they make decisions about eating. I ask about quantity and quality, and when and where they fall asleep (many eating-disordered patients fall asleep on the couch, never making it into bed after a binge). I inquire about personal hygiene, asking how, if, and when they brush their teeth, or wash their face, take vitamins, etc. (it is often a revelation for patients to consider washing their faces before bedtime). We talk about their hobbies, if any, as hobbies interface with relationships to highlight the experience and expression of desire. I am curious about the movies they see, what they watch on television, and what they are reading—books or recipes—and whether or not they cook—and if so, whether they prefer bland or spicy. These questions may seem insignificant or un-analytic, but they are indicative of the ways patients can and cannot soothe themselves as they touch on their dreams, desire, yearnings, or lack thereof. When a behavioral suggestion is offered, it is done without the expectation that the behavior will necessarily be followed. What does it mean to a patient if you provide a behavioral suggestion? What does it mean, as an analyst, if you give a patient a specific suggestion about something they actually do differently? The analytic focus lies in what happens between patient and therapist in these exchanges. Does the patient feel heard, judged, accepted, or criticized as she describes a 'bizarre' food ritual? If the therapist asks a question, does it feel like a demand? As if the therapist always knows better, like 'mother always knew best' which, as Bruch (1973) noted, is often not the case and represents a repetition of the child not being recognized as having her own voice.

Ultimately, what becomes most important in these interactions are the thoughts, fantasies, and discussion that arise from asking questions, working on alternative behaviors, and the obstacles that present themselves when behavioral suggestions are made. These dialogues are opportunities for the patient and analyst to play with a new assortment of ideas and possibilities.

In these interpersonal exchanges, the patient and the analyst live out the 'Levensonian' question "What is going on around here?" (Levenson, 1983). The analyst learns what happens in this relational dyad and sees the patient's maladaptive attempts to solve problems and conflicts. How does "eating food on a plate, counterclockwise, taking one bite from each food group, with food never mixing or touching, and with only even bites," help manage the volcanic anger and feelings of betrayal that lie dormant in her body? Does she feel like "an orange that is peeled and thrown away because there is a peach around the corner"? What parts is she hiding from me so that she can remain 'the good girl,' showing me what she now thinks is the only part of her I care about? To not ask a question is to ignore the parts of her that are dissociated—the parts for which she feels the most disgust, repulsion, and hatred. Dissociation, that is, the numbness or psychic closing off that so often accompanies trauma and follows in its wake, facilitates and contributes to a patient's silence. In the face of trauma, keeping a secret is often not a conscious decision. Powerful internal and external forces are at play and prevent information from surfacing. The defense that helps people to cope at one point ultimately complicates their lives at another. Dissociation is not-knowing there is a secret you are keeping. This secret is an attempt to protect an aspect of self, and sometimes, to also protect others (Petrucelli, 2010). Relating in new ways to eating-disordered patients facilitates the uncovering of secrets so that the patient can move from "*being* the secret" to "*knowing* the secret" (Bromberg, 2011, p. 42).

When a female patient with a history of sexual abuse and an eating disorder was finally able to describe in detail the horrific events of her abuse which related to her difficulties with the ingestion of food, I felt compelled to respond passionately that her abuser was "an unbelievably disturbed pedophile that should be locked away forever or shot!" I knew that I had just thrown my cool, calm 'analytic hat' out the window. Yet, her response was "Thank you . . . it means a lot that you can 'hate' him *with* me. It makes me cry. You are right I have felt very alone with all of this . . . thank you, thank you." Sometimes when we share with our patients our experience of an aspect of their experience—in this case, embodied, expressed hatred for her abuser who caused her horrifying and demoralizing harm—this is a relief. My patient's dissociated hatred was lodged in her body and had taken the form of self-inflicted abuse. Bromberg (2006) emphasized the importance of recognizing the split-off dissociated aspects of self—the various self-states—that enter the room by paying attention to clinical moments, slips of the tongue, or uncanny felt experiences that represent another voice that the patient, and sometimes the analyst, has not revealed or had access to. It had taken years for this patient to begin to verbalize her experience. Speaking about the unspeakable allowed us, as patient and analyst, to authentically connect to the parts of her that were destabilized. Putting words to things unspoken, talking about food, rituals, and considering alternative behaviors gave us access into my patient's 'system,' her organizing principles, and to where she might find hope and the promise of a better life.

Sometimes patients believe that our suggestions will not work. Being interested in what happens when a patient tries or decides not to try to change is part of the data we gather through detailed inquiry, even if the patient does not want to speak about it. Sullivan (1954) is quoted as saying, "I do not believe that I have had an interview with anybody in twenty-five years in which the person to whom I was talking was not annoyed during the early part of my interview by my asking. . . ." Emotions abound between the patient and the analyst in the telling of the story, as well as in the story itself.

Patients, especially in the early stages, may not be able to give you specific information about their eating behavior, because the person who engaged in the behavior is rarely the person who you are asking to describe it in detail. What I mean is that instead, the analyst is confronted by a patient's self-state that knows 'about' the behavior, but does not have the experience of it being personal (Bromberg, 2011). This is true for all patients with serious dissociative mental structures, but it is particularly relevant with eating-disordered patients, as the nature of their symptoms—such as bingeing or purging—enhance dissociative tendencies.

As Wachtel (1993) and others (Frank, 1990; Mitchell, 1988) have noted, deepening the process of exploration and promoting greater access to warded off parts of the self (i.e., transitioning between the intrapsychic and interpersonal, between psychodynamic and behavior)—can be viewed as analytic explorations. Active interventions or suggestions provide more 'grist for the mill.' Sometimes concrete, self-soothing behavioral suggestions are appropriate. Among these are activities to increase mindfulness, such as turning off the TV while eating; activities that occupy one's hands, such as knitting; or activities that shift a mood until the uncomfortable moment passes. For this to be truly beneficial, however, the analyst must work in the here-and-now, with the patient's absence of mindfulness as it is manifested, even while these suggestions are being made. It is not uncommon for the a patient to have a dissociative response while we are making recommendations, even when these are fairly benign, such as suggesting playing a game, making a cup of tea, taking a walk, yoga, calling a friend, taking a bath with candles, dancing to a favorite song, or using music in novel ways. However, it is not just about real life interventions to promote mindfulness or helping patients look at what goes on between them and others. It is also important, if not more so, to keep the patient's mind, not just his or her life and eating habits, as a primary focus in the here and now. A patient who night binges rigged his refrigerator door to play music when he opened it, hoping a favorite song would wake him sufficiently and prevent him from his nightly eating ritual. The music also woke up other people in the house who entered the kitchen, preventing him from eating. This led to our discussion of how unconsciously creative this patient was to finally 'demand' the help and recognition he needed from his family and from the treatment as well.

What is said and not said, or what is seen and not seen, often creates a challenge for the analyst as to when to focus on the eating-disordered behaviors/symptoms or on underlying emotions and relational dynamics. Moving back and forth in this terrain is often intuitively felt, if the therapist stays mindful. It is often the unspoken agenda that is most important. Sullivan (1956), in his concept of selective inattention, described the process of shifting awareness away from anxiety-laden interpersonal situations and how doing this served a dual function. On one hand, the useful aspect of selective inattention is that it places out of awareness things that don't matter or that could be forgotten, freeing up the awareness of new, useful, and currently needed information. On the other hand, selective inattention operates to ignore or exclude aspects of experience that really do matter and thus prevents one from learning more effective interpersonal patterns. Sullivan (1956) contended that selective inattention operates 'backwards.' When interpersonal situations in the present trigger the recollection of a past anxiety-laden situation, selective attention operates to exclude the experience, even if attending to it was important (Evans, 1996, p. 143).

Attending to what is *not* said magnifies the possibility of revealing the unspoken agendas—what is being selectively inattended to—that interfere with a patient's attempts to self-regulate eating. For example, one patient who was very obsessive about her food plan spent two to three hours per day writing down her meals for that day. Not only did she count calories, but she also thought at length about her afternoon classes and what she should wear to them, given what she was going to eat. She also thought about who she was likely to see during the day and how she should adjust her food plans, depending upon whom she might run into. But her struggles with time management were only really uncovered when I discovered why she *needed* to change her appointment time: It took her two hours to walk to her session, no matter what her body was experiencing. It had never occurred to me that she would walk to the Upper West Side in Manhattan from Brooklyn! She revealed that she never takes subways or buses; she *had to* walk. Such information, as in this example, unfolds when you do a detailed inquiry, but, to be clear, it unfolds only when the patient is not dissociating during the process. Dissociation is not amnesia for events in and of themselves. Rather, it is an ability to 'sort-of-know,' which means 'knowing about,' but not knowing 'it.'

Curious Encounters of the Starving, Purging, or Bingeing Kind: Contracting

A verbal contract is an agreement made between patient and therapist regarding substituting alternative behaviors for disordered eating behaviors or thinking. Here, the analyst can get creative. The alternative behaviors are those that the patient is willing to engage in instead of, or before, turning to food. They may include self-soothing, communication, self-exploration, use of food in a structured manner, and, sometimes, pure distraction. But most important, they begin to create the idea that there can be a relationship to others—and that relationship can start with you, the therapist—standing in the space where disordered food behaviors have been. The goal of the contract is not merely abatement of eating behavior but also understanding what making the contract means to the patient, as the patient trusts you with more of her life (Brisman, 1998; Petrucelli, 2004).

Contracting is a way of beginning to mentalize, or holding the other in mind. Patients have to hold you holding them in mind. Adhering to or breaking the contract is equally important in understanding who the patient is and how he or she functions in a relationship—in this case, the relationship with the therapist. I have done various kinds of contracting with patients, but with each patient I keep a book, in which I take notes. This activity itself is an interpersonal dynamic. Some patients love it when I write, some patients want to read their book, and some ask, "Is that book all me?" Some patients see it as a barrier between us and become too focused on me writing, so I stop taking notes. All these interactions have a dynamic meaning in our relationship, and become ways in which our relationship inches its way into the patient's once covert and closed relationship with food—and then, transferentially, to other relationships in their lives.

Over the years, contracting tools as well as the process have changed with advances in technology. Beepers, phone machines, and voicemail have given way to emailing and texting, which sometimes enable patients to reach me more quickly. What has not changed is the underlying point of the contracting: to build mentalization through the medium of a strengthened relationship with the analyst. Another purpose of contracting, also unchanged, is that the patient first begins to entertain the idea of an alternative behavior and, second, learns to delay, when only impulse existed before. Contracting does not work for all patients, some of whom experience it as 'forced feeding.' Others, hungry for symptom relief and symptom substitution, are hungry—that is, they are hungry to for relatedness with another person. In other words, with contracting, the patient begins the process of taking me in, digesting my words, holding feelings, and using me as an alternative to using food.

What does it mean to a patient to hold the idea of an agreement in one's head? When a patient chooses to call, either when about to break our contract or when the contract is already broken, we discuss what it feels like to be attuned to our agreement, even though she feels that calling me is the last thing in the world she wants to do. When a patient does not call, and then tells me about it in the next session, we talk about why she didn't call. This conversation includes exploring the feelings before the binge, the planning and timing, how she binged or purged, whom she told, if anyone; and what she imagined would happen if she had called me. By understanding what the patient does in keeping or breaking a contract, the analyst begins to see the relational components of the eating disorder, in other words, the patient's capacity to self-soothe and regulate internal experience.

For example, I contracted with a young female patient with a history of buli-marexia with the idea of trying new behaviors. She is a dog lover and wanted to bring her dog into session. I am terrified of dogs and revealed to her my dog fears. She was floored and began a mission to 'cure' me. In treatment we were work-ing on desensitization of some of her anguish and disordered food behaviors. I challenged her to a day with no purging and to keep a food log. She agreed. That evening, I received a photo and following text where she sent me a dog picture (see Figure 1.1), and she wrote under it, "Least scary dog picture ever."

Within seconds I received a second text and picture of her other dog (see Figure 1.2). "OK . . . I can see how the ears are a little intimidating, but can you really resist that face?"

Over the weekend, after having contracted with her to keep a food journal, I received the following text and picture (see Figure 1.3) hours before her next appointment.

She texted, "Here's another angle . . . it was so perfect I had to take pictures before I took the journal from her." She offered this in the context of why she failed to bring her journal into session. "I swear I didn't give her this to destroy . . . she took it out of my bag . . . I rescued it." (see Figure 1.4)

Doing this contract served several purposes in that it shed light on disowned parts of her. On one level she turned the kitchen table on me where she attempted to desensitize me while not letting me desensitize her. On another level, in a funny, playful, and poignant way, she leveled the playing field by letting me know how hard and real the undertaking of contracting was. She needed me to engage in the facing of a fear and feel something else—so I could viscerally experience how hard it was for her. Her child self-state needed to have a safe place to be in where that part of her could express its own fears, traumatic responses and also play and

Figure 1.1 Least scary dog picture

Figure 1.2 Pure sweetness

be comforted. She needed to know that I could contain and be playful about fear before she could trust that I could contain and respect her fears as well. You don't disabuse the baby about the blanket. She got a kick out of me being afraid of dogs, and I was comfortable sharing that part of me with her. It put us on equal footing in a way that seemed helpful.

29

Figure 1.3 What could possibly go wrong

Figure 1.4 Playing with ambivalence

Getting Gritty, Coming Clean: Food Journaling and Texting

Another way to invite the symptom in the room is to ask eating-disordered patients to keep a journal in which they record their weekly food intake as well as other ingested substances (alcohol, laxatives, diuretics, drugs, etc.). Texting has infiltrated this arena as I receive picture texts of plates of food as well.

Food charts involve recording the time, place, food, levels of hunger and satiety, substance use, feelings, and eating disorder symptomatic behaviors. Often patients are recording this with a nutritionist, but I sometimes start the process to get a baseline and ascertain the extent to which a patient can use this effectively. Some patients prefer to write just for themselves, while others will use writing as a tool of interpersonal exchange. One patient will say that writing is calming and centering; another will report that it makes her tense and anxious for she can never find the 'right' words. Patients may write as little or as much as they choose. When it is helpful, they continue writing, even when I suggest they can stop. Some patients initiate a break from writing, and return to it when they feel that they are becoming more symptomatic. The relational exchange of decision making and implementation is important information as patients gravitate towards, or away from, a tool—such as journaling, emailing or texting.

Writing may be used as a vehicle to connect to one's internal process as it facilitates knowing and trusting one's self. For an eating-disordered patient, writing can be excruciatingly painful as one goes through the process of recording the time one eats, what one eats, how much one eats, bingeing and purging behavior, and what one is feeling around food. However, it begins the process of naming the affective experience, formulating for patients what they are experiencing, and facilitating interpersonal trust as they share it with another. On the other hand, revealing one's secret world to the therapist may also elicit myriad feelings of being judged, of shame, disgust, self-loathing, and even relief. Food journaling may also serve as a container for the out-of-control feelings related to food.

Likewise, journaling helps patients to gain access to a place untraveled within them. To put something on paper requires the person to develop the ability to stand back and observe. When all goes well, the process of journaling food and behaviors teaches self-monitoring, while serving as a transitional object often providing the patient with a sense of safety.

Journal writing, as well as the anticipated reading and sharing of one's thoughts and feelings concerning food with the therapist may facilitate the patient's "ability to be alone in the anticipated presence of another" (Winnicott, 1958, 1971). Journal writing also facilitates 'potential space,' a place from which to become aware (Rabinor, 1991). The writing provides an opportunity to access cut off aspects of one's own self-experience. The hope is that a patient may initially open up to herself and then may later share this awareness with her therapist.

31

Conclusion

In this chapter, what I hope to demonstrate is not merely the efficacy of utilizing these techniques but the necessity of doing so. I want to highlight how interpersonal and relational traditions are the bedrock for this kind of integrated work, which combines active interventions while still being analytic.

The work of any treatment is an ongoing, complicated mixture of direct intervention with the symptom and exploration of what the intervention means to the patient, including the role the symptom plays in the patient's intrapsychic and interpersonal world. Understanding this as it unfolds relationally allows the intersubjective experience of both patient and therapist to collide, mingle, and ultimately coexist. As clinicians, we are fortunate to have the opportunity to share in a patient's journey towards health and recovery. On this passage we come face-to-face with our patients' courage, strengths, limitations, and perseverance, which often fly in the face of severe medical and psychosocial stressors. Zerbe (1993) has noted that it is a humbling and inspiring experience, one that keeps us striving to make fresh assessments of what really works, what is helpful, and what is not in making those shifts.

Cultivating our curiosity and the curiosity of the patient means finding and reconnecting the parts of the patient that have been disconnected for so long. It means allowing the frightened shadows of self to ally with a new sense of being that moves towards acceptance of health, in mind and body. Our hope is to inspire patients to tell their story, as well as to accept our willingness to hear their pain without judgment, to hold their disgust, their skeletal pieces, their fat, and their hurts. Curiosity converts strangers into people with whom we can empathize, even the garbage-eating-violent-vegetable-purging ones. Our goal is to help our patients through a process of reflection, exploration, and self-discovery to order to increase their capacity for more fulfilling relationships, and to experience less guilt and shame. We help our eating-disordered patients tolerate a wider range of affects and face their challenges with greater flexibility and less fear of the unknown. We help them learn to live in the 'grey,' to endure imperfection by accepting their bodies with the idea of a body being 'good enough,' and probably, above all, to help them establish a sense of self that is not based on their eating disorder. This means making peace with both whom one is, and who one is not, respecting personal histories and limits without letting these define the individual. Sullivan (1956) said that it is easier to act yourself into a new way of feeling than to feel yourself into a new way of acting. The simple, yet complicated message we impart might ultimately be: Create the life you want to live and *live* the life you are trying to create.

Acknowledgement

I would like to thank the following people for reading versions of this chapter and for their invaluable insights: Philip M. Bromberg, Joseph Canarelli, Don Grief, Ruth Livingston, Nicholas Samstag, and Sarah Schoen.

References

Barth, D. (2001). Thinking, talking and feeling in psychotherapy. In J. Petrucelli & C. Stuart (Eds.), *Hungers and compulsions: The psychodynamic treatment of eating disorders & addictions* (pp. 41–52). Northvale, NJ: Jason Aronson.

Barth, D. (2008). Hidden eating disorders: Attachment and affect regulation in the therapeutic relationship. *Clinical Social Work Journal, 36,* 355–365.

Brisman, J. (1994). Learning to listen: Therapeutic encounters and negotiations in the early stage of treatment. *Eating Disorders, 2*(1), 68–73.

Brisman, J. (1995). Psychodynamic psychotherapy and action-oriented technique: An integrated approach. In I. Yalom & J. Werne (Eds.), *Treating eating disorders* (pp. 311–370). San Francisco, CA: Jossey-Bass.

Brisman, J. (1998). When actions speak louder than words: Verbal and non-verbal wrangling in the therapeutic arena. *Psychoanalytic Dialogues, 8*(5), 707–714.

Bromberg, P. (1998). *Standing in the spaces: Essays on clinical process, trauma, and dissociation.* Hillsdale, NJ: Analytic Press.

Bromberg, P. (2006). *Awakening the dreamer: Clinical journeys.* Hillsdale, NJ: Analytic Press.

Bromberg, P. (2011). *The shadow of the tsunami and the growth of the relational mind.* New York: Routledge.

Bruch, H. (1973). *Eating disorders, obesity, anorexia and the person within.* New York: Basic Books.

Davis, W. (1991). Reflections on boundaries in the psychotherapeutic relationship. In C. Johnson (Ed), *Psychodynamic treatment of anorexia and bulimia* (pp. 68–85). New York: Guilford Press.

Davis, W. (2009). Individual psychotherapy for anorexia nervosa and bulimia: Making a difference. In M. Maine, W. David, & J. Shure (Eds.), *Effective clinical practice in the treatment of eating disorders* (pp. 35–48). New York: Routledge.

Evans, F. B. (1996). *Harry Stack Sullivan: Interpersonal theory and psychotherapy.* New York: Routledge.

Fink, B. (2004). *Lacan to the Letter.* Minneapolis: University of Minnesota Press.

Frank, K. A. (1990). Action techniques in psychoanalysis. *Contemp. Psychoanal., 26,* 732–756.

Glennon, S. S. (2012, June). *Therapeutic action from a relational perspective.* Paper presented at a meeting of the Comparative Psychoanalysis Group, NYU Postdoc, New York, NY.

Kohut, H. (1972). Thoughts on narcissism and narcissistic rage. *Psychoanal. St. Child., 27,* 360–400.

Krueger, D. W. (2001). Body self: Development, psychopathologies, and psychoanalytic significance. *The Psychoanalytic Study of the Child, 56,* 238–259.

Kuriloff, E. (2004). When words fail: Psychosomatic illness and the talking cure. *Psychoanalytic Quarterly, LXXIII,* 1023–1040.

Levenson, E. A. (1983). *The ambiguity of change.* New York: Basic Books.

Levenson, E. A. (1988). The pursuit of the particular: On the psychoanalytic inquiry. *Contemporary Psychoanalysis, 24,* 1–16.

Maine, M., & Bunnell, D. (2010). A perfect biopsychosocial storm: Gender, culture, and eating disorders. In M. Maine, B. Hartman McGilley, & D. Bunnell (Eds.), *Treatment of eating disorders* (pp. 3–16). London: Academic Press/Elsevier.

Mitchell, S. A. (1988). *Relational concepts in psychoanalysis: An integration.* New York: Harvard University Press.

Mitchell, S. A. (1999). Attachment theory and the psychoanalytic tradition: Reflections on human relationality. *Psychoanalytic Dialogues, 9,* 85–107.

Orbach, S. (2009). *Bodies.* New York: Picador.

Perry, H. S., Gawel, M. L., & Gibbon, M. (Eds.). *Clinical studies in psychiatry.* New York: Norton.

Petrucelli, J. (2004). Treating eating disorders. In R. H. Coombs (Ed.), *Handbook of addictive disorders: A practical guide to diagnosis and treatment* (pp. 312–352). Hillsdale, NJ: John Wiley & Sons.

Petrucelli, J. (2010). Things that go bump in the night: Secrets after dark. In J. Petrucelli (Ed.), *Knowing, not-knowing & sort-of-knowing: Psychoanalysis and the experience of uncertainty* (pp. 135–150). London: Karnac Books.

Pitts, C. (2014). "Look at me—What am I supposed to be?" In J. Petrucelli (Ed.), *Bodystates: Interpersonal and relational perspectives on the treatment of eating disorders.* London: Routledge.

Rabinor, J. (1991). The process of recovery from an eating disorder: The use of journal writing in the initial phase of treatment. *Psychotherapy in Private Practice, 9*(1), 93–106.

Sands, S. (1997). Protein or foreign body? Reply to commentaries. *Psychoanalytic Dialogues, 7,* 691–706.

Stern, D. (1997). *Unformulated experience: From dissociation to imagination in psychoanalysis.* Hillsdale, NJ: Analytic Press.

Stern, D. (2008). On having to find what you don't know how to look for: Two perspectives on reflection. In E. Jurist, A. Slade, & S. Bergner (Eds.), *Mind to mind: Infant research, neuroscience and psychoanalysis* (pp. 398–413). New York: Other Press.

Stolorow, R. D., & Atwood, G. E. (1991). The mind and the body. *Psychoanalytic Dialogues, 1*(2), 181–195.

Sullivan, H. S. (1953). *The interpersonal theory of psychiatry.* New York: W. W. Norton.

Sullivan, H. S. (1954). *The psychiatric interview.* New York: W. W. Norton.

Sullivan, H. S., with Perry, H. S., Gawel, M. L., & Gibbon, M. (Eds.). (1956). *Clinical studies in psychiatry.* New York: Norton.

Wachtel, P. L. (1993). Active intervention, psychic structure, and the analysis of transference: Commentary on Frank's "Action, insight, and working through." *Psychoanal. Dial., 3,* 589–603.

Winnicott, D. W. (1958). The capacity to be alone. In *The maturational processes and the facilitating environment* (pp. 29–36). New York: International Universities Press.

Winnicott, D. W. (1971). *Playing and reality.* New York: Basic Books.

Zerbe, K. (1993). Treatment: The body reclaimed. In *The body betrayed: A deeper understanding of women, eating disorders, and treatment* (pp. 347–374). Carlsbad, CA: Gurze Books.

2

'MY BODY IS A CAGE'

Interfacing Interpersonal Neurobiology, Attachment, Affect Regulation, Self-Regulation, and the Regulation of Relatedness in Treatment With Patients With Eating Disorders

Jean Petrucelli

> Escape as a thankful word both makes one grateful and gives thanks itself that we can imagine alternatives for ourselves. . . . Escape is a possibility made in language.
>
> Adam Phillips (2001)

Eating Disorders are maladaptive attempts to survive the unbearable, both psychologically and psychophysiologically. This is immensely helpful and important to keep in mind, partly because it adds a science to our understanding and anchors our understanding in an organic structure, which has psychological implications. Offering this insight to eating-disordered patients can alleviate the degree to which these patients blame themselves and some failure of will for their struggles. It also helps prevent people from using the notion of blame as a way to explain all things disordered. As clinicians, it offers us a textured dimension to our growing knowledge and much needed empathetic resonance. When my patient says to me, 'My body is a cage,' she is not just quoting the Peter Gabriel song. She is conveying to me her unbearable pain and the level of relational entrenchment she experiences with her symptoms.

This chapter will explore how we can thoughtfully integrate the neurobiological workings of the brain, the psychological experience of self and self-as-embodied, and the interpersonal context of relationships, as we address and alleviate eating-disordered symptoms and underlying psychological conflicts with our patients. It is a clinical mindbody–bodymind conundrum.

The brain is not a static entity: it is built and rebuilt within the context of experience, especially interpersonal experience. Our challenge is to find the empirical body and to simultaneously attend to the lived body—the body as it is subjectively experienced—and to expand on the implications for treatment.

For the patient with an eating disorder, the body is center stage as, Joyce McDougal (1989) and many others have said—we witness how unthinkable thoughts often get 'stuck' in the body, and these bodily actions and nonverbal communications can often be dramatic in nature. Eating-disordered patients, for the most part, are not adept at communicating in words, since their distress is communicated through food rituals. And because they often have no words to describe their feelings, they can only feel completely overwhelmed by their emotions. This inability to regulate affect creates a numbing or anesthetized state, a state that, to the eating-disordered patient is preferable to the state of being overwhelmed by emotional chaos. An eating disorder is an attempt at self-cure, which fails and leads to further isolation, chaos, and helplessness—it is never simply a matter of self-control. It is a maladaptive attempt to be self-constructive or self-protective rather than simply an expression of self-destruction. This deeper psychic pain sometimes manifests itself in an 'antsyness' of being. When we help patients expand their consciousness and perceptions of their internal and external states, they also come face-to-face or body-to-body, in a manner of speaking, with the absence of disconnect and integral aspects of self.

There are many ways in which the meanings of the body play a prominent role in our understanding of human subjectivity. The role of the body and the self-reflexive function of the mind meet in the interpersonal treatment of eating disorders. The mutual impact of the mind and the body on each other, as part of the clinical treatment process, involves both patient and analyst jointly processing, experiencing, and reflecting on psychosomatic experiences. Is the body something we have, something we are, or something we become? What exactly are these bodies that we are trying to live in? The relationship between bodies and identities is fascinating. We understand and accept that identity and bodies are formed with reference to our cultural world, but understanding the role of interpersonal neurobiology and its relationship to interpersonal experience is also key.

With this is in mind, I'm going to try to weave together four aspects that relate to our understanding of eating disorders and treatment considerations.

One: Interpersonal Neurobiology

We can begin with understanding and respecting our neurobiological foundation, because the underlying genetic structure of a person plays a role in shaping vulnerability and resilience, which, in turn, affects how one perceives, organizes, and responds to experiences. We know there is a genetic underpinning for anorexia and now better understand the role of neurotransmitters and genetics in terms of depression and anxiety. The part played by genes has to be acknowledged, but the limitations must also be understood. LeDoux (2002) explained that "genes only shape the broad outline of mental and behavioral functions . . . inheritance may bias us in certain directions, but many other factors dictate how one's genes are expressed" (p. 66). He concluded that nature and nurture are not different things but rather are different ways of doing the same thing, which is wiring synapses in the brain.

We could say that we are the product of how our brains *and* our bodies operate, in that all of our subjective experiences cannot be precisely explained by anatomy and physiology of the brain. Nor is everything we feel, know, and experience understandable by how the brain functions. Are we constrained by the brain's influences and operations on our bodies? Or are we free to explore knowing ourselves and our bodies to see the bodily reactions—ours and those of our patients—as gateways to understanding the ways in which the body has a mind of its own? Mind, brain, and body are inextricably linked: This proverbial cake has many layers.

There is increasing interest in the particular role of the right hemisphere of the brain in human development. The right hemisphere is thought to be preferentially involved in both maternal behavior and the early emotional experience of the infant. Most mothers and many higher primates carry their infant with their left arm so that the infant's head is against the mother's left breast, Thus, the infant has more direct visual communication with the right hemisphere (Sieratzki & Woll, 1996), as the mother's face is key in transmission of affect (Schore, 2003, p. 18).

Neuroscientific research is confirming that our ability to manage emotions is directly tied to our early attachment experiences (Fonagy, Gergely, Jurist, & Target, 2002; Schore & Schore, 2008; O'Kearney, 1996; Schore, 2010; Treasure, Tchanturia, & Ulrike, 2005; Zhang, Li, & Zhou, 2008). Schore (2003) has gathered a substantial amount of research that illustrates the effect of different experiences of parenting on early brain development. He concludes that it is the interaction of constitutional predisposition and exposure to stressors in the early environment that leads to deficits in frontal lobe functioning. In terms of early childhood, psychosocial neglect and deprivation have been shown to be the strongest predictors of such damage, along with the inevitable parental misattunements and/or sometimes psychopathology. The effects include dysregulation of affect, impairment of attachment, impaired cognitive processing, and a greater reliance on external stimulators (i.e., food or mind-altering drugs) as soothing mechanisms. There is a psychoneurobiological factor underlying the cyclical nature that is fear based related to early attachment. This is then patterned and repeated throughout life (Schore, 2009). Such overreliance on a defensive system can be neurobiologically explained and psychologically understood as we piece together how early experience affects the development of neural pathways in the service of self protection.

Brain researchers are now able to measure and trace neural pathways. Increased activity in the developing brain leads to increased synaptic complexity. Since each person's experience is different, there are different patterns of connectivity in every brain-mind. As Greenfield, in a 2001 BBC Breakfast TV broadcast said, "The brain consists of brain cell connections. It is your personal configuration of these that gives you your mind" (Wilkinson, 2004, p. 83). People with trauma and addictive disorders have a smaller number of neural pathways in the hippocampus (Berthoud, Lenard, & Shin, 2011). The hippocampus is involved in the formation and retrieval of implicit and explicit memories, and what happens in these neural networks is something like 'cells that fire together, wire together' (Edelman, 1989, 2004), meaning that information keeps going down the same path so that, in essence, the person has a more limited access to other choices of behaviors. If the hippocampus cannot do its job, all intense feelings and affect above the person's threshold level cannot be processed. Instead, they are stored in the amygdala. The amygdala has a central role in the processing of emotions. It is responsible for evaluating the affective significance of external stimuli as well as information coming from within, which takes the form of thoughts, images, and memories. This system, which operates outside conscious awareness, is particularly primed to react to fear and anger, but the amygdale has no ability to allow for self-reflection (Schore, 2003).

Experiences, then, are 'held' in the body without symbolization; because one cannot reflect, their ability to make thoughtful choices is affected. And without the capability of using symbolic or metaphoric thought, it is often the body that is left to keep score (Van der Kolk, 1994; Aron, 1998) and the flesh becomes the storehouse of subjectivity. The amygdala is the receiving and sending station between input from the outer world and emotional response. It has a crucial role in coordinating perceptions with memory and behavior. It is sensitive to social interactions. The point is, the amygdale nonconsciously assigns significance to stimuli, only allowing access to concrete language as it shuts down higher symbolic emotional processing pathways and access to symbolic language, memory in language, and reality testing and planning functions (Pearlman, 2014).

What we see in the therapeutic setting are these patients enacting dysfunctional patterns of eating or relationships to food played out again and again in a manner that often seems automatic (or without conscious thought), or dissociated—same old, same old response; same neural road. And they enact these patterns without being able to articulate them in a way that makes them understandable in light of previous experience (Bromberg, 2008, pp. 98–100). What you often hear when you ask about a binge is, "I don't know why I did it and don't see the relevance of talking about it. That was yesterday. I'm going to be good today. I don't want to think about that episode again." The patient is actively trying to keep apart the past and the present, dissociating that part of his or her self-experience or self-state that was actively engaged in the disordered behavior.

The neurobiological findings now suggest that changes in the hippocampus are linked to remembering past relationships; without this ability 'to hold those thoughts,' the repetition of dysfunctional patterns is more likely to occur. Here is a clinical illustration.

Carla: Witnessing a 'Kentucky Flying' Chicken

Carla won't ask a question of others because she fears they would 'want' something from her—they might ask a question back, and then if she answers it she is revealing or 'giving up' something that is privately hers. To reveal something on the inside reflects the loss of something that lives inside of her. Carla is a binge eater who was 5 feet tall and weighed 280 pounds when she started treatment. She has many compulsive food rituals. In her field of work, she is surrounded with medically compromised and often terminally ill people where she is the 'captain' and a model of compassion and care. However, she is terrified of her own experience of wanting—of wanting anything. She is often upset with me that I have 'made' some of her dissociated feeling states more known now and conscious. For Carla, not being able to *not* know and losing weight (about 120 pounds), she feels like she has no place to hide. The more she feels, the more she questions whether she can continue to do her job because the pain of her job now seems unbearable, and without her job, she feels she has very little. Her history revealed one traumatic relationship where a long-term boyfriend led a double life, living with another woman while being with Carla for several years. Neither of the women knew of this until Pandora's lid flew open. The deceit led to a precipitous breakup. Soon after, Carla developed breast cancer. Without using food as her anesthesia, without a sensed ability to modulate overwhelming affective states, and without a mind that had solidified new neural templates, she struggled and often felt ungrounded.

Carla would tell me that she had no desire or curiosity to explore and uncover her desire. She would tell me that she did not know what was in her mind or even really know what the mind is. I told her that according to Dan Siegel (personal communication) there was no definition of the mind in the field of mental health—yet ironically we are all interested in getting the 'mind' healthy. We talked about how she could use her mind to get her brain to get its act together—how to become more aware of the subtle shifts in what she 'might' be feeling and thinking, and where these shifts might be located in her body. Carla did not allow herself to want to lose weight for a long time because she felt she had a 'problem with her mind' and how all the information in it hooked up. She was invested in not increasing her awareness and did not want to 'use' her mind to change her brain until she felt safer with me.

Carla's dysregulated system of functioning was rigid in its attempt to avoid chaos because she had been traumatized in an environment where she was exposed to intense rage. All strong feelings had to be muted. She could never have food in her fridge. Everything she purchased or consumed had to be in even numbers—she had to eat six grapes, not five. Foods couldn't mix on a plate; she would fold her dirty laundry before putting it in the hamper. I asked her to share with me some of her rituals around food. I started by having her write one word a day in a journal: This one word became one sentence, then two paragraphs, and finally a few pages.

Carla's food rituals were attempts to keep 'wanting or yearning' at bay. She made me wonder if it is our therapeutic job to bring 'yearning' into the treatment room? Or do we just let the absence of 'yearning' exist, honoring our patients' different parts by promoting compassionate links through respectful communication?

As human beings, we are hardwired to connect—our mirror neurons are firing all the time. Mitchell (1999) said that we develop intense attachments because we crave relatedness. But what happens when there has been trauma? What happens when we need to allow a patient to want in ways that we cannot understand? We could think about how Carla's early attachment difficulties impacted her affect regulation and neurobiology as well. One poignant memory she tells is of witnessing her mother's unbridled anger. On this particular day, her mother, while raging at the dinner table, picked up a whole chicken by the leg and threw it across the room. This memory was significant for Carla as a food story and as a traumatic remembering of affect 'gone wild.' Her distress was communicated through her food rituals since she had no words to describe her affect. She could only feel completely overwhelmed by her feelings. Here, it is important to note that, although she blamed me—her therapist—for making her painfully conscious of her dissociated self-experience, Carla was able to lose all that weight because new neurons wired into the old networks while they fired together.

Two: Attachment

The second idea woven into this relational matrix is to understand that attachment, self-regulation, and affect regulation are all necessary interlocking components of human development. Attachment styles, even when problematic, are also adaptive. How do we understand and utilize the therapeutic relationship, through the lens of an attachment system, to effect change? Is it a matter of mind or 'not-mind'—having no cognitive or verbal representation? For example, Dan Siegel (1999) described attachment as, "an inborn system in the brain that evolves in ways that influence and organize motivational, emotional and memory processes with respect to significant care giving figures" (p. 67). He believed that attachment establishes an interpersonal relationship that helps the immature brain use the mature functions of the parent's brain to organize its own processes. Thus, it is a crucial component of emotional and cognitive development. Later, Siegel (2010) wrote, "At the most basic level, therefore, secure attachments in both childhood and adulthood are established by two individual's sharing a nonverbal focus on the energy flow (emotional states) and a verbal focus on the information-processing aspects (representational processes of memory and narrative) of mental life" (p. 55). Siegel (2010) believed, "the *matter of the mind matters* for secure attachments" (p. 189, emphasis is mine).

Bromberg (2011) and others (Schore & Schore, 2008) present a different view from Siegel. They take the position that attachment is a totally procedural process that is interpersonally organized by patterns of behavior without thought. It is an evolutional survival system designed to enlist parental rescue in emergency situations and, because it is procedural, it has no cognitive or verbal representation. Emotion is initially externally regulated by the primary caregiver, but over the course of infancy, it becomes increasingly internally regulated as a result of neurophysiological development (Schore, 2010). Schore (2010) wrote that these adaptive capacities are central to self-regulation, which includes one's ability to flexibly regulate states of emotion through interactions with others, interaction in interconnected contexts, and also in times without others. When trauma is attachment related, *thought* is impossible since one of the elements *cannot* reach the level of thought. The interpersonal relationship that is established by attachment is *enacted*, not thought. It is attuned to affect and behavior patterns (Bromberg, 2011). In working with eating-disordered patients, I feel it makes sense to think of attachment patterns as being affected by the regulation of biological synchronicity between and within people rather than as involving thought and self-reflection. In treatment, the therapist, as other, helps makes the self-reflective capacity of the patient become possible.

The Cat's in the Cradle: Attachment and Development

Infants are born with a great deal of affect and little capacity to regulate their own rapid shifts between high and low arousal states. As their only self-regulating capabilities are limited to sucking, gaze aversion, and dissociation they need comforting and nurturing caretakers to experience and learn ways to self-soothe and modulate affect (Lapides, 2010). Attachment is affected not only by the external environment (i.e., mothering), but also by the internal environment (i.e., the genetic makeup of the child, along with personality factors). Thus, the fit between the mother and child is crucial because it is about mutual attunement. Siegel (2010, p. 35) differentiated between the idea of presence—the state of being open—and attunement, which requires presence but is a process of focused attention and clear perception. Taking in another's internal state is necessary for interpersonal attunement. Mothers are not always available to fill the requirements of maternal preoccupation. Optimally, the caregiver must be psychobiologically attuned to the dynamic crescendos and decrescendos of the infant's bodily based internal states of arousal. To effectively accomplish this interactive regulation, the mother must modulate too high or too low levels of stimulation, which would induce either super heightened or extremely low levels of arousal in the infant. Alternatively, a child who is unable to demand the mother's attention may withdraw and allow poor mothering to continue, whereas a more forceful child might draw out appropriate attention from the mother. In addition, some children may be less affected by their mother's anxiety than others (Schore, 2001).

When a parent is alexithymic ('no words for feelings'), there is a high likelihood that he or she will have impaired attunement to his or her infant's emotional states and nonverbal communications. We have some evidence that alexithymia is associated with insecure attachment styles (Fonagy et al., 2002; Damasio, 1999; Barth, 2008). Lapides (2010) wrote, "Parents who are regulated themselves can be responsively attuned, moving toward the child to attend to them, or picking up the infant to stroke, rock or walk the child, while cooing soothing sounds or singing lullabies. These are all RH (right hemisphere), nonverbal communications; a child has no verbal processing LH (left hemisphere) until the age of 2 years, as this area of the brain does not begin to myelinate until the end of the second year of life" (p. 39). Once left hemisphere neural pathways are in place, given sufficient processing time, the slower left hemisphere can exert a regulating influence over the more emotional right hemisphere. This means we can use the verbal capacities of the left hemisphere to both dysregulate ourselves with anxious thoughts and imagined catastrophes, and to regulate ourselves and one another through calm, soothing thoughts and verbal reassurances, distraction, or reframing. By introjecting these soothing moments, the infant learns to self-soothe internally. On the other hand, when infants are left unregulated with body distress, too often and for too long, their capacity for affect regulation is impaired; we see this in insecure attachment patterns. With an insecure attachment, the primary caregiver can induce traumatic states of enduring negative affect in the child. This occurs when a caregiver is inaccessible and reacts to his or her infant's expressions of emotions and stress in inappropriate, rejecting, or unpredictable ways. Instead of modulating levels of arousal, an abusing or neglectful caregiver then induces extreme levels of stimulation and arousal, for example, very high levels in abuse and/or very low in neglect. Without the caregiver providing the necessary interactive repair, the infant's negative affective states can last for long periods of time.

Subsequent dysregulation can take the form of chronic hyperarousal or dissociation (hypoactivation), and can leave the child predisposed to an eating disorder or substance use because the child turns to external sources to soothe or regulate internal distress (Schore, 2003). With hyperarousal, you see alarm or startle reaction of the infant's right hemisphere (the locus of both the attachment system and the fear motivational system); that is, an infant too aroused becomes too anxious. When a person is left in a state of hypoarousal too often or too long, this individual may lose the ability to sense his or her own corporeal self. Such a reaction to relational trauma is dissociation, in which the child disengages from stimuli in the external world (e.g., 'staring off into space with a glazed look' or the 'deer in the headlights' look). This withdrawal occurs in helpless and hopeless stressful situations: The individual becomes inhibited and strives to avoid attention to become 'unseen' (Schore, 2003).

I have a patient with severe anorexia who describes this phenomenon as the 'dead spots' in her subjective experience—when she feels 'slowed down' and lost in a black hole. "I feel nothing," she says, and demonstrates a passive wave of her arms and head. She is trying to put words to this early experience.

The dissociative metabolic shutdown state is a primary regulatory process, used throughout the life span to survive. When we are stressed, we slow down and conserve our energies, which allow us to regroup. We usually don't think twice about doing this, but it is not so automatic or comfortable if we live in fear of the 'black hole of nothingness.' But here is the psychological pull: In this passive hypometabolic state, heart rate, blood pressure, and respiration are decreased, whereas pain numbing and blunting endogenous *opiates are elevated.* It is this energy conserving parasympathetic (vagal) mechanism that mediates the 'profound detachment' of dissociation. The 'profound detachment' is what you see in both anorexia and bulimia with the experience of bingeing and purging. It also speaks to the 'immediate relief' or 'short-lived good feeling' to which patients become addicted: they are not kidding when they tell you they 'feel better'—and physiologically they do—for a bit. Yet, this emotional anesthesia serves a defensive function against the destabilization of the self; therefore, eating, bingeing, or purging becomes an attempt to control what can't be regulated on both physiological and psychological levels. Bromberg (2011) stated, "a primary attachment figure, a parent or an Other whose significance is interpersonally similar to a parent's, . . . holds the power to destabilize the child's mental state by rupturing a relational connection that organizes the child's sense of self-continuity" (p. xvi). The mind then triggers a survival solution and is pulled to dissociate or sometimes use external actions that might aid in the dissociative process, such as bingeing and purging. If defensive overregulation becomes an adopted pattern of behavior, then strong feelings in the body may be unable to rise through the neural chain into consciousness; instead, these may be regulated by external behaviors (Schore, 2010) like bingeing, purging, cutting, or other forms of self-mutilation.

Eating-disordered patients have difficulty titrating anxiety, and their thinking is rigid. If the functions of the right hemisphere, as Schore (2003) and others have described, are involved in the development of 'one's implicit self system,' then knowledge of one's self-states are below conscious awareness for these patients. Schore (1996) posited that this 'below-awareness' is the biological substrate of the dynamic unconscious. When placed in therapeutic situations that demand fluent responses and knowledge of self-states, eating-disordered patients typically cannot function. Operating, as they often do, in a concrete paradigm in response to emotional challenges, they become aware of their body state and not their feeling state. A common response of these patients to their therapists' attempts to communicate is silence or to speak of how fat and disgusting they feel. This is why eating-disordered patients typically do not understand what is being asked of them in traditional analytic or psychoanalytic psychotherapy and, in fact, often find the whole process bewildering and threatening (Bruch, 1978; Sohn, 1985).

When there is little ability or connection to the well of nonverbal, ongoing, out-of-consciousness experience, asking an eating-disordered patient to freely associate to ideas as they come to mind is often beyond their capacity. Instead, we often get highly intellectualized language rather than expression of the self-state or 'implicit self system' or 'dynamic unconscious.' There is a split or dissociation between feeling states and conscious language: The patient may sound as if her language functions are intact and it may seem that she is responding 'normally' to the therapy, but the material may be unrelated to her feeling state, both expressively and receptively (see Chapter 20).

Understanding the neurobiological component is interesting and crucial, because it also explains why you can't talk logic or rationality alone. Asking a patient if she really wants to be sticking the fork down, ripping her throat, won't get you anywhere because—in that moment—it's a case of the 'f—k-its.' So instead I might ask the patient if she might consider suspending the rational part of her brain for a moment. I might say something like, "Because I know that you know that I know that you know . . ." (i.e., that purging five times a day isn't doing

43

wonders for your body, etc.). Or, I might ask if we could convey to each other the irrational/emotional 'other voice' that sometimes only shows itself through the body. I do this in the hopes of creating greater empathy for the patient's experience, empathy that can be felt between us while hoping for the gradual creation of a relational unconscious to emerge. It's also important to hold eating-disordered patients' neurobiology in one's mind as a patient becomes asymptomatic: initially patients feel raw and unable to deal with or make sense of their strong emotions, emotions that have been unformulated. They now need a different kind of communication. We must connect to our patients' right hemispheres and create attachments, with an emphasis on their felt experience. And we must do this with attunement, empathy, and resonance rather than with intellectualized language.

Three: Affect and Self-Regulation

Attachment relationships are decisive because they facilitate the growing development of the brain's self-regulating system. Attachment and self-regulation affect each other. Self-regulation is influenced by one's capacity to regulate affect. The third notion to weave into our integrative understanding of bodymind is the idea that self-regulation, which shows up in self-care issues (Stern, 2007; Petrucelli, 2004), and the concept of affect regulation relate to each other—from the symptoms themselves, to resistance to the therapeutic process, to transference and countertransference issues, to the overwhelming feelings. The inability to regulate affect creates a numbing or anesthetized state that, to this patient, is preferable to being overwhelmed by emotional chaos. Given the difficulties eating-disordered patients experience with self-regulation, affect regulation and dysregulation, there are special concerns; that is, these patients are likely to dissociate.

How does one determine regulation of intake and processing of information when the 'normal' filters and abilities to digest that information are not in place? It is harder for patients with eating disorders to experience change or to be comfortable with uncertainty.

Self-regulation can be thought of as the ability to successfully integrate external and internal demands, while at the same time sustaining a feeling of safety, self-continuity, and desire. With limited ability to self soothe, self-regulate, and self-enliven, eating-disordered patients are vulnerable to feelings of depletion, fragmentation, and overstimulation (Goodsitt, 1983). Affect regulation refers to the way our nervous system manages the arousal in response to stress—basically, the way we manage energy. Through the lens of affect regulation theory, eating disorders can be thought of as strategies to manage excessive and disruptive arousal in combination with the failure of early attachment relationships to teach sufficient self-regulation and co-regulation capacities (Lapides, 2010, p. 39). In other words, eating-disordered patients are not adept at communicating in words, and they feel affectively overwhelmed. Since they cannot practice dealing with conflict—they don't learn how. In the absence of a more direct or effective way to modulate arousal, the eating-disordered patient relies on external regulators related to the seeking or avoidance of food. Some patients turn toward food; others see it as the enemy. Attempts to self-regulate take the form of compulsive overeating, bulimic bingeing/purging to create a dissociative 'numbing' state, anorexic avoidance of food, or often a combination of all three (Lapides, 2010). If you can't self-regulate or have difficulties with self-regulation, your capacity for relatedness with others is affected. What you will often hear from an eating-disordered patient is, "I'd rather stay home and binge than go to the party."

Regulation of Relatedness

When a person's capacity for relatedness is affected, it creates anxiety and instability in one's multiple self-representations—that is, how this person sees him- or herself. This then leads to further difficulties. These difficulties are intrapsychic as well as interpersonal. That's why the regulation of relatedness becomes important, because you get to experience firsthand *how your patients struggle*. Patients also regulate how much of you, the therapist (like the food or substance) they can take in or spit out. They do this by playing with the boundaries or pushing issues around the frame. They try to merge, become enmeshed, shove you away, keep you at arms distance, or try to 'eat' you up.

In struggling with their disorders of desire, wanting immediate gratification or not being able to make a choice or live with the thing not chosen, the therapeutic arena becomes a playground of what these patients can and cannot digest at any given moment. Thus, these issues of self-regulation have an impact on the therapeutic dyad. The going back and forth within the relationship—how they do this with us—becomes the field *for growth and change* as they try to effectively use us, our minds, and sometimes our bodies, symbolically and creatively, while we try to stay responsive to our own self- and body states as well as to the self- and body-states of our patients.

Four: Clinical Relational Moments

Lastly, it is often through the understanding of clinical 'moments' or enactments that occur in treatment that we see how this dynamic occurs clinically, and this is the fourth idea to integrate into treatment. The therapeutic action is about negotiation and interpersonal use of the relationship as a method of mutual and self-regulation. Meeting points between the patient and therapist often occur in a split-second exchange (or moments), whereby the level of involvement and/ or relatedness will shift back and forth between patient and therapist (Petrucelli, 2001, p. 101).

Whether such co-created moments between patient and therapist feel safe but 'on the edge,' what Bromberg (2006, 2011) called 'safe surprises,' depends on what the two do together in the space between what is perceived as potentially traumatic and what seems safe enough, though edgy. In the face of experience that is too much for the mind to bear, a person is traumatically impaired in her ability to cognitively process her own emotionally charged mental states in an interpersonal context. The patient 'checks out.' She does this outside of the treatment room as well as during a session; when she checks out with us; it gives us an opportunity to explore 'what just happened here.'

Bromberg (2006, 2011) described such moments as examples of how the brain triggers its failsafe mode of evolutionary self-survival: The protective function of dissociation, to preserve self-continuity, has replaced the brain's normal function of balancing growth and affective safety. "Dissociation is what the mind does. Self-states are what the mind comprises" (Bromberg, 2006, p. 2). To this I would add the following: Body-states are what the body experiences. I would then expand Bromberg's (2006) assertion that "the relationship between self-states and dissociation is what the mind is" (p. 2) by adding that the relationship between body-states and dissociation is what the *body does.* It is the stability of these relationships that enables a person to experience continuity as 'I' in mind and in body. A flexible relationship among self-states through the use of ordinary dissociation is what allows a human being to engage in the ever-shifting requirements of life's complexities with creativity and spontaneity. It is what gives a person the capacity to negotiate character and change simultaneously—to 'stay the same while changing' (Bromberg, 2006). And it is this relationship that determines what is meant when we speak of 'conscious' and 'unconscious' (Bromberg, 2006), most robustly so when we include 'body-states' within the domain of self-states.

With historical trauma, which can announce its presence in a *variety* of body-states, the development of an anticipatory dissociative mental structure is, as with mental states, designed to concretize perceptual input as always hiding a potential source of dysregulation that could lead to destabilization. The eating disorder continues after the trauma because there is a collapse of time, which makes the person unable to inhabit her body because it remains a 'thing' that can unexpectedly betray her (Bromberg, 2011). Under moments of stress, self-reflection becomes limited. And disaster feels like it is always around the corner. "I'm upset . . . I binge. I had a fight with my boss . . . I purge. My mother wants something from me . . . I starve." When we have the opportunity to experience these moments in treatment, we witness a microcosm of our patients' issues. Our speaking about it with them provides an opportunity to move towards greater shared intimacy where the relational field shifts into a momentary new configuration that is felt by both patient and analyst. The goal is for the two partners to loosen the grip of their shared cocoon and to create space, not only to simply experience what is happening as individuals, but to *reflect* on the *joint* experience. In order to emerge from the dissociative cocoon where the felt misattunement is so great that each protects him- or herself from high arousal at all costs, an affective shift must take place. Being able to *sustain* the shift is a far-reaching issue and struggle for all patients, but it is particularly interesting for eating-disordered patients because of the physicality of their struggles with regulation. Openness and affective authenticity is especially required to respect the patient's autonomy with all the dissociated parts.

How do we create a new road, a new template, in the brain or the possibility of a new choice or new behavior? One idea has to do with novelty, which is, overriding the old circuits or pathways with new, stronger, and more adaptive circuits/ pathways. With this change in circuitry comes a greater capacity for conscious self-reflection and mentalization that allows the patient to supersede unconscious patterns once they are recognized.

How do we change the circuitry? The work of D. Stern (1997, 2009), Bromberg (2001, 2006, 2011), Aron (1998), Mitchell (1991), and the Boston Change Process Study Group (2005) with their own language (i.e., unformulated experience, continuity of self states, meeting of the mind, intersubjectivity, or implicit relational knowing) suggests that it is through the jolt of an affective moment or shift that the creation of a new template occurs. It is about things we have intuitively known, but now we have a neurobiological explanation for the inner workings. Together, with our patients, we have the opportunity to create new neural templates relationally. We can carve out and co-create new roads together. Our goal should be to enhance our eating-disordered patient's ability for greater affect regulation within a safe environment and with a style of interaction that activates more emotions and felt experiences—turning the 'loud' noises down, improving impulse control, and allowing for a greater and real sense of choice. It is why, in short hand, we say, words and verbal interpretations don't work, but the felt experience of a clinical moment just might. Effective therapeutic dyads use the same processes that occur between parents and infants in secure attachments where patients learn to *respond rather than react.* In order to achieve this, treatment must be an emotional, affective, somatic experience in the context of an intimate relationship; the environment must be safe enough to enable experience of emotions and body sensations, even those that are initially frightening or painful (Lapides, 2010). Sometimes we understand this better when we experience body to body interactions that regulate relatedness in the consulting room. Here are two clinical vignettes illustrating body-to-body interactions.

Alyx: Can I Have This Dance?

If I interrupt my patient Alyx, a compulsive binge eater, she says, "STOP . . . you're existing into me . . . when you don't say anything until I ask you, I can regulate how much of you I can let in." She sometimes orders me, "Don't say anything— just sit!" So I don't speak for awhile, and I become conscious of what I feel in my body as I sit with her as she talks at me, hurling words. My mind races—I feel pushed down, physically stiff, palpably stifled. I try not to wiggle or move in my chair as I sit with her talking, dumping, purging words AT me. I sit in silence with her. I feel the sense of myself as being forced down, and I feel like my body is in a knot. I see she is 'only invested' in talking and getting it out—at me—but not even me personally. I am a container—her personal dumpster. I try to make sense of the content, but it sounds just like more of the same. So I begin to wonder about the process: What is this 'something' that is going on? In my reverie, during a particular session, I drift to imagining if this is *her* experience and what it *felt* like with her domineering mother who insisted on doing and redoing all her homework, from elementary school on. Her mother insisted that Alyx send in her (mother's) projects rather than her own, and then took credit for the good grade with sadistic delight. She would cut her off at the dinner table and not let her speak.

In Alyx's outside world, her interpersonal experiences are riddled with difficult interactions. Most of her communications are misunderstood. She either feels trampled on, or she does the trampling. To protect herself and others, she isolates.

I imagine what she felt, somatizing the terror of her mother's cruel narcissistic, sadistic dictatorship, combined with her father's bland ineffectiveness and passivity. I imagine the rage that must have built up in her body towards both parents and then the residual guilt she also felt for wanting to destroy them. I feel bogged down; my legs are heavy; in that moment I'm thinking and feeling that the weight of the added pounds on her body is only an attempt to insulate herself from any of these feelings. So when she takes a breath and says, "OK . . . you can talk now!" I am still lost in my own reverie, with my thoughts racing, I startle, my calf cramps, and I yell "Owww!!" And she says, without skipping a beat. "Yes, it really did hurt."

It took time for us to fully understand what happened that day. Our negotiations around having space, feeling forced, differentiating between 'good food' and being 'force fed,' and her internalizations of her mother as aggressor have eventually yielded much good 'fruit.' In her interpretation of my "Ow!" as being a dramatic empathetic response to her 'complaints' of the moment, she experienced an unexpected response from me, a surprise that 'forced' her to reflect on my experience of her, even though it was of me—and her—in the sense that my body was having a mind of its own in that moment. But I was also forced to reflect on my experience of her response to my body reaction. And because I could reflect on it, I could relate to her in a way that showed I had learned from her how to be with her. This unexpected moment and our ensuing dialogue opened the door for us to explore the idea that a rupture in a relationship is reparable, and that she has a role in making it so.

In order for me to really know Alyx, I had to loosen my hold on the way I had been defining her—that is, by my experience of her. I had to see and maybe feel another truth about her. My body was 'forcing' me to feel something I had not yet been able to and this, in turn, enabled me to respond by using what I had learned from *her*. Reparability, not optimal attunement, may be a better source of healing. It creates the experience of things being 'good enough,' rather than striving for perfection.

What was my body holding that it tightened up? Initially I felt constrained, but I allowed myself to drift into a dissociated reverie. She had to reflect upon herself in relation to me and hold me in relation to her. Even though I was sitting still as she 'purged' her words on me and I had to contain her disavowed affects, maybe my body just couldn't sit still. By distinguishing our individual experience, our talking helped to make clear how the body and experience of affect can better be integrated. But we were also co-creating a new relational unconscious where we could both hold more parts of the other.

Over time, we were able to expand the awareness that we were co-participating in similar, but now known, repetitions of this pattern. She could feel me being responsive to her so didn't have to either starve herself of me (not hear me at all), or inundate (dominate) me with her words to block me out. She could fear 'the other' (me) less, especially when she could pause, digest, and actually take me in without the terror that I would, like her mother, engulf her. Her need to engulf me was quieted and she became less convinced that this way of being (i.e., engulfing the other) would be the only way an interpersonal exchange could happen.

We were able to metaphorically dance without my legs cramping. She speaks, I can ask her questions—or even interrupt—she smiles, I get to speak freely and remain respectful of her. We agree, disagree, agree to disagree, and she says with a big grin, "Isn't it amazing how I've changed, and how you've changed too, and how well we get along? I'm so impressed with myself!" she says; "I can really *hear* you now." And we laugh. We are both becoming more aware and more at home with a fuller range of our parts, self- and body-states.

Liza: What's Eating You?

Liza, at 5 feet 7 inches was 360 pounds when she came in with the decision to have gastric bypass scheduled in three weeks. She wasn't quite happy with her surgeon. I first wondered if she was really set on going through with this and asked if there was any room to discuss such a major decision. But I found out, come hell or high water, Liza was going forward. However, she was open to consulting with another surgeon, and so I recommended another gastric surgeon with whom she clicked better. She had the surgery, lost 220 pounds in two years, and looks like a completely different person. She has the experience of not being recognized all the time.

Liza was never particularly self-reflective by nature and could also be considered a workaholic. The more weight she lost, the more vulnerable she felt, and she now wanted to explore *our* relationship. In the first weeks after a summer break, she called me a "hooker." She said, "I feel like I've rented you. You sell your time for your mind and I want to know when I'm not here, do you miss me? When you have other patients in the room—are you thinking about me? I want to feel that you are penetrated by me and that I have an echo . . . I want to know . . . are you my friend?"

I was fascinated by her questions, her vulnerability, and the expression of feelings. Her word 'echo' kept reverberating in my head and there was much I wanted to ask about. This was the first time she dared to speak her feelings about our relationship. Gently, I tried to explore this with her. She couldn't hear anything from me, except when I said I was far more valuable to her as her therapist than I could ever be as her friend.

I could feel she felt hurt and that whatever this self-state needed, I was letting her down. She didn't want to talk about it again and did a very good job of steering the conversation to a million places. If I tried to speak about this or, for that matter, anything that required her to 'look' at something, she would get a glazed, dissociated look on her face, open up her pocketbook, and start popping hard candies.

The first time she went into her bag and took a candy, she said it was medically needed, and I went with that 'explanation' for much longer than I should have. I realized that this glazed look was familiar to me and I had let her slide. We would be talking about many things and then, all of a sudden, she would shift the topic in rapid speed and grab a candy. Now, I went back and forth between trying to explore the process of what was happening in the moment and the content of what she was saying. I got nowhere.

Over time, I began to see a pattern: As soon as she felt something uncomfortable on any level, she popped a candy. I would ask her, "What happened-right there?" she said, "Nothing." "Did something I said or something you said make you upset, sad, angry, frustrated?" "No!" she retorted. I tried asking her what she would feel if she didn't put the candy in her mouth—and asked if she could not do it—to which she popped in several, in rapid fire. "So you didn't like it when I asked you to not eat the candies," I responded, and she glazed over with a deer-in-headlights dissociated stare. She could only say that she was trying to feel one thing instead of something else.

Then one session, she said talked to a friend about her experience with me. She told this friend that I look like a better 'Cher' and that she likes me a lot and asked to be my friend. And her friend queried with amusement, "What? You asked her to be your friend? She can't be your friend; she's your therapist! Why would you ask her?" And then Liza said to me, "I thought about it, and I also told her about the candies." I replied, "You did?"

She nodded. In that moment, my stomach started growling, making loud rumbling noises. I remember thinking, oh my, not now! I hope she doesn't hear. I thought, why is my stomach growling? Am I hungry? I'm not hungry . . . I just had lunch! But before I could say or do anything, she said, out of the blue: "I think I'm starving myself—I'm starving myself—and I'm trying to get you to see." "Oh my goodness," I replied sadly, "Have I been missing that with you?"

We went over her foods, made a decision that she would go back to the nutritionist, and decided to review her intake of food in a step-by-step way. I also talked to her very directly about her dissociating in the room with me and she said, "I hear everything you say. I just can't digest. It's like I'm starving myself." I added that she was starving herself of me and others—by keeping everything out—words and all, and even the nutritional stuff. I told her that my stomach was growling in this session and that I thought I was feeling the emptiness she feels inside. I told her I heard that she had been trying to tell me, but I didn't get it until now. And she started sobbing, deeply, with her body quivering. I sat with her. She said through her tears, "I keep remembering how alone I felt growing up when my mother was in one of her rages. She would put her face in front of mine and scream at the top of her lungs with her mouth wide open—within an inch of my face. I think I learned in that moment to not take anything in. I think that's why I can't take you in, even though I want to. You need to feed me bit by bit."

I was quite moved and said I would use my espresso spoons, as we often talked about our shared fondness for Italian coffee. Liza has suffered her whole life from feeling disconnected to her body, her truest feelings, and her core sense of self. What were the parts of my patient, Liza, that were dissociated in the face of her terrifying fear of her mother's rages? She has felt that she could not occupy her body while maintaining a mutually safe and intimate relationship with the people in her life that she needs most—be it her husband, friends, family, co-workers, or therapist.

Bodily experience can be useful in bridging the dissociative gaps. Can working in the dissociative gaps require more than verbally-based descriptions of what's happening? Can we include awareness of what it actually feels like in the body for both analyst and patient as they slip and fall and catch themselves and each other while working in that gap? My attentions to my own bodily experience of hunger alerted me to question what was my countertransferential 'hunger' and also feel the hunger in my patient's body.

Our body-states have body and 'not-body' experiences as well. How do our unexamined mind-body disconnections affect the patient? It was interesting to me that because of Liza's large body size, I had not paid attention in the same way I might have to her losing weight. Was my patient 'redirecting' me because I was 'not there' in the way that she needed me to *see* that she was starving herself? Was my stomach growling a signal that allowed me to connect to my dissociated 'not knowing' that within her large body, she was starving? And was the unconscious communication between us that Liza needed to 'project' into me her 'sense' of being starved for affection as well as her literal experience of starving herself? Or was it a dissociated self-state that could only enter the room by my bodily experiences of her? What was clear was that something was resonating: We were attuned or misattuned, but it was between us. Hoppenwasser (2008) writes about the idea of dissociative attunement as a self emergent moment in which multiple self-states are shared by means other than projection. She feels this can often be healing rather than pathological. In addition, I wondered if her 'wanting to be my friend' was an expression of her desire to be 'fed' by a loving (m)other? By exploring this we came into contact with a particular aspect of her pain—her mourning for an experience that she either had and lost or maybe never had at all. She wanted her 'echo' to be heard and felt.

When we listen from an embodied place, our patients are more able to tell us how they need to use us because they can feel we are more interested in listening to them rather than telling them what we think we know. We need to pay attention to how these clinical moments feel and use them. When we do that, we help our eating-disordered patients discover their personal narrative and body history in relation with recognized others, us, who can help them tolerate the parts that they cannot. And if we can help patients better understand these parts, the parts most hated—and welcome them in rather than colluding to disown the parts they do not want anyone to see—we can help them know what they see and say what they know.

In order to deepen and further facilitate the experience of our eating-disordered patient's interiority, we try to help them move fluidly between self- and body-states to facilitate the transition from dissociation, to enactment, to conflict, to self-reflective awareness. Our interest in and desire to engage a nonjudgmental attitude towards the selves that remain or continue to be symptomatic, and our curiosity about the selves that starve, binge, or purge will facilitate the linking of our patients' body states and bodymind parts.

So much happens in the treatment room between the relational interactions and the bodily communications with the patient and within you. Pay attention to the moments we, as therapists, dissociate. In our encounters with patients, we are always struggling with our being seen and known in a way that can elicit vulnerability in both analyst and patient, regulating our stance of being more open or closed and sometimes regulating being more comfortable with things that feel alien to us. Issues of self-esteem, self-knowledge, self-image, self-regulation, and affect regulation are played out in the treatment room and patients enact a piece of each of these with you.

Notice the things you feel in your body, as it informs you. There are many body-to-body interactions, be it disgust, frustration, fatigue, demoralization, anxiety, fear, impatience, anger, sadness, hunger, negative projections, and—especially—shame and how it destabilizes. We accept the recognition of the therapist's body as information relating to the mutual exchange between patient and therapist. Being aware of our 'body feelings' can give us clues into the unconscious experience and communication of the other and the relational transmission of attachment issues in the body.

Together, when patient and analyst are able to process the mutual experience of holding one another's mind and body, and body and mind—in mind—a new relational ground is created.

Summary

To understand our eating-disordered patients, several constructs must be woven together: interpersonal neurobiology, attachment, affect regulation, self-regulation, and clinical relational moments. Eating-disordered symptoms may be the result of deficits in the child's neurobiological makeup, attunement, and attachment issues in the very early environment. With a limited ability to use and understand symbolic language, and a greater reliance on concrete black-and-white thinking, patients are more vulnerable to use external regulators to self-soothe. Difficulties with self-regulation and affect regulation ensue, and result in splitting off parts of themselves and dissociation or behaviors that require further dissociation as a maladaptive attempt to survive.

A complicated neurobiological organization and response system underlies dissociative states (Howell, 2005), and the understanding of this extends further than the scope and intent of this chapter. But, can we better understand and clinically treat these interwoven dynamics by utilizing multiple self-states theory (rather than a linear model), taking neurobiological constraints into account? I think so, because, with eating-disordered patients, parts of the self are split off without self-coherence. Given the prevalence and connection between underlying trauma and eating disorders, eating-disordered patients are more prone to dissociation as a style of coping, because they are more prone to automatic reliance on dissociative mental structure. They experience different self-states and different body-states that cannot coexist or be consciously linked to each other. The neurobiological effect of trauma also contributes to decreased links between and among self-states and decreased reflectiveness. Linkages of self-states and body-states contribute to an awareness of context both within the self and within the world and to the capacity for increased self-reflectiveness and intersubjectivity.

Without an increased capacity for self-reflectiveness and intersubjectivity, the interruption in eating-disordered patients of self-state linkages and the ensuing difficulty in understanding emotions will increase their automatic tendency to use externalized measures to explain circumstances. What we witness is a greater reliance on dissociation and the repetition of habitual patterns as they travel down the same old, same old neural pathways that 'show up' as greater resistance to change.

Direct interventions, supported by empirical findings of changes in brain circuitry, might include consciously altering unconscious, interpersonal procedural expectations when the eating-disordered patient is in "an optimal affective state, by verbally exploring the nature of the interaction, the context in which it was developed, and the potentially maladaptive nature of the pattern both in present interactions and in interactions with the therapist" (Divino & Moore, 2010, p. 344). Seeing maladaptive patterns in others is also a function of why group therapy is so vitally important with eating-disordered patients. It allows them to recognize, compare, and imagine alternative behaviors. Sometimes this 'witnessing' occurs without patients being as affectively charged in their own bodies. Other times, being affectively charged and their conscious recognition of their feelings alerts them to a deeper understanding of triggers for their symptomatic behaviors. They can speak with clarity and precision about the other. Patients can practice and imagine acting differently *through* the other. The new neural templates that may be formed must be repeated multiple times before new behavior emerges and feels organic.

Patients and therapists can have body-state visceral reactions—experiences we feel in our bodies rather than in words—that need to become known and understood together. Understanding eating-disordered patients' nonverbal responses or enactments that occur in treatment may be used to produce change once they are understood by *both* patient and analyst. Putting this into words, being able to articulate the nonverbal, implicit communicative aspects of dissociative body-states involves increasing our awareness of interpersonal neurobiology, attachment patterns, affect-regulation and self-regulation issues as they contribute to the complexity of clinical experience with our eating-disordered patients. There are many times when a patient has been triggered into a dissociative state as they continue to talk in therapy in their 'typical way,' and it goes unrecognized. When one is in a dissociative place, asking an open-ended question about how one is feeling in the moment, rather than interpreting or giving a factual response about what has been said, opens the door to reconnection through reengaging the left hemisphere (Divino & Moore, 2010). They can begin to voice their felt experience through words with you. This is when reconnection *of affective experience and cognition* becomes paramount as it occurs through authentic curiosity where the therapist can express genuine interest rather than state they *know* what is in the patient's mind. What gets conveyed then and becomes intuitively understood is the felt experience of truly caring alongside the expressed desire to learn and understand each patient's unique way of being. As we think out loud in concert, sometimes in spontaneous unexpected moments, moving between therapeutic content and process, information and affective state changes, we co-create new ways of being together. We inspire hope for the future with increased 'body-fullness' as self to body becomes body to self. Even though "the body keeps the score" (Van der Kolk, 1996, p. 214), maybe we can help the body lose 'the cage.'

Acknowledgement

I would like to thank the following people for their help and visions in reading this chapter: Philip M. Bromberg, Ruth Livingston, Nick Samstag, and Sarah Schoen.

References

Aron, L. (1998).The clinical body and the reflexive mind. In L. Aron & F. Anderson (Eds.), *Relational perspectives on the body* (pp. 3–37). Hillsdale, NJ: Analytic Press.

Barth, D. (2008). Hidden eating disorders: Attachment and affect regulation in the therapeutic relationship. *Clinical Social Work Journal, 36,* 355–365.

Berthoud, H. R., Lenard, N., & Shin, A. C. (2011, June). Food reward, hyperphagia, and obesity. *American Journal of Physiology—Regulatory, Integrative and Comparative Physiology, 300*(6), R1266–R1277.

Boston Change Process Study Group. (2005). The 'something more' than interpretation. *Journal of the American Psychoanalytic Association, 53*(3), 693–729.

Bromberg, P. M. (2001). *Standing in the spaces: Essays on clinical process, trauma and dissociation.* Hillsdale, NJ: Analytic Press.

Bromberg, P. M. (2006). *Awakening the dreamer: Clinical journeys.* Mahwah, NJ: Analytic Press.

Bromberg, P. M. (2008). Shrinking the tsunami: Affect regulation, dissociation, and the shadow of the flood. *Contemporary Psychoanalysis, 44,* 329–350.

Bromberg, P. M. (2011). *The shadow of the tsunami and the growth of the relational mind.* New York: Routledge.

Bruch, H. (1978). *The golden cage.* Cambridge, MA: Harvard University Press.

Damasio, A. R. (1999). *The feeling of what happens: Body and emotion in the making of consciousness.* New York: Harcourt Brace.

Divino, C. L., & Moore, M. S. (2010). Integrating neurobiological findings into psychodynamic psychotherapy training and practice. *Psychoanalytic Dialogues, 20,* 337–355. New York: Taylor & Francis Group/Routledge.

Edelman, G. M. (1989). *The remembered present: A biological theory of consciousness.* New York: Basic Books.

Edelman, G. M. (2004). *Wider than the sky: The phenomenal gift of consciousness.* New Haven, CT: Yale University Press.

Fonagy, P., Gergely, G., Jurist, E., & Target, M. (2002). *Affect regulation, mentalization, and the development of the self.* New York: Other Press.

Goodsitt, A. (1983). Self-regulatory disturbances in eating disorders. *International Journal of Eating Disorders, 2,* 51–60.

Hopenwasser, K. (2008). Being in rhythm: Dissociative attunement in therapeutic process, *Journal of Trauma & Dissociation, 9*(3), 349–367.

Howell, E. (2005). *The dissociative mind.* Hillsdale, NJ: Analytic Press.

Lapides, F. (2010). Neuroscience: Contributions to the understanding and treatment of eating disorders. In M. Maine, B. H. McGilley, & D. W. Bunnell (Eds.), *Treatment of eating disorders.* New York: Academic Press.

LeDoux, J. E. (2002). *The synaptic self: How our brains become who we are.* London: Pan Macmillan.

McDougall, J. (1989). *Theaters of the body.* New York: W. W. Norton.

Mitchell, S. A. (1991). Contemporary perspectives on self: Towards integration. *Psychoanalytic Dialogues, 1,* 121–147.

Mitchell, S. A. (1999). Attachment theory and the psychoanalytic tradition: Reflections on human relationality. *Psychoanalytic Dialogues, 9,* 85–107.

O'Kearney, R. (1996). Attachment disruption in anorexia nervosa and bulimia nervosa: A review of theory and empirical research. *International Journal of Eating Disorders, 20*(2), 115–127.

Pearlman, B. (2014). Body or mind: A discontinuous model of neural emotional processing. In J. Petrucelli (Ed.), *Body-states: Interpersonal and relational perspectives on the treatment of eating disorders.* London: Routledge.

Petrucelli, J. (2001). Close encounters of the regulatory kind: An interpersonal/relational look at self-regulation. In *Hungers and compulsions: The psychodynamic treatment of eating disorders and addiction.* New York: Aronson Press.

Petrucelli, J. (2004). Treating eating disorders. In R. Coombs (Ed.), *Handbook of addictive disorders: A practical guide to diagnosis and treatment.* Hoboken, NJ: Wiley & Son.

Phillips, A. (2001). *Houdini's box.* New York: Pantheon Books.

Schore, A. N. (2001). The effects of a secure attachment relationship on right brain development, affect regulation, and infant mental health. *Infant Mental Health Journal, 22,* 7–66.

Schore, A. N. (2003). *Affect regulation and the repair of the self.* New York: W. W. Norton.

Schore, A. N. (2009). Attachment, trauma and the developing right brain: Origins of pathological dissociation. In P. Dell & J. O'Neil (Eds.), *Dissociation and dissociative disorders* (pp. 107–141). New York: Taylor & Francis Group.

Schore, A. N. (2010). The right brain implicit self: A central mechanism of the psychotherapy change process. In J. Petrucelli (Ed.), *Knowing, not-knowing & sort-of-knowing: Psychoanalysis and the experience of uncertainty* (pp. 177–202). London: Karnac.

Schore, J. R., & Schore, A. N. (2008). Modern attachment theory: The central role of affect regulation in development and treatment. *Clinical Social Work Journal, 36,* 9–20.

Siegel, D. J. (1999). *The developing mind: How relationships and the brain interact to shape who we are.* New York: Guilford Press.

Siegel, D. J. (2010). *The mindful therapist.* New York: W. W. Norton.

Sieratzki, J. S., & Woll, B. (1996). Why do mothers cradle babies on their left? *Lancet, 347,* 1746–1748.

Sohn, L. (1985). Anorexic and bulimic states of mind in the psycho-analytic treatment of anorexic/bulimic patients and psychotic patients. *Psychoanal. Psychother., 1,* 49–56.

Stern, D. (1997). *Unformulated experience: From dissociation to imagination in psychoanalysis.* Hillsdale, NJ: Analytic Press.

Stern, D. (2009). *Partners in thought: Working with unformulated experience, dissociation, and enactment.* New York: Routledge.

Stern, S. (2007). The conundrum of self-care. *Contemporary Psychoanalysis, 43*(4), 605–620.

Treasure, J., Tchanturia, K., & Ulrike, S. (2005). Developing a model of the treatment for eating disorders: Using neuroscience research to examine the how rather than the what of change. *Counseling and Psychotherapy Research, 5*(3), 191–202.

Van der Kolk, B. (1994). The body keeps score. *Harvard Review of Psychiatry, 1,* 253–265.

Van der Kolk, B. (1996). The body keeps the score: Approaches to the psychobiology of posttraumatic stress disorder. In B. Van der Kolk, A. McFarland, O. Van der Hart, & L. Weisaeth (Eds.), *Traumatic stress: The effects of overwhelming experience on mind, body and society* (pp. 214–241). New York: Guilford Press.

Wilkinson, M. (2004). The mind–brain relationship. *Journal of Analytical Psychology, 49,* 83–101.

Zhang, X., Li, T., & Zhou, X. (2008). Brain responses to facial expression by adults with different attachment-orientations. *NeuroReport, 19*(4), 437–441.

Part II

THE MINDBODY AND
THE BODYMIND
Reflections Inside and Outside
Reality and Subjectivity

3

'YOU'RE THE ONE THAT I WANT'

Appetite, Agency, and the Gendered Self

Sarah Schoen

My patient, Isabelle, is 25 and fighting her way out of anorexia. Like many patients with eating disorders (EDs), Isabelle's early attachment to her mother was troubled, bound up in her mother's own anxieties about separation and assertion. Yet in Isabelle's struggle to relinquish her symptoms, her tie to her father feels most at stake. She tells me, "The problem with giving up the idea that I have to be thin to be successful, to be effective, is that it's like giving up on something with my dad. It's not just about feeling good or liking my body. It's also [that] we were supposed to be alike, both thin, both athletic . . . in on some private secret, able to do stuff other people couldn't do." Here Isabelle has captured the ways in which her skinny self expresses her feelings about gender's pitfalls and potentials: who she can be, what she can want, and who, in return, will want to be like—and will want to be with—her.

Isabelle's dilemma can help us deepen our understanding of the ways in which eating disorders, gender, and agency are inextricably bound. Who can *she* be? What can she *want?* The perspective I will elaborate in this chapter is that the disturbances in "wanting" so endemic to ED patients (Brisman, 2002; Petrucelli & Stuart, 2001, 2006) are inextricable from disturbances in gendered identifications and desire.[1] A thwarted sense of personal agency, or "I-ness" (Ogden, 1994; Fast, 1995), is certainly implicated in the dissociated self-states expressed by restricting, bingeing, and purging (Bromberg, 2001; Petrucelli & Stuart, 2001, 2006; Sands, 1991). But, it is also the degree to which one's felt sense of agency—of being a person who can want and act appropriately to fulfill those wants—is included or excluded from one's subjective experience of gendered identity that is central to the ED patient's struggle. The question, "What can I want?" thus becomes, "What can I, *as a girl,* want?" "What can I, *as a boy,* want?" Drawing on contemporary interpersonal/relational psychoanalytic theory, I will argue that EDs are usefully conceptualized as disorders of a gendered, agentic self.[2]

Contemporary models of gender development assume that one's experience of "gender identity," and of agency—in other words, of wanting—are derived from a complex web of same- and cross-sex parental identifications (Benjamin, 1991,

1995; Fast, 1984, 1991, 1999; Harris, 2009). Gender identity is not only defined by an awareness of sex difference and the identification of one's self as male or female, but by the ways that "femininity" and "masculinity" become inscribed by personal meanings elaborated via parent–child interactions. Thus, the difficulties for ED patients in experiencing themselves as "subjects of desire" (Benjamin, 1988) will follow from the patterning of interactions between gendered-self in relation to gendered-other, particularly as these patterns inform conflicts between autonomy and dependency. This has implications not only for our understanding of the psychic meaning of eating problems, but also for our approach to working in the transference/countertransference matrix with the ED patient. With her, or with him, shifting gender identifications in both patient and therapist, as well as the patient's experience of the analyst's *gendered* subjectivity (c.f., Aron, 1991), will shape the way in which aspects of the patient's self will either remain dissociatively encapsulated in eating symptoms, or can be welcomed into an expanded gender "repertoire" (Elise, 1998a) and the ownership of desire.[3]

Gender, Agency, and Eating Disorders

It is virtually impossible to think about eating disorders without thinking about gender. EDs are among the most gender-specific forms of psychological distress and have been overwhelmingly the province of women. Women account for some 90 percent of people who suffer from anorexia and bulimia, although the incidence of male EDs is on the rise (Pope, Phillips, & Olivardia, 2000).

In exploring the connection between EDs[4] and gender, feminist theorists have focused on the cultural contributions to eating and body distress. The majority of this literature addresses women, for example, emphasizing increased pressures in recent decades for women to manage multiple and often contradictory roles (e.g., Boskind-White & White, 1983; Chernin, 1985; Steiner-Adair, 1986); the increasingly slim standards for women's bodies, and the tendency for women with EDs to overidentify with the female role and physical standards of thinness (e.g., Boskind-Lodahl, 1976; Bruch, 1973, 1978; Chernin, 1981, 1985; Garner et al., 1980; Kearney-Cooke, 1991; Orbach, 1978, 2000; Polivy & Herman, 1987; Steiner-Adair, 1986, 1991; Wooley et al., 1980), as well as the influence on women by the economically powerful diet industry (Gutwill, 1994a, 1994b). Some from this perspective have emphasized the cultural devaluation of "feminine" needs for dependency and connection in favor of "masculine" traits such as autonomy and separateness (e.g., Kearney-Cooke, 1991; Steiner-Adair, 1991).[5]

Those who have focused on the rising incidence of EDs among men have similarly highlighted pressures associated with changing gender roles and physical standards of athleticism and muscularity (Pope et al., 2000).[6] Indeed, the increased incidence of EDs among men has underscored, rather than diminished, the role of gender in the development of eating problems.[7] Like their female counterparts, male ED sufferers express their pained relationship to their gendered bodies through attempts to banish unacceptable states of need and desire, while simultaneously idealizing conformity to the physical norms of gender stereotype—for women, those of slimness, and for men those of muscularity.

A cultural perspective has been invaluable in explicating how social influences contribute to the dramatic gender bias found in ED prevalence and in providing a corrective to classical psychoanalytic accounts, which were rooted in assumptions about gender as biologically determined and determining. However, predominantly cultural analyses of eating problems cannot illuminate why women would be more susceptible to cultural influence than men (Sands, 1989), or why some men and some women might be more susceptible than others (Pope et al., 2000; Sands, 1989). To address these questions, we can draw on contemporary psychoanalytic models of development, which have retained the complexity of Freud's innovations on the subjective, psychic representations of body, gender, and sexuality while rejecting their essentialist premises.

Contemporary models of gender development provide rich opportunities to address the ways in which gendered meanings for ED patients are not only culturally imposed but emerge in specific relational contexts and become personally, idiosyncratically inscribed. These models highlight the relational meanings of gendered identifications and the importance of being able to establish a coherent, unified experience of gender identity without sacrificing access to a rich, fluid experience of one's gendered multiplicity. For example, theorists such as Chodorow (1978) and Benjamin (1988) have illustrated how gendered identifications inform developmental processes of separation and attachment in the maternal dyad—processes considered central in the development of EDs. In discussing this contribution, Goldner (2011) wrote, "Where little girls operate from the gender premise, 'I am female like you, and thus we are bonded via sameness,' young boys deploy the opposite axiom, 'I am not female like you, and we are separated via difference'" (p. 161).

It follows that gendered identifications will also be used to express psychic pain when these negotiations go awry. Coates, Friedman, and Wolfe (1991) and Coates and Wolfe (1995), in their work with boys diagnosed with gender identity disorder (GID) who insisted they were or should be girls, have dramatically illustrated ways that rigid gendered identifications are bids for connection, usually in fraught relationships with their mothers. ED patients are not, in most cases, refusing to identify with their biological sex. Yet they tend to be deeply conflicted about the *meanings* with which they have imbued gendered categories and desires. Their symptom reflect these conflicts, for example, in attempts to attain or refuse a particular body as it symbolizes a particular identity, and in attempts to control or eradicate particular appetites as they symbolize particular desires.

One important way of understanding the striking gender disparity in ED patients is the tendency for women, as a group, to have greater developmental difficulty than men integrating agency into their gendered identity. They are more likely to end up on one side—the un-agentic side—of gendered splitting: passive vs. active; wanted vs. wanting; object vs. subject (e.g., Benjamin, 1988, 1991; Dimen, 1991; Gilligan, 2011). Painful splits between mind and body, autonomy and dependency, between the self as desiring and the self as desirable—splits that are often at the core of eating problems—both construct and are constructed by the gendered categories of masculine and feminine.[8]

For girls, "bonded via sameness" to their mothers, masculinity and agency easily become conflated. For boys, "separated via difference" from their mothers, feminine identifications can threaten not only agency but masculinity as well. Female agency tends to be further undermined by the way in which girls inhibit their use of healthy aggression in the service of autonomy in order to protect their connections with their mothers (Harris, 1997). Thus one can see EDs among women as arising from the exaggeration of "normative" developmental challenges in differentiating from their same-sex mothers, exacerbated by particular parent–child interaction patterns (e.g., those derived from a relationship with a narcissistically impaired mother; Sands, 1989).

While one can understand ED symptoms in women as an indication of difficulties in integrating a sense of agentic competence into an experience of self-as-girl, when ED symptoms arise in men, they may be signposts signaling divergence from the more characteristic male challenge of integrating dependency needs into their masculine, agentic identifications. Sands (2003) has pointed to this as another reason for the ED gender bias toward women, noting that men are more likely to express disavowed needs and wants through projections onto others, and thus number more highly among those who develop compulsive sexual behaviors, while women are more likely to use their own bodies to contain disowned desire.

Thus, when we do see a man with an ED, it raises questions not only about the exclusion of agency from masculine identifications but about the degree to which masculinity itself was embroiled in one or both parents' conflicted gender identifications.[9] In this regard, the ED boy's rigid "performance" (Butler, 1995; Riviere, 1929) of masculine identity, often expressed in preoccupation with physical stereotypes of muscularity and "fitness," can be seen as analogous to the GID boy's pained, caricatured embodiment of femininity. Both reflect the gendered contours of projective–introjective processes with attachment figures, and the inability on the one hand to feel grounded in one's gendered sense of self, and on the other to fluidly integrate masculine and feminine identifications. Unlike ED women, ED men bear the additional burden of having a disorder defined as "feminine," further compounding the gendered shame expressed in eating problems. It may be that the adoption of "feminine" symptoms *indicates* the shame-ridden disavowal of feminine identifications and desires.[10]

Further, as I noted earlier, the consolidation of an agentic, gendered self not only entails being a woman or a man who can want, but also being a woman or a man who can *act appropriately to fulfill one's wants.* Thus, it involves being able to translate desire into choice, and choice into action. The paradoxical nature of the "independent" assertion of desire is that it simultaneously renders one vulnerable to needing something from someone else—including the recognition by a valued other that one has, indeed, had an impact (Benjamin, 1995; Gentile, 2001; Mitchell, 1988). This consolidation is especially fraught for ED patients, whose symptoms involve overriding internal longings for external nourishment. Rather, they use eating behaviors to preserve the illusion of self-sufficiency and omnipotent control, and to protect against the vulnerability inherent in personal agency and interdependence (Mitchell, 1988).

In what follows, I will draw on contemporary interpersonal/relational theory to demonstrate the multiplicity of gendered resonances in the ED patient's developmental history and experience of self-as-agent. This expands on other work linking ED symptoms with girls' developmental challenges in integrating agency and femininity (e.g., Brisman, 2002; Charatan, this volume; deGroot & Rodin, 1994; Sands, 1989, 2003), including one noteworthy articulation of the symbolic meaning of eating symptoms for men as they reflect disavowed maternal identifications (Crastnapol, 2001). A handful of previous efforts have begun to address how gendered meanings inform enactments with patients who have eating problems (e.g., Brisman, 2002; Crastnapol, 2001), and I hope to build on those contributions. In particular, I will illustrate how shifts in the ED patient's experience of gendered-self in relation to gendered-other are derived *both* from the patient's relational history *and* from the present interpersonal context of the therapeutic encounter. This conceptualization has important implications for how the analyst attends to and participates in the ED patient's "gender trouble" (Butler, 1990).

The Emergence of the Gendered, Desiring Self

For both men and women who develop EDs, the gendered dimension of self and relational experience is dense and prominent. They are among the people Eve Sedgwick describes when observing, "Some people are just plain more gender-y than others" (1990, p. 16). Dimen, in her elegant description of how intimately "self and gender identity inhabit one another," noted the ubiquity of questions such as, "If I feel womanly, am I at my most feminine? Or am I feeling most fully myself? When I do feel like myself, does that . . . have anything to do with my female identity? If I feel, by contrast . . . unwomanly, am I feeling somehow not myself? If I am not myself, is gender identity also . . . secretly, involved?" (1991, p. 337). Imagine how evocatively eating symptoms and body-image disturbance contour such questions: If I (a woman or a man) starve myself, am I controlling my needy feminine self? Does becoming smaller or bigger make me more female? Less female? Does that depend on whether I am small and muscular? Big and strong? If I punish myself with compulsive exercise, and my body is hard, not soft, is the self I am punishing male? Female? If I conquer my appetite, is that a triumph of will over desire? Is my will, or its failure, associated with femininity or masculinity? How about my desire?

Answers to these questions must unfold through a compelling narrative of the ED patient's developmental history. A wealth of clinical data underscores the centrality of conflicts between dependency and autonomy for ED patients. These accounts emphasize the ways that eating symptoms express embattled themes of merger in the maternal dyad, and the tendency for the mothers of ED patients to be narcissistically impaired (see Sugarman, 1991, for a review). While clinically relevant, this focus on boundary confusion in the maternal dyad can oversimplify the gendered complexity in separation processes, particularly in regard to the emergence of an agentic, gendered self.

Separation–individuation processes take center stage between 18 and 36 months, during a period of "rapprochement" characterized by inchoate capacities for triadic relating and the emergence of the *subjective experience* of agency (Gentile, 2001; Fast, 1991). Given that infants begin differentiating from their mothers at birth, and mothers as primary caretakers facilitate babies' developing agency from that point forward (Beebe, 1988; Beebe et al., 1997; Stern, 1985), what is new during the rapprochement stage is not the presence of agentic action on the child's part, but rather the child's awareness of him- or herself as an agent (Benjamin, 1991; Fast, 1991). "At this point," Benjamin wrote, "the child self-consciously wills to have something, for example, the child needs to eat but wants, even insists on eating from the bowl with the clown picture" (1991, p. 282). Toddlerhood, as we recognize it, is virtually synonymous with the arrival of this agentic self, as well as its expression through food and eating behaviors: "The clarion call 'Do it mineself!' is heard when a coat is to be buttoned, shoes are to be tied, or meat is to be cut" (Fast, 1991, p. 303).

Yet what is simultaneously new is the child's awareness of self as *himself* or *herself*. Awareness of oneself as an agent coincides with the recognition of sex-difference and an elaboration of the meanings of these differences via identifications with both parents (Benjamin, 1991, 1995; Fast, 1991, 1999). In other words, the child's first use of the self-referent *I—of being a person who can want and act appropriately to fulfill those wants*—is rooted in newly established gendered identifications. Thus, the question every child asks, and the one that most haunts the ED patient, "What can I want?" becomes the question, "What can I, as a girl, want?" "What can I, as a boy, want?" How does this question come to hold personally constructed hopes and fears?

Fast's (1984, 1999) influential theory of gender differentiation posits that prior to the recognition of sex-difference during rapprochement, children are initially "overinclusive" in their gender identifications, believing that they can be and have it all. Awareness of sex difference involves an encounter with limits and feelings of loss and envy. Initially, this can be expressed by girls in envy of the penis and by boys in envy of the ability to bear babies. In optimal development, initial feelings of loss are ameliorated by the realization that it is possible to integrate qualities initially collapsed into anatomical distinctions (e.g., the conflation of maleness with power or agency, or femaleness with nurturance or creativity) and imaginatively elaborate one's own gendered identifications through ongoing relationships with same-sex and cross-sex others. Later developmental junctures at which navigating dependency and autonomy collide with questions of identity and sexuality present opportunities to further elaborate or foreclose the complexity of gendered identifications (Bassin, 1996).[11] It is disruption in these processes that make adolescence fertile ground for eating and body image problems. Once an eating problem takes root, the threat of cutting oneself off from options associated with forbidden or rigid gender identifications renders the experience of choice—as it is expressed concretely in choosing to eat, choosing what to eat—charged with dread and loss.

My patient, Evan, cannot choose. He is a 36-year-old accomplished, attractive academic, whose athletic body and grueling exercise regime conceal his shameful nightly binges. His stated need to "always keep his eggs in more than one basket" is not all bad. It has spurred him to attain multiple graduate degrees and interdisciplinary expertise. But the crippling anxiety he experiences when he must commit (e.g., one professional path over another; *this* job, place to live, romantic partner—no*t that* one) is debilitating. He tells me, "Choosing what my next paper is about is like choosing what I want for dinner. I'm fine when it's all in my head. That's why I don't eat all day—I'd rather stay in that space where everything is still possible. . . . But to actually do it? It's exposing something, saying, '*This* is what I like. *This* is who I am.' It's dangerous." How can Evan reveal himself when his brilliant, bookish father withdrew from his own desires for success and his son's desires for him? Alternately, Evan's mother's celebration of his competency was gratifying, but required costly allegiance and was punctuated by unpredictable, explosive attacks.

Like many ED sufferers, Evan can neither sustain the losses nor enjoy the gains of personal choices suffused in gendered meanings. Much of our work has focused on Evan's difficulties tolerating the limits imposed by choice, including the choice to anchor himself in his gender and sexual identity. On the other hand, Evan's commitment problems are constituted by his tendency, when he does choose, to lose too much access to generative possibilities—possibilities that would stem from a richer integration of masculine and feminine identifications.

The developmental importance for a child of cross-sex identifications, of bringing together "likeness with difference" in order to tolerate encounters with personal limits signaled by the realization of sex difference, has been articulated by Benjamin (1995, p. 127). She noted that for "identification with difference" to be successful, the cross-sex parent must be experienced as a differentiated other who can identify with the child in return (Benjamin, 1991). This potential for "identificatory love," arising out of the pleasure of being *like* the loved one, develops alongside object love, arising out of the pleasure of being *with* the loved one, and provides currency to the recognition bestowed by an admired other. Thus, for boys and girls, the capacity to imaginatively identify with the cross-sex parent makes the loss of some options tolerable and promotes an experience of choice in which the glass can be half *full.*

That said, Benjamin illustrated the "crucial role" for both boys and girls of the rapprochement father who stands outside the tangle of dyadic dependency and thus represents "separation, agency, and desire" (1995, p. 129). While for boys these representations are gender-syntonic, for girls they require a successful experience of "identification with difference," a relational process only made possible if the girl's father can identify with her in return, thus recognizing her as a subject

65

of desire.[12] If girls are denied opportunities for paternal identificatory love, their agency is compromised; if boys are denied, their agency, as well as their masculine identifications and sense of belonging among men, is on the line. These are often pathways toward the development of eating problems in women and men.

Of course, fathers, like mothers, can narcissistically *over*-identify with daughters, and Isabelle's experience, introduced at the beginning of this chapter, was one of identificatory love gone awry. Isabelle's anxious, self-abnegating mother made it difficult for her daughter to associate efficacy with femininity, which exacerbated Isabelle's reliance on her "sameness" to her father to consolidate an agentic self. These were transforming themes in Isabelle's treatment as she slowly, painfully untangled thinness from autonomy and desirability, and located a different, *and differently gendered,* experience of identificatory love through the transference relationship. This underscores how women ED patients' idealizations of female therapists can reflect paternal transferences, not only longed for idealizing processes within the maternal dyad (c.f. Sands, 1989).

Yet, a sole focus on how paternal identifications offer a girl the opportunity to represent her own desire and feel separate from her mother—the struggle most consistently emphasized in the ED literature—can mask the loss a girl experiences if her desire *for* her mother goes unacknowledged or unrequited. Early in a child's third year, gender identity elaborations are occurring not only in dyadic relation to each parent but also in romantic wishes to win over one or both parents who are now recognized as having a relationship that excludes the child. In this context, Elise (2008) noted the poignancy of the newly oedipal girl having to contend with her mother's desire for a partner whose body and gender are different from her own.

For the ED patient, disruptions in agency happen at two levels: 1) failures in early maternal facilitation of the baby's awareness of and spontaneous responses to internal cues (i.e., at the level of self-regulation), and 2) failures in recognition during early triadic relating when the newly agentic self requires acknowledgement by a differentiated other, such that loss becomes mitigated by possibility (i.e., at the level of identity). Furthermore, early disruptions of agentic expression will retroactively take on gendered meaning during the separation–individuation phase in the context of recognizing oneself as a *girl* or as a *boy* who does or does feel a sense of agentic competence. For example, a woman whose attempts at restriction set off voracious hunger resulting in a dissociated binge episode is enacting her impaired self-regulation. Yet she will retrospectively accuse herself of being "fat, out of control, and disgusting." These identity signifiers are often ascribed either implicitly or explicitly in gendered terms. Perhaps she is "fat, out of control, and disgusting" squarely within her sense of what it means to be a woman. Or perhaps she is failing to be the kind of woman she wants to be, who may be different or similar to her own mother. Or perhaps she is failing to be feminine at all, and this "self" is associated instead with a disavowed paternal identification, maybe one who is demanding and greedy at the other's expense.

A conceptualization of the relational nature of identification processes is central to understanding the development of gender identity and of eating disorders.

From the time a baby is conceived, parents have conscious and unconscious fantasies about who their child will be, and these hopes and fears are powerfully shaped by gendered meanings (Fast, 1999). What kind of boy will I have? What kind of girl? How do I want him/her to be like me, not like me, better than me, not better than me? Like adult romantic love, being a parent is a rare second chance at symbolic contact with one's own, gendered ego ideal (Davies, 1998). Will a little boy give his father the opportunity to live out an improved version of masculinity? Or his mother an invitation to enjoy her boy-like identifications?

From the moment the baby arrives on the scene, and long before the child identifies him- or herself as "boy" or "girl," parents' gendered fantasies, rooted in their own internal labyrinths of gendered identifications, will inform the infinite, daily, physical, cognitive, and affective interactions they have with their child (Fast, 1999; Harris, 1999). To complicate things further, some of these gendered and sexual meanings will be explicit, but others will be conveyed obliquely in, to use Laplanche's phrase, "enigmatic messages" (1995). In Fast's articulation of how mothers or fathers with prominent gendered conflicts might have children whose subjectivity becomes similarly textured, she refers to Coates's clinical work with a boy whose "mother dresses him in a black leather jacket at eight months and tells him that he is mean and bad just like his dad" (cited in Fast, 1999, p. 645). Now school age and acting out, Fast posits that *this* boy's sense of how to *be* a boy took shape in part through his mother's vision of masculinity.

To this I would add the particular relevance of gendered messages conveyed around food and eating in early development. Perhaps this "mean and bad" boy was also supposed to be "big and strong." If so, his mother might have responded differently to his appetite than to a little girl who was suppose to be, say, "mean and lean." Or maybe the little girl is not supposed to be mean at all, and when she eventually rejects her mother's cooking, she may be shamed rather than celebrated for her willful ways.

The "capacity" for autonomy, as expressed in assertions of will and desire, emerges within, not outside, relational experience (Gentile, 2001; Schoen, 2002).[13] This has implications for how we view both development and therapeutic action. Benjamin's opening of a space in which the tensions between sameness (identification) and difference (recognition by a differentiated other) reciprocally enhance one another (Mitchell, 2000) is invaluable in working with ED patients. For them, gendered identifications are ensnared in binary choices between sameness and difference in relation to idealized or devalued others. Whether symbolized by the anorexic's refusal to choose anything or by the binger's attempt to have it all, choice—the expression of a distinct desire belonging to a defined and gendered self—is rejected. Alternately, choices, when they can be made, eliminate far too much. ED patients cannot maintain the necessary dialectic between their gendered identity and their gendered multiplicity (Aron, 1995), which would, in turn, allow the articulation of desires created by the fruitful interpenetration of "masculine" and "feminine" identifications.

Clinical Implications of an Interpersonal/ Relational Perspective

As noted above, the conceptualization of EDs as disorders of a gendered, agentic self assumes a model of gender identity development based on the idea that children establish their gendered self-experience in interactions with both same and cross-sex parents. These interactions are informed by oscillating processes of projection and introjection shaped by parents' own conscious and unconscious gender identifications (e.g., Aron, 1995; Benjamin, 1991, 1995; Corbett, 2011; Fast, 1991, 1999; Harris, 2009). This perspective on gender-identity development must be anchored in a relational model of mind and therapeutic action. In the last two decades, a number of prominent interpersonal and relational theorists have articulated a model of psychic structure based on the internal representation of relational units made up self-other bonds and interaction patterns (Bromberg, 1991, 1993, 1994; Davies, 1994, 1996; Fast, 1999; Mitchell, 1988).

A person's experience of identity and agency, including their experience of gendered identity and gendered agency, emerges from those internally represented self–other schemes that can be affectively modulated, linguistically encoded, and held in simultaneous awareness with other, conflicting experiences. This is what Bromberg (1998) famously called the capacity to "stand in the spaces." What is kept out of awareness and held in the "relational unconscious" (Gerson, 2004) are mutually incompatible experiences of self that cannot be reconciled with internal representations of self–object dyads and thus threaten psychic integrity. What is conscious and what is unconscious at any given moment will depend on the particular constellation of self- and object-related experience that moves to the foreground in the current interpersonal matrix as it is shaped in part by the "irreducible" (Renik, 1993) subjectivity of the analyst (Aron, 1991; Davies, 2004; Hoffman, 1983, 1991; Greenberg, 1995).[14]

It thus follows that a person's conscious experience of identity, self-continuity, and agency (as delineated above in a relational model of mind) will be derived from experiences tied to gendered meanings. Similarly, irreconcilable self–other experience that is dissociatively split off may be more or less textured by gendered identifications, counteridentifications, or conflicts. Insofar as gendered meanings are salient for a particular patient, the present relational context with the analyst, who will bring his or her own gendered self–other representations into the mix, shapes how this material emerges and whether disavowed gender identifications can become part of the patient's agentic self.

Girls Will Be Girls: A Clinical Vignette

In my consideration of eating problems as disorders of a gendered, desiring self, I have tried to explicate a model that can account for the gender disparity in eating-disorder prevalence, articulate the developmental pathways that are implicated when both girls and boys develop eating problems, and make room for individual variation within same-sex groups. That said, despite the increased incidence in men, when the presenting problem is an ED, the most common therapy dyad will be one in which both patient and therapist are female. Therefore, I will conclude with a clinical vignette based on my work with a bulimic woman. In doing so, I hope, to illustrate 1) the importance of the sameness/difference axis in the ED patient's experience of gendered identifications and agency, 2) the shifts in both patient's and analyst's gendered experience over time, and 3) the analyst's need to become aware of her participation in gender-based enactments.

Maya is a 40-year-old attorney, five years into a three-times weekly analysis at the time of this vignette. When she entered treatment, she was bingeing and purging daily. The first two years of our work focused on her struggles to separate from her invasive, chaotic, but lively mother, punctuated by themes of anger and longing toward her constricted, rigid father. During this time, Maya stopped purging and her binges became few and far between. This period was followed by a time of increased self-care and burgeoning professional ambition, including a more prestigious and satisfying job. While productive in many ways, the analysis was much slower in helping Maya with her desire to have a romantic relationship with a man. She felt stuck in one of two extremes: involvements with exciting, unpredictable men who "fill up all the space," or with "boring," stable men who "can't keep up with her." She wanted someone with whom she had things in common, but which things?

Maya is a study in contrasts, with long dark hair, light eyes, and fair skin. She is of medium height and heavy, although with better regulation of her eating she has lost some weight. She may lose more, as her bingeing declines further, but she will never be thin. Her natural shape is large and curvy. Her father, whom she takes after physically, has a similar body type, although without the feminine lines. Throughout our work together, Maya has been vigilantly attuned to our perceived similarities and differences, and when we first explored how she chose me as her therapist, this compare-and-contrast axis was prominent. She liked it that we were both women, similar in age, both with professional degrees. But she also liked her idea that I had some strengths she did not. I would know things she needed to learn. I was sturdy and independent. This gave her the feeling that she could rely on me instead of always depending on herself. And I was thin, which she found comforting: I was different from her but in line with her aspirations.

Over time we have cycled through many binaries structuring Maya's relational experience: active/passive, resourceful/dependent, analyst/patient, teacher/student, smart/dumb, cool/uncool, fat/thin—each of them organized at least in part by the shifting meanings of masculine/feminine. In addition to liking my slimness insofar as it represented her own bodily ambitions and fantasized options, we discovered that in the early years of the treatment my weight symbolized my authority, and thus my dependability, which were, in turn, entangled with Maya seeing me as a "masculine" woman. In this sense my bodily difference was linked to a cross-gendered relational experience, and one in which differences were welcome rather than threatening.

69

Yet, as Maya increasingly took ownership of her own resourcefulness, her need was not for a masculine other on whom she could lean, but a feminine other with whom she could identify. In particular, as Maya struggled to elaborate her femininity and sexuality within her realistic body-based experience, my thinness became an unwelcome disruption. Faced with giving up her fantasy of the omnipotent thin body-self she would one day attain, Maya no longer felt that my body offered her access to "masculine" strength and efficacy, nor feminine potentials for her ego ideal. Rather, it was evidence that I was the kind of woman she could never be, one who fit neatly into the cultural mold for attractiveness—one with access to goodies she would be denied and men who would not want her.

For a time we made headway, exploring these increasingly negative feelings about our "differences." Given that this was a clear shift, and one that represented Maya's first impassioned expressions of disappointment and anger in the transference, my inclination was to stay with rather than challenge her insistence that I was not who she needed me to be. We did make some useful links to Maya's feeling rejected and abandoned by her relatively thin mother who conveyed to Maya that she had access to pleasure and excitement from which Maya was excluded. But despite this initial traction, we ground to a halt.

In session after session, Maya upped the ante in describing ways I had it good *as a woman,* and she had it bad. When I floated tentative challenges to this thin/fat splitting she became either enraged about the degree to which I did not "get it," or deflated, noting that I was probably "right" and must be tiring of her inability to change. I increasingly found myself struggling to honor her experience of painful difference in both its realistic and psychic dimensions. My compassion was strained. I felt defensive, self-conscious. Was I flaunting my shape if my clothes were tailored? Trying to hide behind layers? And why now? Maya's feelings about my slim build had been a frequent theme in the treatment thus far without this constricting effect. Finally, in a session in which Maya's insistence on my body-based privilege really began to chafe (Stern's [1990] apt description of how it feels to the therapist when awareness of an enactment is dawning), I snapped: "Of course, you're right. Thin women *never* suffer from gender-based stereotypes. We have it *so* easy."

The effects of this were quite interesting. Maya initially felt my anger as an attack, but almost immediately was relieved at suddenly finding us in the same boat. She actually laughed, saying, "I guess I have been assuming an awful lot about you based on your body size. I guess that's the thing I'm also trying to reject for myself." As we explored this interaction and those that led up to it in ensuing sessions, the terrain shifted. Maya described feeling like she hated the sympathy she was extracting from me, which felt distancing and demeaning. She told me: "I didn't want you to feel bad for me; I wanted you to *like* me." Angry exchanges did not devolve into stalemates. I could more confidently challenge her refusals to identify with me despite our different bodies, her beliefs in the magical properties of thinness, and her difficulty tolerating feelings of envy and loss when she did not come out ahead. As these themes unfolded, Maya sought out relationships with heavy women whom she could now find beautiful. She began to take the initiative with men she might like and to date one whom she described as a "nice mix of things." In the transference, she become shyly exhibitionistic, showing off her risk taking, her successes, and her new clothes.

Case Discussion

This vignette condenses material from many sessions. Yet my hope is that it illustrates the salience of gender-based enactments in working with ED patients. Transitions in both session content and the quality of our relatedness were marked by shifting configurations of gendered-self in relationship to gendered-other. For example, Maya's early experience of me contained aspects of the recognizing, idealized, rapprochement father, which allowed her both to depend on me without shame and to claim her own desire for boundaries and agency (Benjamin, 1991). This configuration was central to Maya's eliminating her purging and reducing her bingeing, which symbolized her conflict between wanting to take in her exciting, overwhelming mother, and wanting to protect against intrusion. At other times I was less a symbol of specifically masculine strength, and more the embodiment of a combined parent figure: masculine woman, mommy–daddy joined (Aron, 1995). With *this* me, Maya engaged her own potentials as someone whose dreams and desires could be freed from her stultifying preoccupations with food and weight.

As Maya increasingly tried to locate her agency and power within an embodied sense of femininity, she reengaged her struggle integrating limits and possibilities. Now the omnipotence associated with "thinness" was impossible to attain and too painful to renounce, and our within-gender body difference was one that could not be bridged. As the mother who might invite or forbid entry into more oedipal themes, I became the reminder that her glass was empty, while mine was full. This was importantly linked to Maya's history. We replayed experiences in the maternal dyad of have and have not, seduction and exclusion, promises of false sameness and denied difference.

Yet, while I consciously tried to acknowledge differences *and* potential similarities between us, aspects of my own historical struggles to sustain mutual recognition within *my* maternal self-other schemes were invoked by Maya's splitting, and my acknowledgement fell short. It did not hold enough genuine commiseration with the hurdles most, if not all, women face in making peace with their body selves. It did not admit enough comfortable pleasure in my physical attributes, or enough challenge to Maya's insistence that I should feel bad about what was "good" about my body. And it certainly did not include any comfortable satisfaction in winning this particular contest. Maya's distaste for my sympathy made sense, as she could feel perfectly well the distance—and with that, the traces of disdain—it kept between us. Feeling myself suddenly ensconced in a distinct version of my feminine subjectivity and facing the envy and rage of another, particular woman, I was neither able to openly enjoy my advantage, nor genuinely relate to the fear of losing. How then could I legitimize Maya's experience as both valued companion and worthy competitor?

When we dug our way out of our ditch, we found ourselves on new and fertile ground. Maya felt that she could see clearly for the first time the way that her mother always subtly conveyed to her that she was not "doing the girly thing right." (Benjamin [1995] noted that it is one thing to know you are female, like your mother, and quite another to become feminine, like her, as well.) Maya became aware that she felt rejected by her mother, "almost like a jilted lover." Her mother never seemed to look at her with prideful ownership, with pleasure, with desire. In working with this material, Elise's (1998a) extension of Winnicott's (1952) metaphor of the nursing couple, for whom the potential space holds early sensual meanings, was especially generative. For Maya, this captured her early erotic experience with her mother, her pain about feeling the loss of this connection, and her attempt quite literally to take in food to fill a sense of emptiness that had sexual, as well as emotional valence (see also Elise, 1998b). Maya realized that she was used to a sense of rejection by her emotionally remote father, but now it felt like she had "lost out twice," capturing the way in which oedipal loss for girls can represent not only a generational, but gender defeat (Elise, 2008). Explorations of this theme in the transference helped Maya transform disavowed shame-ridden maternal longings into novel erotic possibilities. This was central to Maya's newfound interest in men who seemed to bridge both masculine and feminine identifications, and thus offer "the right mix of things." It was also central to Maya's successful efforts to stop what was left of her bingeing, as it was no longer necessary to dissociate her desire for more.

Yet none of this would have come to pass had Maya and I been unable to address how the direct collision of our similarly female but differently sized bodies unleashed competitive and envious dynamics that both of us found difficult to face. In this sense, we enacted what can be "typical" difficulties for women in female therapy dyads in harnessing aggressive, competitive strivings in the service of autonomy and agency (Dimen, 1991; Elise, 2008; Harris, 1997). Given the ubiquity of this gender pairing in clinical work with ED patients, the risk of enacting perversions in agency (Gentile, 2001)—with some patients, at some times, in some self-other configurations—is high.[15]

Conclusion

To understand the relationship between gender and eating problems, we need sophisticated analyses of the intersection of cultural, psychological, and physiological forces. In work with ED patients, we need conceptualizations of psychic experience that can account for similarities and differences in the meaning of eating symptoms, both between and within gender groups. Interpersonal/relational perspectives, with their emphases on maintaining tension between a felt sense of stable identity, including gendered identity, and fluid access to multiplicity, including gendered multiplicity (Aron, 1995), can make rich contributions in this arena.

The frequently observed conflicts between dependency and autonomy in ED patients tend to be understood as arising from troubled separation–individuation processes in the early maternal dyad. Yet the meaning of separation (difference) within the ongoing navigation of connection (sameness) needs to be extended by recognizing the multiplicity of both same- and cross-sex gendered identifications and counteridentifications in representations of self-other interaction schemes. ED patients tend to organize their gendered "selves" into binary categories representing mutually exclusive options. Thus therapists must resist narratives that foreclose the development of a space inside "big" enough for the "dialectical interplay of masculine and feminine identities" (Ogden, 1989, pp. 138–139) that are at the foundation of healthy gender identity.

The abundant theorizing on gender by contemporary psychoanalysts is invaluable in work with ED patients. Furthermore, it is no accident that in this literature, efforts to untangle the knots of gender and sexuality draw on compelling clinical illustrations with patients whose eating is troubled (e.g., Dimen, 1991; Harris, 1991). Patients with clinical and subclinical eating problems literally personify the intersection of body experiences, identifications, and desires that are saturated in gendered meanings. Thus an enriched understanding of eating problems may, in turn, help us understand how gendered meanings and identifications are rooted in other disorders of an embodied self.

Patients with EDs suffer debilitating impairments in self-continuity and agency. These impairments are intimately linked to the dissociation of self-other configurations embedded in gendered meanings and identifications, particularly in the thwarted strivings of an agentic self. On the one hand, therapists must help ED patients articulate the gendered meanings in their conscious experience, including concretely in their eating habits, food preferences, and ego/body/weight ideals. One the other, clinicians must remain attentive to the presence of enactments holding gendered self-other configurations, the elaboration of which will be key in transforming the experience of "wanting" (Brisman, 2002) into one that holds possibilities for tolerable loss, creative self-expression, and deep satisfaction.

However, like many clinical ambitions, this is easier said than done. Therapists working with ED patients often have to spend long stretches inside their patients' concrete relationships with food and eating symptoms, laboring to formulate the symbolic meanings of who/what they want to take in or expel, desire or reject, be like or unlike, in order to build a bridge to their internal worlds. In addition, the negotiation of gendered conflicts, which are intimately tied to bodily vulnerability, to our most primal feelings of inadequacy, to our earliest encounters with not getting what we desperately desired, is especially fraught. As Elise noted, "A significant portion of shame is gender-related" (2008, p. 94), and integrating shame-ridden aspects of self, while profoundly transformative, is no piece of cake. It is a tall order—not only for patients but for analysts as well—to be open to their own complex same- and cross-sex identifications, hetero- and homoerotic longings, and experiences of physical limits or flaws. Yet, if we try, and attend to how we fail, we will have our best chance of helping our ED patients play at being and having it all, without forgoing the sustenance provided by personally meaningful choice.

Acknowledgement

I would like to thank Steven Tublin, Ph.D. and Lew Aron, Ph.D. for their help in reading and commenting on earlier drafts of this chapter.

Notes

1. Patients with histories of sexual abuse are susceptible to ED symptoms, which further complicates the link between gender, sexuality, and desire. A discussion of these intersections is beyond the scope of this chapter. See Gutwill and Gitter (1995), Slavin and Pollock (1997), and Charatan (this volume) for discussions of these themes.
2. This formulation resonates with Freud's view of therapeutic action as expanding the degree to which disavowed desire can become part of the agentic self: "Where id was, there shall ego be" (1933, 80). For the ED patient, I am emphasizing that this transformation may be more akin to: "Where id was, there shall gendered-ego be" (Aron, personal communication, 2012; see also Fast, 1995).
3. I will use the terms therapist and analyst interchangeably.
4. I do not differentiate between "types" of EDs in this chapter, all of which reflect appetite dysregulation, body image disturbance, and preoccupations with weight and body size. In addition, one eating extreme usually begets another, and it is common for ED patients to "switch" diagnoses.
5. Throughout this chapter I maintain the perspective that no trait is essentially masculine or feminine; rather these meanings arise from the complex interplay of cultural and developmental context.
6. Clinicians working with male ED patients have identified a new subtype of Body Dysmorphic Disorder called "muscle dysmorphia" defined by preoccupation that one's muscles are small when they are actually big (Pope et al., 2000).
7. I use the terms ED and eating problems interchangeably to include both clinical and subclinical symptom expression.
8. See also Benjamin (1995), Butler (1990), Goldner (1991), Harris (1991), Aron (1995), and Sweetnam (1996) for critiques of binary categories implicated in gender construction.
9. Research shows that boys, like girls, are most likely to develop EDs around puberty when issues of identity and sexuality are in the foreground, but that girls are more vulnerable if puberty is early, and boys more vulnerable when they are "late bloomers" (Pope et al., 2000). This in line with my suggestion, to put it simply, that the ED girl wants less "femininity," while the ED boy wants more "masculinity."
10. I am assuming that such difficulties in integration occur across sexual orientations and do not, in and of themselves, indicate preferences for same-sex or cross-sex romantic partners. Indeed, research on ED men contradicts the assumption that they more typically identify as homosexual, but supports their tendency to report an absence of sexual desire in general (Pope et al., 2000).
11. While critical of the idea that developmental stages are fixed or universal, contemporary psychoanalysis retains the notion of significant phases, while acknowledging contextual influence on inner experience and the recurring nature of psychic conflicts (Aron, 1995, Benjamin, 1995).
12. This formulation assumes traditional family structure, and could shift if the exciting "coming and going parent" is not the father or is the same as the primary caretaker.

However, the import of a parental figure "outside" the early caretaking dyad to the child's establishment of a differentiated, agentic self still holds.

13. Lyons-Ruth (1991) has noted that the separation-individuation phase would thus more appropriately be called the separation-attachment phase.

14. Qualitative research supports the prominence of gendered identifications in patients with eating problems and their use of aspects of their therapists' gendered identities in facilitating the development of agency (Schoen, 2002).

15. This vignette shares some features with the case Dimen (1991) used to illustrate how the thin female therapist/fat female patient pair could not find their place as "like subjects" (Benjamin, 1995), an impasse that ended the treatment.

References

Aron, L. (1991). The patient's experience of the analyst's subjectivity. *Psychoanalytic Dialogues, 1*, 29–51.

Aron, L. (1995). The internalized primal scene. *Psychoanalytic Dialogues, 5*, 195–237.

Bassin, D. (1996). Beyond the he and the she: Toward the reconciliation of masculinity and femininity in the post-oedipal female mind. *Journal of the American Psychoanalytic Association, 44(Suppl)*, 157–190.

Beebe, B. (1988). Mother-infant mutual influence and precursors of self and object representations. In J. Masling (Ed.), *Empirical studies of psychoanalytic theories* (Vol. 2, pp. 27–48). Hillsdale, NJ: Analytic Press.

Beebe, B., Lachmann, F., & Jaffe, J. (1997). Mother-infant interaction structures and pre-symbolic self and object representations. *Psychoanalytic Dialogues, 7*, 29–51.

Benjamin, J. (1988). *The bonds of love: Psychoanalysis, feminism, & the problem of domination.* New York: Pantheon Books.

Benjamin, J. (1991). Father and daughter: Identification with difference—A contribution to gender heterodoxy. *Psychoanalytic Dialogues, 1*, 277–299.

Benjamin, J. (1995). Sameness and difference: Toward an "over inclusive" model of gender development. *Psychoanalytic Inquiry, 15*, 125–142.

Boskind-Lodahl, M. (1976). Cinderella's stepsisters: A feminist perspective on anorexia nervosa and bulimia. *Signs, 2*, 342–356.

Boskind-White, M., & White, W. (1983). *Bulimarexia.* New York: Norton.

Brisman, J. (2002). Wanting. *Contemporary Psychoanalysis, 38*, 329–343.

Bromberg, P. M. (1991). On knowing one's patient inside out: The aesthetics of unconscious communication. *Psychoanalytic Dialogues, 1*, 399–422.

Bromberg, P. M. (1993). Shadow and substance: A relational perspective on clinical process. *Psychoanalytic Psychology, 10*, 147–168.

Bromberg, P. M. (1994). "Speak! That I may see you": Some reflections on dissociation, reality, and psychoanalytic listening. *Psychoanalytic Dialogues, 4*, 517–547.

Bromberg, P. M. (1998). *Standing in the spaces: Essays on clinical process, trauma and dissociation.* Hillsdale, NJ: Analytic Press.

Bromberg, P. M. (2001). Treating patients with symptoms—and symptoms with patience: Reflections on shame, dissociation, and eating disorders. *Psychoanalytic Dialogues, 11*, 891–912.

Bruch, H. (1973). *Eating disorders: Obesity, anorexia nervosa, and the person within.* New York: Basic Books.

Bruch, H. (1978). *The golden cage: The enigma of anorexia nervosa.* Cambridge, MA: Harvard University Press.

Butler, J. (1990). *Gender trouble.* New York: Routledge.

Butler, J. (1995). Melancholy gender-refused identification. *Psychoanalytic Dialogues, 5*, 165–180.

Chernin, K. (1981). *The obsession: Reflections on the tyranny of slenderness.* New York: Harper & Row.

Chernin, K. (1985). *The hungry self.* New York: Harper & Row.

Chodorow, N. J. (1978). *The reproduction of mothering: Psychoanalysis and the sociology of gender.* Berkeley: University of California Press.

Coates, S., Friedman, R. C., & Wolfe, S. (1991). The etiology of boyhood gender identity disorder: A model for integrating temperament, development, and psychodynamics. *Psychoanalytic Dialogues, 1,* 481–523.

Coates, S., & Wolfe, S. (1995). Gender identity disorder in boys. *Psychoanalytic Inquiry, 15,* 6–38.

Corbett, K. (2011). *Boyhoods: Rethinking masculinities.* New Haven, CT: Yale University Press.

Crastnapol, M. (2001). The male experience of food as symbol and sustenance. In J. Petrucelli & C. Stuart (Eds.), *Hungers and compulsions.* New York: Jason Aronson.

Davies, J. M. (1994). Love in the afternoon: A relational reconsideration of desire and dread in the countertransference. *Psychoanalytic Dialogues, 4,* 153–170.

Davies, J. M. (1996). Linking the "pre-analytic" with the postclassical: integration, dissociation, and the multiplicity of unconscious process. *Contemporary Psychoanalysis, 32,* 553–576.

Davies, J. M. (1998). Between the disclosure and foreclosure of erotic transference- countertransference. *Psychoanalytic Dialogues, 8,* 747–766.

Davies, J. M. (2004). Whose bad objects are we anyway? Repetition and our elusive love affair with evil. *Psychoanalytic Dialogues, 14,* 711–732.

deGroot, J. M., & Rodin, G. (1994). Eating disorders, female psychology, and the self. *Journal of the American Academy of Psychoanalysis, 22,* 299–317.

Dimen, M. (1991). Deconstructing difference: Gender, splitting, and transitional space. *Psychoanalytic Dialogues, 1,* 335–352.

Elise, D. (1998a). Gender repertoire: Body, mind, and bisexuality. *Psychoanalytic Dialogues, 8,* 353–371.

Elise, D. (1998b). The absence of the paternal penis. *Journal of the American Psychoanalytic Association, 46,* 413–442.

Elise, D. (2000). Women and desire: why women may not want to want. *Studies in Gender and Sexuality, 1,* 125–145.

Elise, D. (2008). Sex and shame: The inhibition of female desires. *Journal of the American Psychoanalytic Association, 56,* 73–98.

Fast, I. (1984). *Gender identity: A differentiation model.* Hillsdale, NJ: Analytic Press.

Fast, I. (1991). Commentary on "father and daughter: identification with difference—A contribution to gender heterodoxy." *Psychoanalytic Dialogues, 1,* 301–304.

Fast, I. (1995). The dynamic self in psychoanalytic psychology: A formulation. *Psychoanalytic Dialogues, 5,* 435–458.

Fast, I. (1999). Aspects of core gender identity. *Psychoanalytic Dialogues, 9,* 633–661.

Freud, S. (1933). New introductory lectures on psycho-analysis. *The standard edition of the complete psychological works of Sigmund Freud: New introductory lectures on psychoanalysis and other works Vol. 22, 1932–1936* (pp. 1–182). London: Vintage.

Garner, D., Garfinkel, P., Schwartz, D., & Thompson, M. (1980). Cultural expectations of thinness in women. *Psychological Report, 47,* 483–491.

Gentile, J. (2001). Close but no cigar: the perversion of agency and the absence of thirdness. *Contemporary Psychoanalysis, 37,* 623–654.

Gerson, S. (2004). The relational unconscious: a core element of intersubjectivity, thirdness, and clinical process. *Psychoanalytic Quarterly, 3,* 63–98.

Gilligan, C. (2011). *Joining the resistance.* Cambridge: Policy Press.

Goldner, V. (1991). Toward a critical relational theory of gender. *Psychoanalytic Dialogues, 1,* 249–272.

Goldner, V. (2011). Trans: Gender in free fall. *Psychoanalytic Dialogues, 21*(2), 159–171.

Greenberg, J. (1995). Psychoanalytic technique and the interactive matrix. *Psychoanalytic Quarterly, 64,* 1–22.

Gutwill, S. (1994a). Women's eating problems: Social context and the internalization of culture. In C. Bloom, A. Gitter, S. Gutwill, L. Logel, & L. Zaphiropoulous (Eds.), *Eating problems: A feminist psychoanalytic treatment model* (pp. 1–27). New York: Basic Books.

Gutwill, S. (1994b).The diet: Personal experience, social condition, and the industrial empire. In C. Bloom, A. Gitter, S. Gutwill, L. Logel, & L. Zaphiropoulous (Eds.), *Eating problems: A feminist psychoanalytic treatment model* (pp. 28–39). New York: Basic Books.

Gutwill, S., & Gitter, A. (1994). Eating problems and sexual abuse: treatment considerations. In C. Bloom, A. Gitter, S. Gutwill, L. Logel, & L. Zaphiropoulous (Eds.), *Eating problems: A feminist psychoanalytic treatment model* (pp. 205–226). New York: Basic Books.

Harris, A. (1991). Gender as contradiction. *Psychoanalytic Dialogues, 1,* 197–224.

Harris, A. (1997). Aggression, envy, and ambition: Circulating tensions in women's psychic life. *Gender and Psychoanalysis, 2,* 291–325.

Harris, A. (1999). Making genders: Commentary on paper by Irene Fast. *Psychoanalytic Dialogues, 9,* 663–673.

Harris, A. (2009). *Gender as soft assembly.* New York: Routledge/Taylor & Francis.

Hoffman, I. Z. (1983). The patient as interpreter of the analyst's experience. *Contemporary Psychoanalysis, 19,* 389–422.

Hoffman, I. Z. (1991). Discussion: Toward a social-constructivist view of the psychoanalytic situation. *Psychoanalytic Dialogues, 1,* 74–105.

Kearney-Cooke, A. (1991). The role of the therapist in the treatment of eating disorders: A feminist psychodynamic approach. In C. Johnson (Ed.), *Psychodynamic treatment of anorexia nervosa and bulimia* (pp. 296–318). New York: Guilford Press.

Laplanche, J. (1995). Seduction, persecution, revelation. *International Journal of Psycho-Analysis, 76,* 663–682.

Lyons-Ruth, K. (1991). Rapprochement or approachement. *Psychoanalytic Psychology, 8,* 1–23.

Mitchell, S. (1988). *Relational concepts in psychoanalysis.* Cambridge, MA: Harvard University Press.

Mitchell, S. (2000). Juggling paradoxes: Commentary on the work of Jessica Benjamin. *Studies in Gender and Sexuality, 1,* 251–269.

Ogden, T. H. (1989). *The primitive edge of experience.* Northvale, NJ: Jason Aronson.

Ogden, T. (1994). *Subjects of analysis.* New York: Jason Aronson.

Orbach, S. (1978). *Fat is a feminist issue.* London: Paddington.

Orbach, S. (2000). *The hunger strike: Starving amidst plenty.* New York: Other Press.

Petrucelli, J. (2006). (Ed) *Longing: Psychoanalytic musings on desire.* New York: Karnac.

Petrucelli, J., & Stuart, C. (Eds.). (2001). *Hungers and compulsions: The psychodynamic treatment of eating disorders & addictions.* New York: Jason Aronson.

Polivy, J., & Hermann, P. (1987). Diagnosis and treatment of normal eating. *Journal of Consulting and Clinical Psychology, 55,* 635–644.

Pope, H. G., Phillips, K. A., & Olivardia, R. (2000). *The Adonis complex: The secret crisis of male body obsession.* New York: Free Press.

Renik, O. (1993). Analytic interaction: conceptualizing technique in light of the analyst's irreducible subjectivity. *Psychoanalytic Quarterly, 62,* 553–571.

Riviere, J. (1929). Womanliness as masquerade. *International Journal of Psychoanalysis, 10,* 303–313.

Sands, S. H. (1989). Eating disorders and female development: a self-psychological perspective. *Progress in Self Psychology, 5,* 75–103.

Sands, S. H. (1991). Bulimia, dissociation, and empathy: A self-psychological view. In C. Johnson (Ed.), *Psychodynamic treatment of anorexia nervosa and bulimia* (pp. 34–50). New York: Guilford Press.

Sands, S. H. (2003). The subjugation of the body in eating disorders: a particularly female solution. *Psychoanalytic Psychology, 20,* 103–116.

Schoen, S. (2002). *What comes to mind: A multiple case study of patients' experiences of good-enough outcome in long-term psychodynamic psychotherapies.* Unpublished doctoral dissertation, University of Michigan.

Sedgwick, E. (1995). Gosh Boy George, you must be awfully secure in your masculinity. In M. Berger, B. Wallis, S. Watson, & C. M. Weems (Eds.), *Constructing masculinity.* New York: Routledge.

Slavin, J. H., & Pollock, L. (1997). The poisoning of desire. *Contemporary Psychoanalysis, 33,* 573–593.

Steiner-Adair, C. (1986). The body politic: Normal female adolescent development and the development of eating disorders. *Journal of the American Academy of Psychoanalysis and Dynamic Psychiatry, 14,* 95–114.

Steiner-Adair, C. (1991). New maps of development, new models of therapy: The psychology of women and the treatment of eating disorders. In C. Johnson (Ed.), *Psychodynamic treatment of anorexia nervosa and bulimia* (pp. 226–244). New York: Guilford Press.

Stern, D. B. (1990). Courting surprise—Unbidden perceptions in clinical practice. *Contemporary Psychoanalysis, 26,* 452–478.

Stern, D. N. (1985). *The interpersonal world of the infant.* New York: Basic Books.

Sugarman, A. (1991). Bulimia: A displacement from psychological self to body self. In C. Johnson (Ed.), *Psychodynamic treatment of anorexia nervosa and bulimia* (pp. 3–33). New York: Guilford Press.

Sweetnam, A. (1996). The changing contexts of gender: Between fixed and fluid experience. *Psychoanalytic Dialogues, 6,* 437–459.

Winnicott, D. W. (1952). Anxiety associated with insecurity. In *Through pediatrics to psycho-analysis* (pp. 97–100). New York: Basic Books.

Wooley, S., Wooley, O., & Dyrenforth, S. (1980). The case against radical intervention. *American Journal of Clinical Nutrition, 33,* 465–471.

4

'STRETCHED TO THE LIMIT'

The Elastic Body Image in the Reflexive Mind

Elizabeth Halsted

"I feel fat," my patient Lucy announced after settling into her seat in front of me. This kind of comment is so familiar to all of us that we can become numb to its implications. *I feel fat* is a prototypical expression of a body-image problem. My patient was expressing how in that moment or that self-state her sense of her body self was bad and dominated by fat. All the nuances of affect, identity and physicality had been collapsed into one attribute. This is the result of integrative psychic failures. Her affective experiences, longings, and views of the self had been poorly integrated into a confused expression of bodily appearance saturated with negative affect mislabeled as "fat."

Most clinicians can identify body image material when it presents itself in the consulting room. We know it when we hear it. The quandary is how to engage the issue in our psychoanalytic conversation, and how to provide a therapeutic intervention that addresses its pathological forms. Too often our inquiries lead us into confused discussions about diet and exercise that are awkwardly concrete and not psychological. We might respond to our patient with an open inquiry, such as "why is that?" We often get strange concrete replies (i.e., "Because I am" or "Really?"). These forays do not bring us new or useful information, nor do they broaden our patients' awareness. These conversations are neither psychological nor therapeutic. They leave both the therapist and patient feeling powerless and bad about themselves, replaying the patient's painful experiences in the world at large. We fall into to these dead-end conversations with patients when we get caught in a cul-de-sac of objectifying cultural messages and limited psychological conceptualizations. We need more ways to think about what body image is, how it is made, and what are its functions? Although psychoanalysts understand the complexities of major disorders, as well as the character issues that manifest in body image problems, we do not have the conceptual tools to formulate intervention strategies to intervene around body image specifically.[1]

I define body image as the imagined body, an internal representation of the external view of the body in any given self-state. Body image is made up of elements of interpersonal and cultural experiences that occur outside the body, combined with elements that occur inside the body, such as feelings and moods; physiological states such as hunger, sleep, or arousal; cognitive contents such as fantasies, imagination, and memory; and personal ideas of identity, values, and purpose, as well as neurological body maps combining spatial, sensory and kinesthetic input. In order to conceptualize how body image is created or how it functions, additional concepts are needed.

Aron's (1998) concept of reflexive functioning is an exceptionally useful idea in considering the question of how body images are made, what is required to make one that is stable and coherent, and what happens when it becomes out of balance. Aron uses the term *reflexive functioning* to "refer to the mental capacity to move back and forth, and to maintain the tension, between a view of the self as a subject and the view of the self as an object" (1998, p. 5). He focused on the place of the body in the mind's self-reflexive capacity. I want to focus more specifically on the relationship of the body image to self-reflexive functioning. The crucial distinction between *reflexive* functioning and *reflective* functioning is that reflexive functioning is a dynamic process, a capacity to move back and forth between an objective and a subjective perspective. Reflexive functioning is also integrative. By maintaining the tension between the two perspectives integration must occur. Reflexivity combines subjective, affective, and experiential aspects of self with an objective view resulting in various selves, self-states, and identities. Reflective functioning (Fonagy & Target, 1996) is the ability to understand one's own or someone else's mental state as a being mental state. It is related to the capacity to have implicit or explicit theories of mind. Self-reflective functioning fuels the subjective pole of self-reflexive oscillations by allowing one to think about one's own feelings and moods and the minds of others. Self-reflexivity is usually better regulated and includes more complex integration when there is the capacity to reflect on mental states, but reflexivity occurs with or without the capacity to reflect on mental states. Self-reflexivity creates a complex self-image in a complex interpersonal and cultural narrative. In the case of body-image formation, reflexive awareness combines a sense of being a body among other bodies and a body that reveals or harbors subjectivity. Aron very nearly makes this point but does not extend his assertion to body image and body-image disturbances. He writes, "Our bodies and especially our skin surface, have the quality of being both me and not me, subject and object: and as such it is our skin sensation that mediate between inside and outside . . . Our experience of our bodies, more than any other experience, partakes of this duality" (1998, p. 22). Body image lies in the transitional boundary and holds elements of both worlds. Reflexive functioning can be seen as the integrative process that creates the body image. Body image is the mental representation of how one's body looks as created by the complex integration of subjective body-self experiences and objective/external body appearance experiences. Body image will always reflect the degree of integration, or the lack of it. Reflexive functioning is the oscillating weaving action between subjective and objective perspectives of the body self. The body image is the consequent psychic product woven by those oscillations reflecting the integrative capacity.

Varying capacities to integrate the dual realities in all realms of experience has been noted by many clinicians (Bach, 1985, 1994, 1998; Bromberg, 1998; Auerbach & Blatt, 1996) and has been useful in explorations of pathological presentations; particularly those marked by dysregulation of affect and dissociated self-states such as eating disorders and pathological narcissism. Difficulties with self-regulation and the disturbed body image seen in patients with eating disorders can be usefully understood as evidence of a poor capacity for reflexive integration.

Everyone oscillates between subjective and objective points of view of the self and the body self. Different character styles prefer one mode to the other, with hysterical styles more often in the subjective realm of impulse, emotion and fantasy, while obsessionals prefer the objective mode of data and reality. Emotional regulation requires the capacity to flexibly oscillate between the two perspectives using the external world to soothe and ground the limitlessness of the internal world, and the ability to retreat into the internal world when reality is overwhelming or painful. Bach (1998) explained how "normally, it is the caretaker who helps the child regulate between the extremes of elation and despair, between self and other, and between the subjective and objective states of consciousness" (p. 667). Under optimal circumstances, parents foster a child's ability to reflect on mental states (Fonagy & Target, 1996) through play, fantasy, and transitional objects. Bromberg (1998) extends this important balance to adults, describing how "if all goes reasonably well developmentally, an adult should not experience a fundamental discontinuity between internal and external reality" (p. 130). Bach (1998) elaborated on what occurs in a child's development;

> What occurs as the child matures is not just better regulated and more appropriate oscillations between subjectivity and objectivity or between self and other but rather a more complex synthesis, a blending and interpenetration of the two in the transitional area so that they are no longer dichotomous.
>
> (p. 667)

Body image is the boundary and transitional area created and shaped by the weaving together of these two modes of being. It is a complex psychic fabrication. It exists in the boundary between the "me" that feels real and undeniably alive and the reflected image that feels more like a "what" that must be cognitively constructed (Bach, 1998, p. 666). The consequent body image reflects the nature of the oscillations, the nature of the perspectives and the mind's capacity to integrate the varying and often conflicting inputs.

A stable body image is evidence of integration and serves important regulatory functions. Emotional stability, self-esteem, and identity are all supported by a stable body image. Its stability reflects the nature of the oscillations from one mode to another within the unique character structure and the interpersonal and body history of a person. The nature of the oscillation varies such that individuals with poor reflexive functioning do not oscillate smoothly but lurch violently and unexpectedly. Furthermore, the data from these dual sources can be highly discrepant; reflexive self-awareness inevitably produces psychic conflict. Depending on character structure and defenses, the psyche may be more or less capable of tolerating the resulting conflict and may produce poorly integrated mental constructs and dysregulated emotions. When reflexive functioning fails to integrate subjective and objective elements, the resulting body image often has qualities that fuse the dual realities. This is the source of collapsed concretized expressions, such as "I am fat" or "I am damaged." My body is fat, bad, damaged, weak, unacceptable, and so forth. These are failed efforts to integrate body-self experience and to self-regulate.

By working in a focused manner on body-image material, our interventions can usefully work to understand and symbolize the history that has consciously or unconsciously shaped body image, and to observe the failures in reflexive functioning while endeavoring to improve it. Returning again to the opening clinical example, "I feel fat," one might wonder what the patient means by *fat*. What are the layers of reflexive self-awareness woven into this body image? Is she talking about a negative feeling about her subjective/internal self? Is she referring to her objective body in the world of body ideals? Is this negative body image a sign of instability? Has it been triggered by an event that could not be integrated? What in her interpersonal history contributes to a negative objective view? If we were to pursue this type of inquiry while holding the goal of improving self reflexive functioning our endeavor might bring positive improvement in self and affect regulation and in the stability and affect tone of the body image.

When body image is integrated into a stable psychic structure it fits seamlessly into self-experience. Internal states reside comfortably within an imagined view of external appearance. A stable body image fits like a comfortable suit. We wear it without being preoccupied by it. It represents us adequately and allows us to use other modes of self-expression such as language, body movement, gesture, and behavior. When body image is disturbed or unstable it is like an ill-fitting garment. It causes painful self-consciousness and is easily disrupted, as when a glance in the mirror causes a complete change in emotional stability and body image. Effective reflexive functioning allows for smooth and flexible oscillations and integrates various and conflicting strands of experience weaving new body images.

Body-Image Development

The body image first appears between 25 and 36 months of age when a child first recognizes his or her image in the mirror (Lemche, 1998). The body image takes shape in the discovery of the child's reflection. It is infused with relational and personal meanings as well as imaginative fantasies that the child has begun to develop and will continue to generate. Body image lies upon a framework of the previous months of body self-awareness, emerging self-awareness and interpersonal regulation (Stern, 1985; Krueger, 2002). The capacity for self-recognition heralds the beginning of self-reflexive functioning. The child discovers that he or she is an object in the eyes of others (Auerbach, 1998), thus opening the possibility of inter-subjectivity and oscillating reflexive functioning. As a child continues to develop, experiences of self are organized into psychic structures or neural pathways. Each self organization includes an image of the body and a sense of how the body is per-ceived by the outer world. Body image will vary on many dimensions. It will vary in its vividness and importance as either a defining or less defining aspect of the self-experience. It will vary in carrying a positively or negatively skewed affective load. And it will vary in its stability, depending on the quality of the integration within individual self-states and between many self-states.

The next major phase for body image development is adolescence, when the body changes and issues of autonomy and independence are prominent again. Eating disorders most often emerge during this phase when reflexive function-ing becomes more complex in an adolescent mind capable of abstract thought and introspection. Reflexive functioning often strains to integrate a new, sexually mature body as well as a new more independent and separate sense of internal self-organization with all its attendant complications, conflicts, and emotional tensions. Many girls with eating disorders have relationships with their mothers that complicate the separation process (Sands, 1989; for a review, see Sugarman, 1991). Difficulties with separation diminish the capacity for reflexive functioning as experiences of merger blur boundaries between self and other and on the level of body image between inner and outer. In addition, identifications on the body dimension can challenge and often strain reflexivity.

The Role of Culture

Cultural messages and societal norms are potent sources of the external point of view as are the pressures to conform or compare. Culture has loaded the air-waves and our minds with objectifying messages about the ideal body. Orbach (2009) pointed to current Western culture as conveying a more potent, penetrat-ing, and pervasive objectifying message than ever before. Physical appearance is increasingly conceptualized as being equivalent to the self: You are what you look like. This construction conflates the external body with the subjec-tive self within. Increasingly appearance is our "canvas to be fixed, remade and enhanced" (Orbach, 2009, p. 1). Culture tells us that our bodies should be controlled, modified, and improved. Furthermore, failure to do so is evidence of low self-worth. Similarly, one's families and peers can be the source of destruc-tive messages that become personal truths engrained in relationships and in one's sense of self. A common social truism is that love, success, or worth is contingent upon having an attractive/ideal body ("You'll never get a man look-ing like that." "You won't be taken seriously looking like that."). Our visually saturated culture offers an extremely narrow aesthetic that poorly represents the realities of human variation. Pressure to conform results in impatience and criticism of people who are not focused on changing their bodies to meet the cultural norm. This sociocultural environment has created pervasive feelings of dissatisfaction, shame, and a general agitation about the body (Orbach, 2009, p. 9). Almost everyone's body image is being damaged by this point of view. If you do not feel bad or worried about your physical appearance, you are out of step with cultural norms. Feminist theorists and feminist psychologists have effectively elucidated the cultural contribution to creating eating disorders and body-image disturbances in women (Thompson et al., 1999). More recently culture's effect on eating-disordered men has been described by Pope et al. (2000). The objectifying messages override integrative possibilities requiring appearance to carry the heavy load of conveying subjectivity, identity, and authenticity in a culturally acceptable way.

We, as psychotherapist, are not immune to our cultural zeitgeist and may therefore formulate interventions, including the negative body ethos. Some conversations in the consulting room may have a subtext that overvalues appearance or believes that changing one's appearance is the most acceptable solution. For example, I might respond to my patient in the introduction who feels fat by inquiring as to whether she has actually gained weight. This inquiry is about her actual body and sets the stage for a discussion of an external point of view of her body. A body-image inquiry would explore what is happening inside her mind. What is her body image representation made of? What feelings, reflections, and interpersonal meanings are woven into it?

The clinical encounter is a new and potentially potent experience of reflexivity in the dimension of body image. In each encounter we convey how we see our patients and how they affect us. Through the many avenues of the intersubjective exchange (facial expression, tone of voice, interpersonal responsiveness) they see their reflection in our eyes, in our words, and in our treatment of them. The transference/countertransference matrix always includes the dimension of the body, and body images are at play to be explored.

Case Example

Sharon is a 30-year-old professional, the daughter of Korean immigrants. She came for a consultation with complaints of depression and episodes of explosive anger. She described having struggled with her weight and having binged and purged while in college and occasionally doing so now. She had never had a romantic or sexual relationship. She avoided dating and many social situations, always postponing entrance into that arena until after she had lost 10 pounds. In fact, her weight was average for her build.

In our initial conversations a model was offered as to how we could approach body image issues.

P: Well, I don't feel comfortable with myself, with my body. I have a bad body image. I guess its low self-esteem but I feel very self-conscious about my body.

T: I think a lot of things probably contribute to that bad body feeling. Let's see if we can unpack them and look at them together.

In subsequent sessions we reviewed her body history, inquiring about health, trauma, puberty, family practices, and peer-group experiences as well as her memories of how she had thought and felt about herself and her body at different times in her life.

For Sharon, the most emotionally charged and conflictual material was about her family's expectations. She had been raised with a powerful message of duty to family and assimilation. The message was that educational success would bring prosperity to her and her family, with the perceived expectation that she would provide for her family here in the U.S. as well as her extended family in Korea. Sharon carried the burden of expectation to succeed and provide. In the arena of work and money she had followed the road map quite successfully. But even there she felt intense guilt that her contributions were inadequate. The family provided very little input or focus on her body or her emotional needs. She was supposed to fit in and succeed. She was now of an age when she was being pressured by her family to find a husband and marry.

We talked about how this emotional weight, pressure, and her feelings of guilt and insufficiency, greed, and anger had resulted in avoidance of social relationships. The emotional weight had been organized in her body image as 10 burdensome pounds. Her body image had become negative and the perceived obstacle to her progress. We constructed several ways to think about this. She had put her emotional needs for social connection aside. Bingeing had become her greedy pleasure, compensating for the deprivation she felt due to her tireless work. She had also adopted mainstream commercial messages about body perfection being the key to romantic connection and felt inadequate and insecure about her average body that might in its imperfect largeness belie her angry and greedy needs for satisfaction. Secondly, Sharon had very little guidance and few expectations in the arena of personal relationships. Her resulting body image had fused feelings of pressure and inadequacy in her family life with similarly pressurized cultural messages of body perfection. With the concept of reflexive functioning in mind, I could have some confidence about what I hoped our conversations could achieve by teasing apart the various elements that had been collapsed into 10 pounds, creating more and better opportunities for her to integrate her feelings and her sense of her identity with an external view of her body. For instance:

P: I had another rage attack. I was unfairly angry at a cab driver and then my doorman. They both made small but forgivable mistakes and I just ripped into them. Afterwards I wanted to binge.
T: It sounds like they were not demanding as much of themselves as you demand of yourself.
P: Yes. But it's not fair of me to expect that of them. I had had a tough day. I hadn't gotten recognition for my work. All this work for what?

T: Might you be able to ease up on yourself a bit?

P: It makes me feel anxious and guilty to think about it. Like I'm letting my family down. And then I start to feel angry again.

T: I think if you could slow down and think some of this through you could calm down some of those feelings. You need to have some fun with people your age without it becoming another job in order to fulfill your parent's expectations.

In a subsequent session our conversation went as follows:

P: I haven't answered the guy who asked to meet for coffee.

T: Hmm. Why is that?

P: Well, I'm not sure he's my type, and I thought I'd wait until I lost that 10 pounds.

T: That's interesting. What do you make of that?

P: Well, you know my parents have put so much pressure on me that I just get overwhelmed and anxious. I knew that it was kind of crazy, but that's what the thought was.

T: Maybe if we slow down and talk through your feelings you might stop putting the pressure you feel on your body.

At this point Sharon's 10-pound burden had been identified as a crazy thought related to feelings of pressure and guilt. It still appeared in her mind as a part of her body image but we were on the road to a new organization. Our repeated conversations placing the feelings inside of her body would encourage a different integration, freeing her body image of these painful feelings and identifying her delay as an emotional choice. Inquiry also includes the immediate experience in our relationship.

T: How does it feel for me to ask about your dating?

P: I know that it isn't really, but it feels like pressure.

T: Like I need you to date so that our therapy can be successful?

P: Yes. And then my next thought is that I have to lose weight.

T: So let's try to pull those elements apart and put them back together in a different way.

As we recognized the same pattern of perceived interpersonal pressure collapsing into a negative body image, we were able to pull these elements apart and make room for her agency.

Comparisons

Body comparisons are a prolific source of data about body image from the objective–external viewpoint. People whose bodies differ from the norm are inundated with negative input as their differences attract comment, criticism and ridicule. This creates a more difficult integrative challenge in establishing a stable body image. This challenge is eased when they find like-bodied people. In "Mirror Mirror on the Wall" (Edut, 2003, pp. 144–155), Leoneda Inge-Barry reflects on her struggle to feel comfortable in her large black body. She writes,

> in helping to mold a more positive self-image, I credit my attending an historically black university. There's nothing like seeing people just like you, who are happy and smart, as you walk across campus . . . No longer too tall or too fat. In fact there were hundreds of me walking around.
>
> (p. 148)

Inge-Barry was relieved of the strain of negative comparison. Because the norm of comparison is so often reflective of the culture's values and power structure, the data of comparison is almost always infused with political meaning. Edut explained, "Scratch away the surface of 'I'm so fat' and 'I hate my hair' and you'll find a sister treading water in a melting pot simmering with every 'ism' imaginable" (2003, p. xxii). With this in mind one can recognize that robust reflexive functioning includes acts of rebellion from oppressive cultural pressures. While teasing out the cultural biases and pressures for conformity we open up fears of being rejected, ostracized, and shunned by one's social group. We may be seen as dangerous as we challenge a rigid external viewpoint, as is the case with many eating-disordered patients. One of my patients explained how she could not trust me entirely because I had shown myself to be in "the fat lovers club." This digestible amount of difference between us allowed us to speak about those unformulated primordial fears of being expelled from the tribe while making room for improved integration of the body self. This patient insisted that in my heart of hearts I too felt disgusted and critical when I looked at overweight people. It took repeated experiences of this truly not being the case for her rigid objective world view to open up to more complex integrations.

Body comparison is also a more or less prominent part of development as the child and then the adolescent both identifies with and differentiates herself from her parents' same and different bodies. The second case illustrates the effects of reliance on comparison for an external point of view and poor integration of the subjective elements of self-experience.

Case Example

Tina entered psychotherapy in her early 30s, having recently married. She was struggling with disruptive feelings of envy and anger vis-à-vis female peers. Her friends, who had been a close group since childhood, enraged her. Every dinner and phone call included questions that to Tina implied comparisons to each other's marriages, homes, children, or jobs. She was becoming increasingly isolated and depressed as she avoided contact because she found the feelings so painful. In her late teens she had a period of anorexia but now managed a stable weight and body image through religious exercise.

Exploration of Tina's history revealed that her childhood peer relationships were rife with comparisons between herself and several close friends. Her circumstance was amplified by the fact that her closest friends all had the same first name. They were the three Tina's. The family's narrative always included the three of them, and comparisons were constantly being made. In addition, she identified herself as being just like her mother, again leaving little room for difference in the integration of her self-image.

Tina adopted comparison as the fundamental building block as she constructed her sense of self and her body image. Interestingly or unfortunately, these three girls were also quite similar in their looks and in their affinities. The metric that emerged for Tina was one that sought sameness. The perception of difference was threatening and elicited stabbing feelings of anger and jealousy disrupting her ability to regulate her sense of self.

Tina did not enter therapy with a body-image complaint. She was maintaining a stable body image in a very rigid way. She kept her weight almost perfectly stable through her exercise regime. When that routine was disrupted, she would complain about feeling fat and in a bad mood, but these fluctuations in mood were minor and controllable by the confidence she had in her ability to return to the target weight.

The rigidity in her body image led me to consider her limited capacity for reflexive functioning. Tina was challenged by difference. She had used simple comparisons to establish a feeling of security and stability. She had always gone from a superficial point of view of comparison that would quickly blossom into an emotional response of either security and stability or painful difference. She did not have enough personal meaning, motive, or identity to integrate into the observation of the external comparison to others and to find safety in differences. She was alexithymic, only naming the rough outlines of her intense feelings. Our conversation added language and metaphor and encouraged imaginative thought as a way of increasing her subjective complexity. We focused on specifics of her subjectivity, her tastes, her opinions, and her aesthetic that she had never elaborated. This process has required me to be a very active therapist, offering my own capacity to name feelings and preferences as well as imagination and fantasy to process feelings. Tina and I have produced collages of images related to a painful exchange in order to increase reflective functioning. Over time, Tina has learned how to use language, imagery, and narrative to modulate her intense emotions in response to difference. Her body image has changed as well, showing flexibility as she contemplates the possibility of pregnancy.

Action Symptoms

When reflexive functioning is inadequate, action is used to bridge the transitional space between inner and outer experiences; action is used in the place of language, fantasy, or symbolic thinking (Krueger, 2002, p. 35). Negative or unstable body image usually coexists with a general action orientation and a concreteness of thought. Action symptoms like those with food are used to integrate self-experience as seen with bingeing in Sharon's case. Although the action symptoms have symbolic content, the patient is not operating in a symbolic mode.

The reflexive challenge benefits from the capacity to think about oneself and one's feelings in language and symbols (reflective functioning). In these case examples interventions are formulated by using the body image as the transitional space where symbols are created. Sharon began thinking of her extra 10 pounds as 10 pounds of pressure. Tina was able to maintain a coherent sense of herself when confronted with external difference, which allowed for a more flexible body image.

Clothing

The clothing-designer metaphor is useful in describing the integrative possibilities of reflexive functioning with the body image being the resulting garment. Actual clothing is an adjunct to the body image acting as an additional, more malleable aspect of the external body self. In *Open and Clothed,* Andrea Siegel (1999) describes clothing's integrative function:

> Because we constantly stride through two completely different universes, that of the world around us and that of the infinity inside us, it is useful to think of the boundary of clothes between the inner and outer person as an area where the inner and outer person meet, get to know each other and come to a harmonious agreement.
>
> (p. 115)

Thus, clothing has many of the same ingredients and functions as body image but has endless flexibility and choice that our actual bodies do not. This is the pleasure and excitement that clothing and fashion offer. People's struggles and triumphs with clothes and clothing choice parallel their psychological struggles with reflexive functioning and body image. Clothing choices often try to solve important body-image dilemmas, such as: How do I want to be perceived physically? How do I want my looks to express who I am internally? What works well with my actual body shape and size? If therapists allow for awareness and conversation about a patient's relationship to his or her clothing, there is often access to important body image material (Halsted, 2006). If the issue is approached with a clear formulation including the patient's history and character style, and if interventions are focused on opening up the transitional space where body image and clothing lie, there are opportunities to improve integration. We must enter the realm of the concrete body image to open the transitional space for new personal and interpersonal meanings to be made.

Case Example

Grace entered treatment at 36 for assistance with what she described as a long-standing depression. She described herself as functioning personally and professionally at a low level. She had a powerful physical presence. She looked like a dark Viking warrior, full and strong. Others had always noticed her body, within her family and the larger social world of strangers. She has always felt different and largely rejected as a female, first as a child who was teased and bullied as a "fat girl," then as a depressed adolescent, and now as a young woman identifying herself as queer.

Grace was large, loud, and very anxious—fearful, in fact. Her speech was interrupted with so many anxious asides that it was hard to follow her thought. "Do you know what I mean?" "Am I making any sense?" She would ask between sentence fragments that did not add up. Connection was difficult. The themes of large and small roiled through our interactions with an unsettling and unsafe effect. "I'm too big for you to handle." "I'm too large to love." "My needs are too large." "I want to crush those small people." "Your comments are small." Conversations about her clothing and sense of style were less labored and felt safer. She often wore clothes that invited comment, clothes that complimented her unusual figure, that were loud but pleasing. Her difficulty living in her own skin and being accepted and loved had a long and painful history. Our relationship found an oasis of safety and connection when talking about her clothing choices. The repeated conversations that held the oscillating reflection on her internal and external self allowed for integrative opportunities in general and in her body image specifically.

Summary

Body image as a psychological term has had significant obstacles in definition and conceptualization, limiting its usefulness in psychoanalytic formulations and interventions. The concept of reflexive functioning is a useful addition to understanding the ingredients contained in a body image and its key functions in affect regulation and character. The degree of integration of a body image reflects the individual's capacity for reflexive functioning on the dimension of the body and appearance. By sorting through the subjective and objective components of the body image, we discover the reflexive challenges for that individual. Clinical interventions can be formulated to increase integrative capacity by generating and then organizing the ingredients, and analyzing and reworking their meaning and affective charge. Such interventions, in the context of the interpersonal exchange, offer unique possibilities for new and more robust body images to emerge.

Note

1. For a comprehensive review of the body image concept, see Cash and Pruzinsky (2002).

References

Aron, L. (1998). The clinical body and the reflexive mind. In A. Lewis & F. S. Anderson (Eds.), *Relational perspectives on the body* (pp. 3–39). Hillsdale, NJ: Analytic Press.

Auerbach, J. S. (1998). Dualism, self-reflexivity, and intersubjectivity: Commentary on paper by Sheldon Bach. *Psychoanalytic Dialogues, 8*(5), 675–683.

Auerbach, J. S., & Blatt, S. J. (1996). Self-representation in severe psychopathology: The role of reflexive self-awareness. *Psychoanalytic Psychology, 13,* 297–341.

Bach, S. (1985). *Narcissistic states and therapeutic process.* New York: Aronson.

Bach, S. (1994). *The language of perversion and the language of love.* Northvale, NJ: Aronson.

Bach, S. (1998). Two ways of being. *Psychoanalytic Dialogues, 8*(5), 657–673.

Bromberg, P. M. (1998). *Standing in the spaces: Essays on clinical process trauma and dissociation.* Hillsdale, NJ: Analytic Press.

Cash, T. F., & Pruzinsky, T. (2002). *Body image: A handbook of theory, research and clinical practice.* New York: Guilford Press.

Edut, O. (2003). *Body outlaws: Rewriting the rules of beauty and body image.* Emeryville, CA: Seal Press.

Fonagy, P., & Target, M. (1996). Playing with reality: I. Theory of mind and the normal development of psychic reality. *International Journal of Psychoanalysis, 77,* 217–233.

Halsted, E. (2006). A shoe is rarely just a shoe: Women's accessories and their psyches. In J. Petrucelli (Ed.), *Longing: Psychoanalytic musings on desire* (pp. 101–112). London: Karnac.

Krueger, D. W. (2002). *Integrating body self and psychological self: Creating a new story in psychoanalysis and psychotherapy.* New York: Bruner-Routledge.

Lemche, E. (1998). The development of the body image in the first three years of life. *Psychoanalysis and Contemporary Thought, 21*(2), 155–275.

Orbach, S. (2009). *Bodies.* London: Picador.

Pope, H. G., Phillips, K. A., & Olivardia, R. (2000). *The Adonis complex: The secret crisis of male body obsession.* New York: Free Press.

Sands, S. H. (1989). Eating disorders and female development: A self-psychological perspective. *Progress in Self Psychology, 5,* 75–103.

Siegel, A. (1999). *Open and clothed: For the passionate clothes lover.* New York: Agapanthus Books.

Stern, D. N. (1985). *The interpersonal world of the infant.* New York: Basic Books.

Sugarman, A. (1991). Bulimia: A displacement from psychological self to body self. In C. Johnson (Ed.), *Psychodynamic treatment of anorexia nervosa and bulimia* (pp. 3–33). New York: Guilford Press.

Thompson, J. K., Heinberg, L. J., Altabe, M., & Tanteleff-Dunn, S. (1999). *Exacting beauty: Theory assessment and treatment of body image disturbance.* Washington, DC: American Psychological Association.

5

'I CAN SEE CLEARLY NOW THE RAIN HAS GONE'

The Role of the Body in Forecasting the Future

Pat Ogden

Human beings are meaning makers. We make meaning every moment through a range of automatic, nonverbal capacities such as observing, inferring, and compiling data, not only from environmental stimuli but from our own internal reactions. This data are compared to our past experience by brains capable of processing a colossal amount of information in a split second through operations that are so complex they elude the understanding of even the most brilliant neuroscientists. The most critical result of this comparison to past experiences is movement: We make a physical action (Llinas, 2001). In a millisecond, we assimilate our internal sensation, images, thoughts, emotions, and memories, as well as the myriad of sensory input from the external world. In the same moment, we forecast the future and act (even if by remaining still).

The overarching purpose of this largely implicit process is to anticipate the future accurately enough so that the actions we make preserve our survival. But "surviving" is not the same as "living." Bromberg (2011) clarified:

> Through their anticipatory protective system, people are able to more or less survive. But many are also more or less unable to live because full involvement in ongoing life is drained of meaning by the affective residue of developmental trauma that in adulthood serves as a perpetual reminder that stability of self cannot be taken for granted and requires that life be managed with vigilance rather than lived with spontaneity.
>
> (p. 276)

Our patients come to therapy because they want to move beyond surviving, and to do so, the restrictive predictions of self-states that are rooted in the past must be revised to fit current reality.

The meaning we make of each moment precipitates our predictions of the future. Meaning making is typically perceived as a conscious and verbal process, but meaning is shaped and expressed through a wide variety of human capacities and phenomena. Tronick (2009, p. 88) stated the following:

> Meanings include anything from the linguistic, symbolic, abstract realms, which we easily think of as forms of meaning, to the bodily, physiologic, behavioral and emotional structures and processes, which we find more difficult to conceptualize as forms, acts, or actualizations of meaning.

Meaning making is thus explicit, described through symbols and language, and implicit, gleaned through a plethora of automatic processes. The nonconscious meaning makings that take place beneath the words are arguably more significant than the meaning we make with language. This chapter will focus on nonverbal behaviors of gesture, posture, prosody, facial expressions, eye gaze, and movement habits that visibly reflect and sustain the meanings that fuel predictions. This "somatic narrative" is a powerful determinant of behavior. It reveals implicit expectations that not only flavor the manner in which content is explicitly expressed but determine the content itself.

While we might view our behavior as logical and conscious, Schore (2011) asserted that it is the brain's right hemisphere, responsible for implicit emotional processing and communication, that dominates human existence. Taking shape long before the more rational and linguistic neocortex and left brain are fully developed, the implicit self "represents the biological substrate of the human unconscious mind and is intimately involved in the processing of bodily based affective information associated with various motivational states" (Schore, 2009, p. 114). Implicit selves, or self-states, and their predictions are echoed in the movement patterns of the body. Our ability to forecast or imagine the effect of our actions is the most potent determinant of which actions we execute and how we execute them.

When certain actions are consistently ineffective in eliciting the desired response, they are abandoned or distorted. We stop reaching out if no one is there to reach back; we cease proximity-seeking behavior, such as eye contact, if such overtures were not responded to in an attuned manner. We learn to slump and keep our heads down if standing upright with our heads held high brought unwanted attention, abuse, or shame. Such actions can be explored not only through engaging in conversation, or "talking about," but through body-based mindfulness interventions embedded within the therapeutic relationship (Kurtz, 1990; Ogden & Minton, 2000; Ogden, Minton & Pain, 2006; Ogden, in press).

As we grow, our repeated interactions with our attachment figures instill us with "implicit relational knowing," or in other words, "how to do things with others" (Lyons-Ruth, 1998). Eluding conscious understanding and verbal description, implicit relational knowing powerfully predicts what vocalizations, expressions, and actions will be welcomed or rejected by others. This knowing is shaped by memories that are organized on a primitive and fundamental level (Piaget, 1962), carrying with them forecasts of the future that "live" in action sequences brimming with unconscious meaning.

Implicit relational knowing depends upon the infant's attachment figure's implicit, embodied "mentalizing," which is crucial for developing the experience-dependent brain. Mentalizing is often described as an explicit process of making sense of our internal experience and that of others through conscious, deliberate, verbal reflection. However, most mentalizing is implicit, strongly determined by nonconscious sensations, emotions, meanings, and how we hold our bodies and execute actions. Embodied mentalizing is expressed through a somatic conversation made up of back-and-forth movements and expressions. Parents must "implicitly conceive, comprehend, and extrapolate the infant's mental states (such as wishes, desires, or preferences) from the infant's whole-body kinesthetic expressions, and adjust one's own kinesthetic patterns accordingly" (Shai & Belsky, 2011, p. 3). Mentalizing includes identifying, distinguishing, and predicting another person's actions at a visceral, affective, and motor level and responding accordingly through movement, expression, gesture, posture, and so on. Infants develop affect regulatory capacities when their attachment figures match, attune, and respond to their continually changing states (Beebe & Lachman, 1998).

These rapid, moment-by-moment, nonverbal interactions with attachment figures shape infants' nonverbal physical tendencies, exposing their relational expectations. As Beebe (2006) asserted, "infants form expectancies of how these interactions go, whether they are positive or negative, and these expectancies set a trajectory for development (which can nevertheless transform)" (p. 160). In a secure attachment, the infant's experience is by and large relationally confirmed so that he develops generally positive expectations of interactions with others and becomes increasingly effective at nonverbal signaling, engaging, and responding to others (Brazelton, 1989; Schore, 1994; Siegel, 1999; Stern, 1985; Tronick, 2007).

An infant's predictions and developmental trajectory are unmistakable in Tronick's (2007) Still Face experiments, when an attachment figure is directed to be unresponsive to the infant. When the lack of response continues past a few moments, the infants exchange active proximity-seeking actions, like eye contact, reaching and crying for more passive postural collapse and auto-regulatory behaviors, like thumb sucking (Tronick, 2006). The meaning is revealed in the procedural organization of these actions. Over time, whether infants are securely or insecurely attached, they will learn to repeat the expressions, postures, movements, and gestures that elicit a desired response from their attachment figure, or at least, in traumatogenic environments, minimize the effects of abuse and neglect. These actions express their implicit relational knowing—their expectations of human interaction.

Repeated executions of particular movements shape the body itself; form is determined by function. As Todd (1937) claimed, "for every thought supported by feeling, there is a muscle change . . . man's whole body records his emotional thinking" (p. 1). Predictions and related emotions can be surmised from habitual affect-laden postures and movements. Habitual tension in the upper body and a forward thrusting of the chest may contribute to chronic anger. A sunken chest and downward turning head may perpetuate long-drawn-out feelings of sadness and grief. If the loss of the postural integrity seen in the slumped postures of Tronick's babies, when the mother is unresponsive, is repeated over time, that posture can become chronic, which in and of itself impacts emotions, meaning making, movement forecasts, as well as movement potential. A slumped posture usually reflects and sustains feelings of helplessness, and in turn contributes implicitly to particular expectations and constrains actions. Since the spine is an axis around which movement can be made, a collapsed spine will render proximity-seeking actions, such as reaching out, more difficult. Range of motion and even eye contact is more effortful with a slumped spine that disrupts the position of the head and neck.

Siera was a 13-year-old girl I treated in private practice. Her carriage was similar to that of Tronick's infants. Her body was constricted, her spine was slumped, her neck was pulled into her shoulders, her head was held stiffly to one side, and her shoulders were hunched. She vacillated between blank but unflinching eye contact and staring into space. As the third of four children born to first generation immigrants from Latin America, Siera has become increasingly isolated and nearly nonverbal. Her mother, Rosa, works seven days a week and has little time to spare for her daughter. Her father is unemployed. Siera hid behind her long, thick hair, letting it fall in front of her face to avoid eye contact, and her school counselor requested that Seira's hair be cut short to improve peer interactions. Needless to say, the haircut did not solve the difficulty. Siera was referred to therapy because teachers were fearful that she might follow in the footsteps of a classmate who had committed suicide. Unbeknownst to her parents, Siera had not spoken at school for nearly a year, and although her mother reported that she had not wanted to go to school and had refused peer activities, the family had believed that this was "typical teenager" behavior. Formerly an excellent student, Siera's grades had plummeted.

At the time of commencing therapy, her mother had decided to homeschool her because she assessed that Siera wasn't "ready" for the stresses of public education. During the initial intake, Siera sat silently, head pulled down and to the left, avoiding eye contact while Rosa did all the talking. Rosa seemed confused by her daughter's behavior, claiming that she had no idea until recently that there was a problem. She reported no abuse, although Siera exhibited typical symptoms of both trauma and eating disorders—difficulties in her family, an enmeshed relationship with her mother, and, as Courtois described, problems with "intimacy, shame, low self-esteem, mistrust of others, guilt, conflict and anxiety about sexuality, a negative body image, the need to succeed, and powerlessness and depression" (2010, pp. 559–560). Siera had never been to previous therapy.

In our private sessions, Siera stated to me that her problems began much earlier than her mother thought. Speaking in a nearly inaudible whisper, Siera attributed her difficulties to repeated experiences of "humiliation" but had not conveyed to anyone the depth of her anguish, nor had she ever sought help. Her solution was to remain quiet and shut down, fearful of taking risks, implicitly predicting that doing so would decrease the chances of ridicule and humiliation. She felt many things were out of her control, and her bingeing and purging may have offered her some sense of control over her body.

In 1952, the Nobel Prize winner Roger Sperry asserted that all the various functions of the brain are secondary to its primary purpose of making our bodies move (van der Kolk, 2006, p. xviii). In order to move our bodies, we must be able to predict the immediate future. Siegel (1999) described the brain as an "anticipation machine." Every single move we make, from reaching for a cup to reaching for help, is the result of our anticipation of what will happen in the next moment. Siera's forecast that the future would hold only more humiliation influenced her actions and how she executed them. Although she did not recall memories before five or six years old, her early experiences are remembered "as a series of unconscious expectations" (Cortina & Liotti, 2007, p. 205). Implicit predictions are all the more potent and influential precisely because the experiences that shaped them are not available for reflection and revision. We know memories are constructive; each time we "remember" something, we can add new associations to the memory, changing how it is encoded in the brain. But when we do not remember what happened, the memories remain unchanged, yet shape subsymbolic processes that, as Bucci wrote, "operate in sensory, motoric and somatic systems, as sounds, smells, feelings of many different sorts" (2011, p. 210). Siera's constricted body; monotone voice quality; low-volume, restrained movement; and lack of engagement coupled with pervasive emotions of shame and fear told the story of her unremembered past.

Bromberg (2012) asserted, "Trauma occurs in situations (explicitly or implicitly interpersonal) in which self-disconfirmation cannot be prevented or escaped, and from which there is no hope of protection, relief, or soothing through communication with another human being" (p. 274). In one self-state, Siera seemed to have given up on human comfort and became increasingly isolated, but in another, she talks in baby talk, "acts like a baby," constantly seeking "hugs and kisses" from her mother who (explicitly) finds Siera's neediness too much and wants her to grow up. At the same time, Rosa protects Siera, keeping her out of school, isolated at home without contact with friends, explaining that Siera was not "ready" to be with her peers. Rosa afforded her daughter little privacy, often entering her room suddenly and uninvited. In therapy, Rosa requested that Siera tell her "everything," while stroking her daughter's face and arms. When Rosa asked Siera to stop "acting like a baby," Siera expressed fear that her mother did not "accept" her, and defended her behavior as "just having fun." It appeared that Rosa's behavior encouraged Siera to remain dependent, while at the same time refusing Siera's "inappropriate" neediness. Siera's needy self appeared in behaviors that served to push Rosa away rather than elicit the physical contact this self-state of Siera craved.

Different self-states, both explicit and implicit, make different meanings and thus have different predictions. Bromberg (2011) clarified how these different selves come about:

A person's core self—the self that is shaped by early attachment patterns—is defined by who the parental object both perceive him to be

96

and deny him to be. That is, through relating to their child as though he is 'such and such' and ignoring other aspects of him as if they don't exist, the parents "disconfirm" the relational existence of those aspects of the child's self that they perceptually dissociate . . . The main point is that "disconfirmation" . . . is relationally nonnegotiable.

(p. 57)

Siera seemed to find it impossible to reconcile her needy young self with the demands of adolescence, and Rosa seemed conflicted in her interactions with each of her daughter's self-states.

Making the meanings that fuel forecasts of the future is a complex endeavor that is not static. As Tronick (2009, p. 87) asserted, "meaning is not one thing—one meaning. Meaning is a layered flow over time of the different meanings emerging from the multiple levels and processes that make meaning." Siera alternately described Rosa's behavior as "controlling" and as "caring," depending on her own self-state. Llinas (2001) asserted that when our brains compare present-moment data with past experience, "an 'upgrading' [occurs] of the internal image of what is to come to its actualization into the external world" (p. 38). Yet, particular self-states in Siera continued to hold forecasts fixed in the past, and her movements were both constrained and reinforced by these predictions.

Trauma and attachment experience, with their consequential neuropsychological deficits, often prevent "upgrading the forecast" because brains are conservative in taking the risk that outcomes of certain actions might be "safe" when they were once "dangerous." The lack of upgrading, of course, serves survival functions (better to mistake a stick for a snake than a snake for a stick) but also can thwart adaptive action in favor of what has worked in past circumstances. One part of Siera remained fearful and withdrawn even in accepting environments, unwilling to take the normal risks of adolescence, fearing that by doing so she would again become a target of ridicule.

Each self-state within Siera had its own perspective of reality, which they did not communicate to one another explicitly. As Bromberg (2012) confirmed, "The felt otherness between one's *own states* becomes an alien 'thing' to be managed because it can no longer be contained as negotiable internal conflict that is mediated by self-other wholeness" (p. 274). Siera had great difficulty holding the differing "truths" of different self-states in her mind at the same time. Conflicting simultaneous or sequential nonverbal indicators often reveal signs of dissociative self-states and their opposing meanings and predictions. These indicators comprise the "language of eating-disordered patients," who tend to act on rather than discuss their emotions (Petrucelli, 2008, p. 245). When Siera wanted me to cease my questioning, her voice would become inaudible and her words slurred. Her compliance was evident in ducking her head, lack of eye contact, and hunched shoulders. Verbal and nonverbal messages often contradict each other and can seek to hide certain self-states as well as make them known. Siera giggled uncontrollably when she attempted to say "no" to her mother in therapy, saying that she felt bad pushing Rosa away and not telling her "everything."

Siera's conflicting self-states were clearly revealed when she expressed her aspirations of becoming an actress. However, her body told a different story: Her lack of meaningful eye contact, slowed movement, and constricted stance exposed a fear of attention that she did not acknowledge. If the self-state who wanted to be an actress and expected that risk taking would bring her happiness, if contentment had not been opposed by her "unconfident" self-state, and if communication had not been explicitly foreclosed between these two self-states, Siera would be more likely to be curious about her environment and engage in "approach" behaviors that would bring her the recognition she explicitly desired.

The conflict between these two self-states was apparent when I remarked on how attractive she looked in her new outfit. Siera unconsciously turned her head to the side, stiffened, pressed back in her chair, seemed uneasy, and smiled uncomfortably, although the explicit wish of the self-state that wanted to be an actress was to be perceived as attractive. This part of her strove to be "thin" and wanted to wear skinny jeans like the girls at school she admired, but another part found it dangerous, implicitly predicting that being attractive would draw attention that would only bring humiliation. Although Siera was not obese, she was also not slender, and like many adolescents with eating disorders, she perceived herself as "fat" and feared being teased for being so (which had happened in the past). Siera had fallen prey to the media's portrayal of ideal size and weight, combined with an appetite for "junk food" for which she criticized herself. She could provide no information about what happened during her bingeing and purging episodes, which presumably took place in a dissociated "not-me" self-state.

The somatic narrative not only reveals self-states to others but also tells us about ourselves. Siera's sense of self was greatly impacted by the nonconscious meaning of her body's chronic posture. The slump in her spine seemed to diminish her self-esteem and perpetuate and possibly even catalyze her feelings of shame, helplessness, and fear. A variety of studies demonstrate the impact of posture and other physical actions upon experience and self-perception. Participants who received good news in slumped posture reported feeling less proud of themselves than participants who received the same news in an upright posture (Stepper & Strack, 1993). Schnall and Laird (2003) evidenced a correlation in subjects who practiced postures and facial expressions associated with sadness, happiness, or anger, with a tendency to recall past events that contained a similar emotional valence as that of the one they had rehearsed, even though they were no longer practicing the posture. Similarly, Dijkstra, Kaschak, and Zwann (2006) showed the tendency for participants embodying a particular posture to recall memories and emotions in which the posture had been operational. With keen attention to her physical pattern in therapy, Siera was able to shed the old thoughts of self-loathing that reflected the "truth" of one of her self-states, and open communication with it.

Tronick (2009) stated, "Some meanings [and some predictions] are known and symbolizable, some are unknown, implicit but with 'work' can become known" (p. 87). By directly addressing the predictions forecast by the body's indicators of implicit self-states, patient and therapist can bring the relational *experience* of these indicators into the present moment. I recognized Siera's habitual holding of her head to the left, pulling it into her shoulder girdle and hunching her shoulders as just such an indicator and asked her to notice the way she held her head. She identified her carriage as representing a part of her that lacked confidence. I wondered aloud what would happen if she explored aligning her head, and as she did so, the self-state that had learned to inhibit that action became frightened and anxious. Having made up its mind that her "humiliation" would be minimized if she made herself small and insignificant, this part of her believed aligning her head would only bring more shame. Every action has a purpose and it made sense to both Siera and me that it was no wonder she held her head to the side. New actions, like new words, can be viewed as threatening and adversarial by other self-states whose reality is challenged by such actions. Keep in mind that these actions are not simply physical exercises: They are rich with strong emotions and painful memories of what happened before when that action had been executed. Processing these actions and their affects can ultimately encourage self-states to get to know one another and increase the ease of transitions between states.

As we explored her carriage, Siera recounted a childhood experience in which she felt "humiliated." In a quiet voice, full of held-back pain, she said,

> *I guess like I wrote something. I wrote an essay, and I went up there. I . . . I . . . I like I glitched a little bit. And then when I read it people laughed at me. And I kept reading. But I didn't say anything afterwards. Never told my teacher or anything that people are laughing . . . And I'm wondering is . . . is anything I do worth worthwhile?*

The self-state recounted in this painful experience was that part of her that completely lost her confidence and remained small and withdrawn. When I asked Siera what that eight-year-old part of her might want to know, she was able to explicitly communicate with this self-state whose need for comfort and acceptance she had not before addressed. "I guess I would tell you (the child part of her) you . . . you're up there. It's all about you. It's seven minutes of fame, kind of, I guess. Don't worry about what people think. Think about yourself." Acknowledging her ability to communicate with and know what this younger part of her needed, I asked if in her imagination if she could envision being with herself when she was eight years old and tell this child part of her "It doesn't matter what they think. It's about you." I felt that together we were communicating with this particular vulnerable and hurt self-state. With this "act of recognition" of the self-state she had pushed aside, Siera began to cry softly, murmuring "these are good tears." Subsequently, we were able to facilitate communication between these self-states physically as well. We discovered that if Siera held her head straight on her shoulders, and placed her hands on her belly where she felt the anxiety, the anxiety lessened, and she felt safe. Together, we had found actions that recognized and soothed the self-state that had felt humiliated and was able then to take the risk of being seen by straightening the position of her head. Through these actions she was able to hold both self-states literally in her body as well as in her mind.

This chapter would be disquietingly incomplete without highlighting how the therapist's own nonverbal expressions and the self-states they represent have a strong impact on what takes place within the relationship. Therapists tend to invite and interact with the parts of the patient they are most comfortable with, disconnecting from and ignoring the patient's self-states they would rather not deal with (Bromberg, 2006). Physical actions that are familiar, easy for the therapist to execute and that do not challenge or stimulate "not-me" self-states of the therapist are those he is likely to explore with his patient. Ignoring or rejecting actions would make him uncomfortable. If the therapist is uneasy with an aligned posture that reflects confidence, he will be unlikely to explore this action with his patient. If he attempts to do so, he will probably be unable to demonstrate an emotionally and physically integrated and aligned posture, so the exploration will have little chance of producing the explicitly desired outcome. But this is not cause for undue concern for the therapist who is curious about his own contribution to the nonverbal aspects of what takes place in treatment. In fact, the mysterious power of relational growth often emerges from the unsymbolized bearing of therapist and patient upon one another, which reflects the relational histories of both parties.

Therapy is always a dance of safety, uncertainty, and risky challenge. Bromberg (2006) discussed the atmosphere of the therapeutic relationship as being "safe but not too safe." If patients' emotional and physiological arousal consistently remains in the middle of a window of tolerance (e.g., at levels typical of low fear and anxiety states), they will not be able to expand their capacities because they are not in contact with disturbing traumatic or affect-laden attachment issues in the here and now of the therapy hour. However, if arousal greatly exceeds the regulatory boundaries of the window of tolerance, experience cannot be integrated.

Together, therapist and patient must navigate the perilous terrain of working at their own regulatory boundaries. This is challenging for both parties, as unpredictable interactions between them elicits self-states from each that want something from the other that is not obtainable at the time it is desired. Thus, while safety is essential to establish a context in which psychotherapy can begin, it is impossible to sustain. Therapist and patient are both privileged and compelled to negotiate the inescapable enactments fueled by dissociated self-states—"privileged" because through the intimate encounters of the enactment, higher levels of organization are attained by both parties, and "compelled" because this negotiation often takes place against the desire of some of their self-states that would rather not deal with "not-me" ones.

Each therapeutic relationship travels two paths. The explicit, conscious path represents what therapist and patient believe they are doing together, supported by theory and technique. My intention with Siera was to help her become assertive and empowered, to live more fully instead of merely surviving. For this explicit journey, body-oriented, embedded relational mindfulness interventions from Sensorimotor Psychotherapy are employed to help Siera's self-states find new physical actions that foster integration between explicit and implicit selves. In contrast, the implicit journey pertains to what we enacted beneath the words, beyond technique. Elusive and unconscious, this journey may feel vaguely familiar to one or both, but leads to outcomes that were not intended or predicted.

At the beginning of our work, I noticed I mirrored Siera's collapsed posture, empathically attuning nonverbally to her vulnerable self-states. As time went on, my posture became more erect, especially when we explored Siera sitting tall and pushing away with her arms in a gesture of assertion and boundary setting. Siera obediently explored these actions but she sometimes seemed detached, and her voice reverted to its old monotone quality. I was disappointed in subsequent sessions that her posture had not changed. I did not "understand" what I was feeling, and could not think about it with any clear meaning. Upon reflection, I realized her infantile self was aversive to one of my self-states, and the words of my own mother came back to me: "Where there's a will, there's a way; just tough it out." An implicit tête-à-tête was taking place between a part of me that wanted Siera to become empowered and abandon her regressed self-state, evidenced in my aligned posture and assertive prosody, and a part of Siera that could not authentically meet those expectations, reflected in her lackluster actions of compliance. The meaning of our relational dance belonged to both Siera and me, and in subsequent sessions, it would become our task to share our respective experiences both verbally and nonverbally to discover together the "safe surprises" (Bromberg, 2006) of relational negotiations that would emerge from our interaction.

The communication of the somatic narrative may be intentional or unintentional, conscious or unconscious, clear or confusing, and often represents contradictions among dissociated self-states of both therapist and patient. The heartbeat of the therapeutic dance is the somatic representation of self-states and the body-to-body dialogue between them. A wealth of nonverbal indicators that reflect and sustain implicit "me" and "not-me" self-states lies waiting under the surface and beneath the words to be discovered in the relational context of therapy.

References

Beebe, B. (2006). Co-constructing mother-infant distress in face-to-face interactions: Contributions of microanalysis. *Infant Observation*, 9(2), 151–164.

Beebe, B., & Lachmann, F. (1998). Co-constructing inner and relational processes: Self- and mutual regulation in infant research and adult treatment. *Psychoanalytic Psychology*, 15(4), 480–516.

Brazelton, T. (1989). *The earliest relationship*. Reading, MA: Addison-Wesley.

Bromberg, P. M. (2006). *Awakening the dreamer: Clinical journeys*. New York: Analytic Press.

Bromberg, P. M. (2011). *The shadow of the tsunami and the growth of the relational mind*. New York: Routledge.

Bromberg, P. M. (2012). Credo. *Psychoanalytic Dialogues, 22*(3), 273–278.

Bucci, W. (2011). The role of embodied communication in therapeutic change: A multiple code perspective. In W. Tschacher & C. Bergomi (Eds.), *The implications of embodiment: Cognition and communication* (pp. 209–228). Exeter, UK: Imprint Academic.

Cortina, M., & Liotti, G. (2007). New approaches to understanding unconscious processes: Implicit and explicit memory systems. *International Forum of Psychoanalysis, 16,* 204–212.

Courtois, C. (2010). *Healing the incest wound: Adult survivors in therapy* (2nd ed.). New York: W. W. Norton.

Dijkstra, K., Kaschak, M. P., & Zwann, R. A. (2006). Body posture facilitates retrieval of autobiographical memories. *Cognition, 102*(1), 139–149.

Kurtz, R. (1990). *Body-centered psychotherapy: The Hakomi method.* Mendocino, CA: LifeRhythm.

Llinas, R. (2001). *I of the vortex: From neurons to self.* Cambridge, MA: Massachusetts Institute of Technology Press.

Lyons-Ruth, K. (1998). Implicit relational knowing: Its role in development and psychoanalytic treatment. *Infant Mental Health Journal, 19,* 282–289.

Ogden, P. (in press). Beyond conversation in sensorimotor psychotherapy: Embedded relational mindfulness. In V. M. Follette, D. Rozelle, J. W. Hopper, D. I. Rome, & J. Briere (Eds.), *Contemplative methods in trauma treatment: Integrating mindfulness and other approaches.* New York: Guilford Press.

Ogden, P., & Minton, K. (2000). Sensorimotor psychotherapy: One method for processing traumatic memory. *Traumatology, 6*(3), 1–20.

Ogden, P., Minton, K., & Pain, C. (2006). *Trauma and the body: A sensorimotor approach to psychotherapy.* New York: W. W. Norton.

Petrucelli, J. (2008). When a body meets a body. In F. Anderson (Ed.), *Bodies in treatment: The unspoken dimension* (pp. 237–254). New York: Analytic Press.

Piaget, J. (1962). *Play, dreams, and imitation in childhood.* New York: Norton.

Schnall, S., & Laird, J. D. (2003). Keep smiling: Enduring effects of facial expressions and postures on emotional experience and memory. *Cognition and Emotion 17*(5), 787–97.

Schore, A. (1994*). Affect regulation and the origin of the self: The neurobiology of emotion development.* Hillsdale, New Jersey: Lawrence Erlbaum.

Schore, A. N. (2009). Right-brain affect regulation: An essential mechanism of development, trauma, dissociation, and psychotherapy. In D. Fosha, D. Siegel, & M. Solomon (Eds.), *The healing power of emotion: Affective neuroscience, development and clinical practice* (pp. 112–144). New York: W. W. Norton.

Schore, A. N. (2011). The right brain implicit self lies at the core of psychoanalysis. *Psychoanalytic Dialogues Psychoanalytic Dialogues, 21,* 1–26.

Shai, D., & Belsky, J. (2011). When words just won't do: Introducing parental embodied mentalizing. *Child Development Perspectives, 5*(3), 173–180.

Siegel, D. (1999). *The developing mind.* New York: Guilford.

Sperry, R. (1952). Neurology and the mind-brain problem. *American Scientist, 40,* 291–312.

Stepper, S., & Strack, F. (1993). Proprioceptive determinants of emotional and nonemotional feelings. *Personality and Social Psychology, 64*(2), 211–220.

Stern, D. (1985). *The interpersonal world of the infant: A view from psychoanalysis and developmental psychology.* New York: Basic Books.

Todd, M. E. (1937). *The thinking body.* New York: Dance Horizons.

Tronick, E. Z. (2006). Self and dyadic expansion of consciousness, meaning-making, open systems, and the experience of pleasure. In G. B. La Sala, P. Fagandini, V. Lori, F. Monti, & I. Blickstein (Eds.), *Coming into the world: A dialogue between medical and human sciences* (pp. 13–24). Berlin: Walter de Gruyter GmbH & Co.

Tronick, E. Z. (2007). *The neurobehavioral and social-emotional development of infants and children.* New York: W. W. Norton.

Tronick, E. Z. (2009). Multilevel meaning making and dyadic expansion of consciousness theory: The emotional and the polymorphic and polysemic flow of meaning. In D. Fosha, D. Siegel, & M. Solomon (Eds.), *The healing power of emotion: Affective neuroscience, development and clinical practice* (pp. 86–110). New York: W. W. Norton.

Van der Kolk, B. (2006). Series editor's foreword. *Trauma and the Body: A Sensorimotor Approach to Psychotherapy* (pp. xviii–xxvi). New York: W. W. Norton.

6

'LOOK AT ME. . . . WHAT AM I SUPPOSED TO BE?'

Women, Culture, and Cosmetic Splitting

Catherine Baker-Pitts

> Extreme bodily acts are practically wired into the job description of femininity.
>
> Virginia Goldner, 2010, San Francisco

Propped on the surgeon's couch in the waiting area, the stitched pillow reads: "Mirror, mirror on the wall, I am my mother after all." A woman who elects cosmetic surgery may feel drawn by a wish to identify with her mother or to cut her mother out. Most compelling is the need to surgically fix what has felt unacceptable in the (m)other's eyes (Lemma, 2010a). Here I look at the possibilities for cosmetic change when psychological splitting leads a woman to view her body, as the public does, in terms of its parts. In the absence of attuned mirroring, I suggest, intrusive aspects of visual culture, namely sexual objectification, fill in for the missing reflection from loving caregivers. Without help in knowing her own mind through an affective mirror, or knowing her body through affectionate contact, a woman who pursues an aesthetic intervention to repair her shame-filled body unconsciously recreates, in concert with her surgeons, the original trauma of being viewed as a part object.

Bodies in Mind

Earlier psychological explorations of cosmetic surgery have tended to pass judgment on women in a social vacuum. The conversation among seasoned analysts at the Freud Museum in London began with a trivializing remark: "It seems to me that these women [who elect cosmetic surgery] just have too much time on their hands." On this side of the split, cosmetic surgery is viewed as frivolous, if not as exclusively pathological (Pitts-Taylor, 2007), reflecting an historical bias in psychoanalysis against giving due heft to the deep internalization of culture, including beauty mandates and gender inequalities.

Outside of psychoanalysis, gender conscious thinkers have shifted the lens away from individual minds to interrogate social conditions that position women as creators and consumers of cosmetic cultures (e.g., Heyes & Jones, 2009; Pitts-Taylor, 2007). Gimlin (2012), for instance, situates cultural repertoires for describing participation in makeover culture within particular health-care structures. In a climate of job insecurity and globalization, cosmetic surgery is acknowledged as a reasonable economic investment (Gimlin, 2012; Holliday & Cairnie, 2007), and even a positive marker of flexibility and marketability (Elliott, 2008; Jones, 2009).

Feminist scholars grounded in the philosophical tradition of Foucault critique the view of body modification as tantamount to self-mutilation, as a surface level communication about deep psychic suffering, and as revealing something profound about the inner "truth" of an individual (Sullivan, 2009; Pitts-Taylor, 2009; Jones, 2009; Heyes, 2007). Skepticism towards an intrapsychic focus that isolates the subject from her social surround is warranted. Still, the contemporary poststructuralist antipathy towards unconscious life and the predominant focus on macro dynamics leaves the surgery subject disembodied, without a deep psychology, and reifies a false dichotomy between cultural theory and psychoanalysis.

In what follows, I analyze how internal psychic structures map onto cultural narratives and show how surgical cultures contribute to—rather than remedy—anxiety, shame, and insecurity centered on the body. Two vignettes illustrate the use of cosmetic surgeries to replicate traumatic relational/social configurations and to strive towards self-protection, self-restoration, and self and interpersonal-regulation.

Cut-and-Paste Culture

Consumer cultures promote and thrive on splitting. Bodies are marked as feminine or masculine, passive or active, fat or thin, fake or authentic, black or white. As is always the case with splitting, one side is idealized and the other devalued, while the binary is perceived as a natural given in the social order (Solomon, 2012; Alexander, 2012). Cosmetic surgery offers the potential to create bodies that "fit" into categories deemed as normative along the idealized side of the split.

In paranoid-schizoid states, defensive splitting is used to isolate contradictory feelings by projecting negative affects out, exacerbating an anxiety of persecution—a fear that the goodness in one's emotional environment will be spoiled by external attacks (Klein, 1940). In beauty-centric cultures, visual technologies enable narcissistic relating, predicated on splitting, in the intrusive evaluation of bodies. A therapy patient introduced me to Tinder, a smartphone application that has logged billions of profile ratings and allows users to "like" an image of a person within a given radius—to cut to the chase of superficial attraction. The iVanity application provides a more "objective" assessment; anyone can take a photo of a passerby and then glean an attractiveness score based on the Golden Ratio, a pattern of balanced proportions developed by the ancient Greek mathematician Euclid that has been used by artists, architects, and now cosmetic surgeons to quantify beauty in symmetrical terms. Imagine walking down the street, lost in your thoughts, and then—click—you are being sized up—by a technological device, no less. This calculating gaze contributes to an atmosphere in which the threat of being visually scrutinized necessitates a vigilant, outwardly focused stance. Cumulatively, such symbolic violations undermine a state of non-impingement, or what Winnicott (1956) called "going-on-being."

Cosmetic surgery is offered up and undertaken to mend splits between mind and body, and to reposition the objectified female as a subject with agency. By internalizing the gaze, a woman takes control of cultural mandates; beauty imperatives are embraced as playful, pleasurable, and self-chosen projects (Gill, 2008). The total privileged scenario of creating a wish-list of procedures, choosing an esteemed surgeon on one's own timeline, and being attended to in a spa-like setting is a distinctly gendered expression of self-pampering (Pitts-Taylor, 2007) that allows for customization above and beyond mere conformity of the malleable subject (Morgan, 2011).

The shift from objectification to an attempt at mastery is made visible on various online sites (e.g., www.makemeheal.com, www.facetouchup.com) and applications (e.g., iSurgeon, iAugment) that allow a consumer to try on breast implants, to reshape her nose, to augment her lips, and to tuck her tummy with the convenience of a few taps. In a sea of objects in virtual reality, she can morph her own image using celebrity body parts and then enter chat rooms with other women who offer advice on the best doctors and procedures.

Cosmetic surgery patients are now cast as semiequal "collaborators" who are encouraged by industry insiders to do the bulk of their decision making before they enter the consultation (Jones, 2009). This research, I suspect, is misconstrued as an act of deep contemplation and prolonged preparation prior to meeting with the surgeon online or, if the surgical candidate prefers a more intimate encounter, in a surgeon's office armed with a portfolio of sought-after body parts. When the surgical candidate invites commentary on her unacceptable body parts, her emotional longings—for connection, recognition, acceptance—are disguised and bracketed. In the most promising scenario, the assessment of her body in the consultation provides a window into the benevolent gaze and a feeling of mastery over the rejecting gaze. Temporarily, the woman's body is held very much in mind by all involved in her surgical endeavor.

To Bequeath a Body

Self-image is a reflection of how we have been seen by others (Kernberg, 2006; Schachter, 1997). A secure sense of self grows out of "acts of recognition," through the internalization of a loving, responsive gaze (Stern, 2009); likewise, a stable body felt to be good enough emerges out of positive interactions of feeling well held and seen, accepted, and valued as whole. Winnicott (1972) recognized the importance of skin-to-skin affectionate contact for the development of an alive body that is a source of pleasure: "Being loved at the beginning means being accepted" (p. 264). In "On the basis for self in body," Winnicott (1972) described the case of a young boy, nine-year-old Liro, who was born with a congenital deformity—webbed hands and feet, a condition he had inherited from his mum. Liro felt that he could only proceed with reconstructive surgeries, he told Winnicott, so long as he knew with confidence that he was loved and accepted as he was presurgery. He needed to feel loved without sanctions—not on the condition of being soft on the eyes, compliant, or good.

A mother who lasers in on her daughter's bodily defects, scrutinizes her skin too closely, and insists that her daughter will "feel better when you look better" calls for accommodation with cultural beauty imperatives and requires submission in exchange for recognition. When a child's developmental struggles are met with prescriptions for endless cosmetic enhancements, approval is, at best, conditional. If the daughter is not able to express her disappointment but instead allies with her critical caregivers, she will assume the burden of feeling bad (Fairbairn, 1952), and this badness is likely to center on her scrutinized body. Hostile features of the misattuned parent take up residence in the self-structure of the child and create a dangerous environment in which to live. This persecutory inner world is then projected out, as the daughter turns to the big "culture parent" for mirroring; her internalized bad feelings attach to the nonbenign aspects of culture wherein she locates critical surveillance of her body coupled with the exciting promise of body-based validation (L. Kogel, personal Communication, January 7, 2013). She cannot detach herself from the cultural lens any more than she can detach herself from a rejecting parent. Furthermore, the daughter's need for approval—from her parents, from her culture—does not go away in response to relentless physical appraisal; instead, her need for missing recognition grows stronger. If she has relied on the defense of splitting to maintain a feeling of safety in her relational world, a surgeon's promise of improving her appearance, of creating a body worthy of positive regard, will be all the more persuasive.

Split into Parts

Cosmetic interventions are marketed and embraced as a solution to impossible cultural standards (Edmonds, 2009): A woman can be sexually experienced and retain virgin-like genitalia with labiaplasty; she can fulfill her reproductive role without losing her sexual allure by going for a three-part surgery called a "mommy makeover" (or she can preemptively couple a tummy tuck with a Caesarean and appear as a "yummy mummy"). If she produces a hard body at the gym, she can turn to the surgeon to add on soft parts or through self-denial she can have an anorexic-like body but, still with breast implants, appeal sexually as a woman rather than as an illicit girl. To avoid incessant attention to her breasts long before she is prepared to explore her sexual desire, a young woman can undergo a breast reduction. Through her body, she enacts and ameliorates social contradictions, and pieces together a fragmented view of womanhood. A waitress who is also in medical school asks, "Do they see me as an aspiring doctor or just as a boob job?"

Adaptation to normative femininity, created in paranoid schizoid terms, requires splitting of mind and body. A highly gendered body is culturally celebrated as easily comprehensible on the surface but, predicated on a rigid paradigm of masculinity or femininity, may be exceptionally fragmented and psychologically unintegrated. Howell (2005) explained that because girls are more likely to be sexually abused and narcissistically used as sex objects, femininity is shaped by self-monitoring, attunement to others, and anticipation of additional bodily violation. She analyzes psychological splitting as a reenactment of posttraumatic dominant–submissive relational patterns and suggests that trauma leads to dissociation of the part of the self that possesses conscious intentionality. This split compromises the fluidity and subjectivity necessary for agency and connection with others (see also Layton, 2004a).

Layton (2004b) extends Benjamin's (1991) gender-conscious analysis of submission and domination to explicate the feminine psychic structure, which she sees as, first, based in the subordination of the female self to the needs of others and, second, as the female need to ally with a powerful (male) other to gain proximity to subjectivity. In contrast, the masculine psychic structure, embedded in narcissistic relating, is organized around grandiose omnipotence and the denial of dependency. Extreme gendered positions play out in cosmetic surgery, as the patient is usually female (9 times out of 10) and the surgeon is overwhelmingly male.

Aspects of the surgery subject's engagement with her medical team may resonate with early experiences of boundary violations, despite the provision of medical care. Relinquishing control to another in an asymmetrical relationship is risky, particularly when the surgeon approaches the female body as his canvas and the aesthetic outcome as a representation of his artistic skill. While sitting in on consultations, I repeatedly witnessed a surgical candidate request a modest breast implant, only to learn later that the surgeon's notes indicated a much larger enhancement. Shannon felt like a "stock body part" at her follow-up appointment when she noticed the uniform bust size of the other women in the waiting area post surgery. As disturbing, Raquel's surgeon consulted her husband on the size of her implants while she was under anesthesia, and together the men agreed on gargantuan breasts that were not her design. Most of the women I accompanied to appointments were silent or complicit with the surgeon's disregard for their consent. Heather noticed her own buttocks on her surgeon's website, but instead of challenging his propriety, she pointed out that he had two "before" pictures posted, and offered to pose for an update.

About Face

The social script is already rehearsed prior to the surgical outcome: On a surgeon's website, Robyn announces preoperation that she is going to feel more confident following her scheduled surgery, described by her doctor as an "ethnic nose job." Her nose thinning procedure is taken as her individual prerogative, reinforcing the cultural myth of a bounded, fully conscious self, capable of choice without constraints, separate from or prior to culture (Fraser, 2003; Wright, 2010; Braun, 2010). The patient's over-determined clarity and ownership serve to justify a cosmetic intervention. As Gimlin's (2012) research shows, in the United States, "accounts" of autonomy assume a defensive tone, as the surgical patient invokes the cultural values of individualism, hard work, and personal sacrifice in an effort to ward off skepticism or judgments.

Beyond the culturally mandated script, the claim of full autonomy is a psychologically necessary stance when historical trauma is unresolved, as discrepant views and truths are experienced as internally threatening and thus cannot coexist (Bromberg, 2008). For a woman whose various self-states are not received, acknowledged, and reflected back by caring figures, a default to a cultural narrative emphasizing self-determination occurs in the absence of alternative voices. Mentalization, the capacity to conceive of conscious and unconscious mental states in oneself and others, is defended against in the aftermath of extreme emotional deprivation, because to know another mind is to acknowledge the traumatic influence of the other (Fonagy, 1991). Similarly, to make room for conscious and unconscious body-states is to imagine the ways that embodiment is shaped by another; to fully acknowledge this co-construction highlights relational failures, and is particularly threatening when one's body has been violated or neglected. When a surgery subject insists she is doing surgery only for herself and minimizes external influences, or downplays and quickly disregards her own doubts, she denies her dependency on others.

For some, the *process* of contemplating surgery, consulting with the surgeon, choosing which body parts to tweak, surrendering to the anesthesia, and convalescing post-operation offers opportunities for covert dependency, and is more compelling than the aesthetic alteration. The prohibition against having needs in Sasha's childhood home manifested in her refusal to eat, and in her family's denial of her eating disorder. Her collapse in the hands of another who tended to her physical needs post-surgery presented a rare occasion to receive care outright.

A single narrative of cosmetic surgery is frequently filled with contradictions, reflecting isolated self-states and defensive adaptations. Jennifer describes in one moment her resolution not to pursue more surgery for the sake of her daughter's own body image, but within the same storyline, this mother insists that she will definitely tighten her face when needed. In describing her terror at the internal bleeding that ensued following her facelift, Eloise declares she will never again elect surgery, but moments later she remarks that the surgeon was right: she should go ahead and take care of her eyes through blepharoplasty. A surgical fix may fit with one self or body-state, but if a surgical patient sees herself as part objects, and if her different self and body-states cannot contain conflicting needs and desires, her body narrative will be fragmented.

When interpersonal trauma and non-recognition in childhood lead to an internal split, parts of the self become isolated; the unseen person clings to one self-state, one single view, one solitary truth, and is unable to move between and reflect on competing feelings, views, and pressures within oneself (Chevetz & Bromberg, 2012). Irena intermittently asks, "What was so damaged about me that I had to go and try to cut that out?" True, the cultural home promised to be a kinder, more profitable place when she filled out her "pendulous" breasts or Aryanized her nose, but she was reluctant to reckon with the interpersonal source of her shame that imbued these body parts. Because she sees her body as part objects, like the culture does, she feels less dissonance when the surgeon focuses sharply on the body parts he plans to cut.

With less impingement/neglect and more attunement, a person is able to hold multiple states of being within a single state of consciousness. She can reflect on and explore the little doubts and listen closely to the parts of the self that hold conflict. She recognizes relational influences on her body and she feels her vulnerability—physically, culturally, emotionally and interpersonally—if she is connected to multiple parts of her experience during the surgical process.

Vignettes

The following illustrations from a qualitative research project show the repetitive use of psychological splitting of affects, good and bad, into dissociated self and body-states—to protect early caregivers, to forge connection and separation, and to transcend early dependency needs. For both Maya and Irena, cosmetic surgery holds great promise for maintaining inner fragmentation and protecting the self from consciously reckoning with the failures in their primary relationships.

MAYA: "I was hoping to get love. Like this will just fix it."

Like other women who elect an aesthetic makeover, Maya describes herself as a trailblazer, ahead of the pack, the ultimate risktaker. Invoking the rationale of her surgeon, Maya explains her breast implants: "I did it to enhance my femininity." Still, she moves back and forth between associating her surgeries with self-improvement and self-mutilation.

Maya's father, a celebrity in the music industry, was mostly absent during her upbringing and, as the predictable paradox goes, he figures prominently in her internal dynamics, particularly those driving Maya's body makeovers. When she was three years old, he left one evening to go to the movies and disappeared for five years. He had created another life and family across the country, in Hollywood, while her mother coped with the abandonment by daily drinking until she passed out on a lawn chair in their kitchen. Maya's father resurfaced when she was eight years old and, by the time she was 12, Maya was well aware of the currency of female sexuality in acquiring male attention. She recalls her father making out passionately with a girl from her school, a vivid memory that conflated her desire for paternal recognition with a fantasy of sexual seduction and power. Soon after, Maya was sauntering down 42nd Street in her miniskirt, eager to capture the penetrating gaze of older men. Maya describes feeling "powerful, beautiful, special, all those feelings like on top of the world in a way I'd never felt before. I liked it." Her fantasy of sexual control, however, could not thrive against the reality of her vulnerability, brought to life by a series of sexual violations.

110

When she was 18 years old, Maya was introduced to cosmetic surgery by her mother, who invited Maya on a "surgery getaway" in Germany. Maya's mother needed her daughter as support following her own face-lift abroad, and she threw in a breast augmentation procedure as bait. Her mother's demands for conformity did not allow Maya to experience her body as distinctly her own; hence, she felt her body to be boundaryless and easily invaded (Krueger, 2001). At a remote location, with the oxygen mask over her mouth as she lay beneath the anesthesiologist towering above, Maya recalls struggling without words to communicate, "I don't want to do this." This moment of imposed voicelessness and psychological merger would foreshadow her limited abilities to protect and defend herself. On the flight home, Maya's body was tightly swaddled in surgical wrappings, but the low air pressure in the cabin still caused her incisions to leak blood, a medical emergency that her mother attempted to cover up rather than tend to, while Maya denied real danger under the pretense of female bonding.

Her mother's excessive vigilance, in place of attuned interactive regulation, led Maya to develop a "traumatically compliant false self system" (Goldner, 1991) and initiated an ongoing process of multiple surgeries to correct what Maya now sees as a damaged body. She is fascinated with public displays of botched surgeries, a group called the "gone wrongs," and she casts her vote online after inspecting "the best, worst and most awful cosmetic surgery." Detectable scars and disfigured body parts associated with surgical cuts threaten to expose her pain, and thus Maya joins in the scrutiny of other women's surgically altered bodies, idealizing and then destroying the other, the mirror of her own desperate, shame-imbued self and body-states. In her attempts to surrender to care (i.e., her mother's, her surgeon's), submission invariably takes the place of her longing to let down her defensive barriers (Ghent, 1990). Her disappointments go unexplored as Maya describes her commitment to future elective surgeries as severed from relational threads. Endless revisions and updates, a lifelong investment, are par for the course. Maya turns to cosmetic surgery, she insists, inspired by technological and medical progress to connect with and reclaim her body (Adams, 2010).

During an interview in my office, Maya unabashedly lifts her shirt to show me her latest purchase: cantaloupe-shaped breasts. Her exposure leaves me wondering what else she is asking me to see, as we stand before the mirror gazing at her new parts, as though looking at accessories on a mannequin in a shop window. Is she looking for the person who resides in that body (Eichenbaum, 2012)? Maya explains "I am able to detach from my body and treat it as an object." She tends concretely to her dissociated body, massaging her breasts daily and watching for hardness and lumps, signs that her body does not recognize the foreign silicone implants. On this particular day, Maya is feeling hopeful about her still squishy breasts, though they will inevitably harden due to capsular contracture, a complication to which she is susceptible, according to her surgeon, given her American Indian skin. (The surgeon does not mention that a larger breast implant increases her risk.)

At the time of our next interview, the aura of Maya's latest surgery has faded, and her self-consciousness has set in. Maya covered all the mirrors in her home and by now has avoided her reflection for five months. What does she fear is so despicable in the mirror? Does she envision the partial aspects of her body that are unacceptable to her own mother, or the body parts that could not hold her father's attention? Does she avert her eyes because of anticipated disapproval (Kernberg, 2006)?

Rather than alluring objects, her hardened breasts feel to her like physical barriers, and the enlarged scars left over from multiple incisions confirm her ugliness. Reluctant to look at her history of neglect and boundary violations or to feel her rage and destructive fantasies, Maya is still unclear about the source of her intimacy issues;

> I dread being touched. I push people away, like, when they find out about this, they can't find out. Like they will reject me in some way. That has been very powerful for me. But I just think with the next surgery it will be fine.

In relation to her surgeons, Maya grapples with competing needs for assertion and recognition, a conflict that collapses through the idealization of the other and devaluation of self (Benjamin, 2004). She transfers onto her surgeons unmet needs, or what Davies (2003) referred to in the parent–child dyad as the longing for "a sense of knowing and being known, and an interest in penetrating—and being penetrated psychically, emotionally, and physically" (p. 7). She allies with the surgeon who embodies paternalistic qualities of free subjectivity and desire: "It is like having a relationship with my father. What I can imagine it being. Acting that out and getting my father to, you know, fall in love with me." Unlike her unavailable father, the surgeon joins Maya in search for solutions to her suffering as they mutually engage in the charade that Maya's feelings of defectiveness are located on her body's surface, only skin deep. She attaches herself in particular to surgeons who enforce limits, even if they later sell her on procedures for tweaking other body parts. Responding conservatively to the patient's requests while offering additional interventions on areas of the body that were not the presenting concern is a business tactic used to enhance the patient's confidence in the boundaries and ethics of the surgeon (Baker-Pitts, 2008). For instance, one doctor told Maya that he could not help her with her problems of tissue hardening, but he could fix indentations in her scar line below her breast by injecting silicone and fat harvested from her stomach.

Maya's surgeons, like her parents, frequently turn a blind eye to her desperation. In self-protection mode, some surgeons have ignored Maya's complaints about poor surgical outcomes and repeated operations when the results were bound to be disappointing. A surgeon who refused to acknowledge the distorted relocation of her nipple also failed to tell her that he had ruptured her lung and, in a panic, done a quick stitch-up. When she complained about the dramatic asymmetry of her breasts, he dismissed her with a mental diagnosis of body dysmorphia. The surgeon expected Maya to fixate on the body part she wished to change earlier in their consultation but blamed her for being too concerned about the aesthetic outcome (Blum, 2003). In the midst of a medical emergency involving internal bleeding, Maya felt ashamed, and she was reluctant to step outside of her accommodating role or to relinquish her loyalty to the surgeon on whom she depended. Her tolerance for bodily intrusion, made possible by her dissociation and general numbness in her body, rings of Howell's (1996) analysis of "a torture that is administered by one dissociated part of the self onto another" (p. 435).

When Maya acknowledges her role as the dependent object in the doer/done-to dance (Benjamin, 2004), she can look at herself, but only with recrimination: "To tell you the truth, I was manic when I went into those surgeries. The doctor I chose was a horrible surgeon, but I didn't care. He would do it." Invoking a sexist image of herself as sexually used up, she concedes, "A lot of people just won't touch you at a certain point." When she did suggest to a doctor that he remove her implants altogether, he responded, "Only if you want to go National Geographic," associating nonimplanted breasts with sagging tissue of aborigines far removed from the aesthetic values of Western culture. Being an object of derision was not Maya's conscious desire, and thus she turned again to surgery to master feelings of stigmatization, while dissociating from her shame-filled body.

Recently, Maya practically relocated to Southern California in order to pursue corrective surgery with a doctor whose latest invention holds what she heralds as great promise. Her passionate letter requesting to be part of his trial was chosen— she was chosen—and she eagerly agreed for the local station to broadcast the surgery in which she would be opened up once more, this time to receive the "pocket protector," a protective lining made of a Gore-Tex like product to encase the implant. The surgeon/inventor (father/savior) had already performed thousands of breast augmentation surgeries and, awaiting FDA approval, was prepared to offer his product to former patients and thousands more. After Maya had fallen in the wrong hands too many times, he assured her, "Not only can I fix it. I can guarantee to make it all better."

IRENA: "I craved that reflection."

At nearly 70 years old, Irena has the impish flair, bright red hair, and vivacious eyes of a young girl, which matches her petite figure. Her vivacity sets her far apart from the image she holds of her mother, who was too burdened by her mood to get out of bed and whose heavy shadow threatens to immobilize Irena. Early on, her mother warned her, "Whatever you do Irena, don't be like me." Irena took on the challenge: "The first time I looked in the mirror and I saw my mother's face, I knew deeply that I wanted to destroy it. With the plastic surgery, I was trying to cut my mother out, but I didn't know that until now. I never knew why I did it." Ideally, the mother figure dwells symbolically inside of the self as a soothing, caring presence, but in the absence of emotional attunement and sensitivity, Irena could only conjure up a haunting image—a cold, blank stare.

Irena's grandmother died in the Holocaust in 1942, and Irena was born prematurely that same year, desperate to be out of her grieving mother's womb. As she put it, "There was no nourishment for me in there." She spent the first months of her life in an incubator, or what she refers to as a chicken coop, deprived of loving touch and contact; she was not breastfed or provided emotional sustenance and, consequently, she states, "I knew organically that was something I was missing." Irena explains, "You look at your mother and you want your mother to say, 'You're cute, you're beautiful,' but my mother was so depressed that she couldn't give me any of that. So, I'd be in front of the mirror a lot, dancing in front of the mirror, looking in the mirror." Irena's mother's questions, still with a tinge of annoyance, resound in her head, "Who's looking at you? Why are you looking at yourself so much?" Irena is looking, she reveals, "for some reflection and with the plastic surgery I'd have somebody looking at me—to create somebody and some form of separation I was making from my sick mother."

I can easily envision Irena teaching movement classes for elderly people in senior centers, as she has been doing for 25 years. She found the missing reflection, a perfect scenario: She sways her hips and arms and taps her feet, looking at the old people, who laugh and gaze at her attentively. She impresses, "The deepest thing that I can do is to move with someone, to mirror somebody moving, as they mirror me." She relates to the seniors who frequently visit their doctors to ask, "Am I okay? Is there something wrong with me?"

In an exhibitionistic spirit similar to Maya's, Irena revealed to me her breasts and the scars from the areola down and across the bottom. They are asymmetrical, but the end result never matters to Irena. Eventually, the thrill of her latest purchase dissipates. Each procedure, stimulated by hope, brings inevitable disappointment. A feeling of deadness, Irena explains, draws her to the operating table, in hopes of creating a body that feels something. During her visits to surgeons' offices over the last 30 years, she feels compassion for herself when she is sitting in the waiting areas with the other bandaged and bruised women there for postsurgery check-ups. She recognizes their shared pain, externalized, transferred onto each woman's body.

Irena's best efforts to rid herself of her mother prove to be futile when, walking down the street, she cannot erase her sad face. Men still whistle at her shapely figure from behind, attention she deeply craves, but she complains, "You know what they say? 'Why so sad?' Can you imagine? They can't say, 'Nice ass.'" She has created a body, part by part—perky breasts, her face pulled to her mid hairline, her eyes tightened, her eyebrows arched, and her nose slimmed following her mother's legacy of "always running from being a Jew." Yet, she has not been able to create a happy face to conceal her mother's sorrowful imprint.

Irena can momentarily reflect on the meanings of her multiple surgeries, as both a tool of emotional survival and "so unloving." She elaborates on her process of working towards a depressive, more integrative stance involving her internal mother:

> She just didn't like herself and she did not want me to be like her, and I totally turned around when she passed away. I love her face now when I

think of her. I think growing to love your own mother deeply, and appreciating her, and having compassion for her is the best plastic surgery you could ever have. And looking for an identity or a person in a magazine to look like, let's say, all that had something to do with her.

Irena's reparation with her mother as a whole person, with good and bad parts and provisions, has allowed her to soften her manic triumph and attacks on her own body. Irena still pursues cosmetic surgeries, but she defaults to the surgeon's office with less hope and less paranoid splitting, and with the sobering reality of her loss, her limitations, and her own mortality. Recently, Irena has allowed her strands of gray hair to sparkle.

More Than the Sum of Her Parts

Our basic human sense of self depends on recognition from another who possesses subjectivity of both sameness and difference (Slavin, 2010), an other who helps construct experience into a meaningful narrative (Benjamin, 1995). For women like Maya and Irena, the turn to cosmetic surgery is a response to the emotional pain of non-recognition, dating from the first body-to-body relationship, and reinforced by the objectifying surround. Both women were deprived of early mirroring interactions, and their bodies were violated and neglected. Cosmetic surgery is the socially prescribed scene in which both Maya and Irena actively shape their relational worlds in conformity with past relationships.

In *Under the Skin,* Lemma (2010b) refers to the compelling pursuit of body modification as serving relational phantasies. The reclaiming phantasy, she asserts, is the expulsion from the body of the hated other; the perfect match phantasy employs the perfect body to guarantee the love and desire of the other; and, the self-made phantasy expresses an envious attack and denial of dependency on the other. Each of these fantasies come to light in the interpersonal worlds of Maya and Irena, who vacillate between consciousness of the relational meanings of their cosmetic endeavors and a commitment to not knowing the anxiety and longings that compel them to seek the cosmetic surgeon's care. Maya and Irena repeatedly ask, "What was I thinking?" even as they plan their next elective procedure before their incisions have healed.

Maya and Irena use constant vigilance, splitting, dissociation, and literal cuts to delineate relationships with their mothers—either to separate from the lifeless mother through the manic pursuit of beauty or, in Maya's case, to bond with the fantasy of the good mother by containing, and then expelling, her reviled parts. For both women, the male gaze is located in the surgeon, who possesses desired subjectivity, offers the promise of recognition, and stands in for the absent, tantalizing, and rejecting father.

Maya and Irena both dissociate their shame and organize around what Bromberg (2008) calls an anticipatory protective system. Elective surgery may temporarily shore up a fragile self-structure and offer a fantasy of autonomy, control, and renewal, but it succeeds only partially—it tends to idealized self and body-states within a neoliberal climate centered on separation and triumph over objectification. As a compromise solution, on the most primitive, bodily level, cosmetic surgeries can offer longed-for experiences of a kind of recognition missed earlier in life, while unconsciously reenacting trauma to stay the same (Bromberg, 1998), unable to grow and repair ruptures in the social world.

To Behold a Body

Winnicott heartily grasped the power of the mirroring other to help integrate the soma and psyche, but in collusion with the fantasy of conformity as curative, D. W. Winnicott prescribed a cosmetic surgery procedure in the 1930s to cure his patient, Masud Khan, of shame associated with protruding ears (Hamilton, 2008), a clinical transgression noted at the time within his analytic community. This occurrence predated the growing appreciation of the analyst's influence as a subject, whose own embodiment and value system bear on the analytic situation. At issue, no doubt, was Winnicott's nonneutral, prescriptive stance, but even a contemporary appreciation of the therapist's self-disclosure and intersubjectivity does not explain Winnicott's countertransference to his patient's physical features and his willingness to compromise the potential space for meaning-making (Namir, 2006). His uncharacteristic reductive intervention reveals something about his own biases, blind spots, and projections.

Therapists still refer their patients to plastic surgeons—sometimes with less serious contemplation than when making a referral to a psychiatrist for mood-stabilizing medication. Steeped in an enactment, Karen reasoned, "I loved my therapist, she loved her surgeon, so I knew I'd love him too." Indeed, she received a lower cost for her procedures as part of a group rate, and her therapist congratulated her on her proactive move to seek beauty surgery, in effect inviting the patient to identify with the thoughtless, narcissistic state of the original object, who failed to hold the interests of the patient/child in mind (Fonagy, 1991). In another scenario, a 67-year-old psychoanalyst who has had two facelifts and is planning another, acknowledges, "I look at women—colleagues, patients—and wonder why they do not get a facelift, a little lift." She contemplates, in her next breath, "Maybe not having surgery is just really accepting mortality, or moving into the next phase of life." She recognizes that pointing out the possibilities for cosmetic surgery would be "too hurtful" to her 38-year-old daughter, who has not expressed interest, yet this mother/analyst is personally invested in normalizing and oversimplifying a desire for surgical change, a sentiment she carries into the consulting room, where values about female appearance go largely unpacked.

Relational psychoanalysis has moved towards an embrace of the clinician's important role in validating a traumatic social reality (Thomas, Benjamin, & Mailer, 2010; Layton, Hollander, & Gutwill, 2006). This includes recognition of a collective unconscious—the widespread cultural production of desires and anxieties that inhibit a reflective space wherein life narratives and symbols acquire meaning (Bloom et al., 1994). When relational trauma attacks the meaning-making process and precludes knowing other minds and feeling known, insidious, malignant social influences attach to bad internal objects and go unformulated.

In clinical work, analysts are challenged to access the defensively split off "not-me," banished parts (Bromberg, 1998, 2006), and to speak to multiple, disowned, dissociated, and changing self and body-states. Analysts can inquire which "I" is speaking in the dominant trope "I did it for me!" and how and to what extent is this "I" connected and in dialogue with other self and body states. As witnesses of the emotional toll of accommodation to beauty cultures, we are poised to help patients live between multiple body-states, experience rather than dissociate from conflicting pulls, acknowledge ambivalence, mourn limitations, and accept transience. Collectively, we might even hold out the possibility for resisting, in Shakespeare's words, "the most unkindest cut of all."

References

Adams, J. (2010). Motivational narratives and assessments of the body after cosmetic surgery. *Qualitative Health Research, 20*(6), 755–767.

Alexander, M. (2012). *The new Jim Crow.* New York: New Press.

Baker-Pitts, C. (2008). *Symptom or solution? The relational meanings of cosmetic surgery for women.* Unpublished doctoral dissertation, New York University.

Benjamin, J. (1991). Father and daughter: Identification with difference—A contribution to gender heterodoxy. *Psychoanalytic Dialogues, 1,* 277–299.

Benjamin, J. (1995). Sameness and difference: Toward an "over inclusive" model of gender development. *Psychoanalytic Inquiry, 15,* 125–142.

Benjamin, J. (2004). Beyond doer and done to: An intersubjective view of thirdness. *Psychoanalytic Quarterly, 73,* 5–46.

Bloom, C., Gitter, A., Gutwill, S., Kogel, L., & Zaphiropoulos, L. (Eds.). (1994). *Eating problems: A feminist psychoanalytic treatment model.* New York: Basic Books.

Blum, V. L. (2003). *Flesh wounds: The culture of cosmetic surgery.* Berkeley: University of California Press.

Braun, V. (2010). Female genital cosmetic surgery: a critical review of current knowledge and contemporary debates. *Journal of Women's Health, 19*(7), 1393–1407.

Bromberg, P. M. (1998). *Standing in the spaces: Essays on clinical process, trauma, and dissociation.* Hillsdale, NJ: Analytic Press.

Bromberg, P. M. (2006). *Awakening the dreamer: Clinical journeys.* London: Analytic Press.

Bromberg, P. M. (2008). Shrinking the tsunami: Affect regulation, dissociation, and the shadow of the flood. *Contemporary Psychoanalysis, 44*(3), 329–350.

Chevetz, R., & Bromberg, P. (2012). Talking with "me" and "not-me": A dialogue. In V. Sinason (Ed.), *Trauma, dissociation, and multiplicity* (pp. 155–203). New York: Routledge.

Davies, J. M. (2003). Falling in love with love: Oedipal and postoedipal manifestations of idealization, mourning, and erotic masochism. *Psychoanalytic Dialogues, 13,* 1–27.

Edmonds, A. (2009). "Engineering the erotic": Aesthetic medicine and modernization in Brazil. In C. Heyes & M. Jones (Eds.), *Cosmetic surgery: A feminist primer* (pp. 153–169). Surrey, England: Ashgate.

Eichenbaum, L. (2012). Roundtable: The changing landscape of female desire: The growing chasm between "hotness" and sexual obsolescence in a digitized, surgicized, and pornographized world. *Psychoanalytic Perspectives, 9,* 163–202.

Elliott, A. (2008). *Making the cut: How cosmetic surgery is transforming our lives.* New York: Reaktion Books.

Fairbairn, R. (1952). *An object relations theory of the personality.* New York: Basic Books.

Fonagy, P. (1991). Thinking about thinking: Some clinical and theoretical considerations in the treatment of a borderline patient. *International Journal of Psycho-Analysis, 72,* 639–656.

Fraser, S. (2003). The agent within: Agency repertoires in medical discourse on cosmetic surgery. *Australian Feminist Studies, 18,* 27–44.

Ghent, E. (1990). Masochism, submission, surrender—Masochism as a perversion of surrender. *Contemporary Psychoanalysis, 26,* 108–136.

Gill, R. (2008). Empowerment/Sexism: Figuring female sexual agency in contemporary advertising. *Feminism & Psychology, 18,* 35–60.

Gimlin, D. (2012). *Cosmetic surgery narratives.* New York: Palgrave MacMillan.

Goldner, V. (1991). Toward a critical relational theory of gender. *Psychoanalytic Dialogues, 1,* 249–272.

Hamilton, J. W. (2008). D. W. Winnicott and Masud R. Khan: A tragic misalliance. *Psychoanalytic Review, 95,* 1017–1034.

Heyes, C. J. (2007). Normalisation and the psychic life of cosmetic surgery. *Australian Feminist Studies, 22*(52), 58–71.

Heyes, C., & Jones, M. (2009). Cosmetic surgery in the age of gender. In C. Heyes & M. Jones (Eds.), *Cosmetic surgery: A feminist primer* (pp. 1–17). Burlington, VT: Ashgate.

Holliday, R., & Cairnie, A. (2007). Man made plastic: Investigating men's consumption of aesthetic surgery. *Journal of Consumer Culture, 7,* 57–78.

Howell, E. F. (1996). Dissociation in masochism and psychopathic sadism. *Contemporary Psychoanalysis, 32,* 427–453.

Howell, E. F. (2005). *The dissociative mind.* New York: Routledge.

Jones, M. (2009). Pygmalion's many faces. In C. Heyes & M. Jones (Eds.), *Cosmetic surgery: A feminist primer* (pp. 171–189). Surrey, England: Ashgate.

Kernberg, P. (2006). *Beyond the reflection: The role of the mirror paradigm in clinical practice.* New York: Other Press.

Klein, M. (1940). Mourning and its relation to manic-depressive states. *International Journal of Psycho-Analysis, 21,* 125–153.

Krueger, D. W. (2001). Body self: Development, Psychopathologies, and Psychoanalytic Significance. *Psychoanalytic Studies of the Child, 56,* 238–259.

Layton, L., Hollander, N., & Gutwill, S. (Eds.). (2006). *Psychoanalysis, class a politics: Encounters in the clinical setting.* New York: Routledge.

Layton, L. (2004a). Beyond narcissism: Toward a negotiation model of gender identity. In Layton (Ed.), *Who's that girl? Who's that boy?: When clinical practice meets postmodern gender theory* (pp. 31–64). Northvale, NJ: Jason Aronson.

Layton, L. (2004b). Relational no more: Defensive autonomy in middle-class women. *Annals of Psychoanalysis, 32,* 29–42.

Lemma, A. (2010a). Being seen or being watched? A psychoanalytic perspective on body dysmorphia. *International Journal of Psychoanalysis, 90,* 753–771.

Lemma, A. (2010b). *Under the skin: A psychoanalytic study of body modification.* New York: Routledge.

Morgan, K. P. (2011). Foucault, ugly ducklings, and technoswans: Analyzing fat hatred, weight-loss surgery, and compulsory biomedicalized aesthetics in America. *International Journal of Feminist Approaches to Bioethics, 4*(1), 188–220.

Namir, S. (2006). Embodiments and disembodiments: The relation of body modification to two psychoanalytic treatments. *Psychoanalysis, Culture, & Society, 11,* 217–223.

Pitts-Taylor, V. (2007). *Surgery junkies: Wellness and pathology in cosmetic culture.* New Brunswick, NJ: Rutgers University Press.

Pitts-Taylor, V. (2009). Becoming/Being a cosmetic surgery patient: Semantic instability and the intersubjective self. *Studies in Gender and Sexuality, 10,* 119–128.

Schachter, J. (1997). The body of thought: Psychoanalytic considerations on the mind-body relationship. *Psychoanalytic Psychotherapy, 11,* 211–219

Slavin, M. O. (2010, April 13–17). *Lullaby on the dark side: Existential anxiety, making meaning, and the dialectics of self and other.* Steering Committee Invited Panel, Division of Psychoanalysis, New York City.

Solomon, A. (2012). *Far from the tree.* New York: Scribner.

Stern, D. B. (2009). Partners in thought: A clinical process theory of narrative. *The Psychoanalytic Quarterly, 3,* 101–131.

Sullivan, N. (2009). Somatechnics of bodily inscription: Tattooing. *Studies in Gender and Sexuality, 10,* 129–141.

Thomas, N., Benjamin, J., & Mailer, S. (2010, February). *Collective trauma, reconciliation, witnessing, and the therapeutic intervention.* Panel discussion at the International Association of Relational Psychoanalytic Psychotherapy, San Francisco, CA.

Winnicott, D. W. (1956). On transference. *International Journal of Psychoanalysis, 37,* 386–388.

Winnicott. (1972). On the basis for self in body. *International Journal of Child Psychotherapy, 1,* 7–16.

Wright, J. (2010, June). *Choice feminism on breast implant surgery: mapping feminist theories of consent and coercion.* Paper presented at the Age of Plastic Surgery Conference, Vancouver, Canada.

7

'I WON'T GROW UP, NEVER GROW UP, NOT ME!'

Anorexia Nervosa and Maturity Fears Revisited

Dana L. Charatan

The ways in which clinicians have viewed the traits of women with anorexia nervosa (AN) has historically been inadequate, and it is generally agreed that the explanatory mechanisms we presently rely on are insufficient either to understand or treat AN successfully (Steinhausen, 2002). In this chapter, I explore the construct of maturity fears in these women, hypothesized to be inherent to the psychopathology of AN (Bruch, 1973, 1978; Crisp, 1980, 1997; Garner, 1991; Garner, Olmstead, & Polivy 1983; Strober, 1997), and I will illustrate its particular relevance when there is a history of physical or sexual abuse.

While not every victim of childhood physical and/or sexual abuse develops AN, and not every girl who becomes anorexic was abused as a child, a higher rate of eating disorders exists among this population. Furthermore, when such history is present in AN, individuals are more likely to fall into the binge/purge category than the restricting subtype (Carretero-Garcia et al., 2012; Tice, Hall, Beresford, Quinones, & Hall, 1989).[1] For these patients, AN is a dramatic example of the way in which this self-inflicted violence, in the form of starvation, is also an effort to prevent maturity when maturity itself has come to represent the destruction, rather than the growth, of the self.

Historically, maturity fears in patients with AN have been simplified to fears about taking on the myriad responsibilities that adulthood brings. The result is often a paternalistic and condescending view of women who are paradoxically described in the literature as extraordinary in their intelligence, desire to achieve, and need for perfectionism. Another perspective, one that integrates cultural and interpersonal influences into psychological development, can shed light on why it is not solely pathological but understandable why some women ultimately choose starvation as a means of psychic survival.

My postulation is that an effective approach to working with anorexia begins by understanding that starvation, while a deadly form of self-destruction, also expresses a healthy desire to be autonomous. I use the term *maturity fears* to

refer to the anxiety surrounding girls' physical and emotional development beginning during the prepubescent phase and continuing through puberty (Crisp, 1980,
1997). This definition encompasses the fears of sexual expectancies and desires
that follow the physical changes within the body and psychological motivations
surrounding the emergence and formations of sexual desire. These fears and
desires originate internally through hormonal shifts and externally through others'
reactions to those transformations. Furthermore, these fears may also incorporate
the co-occurring increasing emotional demands for intimacy and vulnerability
in intimate relationships accompanying progression from childhood into adolescence and adulthood. Yet from the perspective I use here, I also focus on the adaptive nature of these fears, given the ways in which girls continue to face particular
hardships and relational burdens growing up in a male dominated world.

Fears regarding the foreclosure of one's agency are particularly compelling
when girls are exposed to early childhood abuse. In these families, the girl's
body and psyche become a literal stage for the imposition of an Other's needs,
desires, and control, negating any recognition of her subjectivity, agency, or right
to physical and psychological limits. Such experiences are tinged with patriarchal
understandings of subject (girl) as object, with a subsequent collapse of the girl's
developing sense of her own mind (Slavin & Pollock, 1997) and her own body.
Instead of helping the girl to navigate her own conflicted experience of her emerging physical, emotional, and sexual needs, the abusive parent[2] shatters the evolution of the girl's understanding of her own needs, desires, and appetites, replacing
them with his or her own forced upon the child.

Eating disorder symptomatology can be viewed as a perverse strategy (Kaplan,
1991) adopted in order to use "a part, a detail, [to stand] for the whole," (p. 34).
Kaplan derived the perverse strategy as a type of fetishism used by women in which
an exaggeration of femininity can be used to negate the differences between the
sexes. In a somewhat similar vein, Davies (1994) uses the phrase "perverse scenario" in order to describe occasions when patient and analyst become entangled
in a collapse of intersubjectivity, each locked in a denial of the other's experience
as an agent, including as an agent of one's own sexual desire. Common to both
Kaplan's "perverse strategy" and Davies' "perverse scenario" is a substitution of
a rigidly held view of binary positions for a broader, more nuanced and inclusive
understanding of both intrapsychic and interpersonal functioning.

In my understanding of AN, I use the concept of "perverse strategy" to under-
score how a symptom, here starvation, comes to serve the function of not only
forestalling physical, hormonal, and relational development, but also represents
an attempt to forge a path toward agentic functioning which ironically renders the
girl subjugated to food, weight, and body obsession. In addition to forestalling
physical maturation, this strategy precludes psychological maturation in that it
inhibits movement from a largely egocentric state (as starvation largely depletes
one of the ability to relate in any real, sustained fashion) to one that is more related
and able to recognize the potential presence of an empathic, nonimpinging or persecutory Other. Such perverse strategies are particularly salient when the anorexic

girl or woman has been exposed to abuse at the hands of a primary caregiver, as illustrated in the case below.

Alex

Alex entered my office at age 24. Tall and slim, she disclosed a long history of sexual abuse and neglect by her alcoholic parents. She fed me tidbits of her upbringing in an upwardly mobile family ultimately ravaged by her parents' alcoholism. No one had ever questioned whether she might have an eating disorder, despite weighing as little as 98 pounds at 5'6". Alex stated that her family "didn't talk about such things." We came to call her anorexia the "unknown known," one of many ways in which "sort-of-knowing" was central to Alex's family dynamic. Unspoken atrocities were experienced, witnessed, and placed in a vault.

Alex's father was a successful professional whose prosperous career trajectory was juxtaposed to her mother's unfulfilled professional ambitions. After becoming pregnant with Alex's older brother, her mother withdrew from graduate school, becoming a stay-at-home mother. While Alex's mother told her children that she was content to be a mother and homemaker, Alex felt guilty for being the perceived cause of her mother's relegation to household duties. Alex was a poor feeder, her nutritional deprivation severe enough to warrant a failure to thrive diagnosis. Alex's childhood memories are of a mother who vacillated between being enmeshed and anxious and emotionally absent and aloof. The former was displayed by her insistence that Alex co-sleep until the age of seven; the latter by her descent into alcoholism that culminated with neglect and severe verbal abuse.

When Alex was 8, her alcoholic father began to molest her. While her father was sexually abusive when inebriated, her mother would fly into "unpredictable rages," terrifying Alex to the point that she would crawl into bed with her father to "protect" herself. As Slavin and Pollock (1997) described, she was trapped between collusion and the destruction of her family. At age ten, Alex finally told her mother, and her father was removed from the home. Alex's mother's drinking then escalated to the point where the house went unclean for weeks at a time, leaving Alex and her siblings to fend for themselves in terms of obtaining food, getting themselves to school, and doing their best to keep the authorities at bay. At age twelve, all four siblings were removed from the home after her mother threatened to kill Alex and her younger brother with a knife. At sixteen, shortly after being reunited with her mother and siblings, Alex received a letter of allocution from her father. It was then Alex learned she had been repeatedly raped by her father in her sleep during the years leading up to his removal from the home.

It was at this time that Alex became preoccupied with weight and dieting. Within a year, this turned into extreme caloric restriction. Despite her severe traumas, Alex's academic performance led to her acceptance at a top undergraduate institution, a testament to her resilience and determination. Upon leaving home again, this time in a supposedly more developmentally appropriate manner, she continued to restrict, without anyone noticing the resulting twenty-five-pound weight loss.

Alex began to experiment with cutting and purging at age twenty. Much pressure was placed upon her to go to graduate school, and Alex was indeed accepted as a doctoral student. Her parents (including her father) were elated. They expressed their belief that her older brother, a high school sports coach, was a "waste of resources" and that Alex was responsible for taking over where he had failed to make something of himself. She developed night eating syndrome, getting out of bed four to six times a night in order to be comforted and soothed back to sleep by food. Referring to these episodes as "binges," she tended to eat what we have recognized to be "kid-food": a handful of grapes, goldfish crackers, a few bites of pasta, apple juice, some strawberries. These are foods that she identifies as being some of her favorites from childhood.

In time Alex shared with me that her mother had been raised by an alcoholic and abusive father whose mother had denied his actions because she did not have the financial means to leave him. And so, in the context of severe abuse and neglect, a more common intergenerational message was passed, that women must rely on men for financial security no matter the emotional cost. Furthermore, growing up was to be feared, as it meant forsaking one's own dreams for another's.

Food Refusal and the Reclamation of Agency

What it is about the refusal of food and the resulting prepubescent physical state that is so compelling to the anorexic girl? Because feeding is one of the earliest preverbal communications between the caretaker and the infant, misattunement to the infant's needs is often played out through food. If the parent is perceived as impinging in this area, the infant may fail to discover for herself how to identify her own needs and states of being. Symbolically, food serves as the first misattunement she experienced, and it may become the foundation for her inability to communicate and assert her needs to others. When puberty arrives with its intense surge of physical and emotional changes, old manners of tension reduction are called upon to assist in coping with these new experiences. Clearly, when abuse of any kind, particularly sexual, is part of the early attachment experience, body memories are even more prevalent and the soma becomes a war zone of encroachment, subjugation, and a "not-me" arena in which confusion arises regarding where one's body ends and the caretaker's begins.

Alex learned at a precocious age that her body was an arena in which her burgeoning sexual longings were collapsed in the shadow of her father's narcissistic gratification. Along with this discovery came a "poisoning of desire" (Slavin & Pollock, 1997, p. 582) for sexual intimacies in adulthood. Alex described experiencing no joy or pleasure from any sexual experience in adulthood. An integral facet of maturity fears is the repudiation of adult sexuality. This disavowal symbolizes a rejection of the engulfment the pre-anorexic girl may have experienced by her parents in any number of ways (Lawrence, 2001), not merely through incest or abuse but also through other forms of excessive impingements (Winnicott, 1956, 1971).

By forestalling the commencement of sexual activity, the anorectic demands to be independent and self-sufficient, therefore eschewing parental dominance on the one hand while simultaneously clinging to her parents, who have not met her relational needs, on the other. Fairbairn (1952) described this type of loyalty to problematic objects as a means of defining and experiencing the self in terms of these relationships. Gentile (2001) gave a more recent illustration of the ways in which a lack of intersubjectivity in parent–child dyads forecloses the development of agency. If a girl has not found a way to safely differentiate herself from her parents, the relinquishment of these ties would mean to suffer from a form of voluntary self-annihilation unless an autonomous self and new self–other bonds can be created. By preempting the creation of new relationships, she also makes clear she will not allow this type of submissiveness to continue. This statement is quite powerful and indeed, potentially quite adaptive.

Growing Up Gendered

While maturity fears originate on the one hand in foreclosed opportunities for agency in early developmental experiences, they find their origins as well in a cultural context that perpetuates binaries between masculinity and femininity and the devaluing of the latter. Before the establishment of a "core gender identity" at around eighteen months (Benjamin, 1991), boys and girls sustain all-encompassing gender identifications (Fast, 1979) and the world of gender is open and fluid. At the same time, immersion in relational configurations constituting the social construction of gender as it is transmitted through particular family structures, is present at birth (Butler, 1990). Gradually, or at times more dramatically, this information as it permeates relational patterns forms the cognitive and self-structures of the child, and she begins to adopt the mannerisms and qualities expected of her.

Fast (1979, 1990) posited that children's initial gender identification is bisexual. Fast (1979), along with Aron (2002), Benjamin (2002), and Butler (1990), stated that a major developmental task in early childhood is letting go of the omnipotence encompassed within the fantasized possibility of bisexual identities and is instead taking on one role without completely disavowing attributes and identifications associated with the other. I prefer the term *omnigendered* to describe this sense of gender-role possibility and fluidity, as it moves away from the prefix "bi," which reifies a binary view of gender that has been discredited by many contemporary gender theorists (Dimen, 2002; Goldner, 2002), and further disentangles sexual orientation from gender identity. At the same time, the concept of an omnigendered identity continues to reject gender and anatomy as inherently equivalent while advocating that individuals may identify with a broad spectrum of gender-associated qualities.

With the navigation of the oedipal phase of development comes the solidification for both sexes that there is a sex that is "not-me," potentially foreclosing the omnigendered state of earlier development. In so far as masculinity has been conflated with autonomy, maturity fears in girls can be conceptualized as an expression of the fear that to grow up female will require repudiation of autonomy and agency. Certainly, for girls who are sexually abused by male figures, their own desire can feel alternately eradicated and dangerous.

In developmental terms, it makes sense that the onset of puberty, which further solidifies the binary between male and female, evokes the acknowledgment of old losses, and for the pre-anorexic girl carries with it an overwhelming sense of despair. This is one way of understanding why the initial modal age of onset of the disorder (age fourteen; American Psychiatric Association, 2000) correlates with this developmental milestone. However, before applying this concept to AN, I want to further address the idea of differentiation between the sexes as it relates specifically to the development of AN. The problem of establishing a sense of one's gender that accepts both limits (i.e., accepting that there is a gender one is not) and the ongoing possibilities for fluid cross-sex identifications has been discussed in terms of gender development in general, not specifically with an eating-disorders population (see Schoen, this volume, for a contribution to this topic). What is the relationship between gender development, wishes for achievement, power, and autonomy in a male-dominant society and the early experience of having one's boundaries violated and ignored? And how might this result in the perverse strategy of food refusal, an act that symbolically turns back time to a pre-oedipal stage where gender difference did not yet exist, a stage where limits were yet to be established and symbiosis is desired as opposed to annihilating?

Maturity Fears and Gender Difference

It is often stated that girls and women who become anorexic are perfectionist and overachieving (Pieters et al. 2005). These girls are likely to be hyperaware, albeit at an unconscious level, that their autonomous and agentic selves are threatened as their feminine position solidifies through expected maturational and developmental processes. Again, in abusive homes, such as Alex's, patriarchal and oppressive frameworks further compound these societal notions in violent and ominous ways. Thus, the preanorectic, particularly one who has experienced such abuse, is faced with a choice, as stated, earlier to relinquish her strivings or relinquish her womanhood. Of course, the latter can only ultimately be achieved by death, necessitating an impossible choice.

I am suggesting a developmental path in which it is not uncommon for the pre-oedipal oedipal girl, to feel that in order to embody the socially and relationally defined female role, she must renounce certain aspects of herself, such as her physicality, agency, and autonomy (Elise, 2008). Yet I want to draw particular attention to the way in which this renunciation is coerced from her when she is the victim of severe abuse, and the way in which AN becomes a form of protest against this loss.[3]

In (sexually) abusive family environments, passivity and femininity are equated both with the experience of having one's agency ripped away and of survival. As with any defense associated with survival, the psychological freeze state the girl must adopt in order to live through the abuse becomes encoded intrapsychically and relationally. Food refusal can become a way to remain in a dissociated freeze state, where one's bodily limits and needs (i.e., eating and sexual urges) are disavowed as part of a procedural pattern (Schore, 2011) in which recognizing and acting upon one's own physical needs is perceived as dangerous and even life threatening. This notion could in part explain why some anorexic girls are unable to see their disease as a threat to their own health, as they have learned through their earliest relational experiences that the only way to survive is to deny the experience of need and agency. This is again a perverse strategy to lay claim to one's own body in an attempt to shield oneself from impingement by an Other.

As any clinician working with someone suffering from an extreme eating disorder knows, this relational impenetrability, while adaptive in an abusive and chaotic household, is a vast obstacle in the creation of an intersubjective, co-constructed therapeutic space. Interpersonal and relational theories posit that it is in the construction of exactly this type of transitional space that offers the new experience of relating in an authentic manner in which both parties are deemed to be owners of their own subjective experience. Each influences the other, but without the need to control or dominate the other in order to sustain one's own psychic integrity. Perhaps such a relationship is the definition of the mature intimacy that the anorexic girl longs for yet is desperately afraid of pursuing, as historically being vulnerable to the other's desire has meant complete subjugation of her own needs and desires. For the AN patient who has been abused, there is no procedural knowledge of how to engage in such a reciprocal relationship, and shutting herself off emotionally, relationally, and physiologically allows her to employ deeply rooted intrapsychic and relational coping strategies that once enabled her to survive. This inability to tolerate the experience of subjectivity and intersubjectivity, the fostering of which is typically the goal of the interpersonal analyst, is where impasse may be likely to occur.

One day Alex arrived proudly carrying a tiny puppy, and we explored how parenting him might create a space for her to recognize the needs of another, and gain confidence in her ability to care for herself. At our next session, I asked about the dog. Alex began to cry, informing me that the puppy was "too much." She had given him back two days later after he had chewed through her sofa and damaged her floor. She had also barely eaten since making this decision. I initially sharing in her pain and disappointment was wondering if I had been pushing her too quickly to take care of someone else when she was still so desperately trying to learn how to take care of herself. I knew my sadness showed on my face, and I tried my best to sustain eye contact without judgment. We sat in silence for some time. Eventually, pressured by my own feelings of guilt, I noted that the puppy's need to chew, to consume, may have been a metaphor for Alex's ravenous needs that remained unmet as a baby. It was a poor interpretation at best, and was met with rage by Alex, who spewed back that I could not understand how pathetic she felt. Suddenly, I realized I was furious she could be so callous toward an innocent puppy and that she could not "take in" my interpretation, even if it was not quite good enough. Silence. Then, quietly, she baited me: "I'm hungry." Feeling overpowered by my own rage, I nearly screamed, "Then eat something, damn it!"

Instead, I said nothing, an act which in its withholding nature felt nearly as spiteful as yelling. Had I become her neglectful mother, ignoring her recognition of needs? Or was I enacting a new experience by giving her space to determine her desires and limits for herself?

I Want Me to Want You

Can the ultimately futile endeavor of "protest[ing] against [the] limits," (Benjamin, 2002) of a unigendered identity shed light on the development of AN? AN can usefully be seen as the ultimate protest against limits on the one hand, and the abdication of all desire on the other. As we mature physically and psychologically, new needs emerge. For the anorectic, agentic sexual longings may be conflated with submission, feelings of oppression, and lack of the efficaciousness necessary to be a subject seeking another subject. Dimen stated, "Desire is gender-syntonic for men, dystonic for women" (2002, p. 50). She posited that it is men who want to want, and women who want to be-wanted. She terms this distinction to be "subject-as-object" (Dimen, 2002, p. 50). In sexual abuse victims who develop AN, we see this in stark relief, and the solution to this dilemma is to disavow all sexual (and relational) desire due to decreased hormonal production (Coovert et al., 1989; Key et al., 2002).

The development and experience of anorexia navigates through many other polarities: male/female, adult/child, fat/thin, weak/strong, active/passive, compliant/obstinate, empty/full, intimacy/isolation, sexually desirous/frigid. The abused anorectic woman tends to have a relational history that reinforces rather than deconstructs these polarities, where doer/done-to (Benjamin, 1988) and persecutor/victim (Davies & Frawley, 1992, 1994) object roles dominate interpersonal experience. When choices are based on dichotomous splitting, one is relegated to a constant oscillating dance between dichotomies. Specifically, sexual maturity is feared because it cannot be conceived of as an act between two consenting subjects but instead as a dominating subject devouring a persecuted object. As Schoen (this volume) has also elaborated, many have focused on the salience of difficulties separating or individuating from the family of origin in the development of eating disorders, while underestimating themes related to the confrontation with and confusion between one's own and the Other's desire and the stalled movement toward agency. It is this that I believe to be at the center of the anorexic girl's difficulties, particularly the anorexic girl with a history of abuse. At the core of food refusal for these girls is the beckoning of maturation associated with sexual, relational, and physical annihilation, which may, in turn, cause the anorectic girl to literally and figuratively shrink back to a prepubescent bodily state. The drop in sexual desire concordant with starvation removes the possibility of again being physically or psychically annihilated. This is, of course, a perverse strategy in that the means actually elicit the end so to speak, as her attempt toward agency leaves her weakened, sickened, and unable to act as her own relational agent.

Furthermore, a girl who wants to disavow her femininity must reject the notion of being one who takes in, who receives (Lawrence, 2002). Consumption of food is the symbolization of this taking in and is such to be avoided at all costs. As the ultimate symbol of taking in, food becomes the focus of these women's lives. The girl can attain a sense of power in her refusal to take in food. Thus, it may be that the anorexic girl is caught between her family's transmission of her culture's tyrannical two-gender system and her own inherent knowledge that this construction is amiss. It may also be that when abuse is the predominant childhood experience, the only response to the family's transmission of oppressive relational paradigms is to remain impenetrable and frozen, both of which are often the way in which the anorectic is perceived by those around her. Through rejection of these relational paradigms via starvation, she attempts to become an active agent of her own authority and gain a sense of empowerment.

Alex's twenty-fifth birthday fell on the day of our session. I wished her a happy birthday. Alex immediately broke into tears, explaining that her mother had called drunk the night before, begging Alex "not to grow up" and wishing she could "be a baby again." Alex cried herself to sleep and had not eaten since. Alex stated that she literally felt "frozen." She was also a week shy of attaining her master's degree, becoming the most highly educated woman in her family. She asked if I had passed my comprehensive exams the first time. I wondered what she imagined. She hoped I had passed with flying colors, providing her with an idealized example of a successful woman who could (in her fantasy) juggle both career and parenthood. (Alex noticed early on that I wear a necklace with two small charms, one for each of my children. This hyperattunement to the other speaks both to her hypervigilance regarding those around her and her ability to be sensitive and acknowledging of another's position. It also demonstrates my need to be seen as a subject in my own right, with my own external life.) I paused, and decided to disclose that my program did not require written comps to receive a master's degree. "Well, there goes that illusion." I asked what she meant; she assumed I had gotten through a rigorous graduate program while having children (which I did), and perhaps I had sold out by getting my degree from a less prestigious institution so that I could be a "decent" parent. Dumbfounded by her dichotomous thinking, I asked if it were not possible to be both ambitious and nurturing. Alex said she never wanted to have children. When I asked what being a mother meant to her, she replied, "Being a mess or giving up your dreams."

Any discussion of AN is amiss without including the dance with death that always entails. In refusing to accept the fact of her femaleness, the AN girl chooses to enter a state of androgyny or phantasied omnigenderality, which also incorporates a state of near-deathness. Thus, in death, she has won the battle against an experience of femininity shaped by subjugation to the Other's desire.

Here we return to the analyst–patient dyad and the elicitation of strong and often hostile reactions in the countertransference, in part fueled by fear and anger at the possibility of watching the patient slowly suicide (Lawrence, 2002; Sands, 2003). Contemporary interpersonal and relational authors would locate the analyst's feelings not only intrapsychically but also as stemming from the analyst's personal participation in the patient's internalized relational configurations

(Bromberg, 1998; Davies, 2004; Mitchell, 1988; Sands, 2003). Instead of reject-ing these emotions, or responding to the patient's disavowal with her own, a rela-tional framework allows the analyst to try to use her subjective experience to help her know how the patient relates to others, both in the past and present.

While on the surface the anorexic strategy appears to be blatantly life threat-ening, with patients like Alex, clinicians would be well served to examine how, from the patient's perspective, the rejection of a feminine body is actually felt to be life affirming. The tenacity of her conviction is a refusal to be further oppressed even if it means obstinately opposing the benign attempts of her treatment team to aid in her recovery. The power of her statement can be used to focus the analysis on what makes her strong as opposed to what makes her weak. This process is the reparation of agency (Pollock & Slavin, 1998). Any therapy that highlights patients' ego weaknesses as opposed to ego strengths is doomed to fail; recogniz-ing this fortitude and capitalizing on it can help the dyad work together in a more mutually satisfying way.

The analyst can work with her patient to pinpoint how this strategy inhibits the incorporation of a healthy sense of feminine identity and to break down perceived gender binaries that do not allow one to be both one whom needs and one who is strong. Furthermore, by sitting with the disconcerting projective identifications and death-anxiety provoking physicality of the anorectic, the analyst can gain some valuable insight into the inner worlds of these patients.

Alex often experiences raw states that I liken to "having her nerves exposed to the world." She talks about the "too muchness" of these periods, when all of her senses are kindled and ablaze. She eats little during the day, supplementing with night-time "nursings." She relies on physical sensations to inform her of her mood state. How concave her stomach is that day often sets the stage for our affective experience together in the room, the essence of inability to differentiate psyche and soma.

One day I asked how happiness and emptiness had become so aligned for her. She stated that when she did not eat she became extremely focused on her bodily sensations and thus could not make any other decisions. I validated her sense of empowerment, how great it must feel to have so much pressure gone to make even the smallest decisions. By not eating, she was making a decision, as unhealthy as it might seem to others. "Are you telling me that it's okay not to eat?" "I'm just noticing that it must be nice to feel like you can have power over what you do or don't do with your body." Alex told me that no one had ever accepted her way of dealing with problems without either ignoring her or shaming her. I pointed out that perhaps in between neglect and condemnation was a middle ground in which I could accept her choices without always agreeing with them. This possibility had never occurred to her. And then, she laughed. Her laughter was contagious and soon, we were both giggling together. Our intersubjective space was filled with a newfound sense of agency; hers with a sense of autonomy and relief, mine with elation, having given her a new experience of being seen and validated. We both felt happy.

Alex still struggles with restriction. Her night eating has become less frequent, in part because she eats more during the day. She has developed friendships, experienced a romantic relationship and the loss of that relationship. She continues toward her PhD, withstanding the uncertainty of how her academic career will potentiate. She is learning to accept the possibility of being in relationships that will not be abusive or exploitative. She has regained a few pounds, enough that her physical condition is not of major concern. Perhaps of greatest salience, she has gained comfort in the process of making decisions, and has begun to differentiate between emotional and physical states. Her happiness is no longer bound to feeling empty, and she is expressing a longing for "more" in many areas of her life. She has chosen a dissertation advisor. She no longer believes that "growing up" means turning into her mother, or her grandmother, and shutting down her dreams for those of a male partner. Through our mutual recognition of the ways in which she has achieved agency, autonomy, and empowerment, despite an incredible history of complex PTSD, she no longer feels frozen, an anachronism in her own body. She is learning to embrace her femininity without foreclosing her desire. In other words, she is learning to enter an adaptive omnigendered place. We continue to explore this arena, and all the possibilities it offers. It is a very full, intersubjective space, one which we navigate together.

Acknowledgement

Earlier versions of this paper were presented at the annual spring meeting of the American Psychological Association's Division of Psychoanalysis (Division 39), New York City, on April 14, 2011, and at the William Alanson White Institute of Psychiatry, Psychoanalysis, and Psychology, New York City, on October 4, 2011. I am indebted to Gary Walls, PhD, and Karen Randall, PhD, for their contributions in the earliest stages of this paper's conceptualization. I would also like to thank Jean Petrucelli, PhD, and Elizabeth Halsted, PhD, for their interest in my work and engendering my participation in this project. Finally, thank you to Sarah Schoen, PhD, and Jonathan Slavin, PhD, ABPP, for their invaluable insights and commentary in preparing this manuscript.

Notes

1. There is also a growing body of research that questions the validity of the AN subtypes of "restricting" and "binge/purge" as there is significant crossover between the two (Eddy et al., 2008; Fichter & Quadflieg, 2007). However, these subtypes remain in the newly published DSM-V (APA, 2013).
2. It is noted that abuse often occurs by individuals situated outside the family of origin and that these experiences can easily result in similar intrapsychic and relational consequences, but for the purposes of this chapter and the clinical example used, I refer to abuse that occurs within the immediate family.
3. It is worth noting that I am erring on the side of describing girls who do not develop anorexia as those who conform to a socially constructed feminine role, devoid of agency, in order to emphasize the adaptive nature of the anorexic's "perverse solution."

To argue this point, I am aware that I am not emphasizing the multiple ways in which agency can indeed be integrated into feminine identity, in so far one's attachment figures do or do not embody this possibility, and one's interactions within the family do or do not facilitate agentic development within feminine identifications (see Schoen, this volume).

References

American Psychiatric Association. (2000). *Diagnostic and statistical manual of mental disorders* (4th ed., text revision). Washington, DC: Author.

American Psychiatric Association. (2013). Diagnostic and statistical manual of mental disorders (5th ed.). Washington, DC: Author.

Aron, L. (2002). The internalized primal scene. In M. Dimen & V. Goldner (Eds.), *Gender in psychoanalytic space: Between clinic and culture* (pp. 119–147). New York: Other Press.

Benjamin, J. (1988). *The bonds of love: Psychoanalysis, feminism, & the problem of domination.* New York: Pantheon Books.

Benjamin, J. (1991). Father and daughter: Identification with difference—A contribution to gender heterodoxy. *Psychoanalytic Dialogues, 1,* 277–299.

Benjamin, J. (2002). Sameness and difference: An "over inclusive" view of gender constitution. In M. Dimen & V. Goldner (Eds.), *Gender in psychoanalytic space: Between clinic and culture* (pp. 181–206). New York: Other Press.

Bromberg, P. (1998). S*tanding in the spaces: Essays on clinical process, trauma, and dissociation.* Hillsdale, NJ: Analytic Press.

Bruch, H. (1973). *Eating disorders: Obesity, anorexia nervosa, and the person within.* Houston, TX: HarperCollins.

Bruch, H. (1978). *The golden cage: The enigma of anorexia nervosa.* Cambridge, MA: Harvard University Press.

Butler, J. (1990). *Gender trouble: Feminism and the subversion of identity.* New York: Routledge.

Carretero-Garcia, A., Sanchez-Planell, L., Doval, E., Rusinol-Estragues, J., Raich-Escursell, R. M., & Vanderlinden, J. (2012). Repeated traumatic experiences in eating disorders and their association with eating symptoms. *Eating and Weight Disorders, 17,* 267–273.

Coovert, D. L., Kinder, B. N., & Thompson, J. K. (1989). The psychosexual aspects of anorexia nervosa and bulimia nervosa: A review of the literature. *Clinical Psychological Review, 9,* 169–180.

Crisp, A. H. (1980). *Anorexia nervosa: Let me be.* New York: Grune & Stratton.

Crisp, A. H. (1997). Anorexia nervosa as flight from growth: Assessment and treatment based on the model. In D. M. Garner & P. E. Garfinkel (Eds.), *Handbook of treatment for eating disorders* (2nd ed., pp. 248–277). New York: Guilford Press.

Davies, J. M. (1994). Love in the afternoon: A relational reconsideration of desire and dread in the countertransference. *Psychoanalytic Dialogues, 4,* 153–170.

Davies, J. M. (2004). Whose bad objects are we anyway? Repetition and our elusive love affair with evil. *Psychoanalytic Dialogues, 14,* 711–732.

Davies, J. M., & Frawley, M. G. (1992). Dissociative processes and transference-countertransference paradigms in the psychoanalytically oriented treatment of adult survivors of childhood sexual abuse. *Psychoanalytic Dialogues, 2,* 5–36.

Davies, J. M., & Frawley, M. G. (1994). *Treating the adult survivor of childhood sexual abuse: A psychoanalytic perspective.* New York: Basic Books.

Dimen, M. (2002). Deconstructing difference: Gender, splitting, and transitional space. In M. Dimen & V. Goldner (Eds.), *Gender in psychoanalytic space: Between clinic and culture* (pp. 41–61). New York: Other Press.

Elise, D. (2008). Sex and shame: The inhibition of female desires. *The Journal of the American Psychoanalytic Association, 56,* 73–98.

Eddy, K. T., Dorer, D. J., Franko, D. L., Tahilani, K., Thompson-Brenner, H., & Herzog, D. B. (2008). Diagnostic crossover in anorexia nervosa and bulimia nervosa: Implications for DSM-V. *American Journal of Psychiatry, 165,* 245–250.

Fairbairn, W. R. D. (1952). *Psychoanalytic studies of the personality.* New York: Routledge.

Fast, I. (1979). Developments in gender identity: Gender differentiation in girls. *International Journal of Psychoanalysis, 60,* 443–453.

Fast, I. (1990). Aspects of early gender development: Toward a reformulation. *Psychoanalytic Psychology, 7,* 105–117.

Fichter, M. M., & Quadflieg, N. (2007). Long-term stability of eating disorder diagnoses. *International Journal of Eating Disorders, 40,* S61–S66.

Garner, D. M. (1991). *Eating disorders inventory-2.* Odessa, FL: Psychological Assessment Resources.

Garner, D. M., Olmstead, M. P., & Polivy, J. (1983). Development and validation of a multidimensional eating disorder inventory for anorexia nervosa and bulimia. *International Journal of Eating Disorders, 2,* 15–34.

Gentile, J. (2001). Close but no cigar: The perversion of agency and the absence of thirdness. *Contemporary Psychoanalysis, 37,* 623–626.

Goldner, V. (2002). Toward a critical relational theory of gender. In M. Dimen & V. Goldner (Eds.), *Gender in psychoanalytic space: Between clinic and culture* (pp. 63–90). New York: Other Press.

Kaplan, L. (1991). *Female perversions.* New York: Doubleday.

Key, A., Mason, H., Allan, R., & Lask, B. (2002). Restoration of ovarian and uterine maturity in adolescents with anorexia nervosa. *International Journal of Eating Disorders, 32,* 319–325.

Lawrence, M. (2001). Loving them to death: The anorexic and her objects. *International Journal of Psychoanalysis, 82,* 43–55.

Lawrence, M. (2002). Body, mother, mind: Anorexia, femininity, and the intrusive object. *International Journal of Psychoanalysis, 83,* 837–850.

Mitchell, S. A. (1988). *Relational concepts in psychoanalysis.* Cambridge, MA: Harvard University Press.

Pieters, G., Hulstijn, W., Vandereycken, W., Mass, Y., Probst, M., Peuskens, J., et al. (2005). Fast psychomotor functioning in anorexia nervosa: Effect of weight restoration. *Journal of Clinical and Experimental Neuropsychology, 27,* 931–942.

Pollock, L., & Slavin, J. H. (1998). The struggle for recognition: Disruption and reintegration in the experience of agency. *Psychoanalytic Dialogues, 8,* 857–873.

Sands, S. H. (2003). The subjugation of the body in eating disorders: A particularly female solution. *Psychoanalytic Psychology, 20,* 103–116.

Schore, A. (2011). The right brain implicit self lies at the core of psychoanalysis. *Psychoanalytic Dialogues, 21,* 75–100.

Slavin, J. H., & Pollock, L. (1997). The poisoning of desire. *Contemporary Psychoanalysis, 33,* 573–593.

Steinhausen, H. C. (2002). The outcome of anorexia nervosa in the 20th century. *American Journal of Psychiatry, 159,* 1284–1293.

Strober, M. (1997). Consultation and therapeutic engagement in severe anorexia nervosa. In D. M. Garner & P. E. Garfinkel (Eds.), *Handbook of treatment for eating disorders* (2nd ed., pp. 229–247). New York: Guilford Press.

Tice, L., Hall, R. C., Beresford, T. P., Quinones, J., & Hall, A. K. (1989). Sexual abuse in patients with eating disorders. *Psychiatric Medicine, 7,* 257–267.

Winnicott, D. W. (1956). *Through pediatrics to psychoanalysis.* London: Hogarth Press.

Winnicott, D. W. (1971). *Playing and reality.* London: Brunner-Routledge.

8

'SPITTING OUT THE DEMONS'

The Perils of Giving and Receiving for the Patient With Anorexia

Jill C. Howard

The giving and receiving of gifts, both in and out of the consulting room, provides a rich external arena to explore the anorexic patients' impoverished inner world. The feelings around gift giving may be understood as a manifestation of forbidden desire. These feelings highlight how the need to stave off disappointment and despair in relationships, as well as the fear of being engulfed, or engulfing the other, creates distortions in the capacity to give, both literally and figuratively. Gifts may either be given excessively or, conversely, objects may be hoarded to manage the intolerable buildup of anxiety around the experience of emptiness.

The giving and receiving of gifts is also fraught with issues around power and control (will you or won't you take what I have to offer?). The swings range from significant withholding to the feeling of something literally being forced down your throat. These enactments may offer a way to explore the anorexic patient's difficulties with self-regulation and desire.

What is it about giving and receiving gifts that is so difficult? Interestingly, this is an area of difficulty in psychotherapy and psychoanalysis in general (Goldberg, 2002; Frawley O'Dea, 1998; Kritzberg, 1980; Talan, 1989). While there is a rich literature around gifts in many other disciplines, the psychoanalytic literature has remarkably few (Otnes & Betramini, 1996). In fact, this paucity of literature suggests a reserve, discomfort, or embarrassment around the subject (Glover, 1955; Goldberg, 2002; Kritzberg, 1980; Talan, 1989). Glover (as cited in Silber, 1969) reporting on a survey of his British psychoanalytic colleagues stated that "the majority [of analysts] . . . do not receive gifts gladly" (p. 338).

Perhaps this stems from Freud's (1917) statement that, "Those who question the derivation of gifts (from anal instincts and libido) should consider their experience of psychoanalytic treatment, study the gifts they receive as doctors from their patients, and watch the storm of transference which a gift from them can rouse in their patients" (p. 131). At best it is a touchy subject; at worst it reeks of corruption (Goldberg, 2002). Clearly, Freud not only accepted gifts from his patients but gave them to them as well.

The psychoanalytic position about gift giving seems to be embedded in the taboo around action rather than verbal production (Frawley O'Dea, 1998; Goldberg, 2002; Kritzberg, 1980). However, with the effort to broaden the range of patients who can benefit from psychoanalytic treatments, contemporary psychoanalysis now includes many ideas that were once considered "parameters" (Eissler, 1953). The "humanness," originally exemplified by Freud, has reentered the consulting room.

This humanness has also become central as both interpersonal and relational psychoanalysis have become increasingly more popular. The move to a two-person psychology that utilizes the relationship between the patient and analyst in a real way has diminished the role of interpretation and altered the hierarchical structure of the analytic dyad. Glover's (1955) survey did include references to accepting gifts so as not to appear inhumane and to reassure the patient that he was not being snubbed. Even in 1955, there was some acknowledgment that to refuse the patient's offering was to risk offending in a way that could not be considered therapeutic.

In her comprehensive discussion of "unwrapping the secret of the gift," Goldberg (2002) pointed out that the gift is perceived as an uninvited "guest" in the consultation room. In addition, a gift demands an action. Whether one chooses to accept, reject, or interpret it, one is forced to act. This "acting," though, may be thought of as "acting in" rather than as acting out (of the consulting room; Frawley O'Dea, 1998). Stein (1965) believed that a gift given during treatment was a special form of communication rooted in unconscious fantasy.

Still, more seemingly taboo, Levin and Warner (1966) considered the analyst giving a gift to a child patient to be part of standard procedure and not a parameter. Freud certainly agreed, despite abstinence and neutrality, and there are other similar references to this in this very small literature.

More recent contributions to this literature emphasize the importance of mutuality (Frawley O'Dea, 1998), reciprocity (Goldberg, 2002), and self and mutual regulation of intense, affect-laden experience (Ogden, 1999).

This evolving interest in self and mutual regulation of affect offers a natural bridge to the discussion of the anorexic patient. These patients have serious problems with the regulation of affect and, more specifically, with the regulation of desire. One has to know one's own thoughts, feelings, and wishes to know what one wants. This inability is at the core of anorexia. Petrucelli (2004) highlighted this when she asked an anorexic patient, "When is the last time you made your own decision about something? When is the last time your parents let you fail or make a mistake, so you could learn that you could actually live through it?" (p. 324).

Hilde Bruch (1978), one of the pioneers in the understanding of anorexia, believed that most anorexics have spent their entire lives wanting to live up to their family's expectations and always failing. Feeling inadequate, incapable, and undeserving, they resort to controlling the one thing they can; their own bodies. Only in starvation can they say, "This is what I want to do and you can't stop me" or "This is how I can feel successful at something and call it mine!"

These girls were never acknowledged in their own right and, instead, were used in the service of their parents needs. The familiar picture of compliance hides a personal reality of deprivation, disappointment, and an inability to lead a self-directed life. The conformity of the child occurs because there is no separation, individuation, or differentiation.

Harold Boris (1984) suggested that anorexia occurs when the dysregulation of desire is connected in infancy with the dysregulation of appetite. Wishing to have everything (greed), the anorexic chooses food over human relatedness, as the thought of being inherently insufficient is unbearable. People disappoint, and relying on another human being is unacceptable. The renunciation of desire is central to anorexia but, ultimately, it represents a failure to trust in human related-ness (Bromberg, 1998; Petrucelli, 2004, 2010)

Bromberg (2001) believed that this renunciation is achieved through dissocia-tion. This process allows the anorexic to sequester different parts of herself so she can regulate intolerable affects and still maintain some form of human related-ness. In this way, she protects against trauma and she ensures that some piece of herself does not die.

Zerbe (1993), like Bromberg, would suggested that the goal of treatment is to hold varying perspectives of ourselves and other people in full awareness in an ongoing way. This can only happen when the anorexic truly knows who she is and what she wants.

For Bruch (1978), the task of therapy is to help the patient to be in touch with her own impulses, feelings, and needs so that she can become self-directed and autonomous. She focuses on failures of self-expression and the deeply rooted conviction of incompetence.

Interestingly, Bruch (1978) speaks directly to the issue of gifts in her seminal book. She states that gifts may be confusing or stressful as they are experienced as undeserved. In addition, the anorexic doesn't even know what she wants so a gift can seem meaningless. The anorexic reports a long history of acting as if she were grateful and delighted when she received a gift (so her parents would feel good) but she remained confused and, essentially, unseen.

The one case that Bruch reported where a patient remembered feeling pleasure at receiving a gift was when her father brought her something when he returned from a trip. Her pleasure came from her awareness that he had thought of her when he was gone.

Tina

At times I see Tina as a tiny sparrow and at times I see her as a predatory vulture. Perhaps that is because I never know whether she will walk in looking for care-taking and warmth or looking to swallow me up. Her diminutive body contains, or doesn't contain, a palpable level of hostility and aggression. Her tiny voice can turn into a roar without even getting louder. She flitters and floats and then takes over.

Tina's cardiologist referred her to me 22 years ago. He described her as an old-fashioned neurasthenic and remarked that it was unfortunate that the diagnosis no longer existed. He also reported a history of anorexia starting at age 15, with hospitalizations, but stated that she no longer reported being anorexic. In fact, she carries food with her everywhere she goes and has been seen in the lobby of my building devouring a sandwich or salad as if she was attacking it.

The reference to neurasthenia captured Tina's general state of fragile health. It is hard to sort out the physical from the psychological as her general state of weakness and fragility did result in her taking a medical retirement. At the same time, the self she portrays to the world is one of being weak, needy, helpless, and not quite tethered to this earth. Her voice, body size, posture, and facial expressions look more like that of a child than a woman of 65 years. Not surprisingly, Tina is always distraught about her physical appearance but could pass for 50.

Tina was not working when we first met. She had retired and had barely been functioning. While she did have pulmonary and rheumatologic issues, the person I met was clearly depressed and struggling to just get through the day. She reported a past history of anorexia with hospitalizations when her weight dropped to 64 pounds. Although she insisted that this was no longer her issue, her weight has fluctuated between 84 and 90 pounds over the 22 years I've known her. Every bone in her chest protrudes, and at 5 feet 1 inch, she looks skeletal.

Tina told, and continues to tell, the story of being totally loved and cared for by two devoted parents who met her every need. She never had to learn to do things because everything was done for her. As an only child, she was the center of her parents' universe. She lived at home when she attended an Ivy League college and finally moved out when she was close to 30.

The only flaw she was willing to admit to in her family was that her mother was quite controlling. As an afterthought, she mentioned that her mother had always loved another man, Uncle Stan, and did not really love her father. Uncle Stan was married to mother's closest friend and the families were part of a very tight, and active, social circle. She brought in photos from the 40s showing her beautiful mother gazing at Uncle Stan and not at her father. To this day, Uncle Stan's son is there to help her if ever needed.

In our early years, the most concerning thing was Tina's insistence that she had not been raised to take care of herself and she had always planned to die when her parents died. Now that both of her parents were dead, the specter of suicide loomed in the air. It was less a threat and more a statement of her inability to imagine fashioning a life that was worth living.

I treaded very lightly in the beginning of our work, as I didn't know how much Tina could really tolerate. She talked freely but never swayed from her tale of the perfect parents. She attended the sessions religiously and always arrived early. She was clearly becoming more attached to me but I wasn't sure what the quality of that attachment really was. She seemed totally compliant, but I felt an underlying aggression that suggested that things were not going to be so easy going over time.

At our first Christmas, Tina sent me a Tower of Treats from a well-known mail order catalog. I was uneasy with it but thanked her and said nothing, as I knew she would be very hurt if I did not receive what she was giving. Every year since, Tina has done the same thing but, in recent years, it has switched to plants or flowers, as my office looks something like an indoor garden. If only it had stayed that simple.

As it turned out, the subject of giving and receiving gifts has been the main playing field for the enactments that have characterized both our relationship and her relationships with others. This has included concrete gifts for occasions and issues of giving and receiving that are akin to the giving of gifts.

For example, Tina was in crisis and called to ask if we could speak for 10 minutes. At her next session she handed me $40. I declined it as I do not charge for phone calls but she would not stand for that. She threw it back at me and said, "I will never be able to call you again if you don't take it." So here was the first round of an analytic boxing match that has gone on for years. The message was clear: you take this on my terms or I will not play. Her terms and mine were diametrically opposed and there was no room for negotiation. The little voice was unwavering but unbelievably powerful as she threw the totally unwelcome money at me. I put it aside and decided to think about it later. I felt like my professional ethics had been totally swallowed up by her need to control me. Whose office was this anyway?

Over time, Tina became more stable and was able to return to work. She went to work, full time, as the office manager for a doctor, who I will refer to as Amy. As their relationship developed, Tina became Amy's friend and confidant. As they got closer it became clear that Amy was more fragile than Tina and, in the end, needed all of the caretaking and support. They maintained this seemingly close friendship with Tina continuing to address Amy as Dr. S. Ultimately, Amy met a man she planned to marry. She asked Tina to be her maid of honor. This unraveled Tina. She would need the "perfect" dress, the "perfect" haircut, and the "perfect" gift to give Amy. After the wedding, Amy basically disappeared and Tina was left bankrupt, literally and figuratively. Throughout their relationship Tina had refused Amy's gifts saying she really did not deserve them.

About 10 years ago, Tina started her own small business helping lawyers with their clerical tasks. She has primarily worked for two lawyers. Both of these relationships have been fraught with a tug-of-war over giving and receiving gifts and issues around unclear boundaries. Once again, Tina has become the confidant to these two lawyers and, once again, the relationships have vacillated between pain and pleasure.

The first year that Tina worked for Mr. R., a man 15 years her senior, he gave her a check for Christmas. She had spent hours picking out the perfect gift for him, and his family, and she was furious. She tore up the check and dropped the pieces into the garbage can in front of him. She told him not to bother to give her anything, as he obviously didn't appreciate her. The next year he picked out a special gift and she was angry because he didn't give her a check to acknowledge her hard work. I reminded her of what had happened the previous year, but she remained hurt and bereft. She could not see that there was no way to please her. She dreamed of being taken care of but spit out anything she was given. At the same time, she insisted the other except her offering.

Suffice it to say, this went on in both offices for years with various occasions, offering various opportunities to repeat this deeply entrenched pattern. This pattern, of longing to be given to, and refusing to acknowledge that it was her fear, of either being engulfed, or engulfing the other that was at issue. Her insatiable hunger did not allow her to take in what others wished to give to her. Instead she felt deprived and angry.

One day I was riding in a cab and I thought of Tina in an affectionate way. I decided to tell her when I saw her having no idea what would happen. I was shocked. Tina broke into a huge, childlike grin and was absolutely delighted. She said, in a very childlike voice, "You did?" You really thought of me? What did you think? I said, "It is Thursday. I'm going to be seeing Tina today." I never could have imagined the impact that that sentence was going to have. Tina took it in and she did not then, or later, spit it out. In fact, she has referred to it in recent years.

That was a turning point for us. Interestingly, Tina had started bringing me flowers occasionally throughout the years. We went back and forth about what she was expressing, what she wanted, and about my discomfort about unreciprocated gifts. Tina said, "You always give me gifts." I tried to point out that that was part of our relationship, but I realized what she was finally able to say and I backed off.

Now we negotiate, periodically, throughout the year. Tina trades one Christmas Tower of Treats for three bouquets of flowers because it costs the same amount and she can spread her giving out from Christmas to my birthday. She also gave me flowers when I had back surgery and when I had a death in my family. I simply said thank you and left it at that.

Tina's ability to divide up her gifts represents the beginning of her ability to regulate the intense emotions that have been the source of a great deal of her pain. She has acknowledged her desire and risked seeing where her hunger would take her. Neither one of us has been devoured and neither one of us is starving.

Our dialogue has been different as well. Sometimes Tina comes in and literally drowns me in words. I can't get a word in and I feel useless. At the same time, I know I am not useless to Tina. That gives me the fortitude to stand up to the barrage and say, "How can we ever sort these things out together if you won't even let me speak?" Tina will now say, "Oh, I did it again" or "I didn't mean to do that" or something else that acknowledges that I am there with her and she's afraid to take in what I might say. I remind her that she always has the ability to stop me if she feels flooded or to ask me to break something down too more manageable bites if she cannot swallow what I am saying.

I have, over time, learned what kinds of things are intolerable for Tina to hear. I know that an argument at work or with a friend will cause her to resort to paranoid projections of the others malevolent feelings toward her. We deconstruct every argument, piece by piece, until it is possible for Tina to see how frightened she is of losing the person and how little she trusts people do not wish to harm her. It is still very hard, though not impossible, to get her to see that it is she who was feeling the malevolence in those encounters. If we go slowly enough, she can begin to see it. At those moments, she needs me to be completely present and emotionally available to her. Afterwards, she may send me a funny email to be certain I am still there for her.

Summary

The enactments that have occurred over the giving and receiving of gifts have provided a rich arena to actually experience Tina's inner world. Like most anorexics, Tina grew up in a family where all of her needs were presumably met and her individuality was not taken into consideration. She was not the initiator of urges; she was the recipient of presumed desire. Tina's sense of herself was infantile and she felt incompetent to navigate a life of her own.

Tina's admission that her mother was controlling, and not perfect, was not a small thing. However, I doubt she was, or is, aware of the impact that her mother's love for a man other than her father has had on her. She describes it as if it was nothing, but our work would suggest that she felt the need to make up for her mother's disappointments in her marriage and in her life. In the compliant way that one would expect, Tina performed her duties beautifully and shrunk to 64 pounds. She actively struggled with anorexia for years but did not return to treatment until after the death of both of her parents. She felt unable to conduct a life when they were gone, but it would also have been too much of a betrayal of her parents had they still been alive.

Through the enactments around giving gifts I came to feel, and therefore really know, what Tina felt when she was growing up. Tina knew what I wanted, when I would get it, and how I would feel. She would not take no for an answer and I had no voice and no way to step into the process. I was enslaved by her desire and allowed none of my own.

My decision to tell Tina that I had thought of her was a turning point in the treatment. Just as Hilde Bruch's patient felt seen when her father brought her a gift from his travels, Tina felt seen, and valued, by me when I thought of her outside of my office.

That moment opened the door that has allowed us to begin negotiating. I do accept what she offers but she tells me, in advance, what she wants to bring, and why, and we decide together what will happen. Without any limits, she would drown me in flowers. This way she has an opportunity to assert her desire whether or not she follows through. She always assumes her childlike voice when she wants to woo me but she sticks to our new "rules of engagement." She has asked me to bring her pictures of my garden, and I have, but I don't think she is ready to accept the fresh-cut bouquet that I know she is longing for.

I do think Tina's choice to bring me flowers or plants is a thinly veiled unconscious communication. Plants need to be taken care of or they will die. Tina longed to be nurtured as the person she really was; not as the compliant child who expressed no desire. Tina's appetites are ferocious and she still needs to learn how to regulate them. At least she now knows that they exist.

I am concerned about Tina's health. I wonder if her "neurasthenic" quality was a result of the many years of starvation she endured. She often complains of bodily pain, and I find it difficult to sort out what is physical and what is her age-old way of locating all of her unregulated emotions in her body. It remains a challenge for both of us.

Twenty-two years is a long time, and I believe Tina really knows who I am. I have been as consistent and real with her as I can be, and I believe it has given her some faith in human connections. She will ask for help if she is in trouble and she will take things in, over time that she cannot initially digest.

I often think how lucky I am that I didn't grow up in a perfect family with people who "met" my every need. Tina's struggle to be seen was truly a life-and-death struggle, and she is still here to let me tell the story of the work we have done together.

References

Boris, H. N. (1984). The "other" breast: Greed, envy, spite, and revenge. *Contemporary Psychoanalysis, 22,* 45–59.

Bromberg, P. M. (1998). *Standing in the spaces: Essays on clinical process, trauma and dissociation,* Hillsdale, NJ: Analytic Press.

Bromberg, P. M. (2001). Out of body, out of mind, out of danger. In J. Petrucelli & C. Stuart (Eds.), *Hungers and compulsions: The psychodynamic treatment of eating disorders & addictions* (pp. 65–80). Northvale, NJ: Jason Aronson.

Bruch, H. (1978). *The golden cage: The enigma of anorexia nervosa.* Cambridge: Harvard University Press.

Eissler, K. R. (1953). The effect of the structure of the ego on psychoanalytic technique. *Journal of the American Psychoanalytic Association, 1,* 104–143.

Frawley O'Dea, M. G. (1998). What's an analyst to do: shibboleths and "actual acts" in the treatment setting. *Contemporary Psychoanalysis, 34,* 615–633.

Freud, S. (1917). On transformation of instinct as exemplified in anal erotism. *Standard Edition, 17.* London: Hogarth Press.

Glover, E. G. (1955). *Technique of psychoanalysis.* New York: International Universities Press.

Goldberg, B. (2002). Unwrapping the secrets of the gift: gift giving and psychotherapy. *Psychoanalysis and Contemporary Thought, 25,* 465–490.

Kritzberg, N. I. (1980). On patient's gift–giving. *Contemporary Psychoanalysis, 16*(1), 98–118.

Levin, S., & Warner, H. (1966). The significance of giving gifts to children in therapy. *Journal of the Academy of Child Psychiatry, 5,* 630–652.

Ogden, J. K. (1999). Love and sex in 45 minutes: transference love as self and mutual regulation. *Psychoanalytic Psychology, 16*(4), 588–604.

Otnes, C., & Beltramini, R. F. (Eds.). (1966). *Gift giving: A research anthology.* Bowling Green, OH: Bowling Green State University Popular Press.

Petrucelli, J. (2004). Treating eating disorders. In R. H. Coombs (Ed.), *Handbook of addictive disorders: A practical guide to diagnosis and treatment* (pp. 312–352). Hillsdale, NJ: John Wiley & Sons.

Petrucelli, J. (2010). Things that go bump in the night: Secrets after dark. In J. Petrucelli (Ed.), *Knowing, not-knowing and sort-of-knowing: Psychoanalysis and the experience of uncertainty* (pp. 135–150), London: Karnac.

Silber, A. (1969). A patient's gift: its meaning and function. *Int. J. Psycho-Anal., 50,* 335–341.

Stein, H. (1965). The gift in therapy. *J. of Psychotherapy, 19,* 480–486.

Talan, K. H. (1989). Gifts in psychoanalysis: Theoretical and technical issues. *Psychoanal. St. Child,* 44, 149–163.

Zerbe, K. J. (1993). Selves that starve and suffocate: The continuum of eating disorders and dissociative phenomena. *Bulletin of the Menninger Clinic, 57,* 319–327.

Part III

TREATING THE FAMILY, THE YOUNG, THE HORMONAL, AND THE RELIGIOUS

Developmental, Familial, and Cultural Contexts

9

'WHAT'S GOING ON, WHAT'S GOING ON?'

An Interpersonal Approach to Family Therapy With the Patient With an Eating Disorder

Judith Brisman

In the field of eating disorders, understanding the family's role with regard to symptom prevention, development, and cure is at the heart of an important controversy. Do families have anything to do with the catastrophic outbreak of a potentially life-threatening disorder, or are they unjustly blamed for a genetically based illness that our perfectionistic culture taunts to the surface? No mental-health disorder is fraught with as much disagreement, heartache, and ambiguity. Girls (and boys now, too[1]) have literally gone mad—and no one is quite sure what to do.

Interpersonal psychoanalysis has played a significant role in opening a thoughtful dialogue in this heated arena. It was indeed the Interpersonalists who initially blamed mothers for the development of schizophrenia, insisting that flawed parent–child relationships resulted in the schizophrenic process (Fromm-Reichmann, 1948). But it was the Interpersonalists again who then began an expansive conversation refocusing the role of the parent from one of blame to one of critical caretaker (Gartner 1995).

The Maddeningly Confusing but Crucial Role of the Family

Each case involving an anorexic child is disquietingly similar and deeply complex. A wisp of a kid is forced into treatment by her parents; she sits in the therapy office, hands crossed over her chest, and offers little in the way of psychological introspection. The parents are distraught.

Such a dynamic was most aptly represented by an 11-year-old, who, upon meeting me, refused to talk at all. Thwarted in the verbal arena, I asked her to draw what she felt. She stared at me without blinking, and then drew one bold and defiant line on the paper. "What are you going to do with THAT?" she asked. Words—finally! But they left me with nowhere to go.

145

In this particular case, a time proven and often recommended direction for recovery was put into play. The patient, who was 5 feet tall and weighed 80 pounds, had to gain weight or the treatment team and family would insist on more intense intervention. Therapy would be focused on restoration of health, not on understanding of dynamic issues.

Initially, the patient was required to gain about a pound a week. If she was not able to do this, she would then have to endure (her word) an increase in the dreaded family and individual sessions. The parents made sure that she did not exercise and they set limits, insisting she could not go on a longed-for, previously planned trip if she failed to gain weight. With this patient, recovery bounced up and down, literally week to week, until residential care was recommended by the treatment team—and put into play by the parents. She came home at goal weight, but proceeded to lose the weight again. When it was clear that the parents meant business and indeed another residential stay was planned, the daughter gained the (exact) weight needed and finally lurched into recovery.

This kind of intense day-to-day involvement with the parents, the patient, and the treatment team is essential. Often, just the threat of consequences—loss of planned trips or imminent hospitalization—results in the needed weekly weight gain. The anorexic patient, the parents, and the professionals wobble back and forth as the eating-disordered child fragilely takes responsibility for the care of her own body.

Parents repeatedly ask me when the "real" problems will be dealt with. Are we discussing the daughter's insecurity or the son's fear that he does not fit in? Are we getting to the crucial issues that started the food crisis in the first place? With teenage kids—likely not.

Here is where interpersonal work, in significant ways, can take center stage. Ironically, this is work that has as much to do with nonverbal action as it does verbal interpretation. In the initial stages of treatment with the eating-disordered (and particularly the anorexic) child, hope of recovery comes from restructuring family dynamics, not necessarily from a spoken understanding of those dynamics. A change in the social context allows for a change in the individual—and vice versa. For change to endure and for there to be an ongoing assessment of how the parents can best be of help, exploration and words must enter the picture, but often not until the behavioral work is well under way. At the heart of interpersonal thinking is this admixture of systemic intervention with ongoing questioning of what change means. Here, the Interpersonalists have much to contribute.

A Brief History

Initially, verbal intervention took precedent regarding the hope for change with the eating-disordered patient. If there was trouble with an individual, certainly there was trouble with the family. The work of the therapy was to explore just what happened and why.

As early as the 1800s, intrafamilial conflict was seen as a potent catalyst to anorexic starvation (Brumberg, 1989). Over time, specific family characteristics and traits (such as conflict avoidance in the anorexic patient's family) came to be seen as the precursors for the trouble with food (Humphrey, 1988). Poor or insecure attachment, for example, was considered causal in symptomatic development (Ward et al., 2000). The use of introspection, exploration and words—the allowing for an understanding of complicated intra- and inner dynamics—became the foundation for therapeutic action.

But therapists such as Minuchin, Rosman, and Baker (1978) disagreed. Minuchin (who was trained as an interpersonal psychoanalyst) looked to dysfunctional patterns of family interaction (such as overprotectiveness, rigidity, conflict avoidance, and triangulation) and urged that these patterns be behaviorally changed, not merely understood. When the families actively changed what they were doing with each other, anorexic behavior seemed to disappear (Minuchin et al., 1978). This treatment modality, termed "structural family therapy" allowed for little discussion of the unconscious process or family dynamics. Here the thinking, interpersonal at heart, was that changes in the social context (i.e., family) could produce changes both in the individual's behavior and ultimately (albeit indirectly) one's inner life (Gartner, 1995). While Minuchin's research was later questioned (Asen, 2002), it set the stage for a focus on systemic interactions as the direction of treatment in families with an eating-disordered child.

A focus on interrelational patterns, as well as consideration of boundaries, communication, and emotional expression within the family, highlighted the thinking in books such as *Surviving an Eating Disorder: Strategies for Family and Friends* (Siegel, Brisman, & Weinshel, 1989). Trained at the White Institute, Brisman carried her interest in interpersonal engagement to the arena of the family. She looked to Levenson's (1983) iconic question, "What's going on around here?" to explore interactional and emotional patterns in the family. Early observations of families noted that well-intentioned and scared parents were telling their eating-disordered kids in no uncertain terms that they should listen to their parents, not themselves; any attempts at self-responsibility on the part of the patient were unwittingly destroyed. Although, by the second and third editions of *Surviving* (1997, 2009), the message changed significantly, initially, families were urged to step aside from the actual battles over weight and eating. Treatment was solely in the hands of the eating-disordered child and her therapist or treatment team.

In this spirit, every time the person with the disordered eating would implicitly or explicitly call out for help from other family members, the work would be to keep significant others out of the struggle regarding food and weight. No question, as a result, food would inevitably be left untouched, vomit remained on toilet seats, and the question "Do I look fat?" would be asked repeatedly. Parents were urged not to intervene but to insist on responsibility for actions that interfered with the rest of the family (i.e., there would not be punishments for the vomiting behaviors—but there could be consequences if toilets were left unclean). The thinking behind this interpersonally based work was that by behaviorally changing the interactional parent–child patterning, the patient would be enlisted to source and enliven her own recovery potential (Brisman, 2010).

What Went Wrong

This interpersonally focused treatment became the baseline for work with the eating-disordered patient and family. However, questions arose over time. Despite the evolving interventions and clinical thoughtfulness, the madness of anorexia continued, disabling child after child. Researchers began to question whether the push to disengage parents from the actual food battles was significantly—and dangerously—off base. Perhaps the trajectory in the field of eating disorders was beginning to parallel the outdated thinking in autism and schizophrenia (i.e., that parents somehow harmfully contributed to the development and continuation of the disorders). Not only was there concern that parents were being unwittingly (or overtly) blamed but there was also concern that the patient was being decoupled from what was potentially the most valuable resource: direct parental care. This thinking embodied the questioning of researchers at the Maudsley Hospital in London, who in the late 1980s took these issues to task (Russell et al., 1987).

New Thinking—or Maybe Not

A treatment modality termed the Maudsley approach (more recently, Family-Based Treatment) emerged as a critical means of engaging families with an eating-disordered child. Here, parents were urgently guided to (literally) feed their starving child. Parents, not therapists, were now in command with regard to restoring normal eating behaviors. The therapist's role was to meet in conjoint family sessions with all members of the family, not to assess relational patterning (and certainly not to explore etiology), but rather to support each family member in actually feeding the person who was in trouble with food. The thinking was that problems in the family, other than the eating disorder, developed as a result of the eating disorder itself, not the other way around.

Initially, when families were involved in this treatment approach, the recovery rate was an extraordinary 90%, with patients manifesting symptom-free behavior at five years posthospitalization (Russell et al., 1987; Eisler et al., 1997; Eisler et al., 2000). With publication of this research, the field changed overnight. Parental management of the food came to be seen as the rule, not the exception.

But, questions soon arose here, too. The straightforward results of the Maudsley-based research were examined more closely, and the implications of this research were deemed overstated (Strober & Johnson, 2012, p. 157). Indeed, safety parameters for the studies necessitated that all participants in the research were medically stable and have at least 75% or more of their ideal body weight. From the start, the patients in these studies were already self-selected and on their way to a positive recovery. Further, despite the loading in the direction of health, a closer look at the results of the research revealed that only half the participants were in fact unremitted. As Strober and Johnson noted with regard to the Maudsley research in general, "Good sense must guide its interpretation" (2012, p. 165).

Researchers, therapists, and families have been daunted and confused by the jolt in directions, zig-zagging at lightning speed, in an effort to evoke therapeutic change. Just what to do with families, is now a central question in the field.

The Interpersonal Contribution

One of the most complicating factors in the arena of eating disorders is that, despite the surge in research, the only consistent predictable factor found to result in recovery is early intervention. The earlier the behavior is abated, the (significantly) higher chance there is of a return to health (Fairburn, 2005; Lask & Bryant-Waugh, 1999). Early intervention means intervention with the food itself, such that clear behavioral changes are made, and made fast. This crucial information means that if a parent suspects there is a problem brewing, the family must act quickly. Given the confusion in the field, however, it is unclear whether acting quickly means direct intervention with the food. There is now general consensus that families must be involved, but the question of how is still very much up in the air.

This is where an interpersonal perspective can ease some of the complexity the field now faces. Brisman (1992, 1995) has examined how an interpersonal approach is critical in the individual treatment of the eating-disordered patient. That is, an approach is needed in which behavioral change regarding the disordered eating is the initial focus of the work. But, equally important as the behavioral changes are initiated with the patient is the exploration of what these interventions mean to the patient. The work—analytic in nature—ultimately involves a combination of behavioral focus and exploration. Attempts at behavioral change with the food are not the end goal of treatment, but rather an ever-present anchor for understanding what taking hold of one's life and working in a potentially collaborative relationship with the therapist means to the patient. Behavioral change (the language of the patient) allows for interpersonal exploration (the language of the therapist). The ultimate negotiation of both languages in the context of the ever-evolving patient-therapist relationship is the overall goal of treatment (Brisman, 1994).

A Child's Gone Mad

With regard to families, this same interweaving of languages, action, and introspection holds true as well. As a point of reference, consider the role of anger in families in which there is an anorexic child. If I am to think about all (yes, all) of the anorexic patients I have seen, the trajectory of treatment inevitably goes in one direction: the child, seemingly out of the blue, loses weight; the family consults with a professional; parents (as per the treatment protocol previously described) set limits with their child; and (when treatment is successful) weight is gained. Then, all hell breaks loose. Kids shriek, scream, pull knives, cut themselves, throw chairs, and turn over furniture—indeed in the most basic and literal of ways, a child goes mad.

One may argue (and many do) that these kinds of emotional brawls can be attributed to the change in the disordered eating, the child's terror of weight gain, and the disruption in the obsessional rigidity with food and weight. There is no doubt that these factors play a profound role in the angry chaos that ensues.

Yet one can also argue that this emotional disarray has to do with the emergence of feelings previously imprisoned by the symptomatology; it is a hopeful sign when overt emotional expression begins to supplant bingeing, starving, or vomiting. Indeed, there is much more work to do with the child or teen once disordered eating is managed. Ongoing psychoanalytic inquiry and exploration of self-care and emotional expression broaden the picture and allow for continued work towards recovery. However, before this occurs, there is much that the family needs to do to ensure that the stage is set for recovery to move forward. Exactly what the family needs to do is the question.

When families initially enter treatment with an eating-disordered child, often (and this is at the heart of the Maudsley thinking) the kids are running the show. Parents are shunted to the side, parental authority is usurped, and the marital unit is often in disarray with couples fiercely disagreeing about what is best for their child. The Maudsley group fought to change this dynamic, putting the parents back in control and urging them to disregard their child's fierce rage at being forced to eat. These researchers eschewed theory (despite the fact they used a structural family-based theory at its core). They felt that examining etiology of the family relations was at best useless, arguing that, in the midst of a crisis, the family was experiencing natural upheaval. Also, they felt theory was potentially dangerous because it would make parents feel blamed for the disorder when they needed to be strong and take charge. But the Maudsley group missed something essential. While they noted that signs of overt parental hostility could preclude the possibility of effective parental involvement in the refeeding process (Le Grange et al., 1992), they failed to focus on why a child's rage and dogged misguided determination might be more difficult for some parents than others. What taking charge means to a parent is an essential question for treatment; when there is no exploration in this regard, the entire point of treatment may well be missed. When weight is gained and emotions run wild, the parents still need to find ways successfully negotiate the chaos and pave the way for healthier self-care for everyone.

For the parents—and all family members—the question about what it means to take an authoritative position and to stand up to one's child's rage is key. For example, consider the father who sees his controlling mother in the face of his starving child. He will likely need to learn to catch his breath to deal with the fury he feels when his daughter demands that she is *not* going to eat. For this father, the daughter's tyrannical assaults are no longer merely about food or weight. Or, think of the mother, who merely by serving a breakfast, is told by her screaming, flailing child that she is stupid, inept, trying to destroy the child (such behavior is not out of the question for meal time exchanges). The mother, who has grown up with the battering verbal abuse of an alcoholic father, cowers and breaks down at her daughter's demands to leave the table. These parents cannot merely be told to "try harder." Unless there is an ongoing understanding of the crisis moment and what the child's maddening demands mean to the parent, the emotional turmoil will likely increase, and hope of successful intervention with food must be abandoned.

Additionally, as in any psychodynamically oriented treatment, each family member's reaction to the therapist and what he or she is doing with the therapist (i.e., the transference) is also critical. All too frequently, in the eyes of the parents, the therapist wafts back and forth wildly from being the savior authority to being the abusive, inept caretaker. In this regard, transference is relentless, powerful, and intractable, no matter what treatment model is used. How the parent experiences what the therapist is doing and who the therapist is to the patient and family must be questioned and interwoven into the work.

As Levenson reminds us, "most parents act badly in good faith. They are doing their best; they are doing what they have been taught to do" (cited in Gartner, 1995, p. 806). Yet, it is the therapist's role to consider how the parents' reaction to us (or to the child and each other) can best be put to use. Consider the compliant, authority-pleasing mother and her authority-questioning, bombastic husband. How can each be nudged to question the relationship with the therapist and translate their fierce reactions back to effective work with their child? Remember, these are parents who are not interested in their own treatment (the Maudsley group had this right). They are interested in helping their child. Therefore, communication needs to focus on what they have done that has worked, and what has not. The mother's submissiveness (wanting to give up or give in), for example, might be used as a barometer to assess when things are getting too heated; perhaps she is the one who knows when to back off and allow their daughter a moment to breath. On the other hand, the father's angry questioning might be understood as an important means of evaluating the treatment process itself.

Listen, as well, to each spouse for an appreciation of where the family lineage may be relevant. "Our daughter is just like my husband's mother," a frustrated mother of an anorexic patient tells me. "Both of them do whatever they want and never listen to him. It makes him crazy." When I asked how he dealt with his infuriating mom, the dad told me he just blocked her out, pretended she did not exist. This led to an interesting discussion of how blocking his daughter out might be of help. But we also had to wonder which parts of the dad's "blocking her out" were not working. For example, I knew the daughter felt neglected by the dad. I suggested a plan whereby the dad would spend more time alone with his daughter and get to know her better. At the same time though, we made positive use of his ability to emotionally blockade feelings to help the mom tolerate crescendoed moments of heightened despair at the dinner table. These parents were able to listen. Had I started with an investigation of the parents' personal life and history, this may have fallen flat. By keeping the focus on how the parents could help their daughter, information flowed more freely.

This kind of work is urgently needed when an eating disorder erupts in a family. No parent can easily regulate the feelings of helplessness and powerlessness evoked when facing the triumph of an eating-disordered child. Without understanding, exploration, and a refocusing of the parent's own relational patterns, interventions with the child's eating will often result in further chaos and crisis. Yet a thorough, traditional analysis of the family situation just takes too long. Parents may not want to know how their history relates to their child's disorder. They may not appreciate its relevance; also such a perspective may feel blaming to parents who feel guilty enough. The question of what the child's rage or road-blocking means needs to be gently questioned, with real curiosity, and with compassion for the child's intractable moments. This work needs to be clear, directive, and intervention-oriented. Otherwise, the risk of not reaching the child—or the parents—and the possible entrenchment of the symptoms is just too serious.

For some parents, moment-to-moment refeeding of their child will be the essential base of treatment. For others though, the rage-filled epicenter of meal times may be the last place they should be. (For others still, time and work obligations may just not allow it.) A team of therapists, nutritionists, and doctors might be a better alternative for these parents regarding the direct management of what is eaten each day, with parents actively supporting this work from the side. For all parents, as they understand more about themselves, their own history, and their (and understandable) reactions to their child's behavior, their role can evolve and be refined to best assess and further the work needed for the child's recovery.

Knowing, Not-Knowing, and the Interpersonal Voice

The interpersonal field is known for its ever-present questioning of tradition and orthodoxy. Past and present, there is a dare to leave the safety of the familiar and encourage challenges of the unknown. In the face of the crises of eating disorders, manualized treatment directions have, at times, dictated therapeutic protocol and allowed for a determined path of intervention. These therapeutic anchors offer answers and new therapeutic territory, but also potentially narrow the options for individualized assessment and treatment. A base of treatment is needed that allows for answers—and questions—as part of the treatment endeavor.

In treatment of the eating-disordered family, an interpersonal perspective provides a steadying base of traditional psychodynamic thinking within a somewhat untraditional framework in which overt behavioral change is directly encouraged. Awareness of how the past plays on the present is gently interwoven into work, in which active intervention is privileged over words. Here, the interpersonal treatment of the eating-disordered family presents a general direction of answers while simultaneously allowing for ongoing questioning and embrace of the unknown with each unique family we see.

Interpersonalists have always encouraged questions at the same moment that answers are provided. They have much to say . . . and much to ask. With regard to the family caught in the chaos of a child gone mad, it is time to listen—hard.

Note

1. Feminine gender will be used to allow for the flow of reading in the text.

References

Asen, E. (2002). Outcome research in family therapy. *Advances in Psychiatric Treatment, 8*, 230–238.

Brisman, J. (1992). Bulimia in the late adolescent: An analytic perspective to a behavioral problem. In J. O'Brien, D. Pilowsky, & O. Lewis (Eds.), *Psychotherapies with children: Adapting the dynamic process* (pp. 171–187). Washington D.C.: American Psychiatric Press.

Brisman, J. (1994). Learning to listen: Therapeutic encounters and negotiations in the early stage of treatment. *Eating Disorders, 2*(1), 67–73.

Brisman, J. (1995). Addiction. In M. Lionells, J. Fiscalini, C. Mann, & D. Stern (Eds.), *Handbook of interpersonal psychoanalysis* (pp. 537–554). Hillsdale, NJ: Analytic Press.

Brisman, J. (2010). When helping hurts: The role of the family and significant others in the treatment of eating disorders. In M. Maine, B. McGilley, & D. Bunnell (Eds.), *Treatment of eating disorders: Bridging the research-practice gap.* London: Academic Press.

Brumberg, J. (1989). *Fasting girls: The history of anorexia nervosa.* New York: Plume.

Eisler, I., Dare, C., Hodes, M., Russell, G., Dodge, E., & Le Grange, D. (2000). Family therapy for adolescent anorexia nervosa: The results of a controlled comparison of two family interventions. *Journal of Child Psychology and Psychiatry and Allied Disciplines, 41*, 727–736.

Eisler, I., Dare, C., Russell, G. F. M., Szmukler, G. I., Le Grange, D., & Dodge, E. (1997). Family and individual therapy in anorexia nervosa: A 5-year follow-up. *Archives of General Psychiatry, 54*, 1025–1030.

Fairburn, C. G. (2005). Evidence-based treatment of anorexia nervosa. *International Journal of Eating Disorders, 37*, 26–30.

Fromm-Reichmann, F. (1948). Notes on the development of treatment of schizophrenics by psychoanalytic psychotherapy. *Psychiatry, 11*, 263–273.

Gartner, R. (1995). The relationship between interpersonal psychoanalysis and family therapy. In M. Lionells, J. Fiscalini, C. Mann, & D. Stern (Eds.), *Handbook of interpersonal psychoanalysis* (pp. 793–822). Hillsdale, NJ: Analytic Press.

Humphrey, L. (1988). Relationships within subtypes of anorexic, bulimic and normal families. *Journal of the American Academy of Child & Adolescent Psychiatry, 27*(5), 544–551.

Lask, B., & Bryant-Waugh, R. (1999). Prepubertal eating disorders. In N. Piran, M. Levine, & C. Steiner-Adair (Eds.), *Preventing eating disorders* (pp. 476–483). Philadelphia: Taylor & Francis.

Le Grange, D., Eisler, I., Dare, C., & Hodes, M. (1992). Family criticism and self-starvation: A study of expressed emotion. *Journal of Family Therapy, 14*, 177–192.

Levenson, E. (1983). *The ambiguity of change.* New York: Basic Books.

Minuchin, S., Rosman, B. L., & Baker, L. (1978). *Psychosomatic families: Anorexia nervosa in context.* Cambridge: Harvard University Press.

Russell, G. F., Szmukler, G. I., Dare, C., & Eisler, I. (1987). An evaluation of family therapy in anorexia nervosa and bulimia nervosa. *Archives of General Psychiatry, 44*, 1047–1056.

Siegel, M., Brisman, J., & Weinshel, M. (1989). *Surviving an eating disorder: Strategies for family and friends.* New York: HarperCollins.

Siegel, M., Brisman, J., & Weinshel, M. (1997). *Surviving an eating disorder: Strategies for family and friends* (rev. ed.). New York: HarperCollins Living.

Siegel, M., Brisman, J., & Weinshel, M. (2009). *Surviving an eating disorder: Strategies for family and friends* (3rd ed.). New York: HarperCollins Living.

Strober, M., & Johnson, C. (2012). Why biology, environment and psyche all matter in anorexia nervosa, why therapists make mistakes, and why clinical benchmarks should guide the management of weight correction. *International Journal of Eating Disorders, 45*(2), 155–178.

Ward, A., Ramsay, R., Turnbull, S., Benedettinni, M., & Treasure, J. (2000). Attachment patterns in eating disorders: Past and present. *International Journal of Eating Disorders, 28,* 370–376.

10

'BRIDGE OVER TROUBLED WATER'

Girls' Growing Bodies, Growing Minds, Growing Complications

Jacqueline Ferraro

Twelve-year-old Nicole enters my office and immediately plunks herself down in my chair. Gone are the days when she first came to see me at age six and we played with an array of dolls and Beanie Babies. I am aware of the changes in her body, her interests, and her behavior. Toys that enabled her to talk about herself, her family, and dilemmas in her life are no longer needed or wanted. My position as the special adult that she could talk to and play with has seemed to disappear. Childhood toys are replaced by a cell phone, iPod, and videogame player that all belong to her, and that she occasionally shares with me. The little girl I towered over is nearly as tall as I am. "You're old!" she mercilessly declares one day. And, indeed, at that moment I do feel old.

With the advent of puberty, fundamental changes are taking place in the bodies of all girls. Prior to this time and except for the sexual organs, the bodies of boys and girls are more similar than dissimilar. Puberty heralds a maturational process in both that begins to identify their bodies as sexual entities capable of reproduction. Prepubescent bodies are forever changed. For girls, powerful forces, in the form of hormones such as estrogen[1] drastically alter and fashion their bodies into a more sexual and adult identity. In moving through these remarkable physiological changes, out of her control, each young girl must find ways to cope with evolving developmental stages that can be thought of as creating changing, disjointed and disconnected experiences of self that must be negotiated.

Navigating all these developmental and physiological changes, and the accompanying social and emotional aspects, can be challenging and anxiety-producing for any young person. Karina, a nine-year-old child whom I've been seeing, is quite aware that something big and dramatic is on the horizon. Recently, when talking with me about puberty, Karina declared: "I won't be me and I like me the way I am." Karina "wonders and worries about how she will change and who she will become. For some pre-teens and adolescents, these anxieties and stressors can be overwhelming and efforts to cope can transform into the development of an eating disorder" (Ferraro, 2013).

This chapter will focus on these developmental issues as they can present in preadolescent girls, their transition through puberty, and on into adolescence. Body image, physiology (including the important role of hormones), and cognitive development will be addressed with vignettes aimed at highlighting aspects of development. Normal developmental changes create a multiplicity of selves, including developmental selves that can arise from the many stages of development, emotional selves (Buechler, 2008), and hormonal selves (Kolod, 2010). All these selves can be seen as an integral part of this maturational process and present ways that the female child (and analyst) reacts to the ever-changing states of this process. An awareness of the depth of the dramatic changes in girls' bodies and the concomitant self-states is an essential part of the treatment of preteens and adolescents. For some but not all prepubescent and adolescent girls, their efforts to cope with these complex changes can involve a focus on controlling weight (restricting and/or bingeing), cutting themselves, drugs, alcohol use, and sexual experimentation and activity.

Body Image

Body image, how a child sees herself, is co-created in relationships with others and encompasses aspects of physical, mental, and emotional being. Personality characteristics of each child are embedded in this perception. The development of body image begins the moment we are born. How a child is held, touched, cared for, and loved becomes part of who she is. "Our self is first, and foremost a body, as experienced being handled and held by other-self" (Aron & Anderson, 1998, p. xx). The development of body image starts in the home with parents, siblings, and other relatives and encompasses their perceptions and ways of interacting with the child. With time and continued growth, it expands to include interactions with teachers, classmates and friends. In these early years, the sense of being female and male can, but not necessarily, have quite distinctive aspects for children in such areas as activities, toy preferences, and types of play. Nonetheless, externally, except for the sexual organs, young boys and girls physically appear more alike than different.

By the time children are in middle school, major changes in the physical developments of infancy and early childhood have receded, and they have grown more comfortable with their bodies. Girls are now familiar with their many bodily sensations and affects, their motoric and academic capacities, and the multitude of ways that others respond and interact with them. Children in the middle school years have moved from the greater security and comfort of home and family into the school environment of learning and the social world of classmates and peer relationships. Physical activity, curiosity, and peer interactions—especially same-sex peers—have come to the forefront for many children. It is a time of reaching out into the larger world as children of this age become more involved with school and learning. These preadolescents are becoming more socially responsible and self-sufficient as compared to earlier stages of development. Middle school–aged

children take all of these experiences and begin to integrate them into their growing sense of self.

Phases of Personality Development

Psychoanalytic theories of development range from Freud's (1938) psychosexual
stages, to Margaret Mahler's (1975) separation-individuation theory of development, to Erik Erikson's (1979) stages of psychosocial development. While these
stages are presented in a sequential fashion, development does not proceed in
such a linear way. There can be overlap, full or partial disjointed returns to prior
stages, and a circling back to earlier elements in development. The key figure
in the development of interpersonal theory, Harry Stack Sullivan, delineated his
lesser known developmental epochs (or eras) and focused on the orientation of
humans toward interpersonal connection (Sullivan, 1953). For purposes of this
chapter—to highlight the potential contribution of interpersonal theory to the
development of eating disorders—I will focus on Sullivan's juvenile, preadolescence, and early adolescence epochs.

Juvenile Epoch

Just prior to preadolescence, Sullivan addresses what he calls the juvenile epoch,
a time when children enter elementary school and begin to develop their social
skills and become more involved with playmates "like oneself" (Sullivan, 1953,
p. 5). Whereas young children tend to play equally with boys or girls, children in
the juvenile era begin to associate more with playmates of the same sex. Thus,
girls tend to congregate and play with other girls. Birthday parties can divide up
along gender lines with parties that focus on activities preferred by one gender.
For example, girls may have parties with an American Girl theme, or boys with a
dinosaur or baseball emphasis.

With children moving out into the larger world, Sullivan describes this earlier
developmental phase as "the time when the world begins to be really complicated
by the presence of other people" (Sullivan, 1953, p. 232). At this time children
begin to develop a capacity for compromise and cooperation. These qualities of
human interaction, begun in the home, are now tempered by exchanges with others, especially peers who tend to be less tolerant than parents, siblings, or other
relatives and more vocal about expressing their own needs and desires. Children
now begin to perceive differences in themselves and others. Exposure to authority figures other than parents—such as teachers and the parents of friends—adds
to an awareness of differences in people, in this instance, between adults in their
world. Thus begins a realization and the dawning perception of parents as "simply
people" rather than idealized figures (Sullivan, 1953, p. 230).

This process becomes important as development continues and parents come to
be seen in greater perspective with both positive and negative traits. However, if
parents "still have to be sacrosanct, the most perfect people on earth—then one of

the most striking and important of the juvenile contributions to socialization has sadly miscarried" (Sullivan, 1953, p. 231).

This growing awareness in the juvenile stage becomes the underlying process in development for preteens and adolescents to gradually see their parents and, more importantly, themselves in greater perspective. Through this process they can become more aware and more accepting of parents and others, and of themselves. The strong connection of children to their parents ideally provides a security that enables children to weather disappointments in a parent (and in themselves) while maintaining their connection to and continuing to love and value that parent (and themselves). If parents do not need to present themselves as perfect, and the child doesn't need to have a perfect parent, then the basis is laid for the development of resilience, even in the face of failure or disappointment in a parent or oneself. This aspect of development is particularly valuable when considering the development of eating disorders. Children and adolescents who develop eating disorders frequently have difficulty in the areas of self-esteem and self-acceptance. Their capacity to internally value and accept themselves—including normal imperfections—is transferred onto external factors, usually distorted, of weight and shape.

Preadolescence Epoch

Sullivan's juvenile era leads into his preadolescence epoch and the "need for interpersonal intimacy" (Sullivan, 1953, p. 245). In this stage, the preadolescent develops an interest in an Other, a special same-sex friend who Sullivan calls a "chum" (Sullivan, 1953, p. 246). The ubiquitous nature of this interpersonal, intimate relationship can readily be seen in the preponderance of girls' necklaces sold with the inscription of "best friends." Actually, the necklace is two chains, each attached to half of a heart that is broken with a jagged line down the middle. Each girl wears the chain with half of the heart and half of the inscription. When their two pieces are put together, they form one heart inscribed with "Best Friends." This talisman, worn by two best friends, attests to the bond and intimacy between them as they wear it around their necks and close to their hearts. It is a kind of love as the preadolescent girl focuses on the happiness of her chum, or best friend, derives pleasure in being a part of that happiness and, in doing so, sees herself positively reflected back through the loving eyes and actions of her friend. Such a powerful relationship contributes to the growth of a positive sense of self. The preadolescent girl has moved a step away from the adoring eyes of her parents towards those of a special "chum."

This intimate connection with a peer and the ensuing mirroring feedback becomes critically important when considering an aspect of eating disorders in which a person can be seen as turning away from human connection toward a relationship with thinness and weight. Rather than focusing on the reflection of self from an interpersonal other, the mirror is an inanimate reflection of projected inadequacy and distortion, untempered by a real and intimate connection with another person.

Early Adolescence Epoch

According to Sullivan (1953), in early adolescence and with the advent of puberty, the preadolescent's intimacy with a best friend morphs into more of a sexual desire for an Other, members of the opposite sex for heterosexual adolescents and transgender teens or someone of the same sex for lesbian and gay teens. Same-sex friends may still be important, but interpersonal interests expand to a more sexual interest in others. Sullivan differentiates intimacy, which he defines as collaboration with another person, from biological maturation and the experience of genital, sexual feelings, or lust, that propel a young teenager toward a greater preoccupation with sexual thoughts, feelings, and activity. He separates early from late adolescence, in which the latter is characterized by integrating lust with intimacy and establishing "a fully human or mature repertory of interpersonal relations" (Sullivan, 1953, p. 297).

However, in early adolescence the focus is on ways to incorporate this newer genital awakening into the rest of the girl's life. With the production of hormones, genital sexual sensations, the secondary sex characteristics of breasts, pubic hair, etc. and a more shapely feminine body, early adolescence is a challenging time for all girls. With this comes an awakening of curiosity and potential sexual experimentation. Parents and society can react with repressive prohibitions that may engender, in some adolescents, a concomitant repression and, for some teens, contribute to the development of eating disorders as normal sexual feelings and tensions shut down or are transferred to controlling food, weight and body. Conflict and resolution are played out on and within the body.

Alicia

Alicia is a 15-year-old girl who is anorexic and whose weight has begun to plunge. She describes herself as proud of her capacity to inhibit her desires regarding food and eating, seeing herself as superior in her ability to avoid even a mouthful of the pizza being consumed by her friends at the local pizza parlor. While she desperately yearns to have even a bite, her resistance excels. This extends to other areas of her life, as she restricts pleasures in multiple ways. Alicia tries to feel invisible even as she actually becomes more visible to others who notice her plummeting body weight. She is aware that her friends are dating or "hooking up" with boys while she remains emotionally aloof and isolated, seeing herself residing in a state of "splendid superiority." She notes that her two older siblings, ages 18 and 19, have yet to date and—in her household—there seems to be an absolute avoidance of anything that even hints at sexuality. Alicia considers it "taboo" to even admit to liking a boy, feels ashamed of any such interest and is appalled at the thought of her parents "seeing" or learning about her having any desire for a boy. She is shocked and a little envious of the ease she observes between other girls and their parents as they freely discuss boys and love interests. Alicia is involved in an intimate and highly critical relationship with her own body rather than with peers and potential sexual partners.

Physiological Development

Around ages six to eight, physiological changes begin in the bodies of children. This section will highlight some of these normal processes and their effect on girls' bodies and potential effect on the sense of self.[2]

Adrenarche

Adrenarche, which begins around age six, starts a process in middle childhood that is currently a focus of research into its effects on biology and behavior (Campbell, 2011; Rosenfeld, 2012). It is a hormonal process that involves the release of androgens, steroids produced by the adrenal cortex, which contribute to physical changes in the bodies of children, including some beginning growth of pubic hair, beginning changes in sweat composition, and some oiliness of the skin that can result in early acne in some children. While adrenarche is considered a separate process from the physiological and hormonal changes of puberty, there can be some overlap through the effects of hormones. These bodily changes beginning with adrenarche can have a mild to a more troubling impact on girls.

Teenager Claire still vividly recalls when she suddenly began to develop some acne at age seven. Unlike her fellow classmates (and similar to her older brother), Claire's early acne was pronounced and set her apart from her classmates. She was embarrassed and sensitive to comments by her peers who didn't understand this process and questioned her hygiene. Claire's sense of her body and her self retained this earlier image of someone unattractive and undesirable. Now, in her midteens, Claire still tries to cope with the residue of the earlier experience and the ongoing challenge of acne. She focuses on her face, continually searching out acne remedies, but also researching plastic surgery options for her nose (too big), her chin (too small) and her lips (too thin). With puberty and adolescence, coupled with other family and social issues, this early vulnerability contributes to Claire's lower self-esteem, as well as some of her social withdrawal from peers and emotional isolation.

Puberty

Puberty typically begins around ages 10 or 11 for girls and can span a wide range of ages, and last approximately four years to full maturation. Under the influence of many hormones, including estrogen and progesterone, girls begin their process of sexual maturation. There is growth in height and weight, with the development of breasts, pubic hair, and changes in the vagina, uterus and ovaries leading to menstruation and the capacity for childbearing. Body shape, greater fat distribution to hips, thighs, and buttocks and an increased percentage of overall body fat, are normal parts of this hormonal process in girls. As this growth in body fat proceeds, especially in the early stages where the body fat has not settled into the shape and curves of the taller and more sexually mature female body, many girls and their parents experience this earlier increase as a significant and troubling weight gain.

It can be a particularly sensitive time for girls as well as for their parents. Some parents come to see me specifically distressed about their child's weight and shape at this time. Addressing and exploring the anxieties of these parents is a first step in helping them to lessen their anxiety and decrease any overt or covert messages about weight and food that could be destructive to a budding adolescent's self-image and self-esteem. Discussing puberty and physiology, combined with giving parents active ways "to do something" on behalf of their child, is invaluable. This can take the form of active listening, encouraging fun activities such as soccer or dancing, and conveying a sense of pride and acceptance of their daughter (and her body). Being able to listen, talk, and hold positive regard for a daughter facilitates both a verbal and nonverbal communication of worth and develops resilience in the child.

When you add sensitivity to the peer environment and the attention of boys to the adolescent mix, girls can become sensitized to their bodies and any amount of perceived fat or difference from their female counterparts. In a vulnerable girl, when these elements are combined, for example, with a level of anxiety, perfectionism, and stress, there is a potential for the development of an eating disorder. Stress and anxiety can come from within (e.g., social shyness and perfectionism) and without (e.g., the family environment, high parental criticism, and teasing and harassment from peers; Strober & Peris, 2011).

Puberty focuses a girl's attention on her body and her sexual desirability, including her physical attractiveness (hence the obsession of looking into mirrors and worries about her body and its appearance); it brings sexual competition for the attention of the desired sexual partner to the forefront. With the advent of menstruation, girls come under the influence of the cyclical hormones of estrogen and progesterone. During an average 28-day cycle, there is a rise and fall of each hormone with peaks of estrogen and progesterone occurring at different points in the cycle.

At puberty these hormones flood the teenage girl's brain.[3] Estrogen and progesterone affect different parts of the brain, particularly in the areas of emotions (amygdala), control of body organs (hypothalamus), and memory and learning (hippocampus; Brizendine, 2006, p. 34). With the menstrual cycle there are fluctuations in the levels of these two hormones. In the first two weeks and under the influence of estrogen, girls can feel calmer, more socially relatable, and a little clearer about issues. With the decrease in estrogen and increase in progesterone of the last two weeks of the menstrual cycle, girls can experience PMS (premenstrual syndrome). Premenstrual syndrome has a wide variety of signs and symptoms including irritability, mood swings, depression, anxiety, fatigue, breast tenderness, etc. These premenstrual changes can vary in intensity from month to month and from person to person. At such a time girls may be more volatile and sensitive to stress.

Currently, research is proceeding with studies focusing on the hormones of puberty and their potential contribution to eating disorders. For example, Dr. Kelly

Klump, of Michigan State University, is studying genetic, environmental, and neurobiological factors and the possibility that ovarian hormones may contribute to the development of eating disorders (Klump et al., 2002; Klump et al., 2003; Klump et al., 2007). Her research is examining the association of pubertal hormones with individual personality traits and other disorders, such as anxiety (Keel et al., 2005).

Cognitive Development

Increased awareness and an appreciation of the role of physiology—including hormones—and the role of the brain in the perception and processing of environmental situations, emotions, and stress is essential to understanding adolescent development and behavior. "*Hormones can determine what the brain is interested in doing.* [emphasis added] They help guide nurturing, social, sexual, and aggressive behaviors" (Brizendine, 2006, p. xvii).

In her book *The Female Brain,* Louann Brizendine (2006) explains that the fetal brains of both girls and boys are similar until the eighth week of fetal development when there is a testosterone surge in the brains of a male fetus, "killing off some cells in the communication centers and growing more cells in the sex and aggression centers" (p. 14). At this same time, girls' brains continue their growth and "sprout more connections in the communication centers and areas [of the brain] that process emotions" (p. 14). These physiological differences mean that the communication and emotional memory centers are larger and more developed in girls while boys' brains, by comparison, are more developed in the areas of sexual drive, aggression, and desire for action (Brizendine, 2006, p. 5). Girls are more wired for mutual gazing and, over the first three months of their lives, girls will increase their capacity for eye contact and mutual gazing at faces by over 400 percent. In contrast, boys tend not to have such an increase in these abilities during that same time period. As Brizendine (2006) stated: "Baby girls are born interested in emotional expression.[4] They take meaning about themselves from a look, a touch, every reaction from the people they come into contact with. From these early cues, they discover whether they are worthy, lovable, or annoying" (p. 15).

After birth, both the male and female brains are subjected to huge amounts of estrogen: for boys this lasts for nine months while for girls this high level of estrogen continues for 24 months. Estrogen "stimulates the brain circuits that are rapidly being built. It spurs the growth and development of neurons, further enhancing the female brain circuits and centers for observation, communication, gut feelings, even tending and caring . . . promoting social nuance and fertility" (Brizendine, 2006, p. 19). In general, girls' brains are more attuned to the social approval of others.[5] When there is attunement, with sensitive mutual gazing, and attentive talking and listening between parent and female infant, there is the potential for a greater growth in self-esteem and self-confidence as these areas of the brain respond to this input. Considering the possible implications of this cognitive development for later preadolescent and adolescent girls may shed light on the tendency of girls towards greater awareness of and sensitivity to interactions with others.

In development, changes are taking place in the body and the brain that affect thinking and behavior. A preteen or teenager's capacity to manage her emotions and experiences are critical aspects of development. Research has broadened our understanding of cognitive development, increasing our awareness that different parts of the brain mature at different times.

The prefrontal cortex is a particularly important part of the brain, involved in judgment, reasoning and problem solving. The prefrontal cortex helps us to prioritize thoughts, and helps us to imagine, plan, control impulses and modulate mood. This part of the brain, so critical to self-regulation and decision-making, does not fully mature until a person reaches their mid-20s.

This relative cognitive immaturity of adolescents leaves them more emotional and vulnerable to hormonal fluctuations and interpersonal experiences just when they are separating from parents, connecting with peers and struggling with powerful sexual feelings. The adolescent girl, given the immaturity of her brain—that is, connections between parts of the brain that are immature, such as the emotional center (amygdala) and the area of judgment and impulse control (prefrontal cortex)—is more vulnerable to being overwhelmed by her emotions. When stressed, she may be less able to think critically and judge situations and respond appropriately. This cognitive immaturity, combined with the tendency of females for greater emotional connection, can make girls highly sensitive to rejection and fearful of exclusion from the female group (Brizendine, 2006, p. 34–35). Adding hormones to the mix, including androgens[6] and hormonal fluctuations, may contribute to aggression that, for girls, frequently comes off as "meanness" as they bond in cliques, excluding and badgering other girls. In my sophomore year of high school, I still remember the "Hate Jackie Club" of my former group of girlfriends, who bonded together more firmly in their alliance against and exclusion of me. Looking back, I believe it connected them and probably assured them of their value and desirability to each other. At the same time, in devaluing me, they enhanced their own self-worth (during an insecure time in all our lives). Needless to say I survived, but I was forced to find new friends and to find ways to maintain my own shaky, adolescent self-esteem.

With development in the prefrontal area of the brain there is a growing ability of adolescents to think in the abstract and a growing capacity to see themselves as they imagine others see them. At the same time, as children enter the teen years and high school, there is the growing separation from parents physically, emotionally, and psychologically. There is less time spent with parents and a relative decrease in parents' influence as adolescents turn increasingly toward peers. Therefore, at the very time that the teen can keenly imagine how others see her, she is more influenced by and closer to her peers (Fonagy et al., 2002, p. 318–319).

Dr. Deborah Yurgelun-Todd, currently at the University of Utah, has been studying the development of the adolescent brain and the emotional and cognitive changes that occur during adolescence (2007, p. 251–257). In some of her work,

163

she raises the possibility that the increase in teenagers' capacity to abstract correlates with an increase in their level of social anxiety. "In adolescence, you may start to become more self-aware and more able to think abstractly or hypothetically about other people's thoughts and feelings . . . but that may also allow you to have more social self-consciousness and worry more about what other people are thinking of you" (2002).

According to Yurgelun-Todd (2002), adolescent brains process emotional information from external stimuli differently than adult brains with a stronger gut response and less attention to evaluating consequences. Her research suggests that, in calm situations, teenagers can think and rationalize almost as well as adults, but when stressed they are less capable of thinking more clearly about a situation, using judgment in decision-making and considering the effects of their behavior. When processing emotions, research indicates that teenagers have greater activity in their amygdala (the more emotional part of the brain) in contrast to adults where there has been a shift to greater brain activity in their frontal lobes (including their prefrontal cortex) to process strong feelings. When immaturity in cognitive development is combined with the physiological changes of puberty, aspects of normal development, separation from parents and the heightened influence of peers, adolescents who are particularly vulnerable[7] may develop eating disorders and other self-destructive behaviors.

Multiplicity of Self-States

The current emphasis on multiple self-states provides a way to think about preteens, teenagers, and their development. From infancy to adulthood, a stream of significant interpersonal relationships enter our lives and then become internalized. Embedded in our relationships are a multitude of experiences that can be affectively overwhelming, potentially threatening to the relational connection, and, when this occurs, experienced as traumatic. These experiences can range from the more ordinary to the more commonly considered traumatic events of abuse or serious neglect. In an effort to cope with overwhelming events, these experiences are disconnected, along with their memories and affects, into discrete parts of the personality. Howell (2007) described a trauma/dissociation model with "dissociated partitions in the mind and parts of the self . . . trauma splits off pieces of living experience, such that parts of experience are no longer accessible to the person" (p. 49). Howell (2005) also speaks of the normality and pervasiveness of dissociation, "when we take into account the internalization of multiple aspects of attachment relationships, plus the likelihood of some relational trauma" (p. vii). She believes that "dissociation perfuses everyday life" (p. 5). These dissociated self-states are discreet structures within the individual that become organized and defined as separate or partial parts of the self, affecting perception, reflection, and behavior.

The developmental stages connected with growing from childhood, to preadolescence, through early adolescence, adolescence itself, and then young adulthood are embedded with multiple self-states that mark the normal, somewhat disjointed steps and experiences in development. Like self-states, each developmental stage can be understood as having "its own narrative, its own memory configuration, its own perceptual reality and its own style of relatedness to others. It is not simply something one feels—it is who one is—at least, at certain times" (Bromberg, 1998, p. 245). When in the throes of powerful feelings—emotional self-states such as anger or love (Buechler, 2008)—teenagers can disconnect from the usual ties that link them to others (parents, friends, classmates, etc.) and to other parts of themselves. Kolod (2010) extends the concept of self-states to include hormonal self-states wherein, under the influence of fluctuating hormones, including estrogen and progesterone, females are different and relate differently at various points in the menstrual cycle. With cyclical degrees of premenstrual syndrome (PMS) and menstruation, girls are invariably forced to connect with their bodies.

With anorexia and significant weight loss, girls can postpone menarche, the start of menstruation, or cease menstruating. Girls who cease to menstruate disconnect from the normal aspects of physical, emotional and social development and also disconnect from their bodies and parts of themselves, that is, their usual cyclical, hormonal experiences of self. Mood and emotional range becomes less dimensional and more contained and restricted, similar to their eating patterns. What do these losses mean for girls and what are the repercussions in their lives and development?

An appreciation of the profound changes in growing girls' bodies and minds, and the concomitant self-states they can engender, is indispensable to an understanding of preteens and adolescents and to their treatment. Writings on self-states (Bromberg, 1998; Howell, 2005, 2007; Putnam, 1997)—including those associated with development, emotional states (Buechler, 2008), and Kolod's (2010) focus on hormonal selves—illustrate the complexity of these transformative processes at work in girls and increase our understanding of the resourceful efforts both young preteens and adolescent girls use to cope with these bodily changes and multiple self-states. The following vignette returns to Nicole and highlights my effort as a psychoanalyst to understand my own bodily changes and perceptions—past and current—illustrating ways they intersect, shape, and inform the treatment.

Nicole: The Nexus of Young and Old

I see Nicole's slender body, now a foot taller than when I first met her and breasts that are already developing. Her clothes—black leggings, purple tunic over a grey skirt, and silver bracelet—reveal a sense of fashion and individuality as she carefully presents herself to friends, schoolmates, and the world. She struts in with an air of confidence and independence as she plunks herself down in my chair. I find myself taking pleasure in seeing her growth.

However, Nicole has just called me "old." My feelings are mixed. I shift and move farther back in my chair. I glance down at the veined hands (not *my* hands) coming together at the center of *my* lap and moving closer to the middle of *my* body. Her declaration hits me in a vulnerable spot. I can claim ownership only in some circumstances; at other moments, I must distance myself from the thoughts and feelings. Old? I don't feel old; but I am in a markedly different phase of my life. (Ah, that sounds and feels so much better!) Yet, Nicole forces me to think about aging, hers in comparison to mine. In quick flashes I see myself in the mirror, someone long past puberty. Select memories and feelings of that long ago time intrude—pleasurable sleepovers at my best friend Maureen's house and two boys in sixth grade who "fought," competing for my attention. However, I also notice that it is hard to fully recall life at age 12, especially any of the difficult moments that, intellectually, I know I experienced.

I return to Nicole and the present. Why did she make such a cruel-sounding remark at this moment? And why does Nicole take over my chair? Is this a potent communication of her readiness to separate and, at some level, surpass me? Sitting in my chair, she almost sounds and acts like the older one in our duet. It is my old, solid and comfortable chair but something about her exudes a sense of newness and ascendency. I am made to feel distant from her and alone. Then Nicole tries to reach out to me, to bridge the gap between us. "Here, let's play this video game, I'll show you how to do it." With her pocket game player, Nicole brings up a video game that involves scoring points. She explains the game, but I have no idea what she is talking about. Looking at the screen I am at a complete loss. She tries to show me through example. As images flash across the screen her thumbs hover over the control buttons, rapidly pressing them. She quickly racks up point after point. I try to make sense of it, but I am at a loss. Without any experience in playing video games I am out of my league. Nicole becomes impatient as I fail miserably. Not only can't I figure out how to play the game, but my thumbs aren't fast enough. Old? Are my reflexes telling me something? Is my body unable to keep up with hers in this very basic way? Do I experience a disquieting sensation in connection to her evolving and budding body and my older, slower (but still vital) self? I am forced to consider her youth and promise in relation to my experience and wisdom gained through the years. These latter qualities provide me with value and comfort, and I find assurance in their essential contribution to my clinical work with Nicole.

In the video-game match with me, Nicole is victorious. She gloats and then dangles the silver bracelet adorning her wrist. "My boyfriend gave this to me for my birthday. Isn't it pretty?" We talk about her boyfriend, school and friends. She wants to terminate therapy. She doesn't need me. For some time, we have been winding down and are planning on ending in a couple of weeks.

Then, in the midst of all of this, Nicole suddenly gets up, comes over, and warmly hugs me. For a brief second she is the little girl I first met. "I think it's going to be harder for you than for me," she declares referring to our upcoming termination. She's probably right. She is moving on; I am being left behind, and I know that I will miss her. In my moment of reflexive anger at her hurtful comment, I had lost that feeling. It now returns in response to her act of tenderness.

Self-States, Preadolescence, and Adolescence:
Hugs and Boys

Nicole and I have a history together that spans six years. Each of us also has a history (more in my case) that is quite separate from each other's lives. She is now on the cusp of adolescence in both her physical and psychosocial development. In this vignette you can hear the voice of the young girl I met six years ago—the one who tries to recreate our earlier way of being together and wants to play another game with me, in this instance a video game; and she is the same one who sweetly and impulsively gives me a quick hug. That little girl is still in the room, making periodic appearances in our sessions. At the same time, Nicole, the now early adolescent, has a more continuous presence. She is separating and becoming more autonomous. She looks to the future and all its possibilities while I am more caught in the past and present. Nicole is dressed in a hip, preteen outfit, has a strut and confidence to her stride, and focuses on boys—or at least one in particular, Ryan. In showing off her shiny bracelet and announcing that her boyfriend gave it to her, Nicole asserts her desirability as a sexual object (albeit at a 12-year-old level) and flaunts her personal success and happiness at having a boyfriend. She is not subtle as she confirms to herself, and to me, a more grown-up state in her development.

What is it like for Nicole to have moments in our short 45 minutes of being all these different selves—the more grown-up and self-assured person in the analyst's chair, the young girl who first came to see me and has such warm and tender feelings for me, and the desirable young woman who is the object of a boy's attention? As Bromberg points out, each state is filled with specific memories and ways of relating. And, as her therapist, I too have moments reacting to her different states, even as I respond to my own memories and feelings called forth in the session with her. How does Nicole, the preteen, bridge the gap with Nicole the almost teenager? Can her effort to engage me in a videogame be seen as her attempt to link her younger self with her more adolescent self, or as a way to connect us? Can it serve both purposes? How do I bridge that gap of time and space within myself and with her? Can I?

Her focus on boys and schoolmates is in keeping with a normal emphasis on peers at this age. In thinking about all the changes that Nicole is going through, it isn't surprising that the role of peers becomes so central to her life. She and her fellow adolescents are colleagues, passing through unchartered territory that is both exciting and scary. They can share experiences with each other and know first-hand and in a here-and-now way, what the other might be feeling. Adults may serve as guideposts but they exist in a space and time that is outside of this adolescent experience. For many adults, adolescent reality is but a distant memory and—at least in my experience and perhaps the experience of others—one gratefully left behind. Peers are fellow travelers.

In calling me "old," Nicole asserts our separateness. She is a young girl blossoming before my eyes even as my body is changing—not so drastically, but ever yielding to the forces of gravity and age. At this moment, Nicole reminds me that I am an outsider—an adult outside of her peer group—who exists, at one of these moments, to admire and confirm her success and development. Somewhat reluctantly I see this as a natural state of affairs. These moments of pride and self-confidence are experiences, given existence in this exchange with me, that form building blocks, contributing to who she is and solidifying a sense of self. I'm also aware of the possible underlying fear and anxiety about losing me that is so well masked, or disconnected and dissociated by her bravado and eagerness for autonomy and separation. Nonetheless, the Nicole she will become will also incorporate the smart and unhappy young girl I first met, the wiser, early adolescent she is, and the young woman she is becoming—a girl with the present insight to say: "I think it's going to be harder for you than for me." These self-states can exist side-by-side and, as Bromberg states,

> there is now abundant evidence that the psyche does not start as an integrated whole, but is nonunitary in origin—a mental structure that begins and continues as a multiplicity of self-states that maturationally attain a feeling of coherence which overrides the awareness of discontinuity. This leads to the experience of a cohesive sense of personal identity and the necessary illusion of being—"one self."
>
> (Bromberg, 1998, p. 244)

For Nicole, at this stage in her development, the "illusion of one self" can be even more elusive when she is in the midst of significant pubertal changes in her body and experiencing the hormonal effects on physiology, mood and behavior as these powerful chemicals course through her body at different times and rates. At the same time, Nicole is in the midst of confronting separation from her childhood, me and increasingly, from her parents. Peers, and how she perceives they see her, now take center stage. Increasingly, at certain moments, parents and analyst exist on side stages.

Through my actions, in quietly listening and admiring, I not only offer Nicole a way of seeing herself but also communicate an acceptance of who she is at these different moments. I offer her a steady presence as I also draw on my own memories of adolescence. For instance, her comment about my age thrusts me back into high school recalling my father's 50th birthday and my loudly proclaiming to him: "You're a half-century old!" As I grew older I came to wince at my awareness of the hurtful aspects to my declaration. Did I have some sense of its power to hurt? Did I want to hurt him? And, if so . . . why? Was I fearful of his, or my, growing older? Was there some other motivation at that time? Could it be similar to or different from Nicole's comment to me? I quickly ponder these questions and grapple with my feelings as I respond to Nicole. I note that my father never complained and seemed to brush it off (at least as I remember that long ago time). The adolescent-me (like Nicole) of this moment feels emotional, conflicted and unable to fully sort out what is happening and what I said many years ago. At the same time, the therapist-older-me, like my father, understands the perspectives of youth and the rash bravado that can cover a multitude of feelings as I struggle with the emotional effects of her comment around aging.

In response to Nicole and—like my father—I, too, simply acknowledge that I am older than she and leave that as the totality of my verbal comments. Lachmann and Beebe (1998) draw our attention to the self and to the mutual regulation that takes place in treatment through the interactional exchanges between the participants. "The nature and range of the patient's self-regulation, that is available over the course of treatment, will depend on the quality of the interactive regulation, and the styles of engagement, and self-regulation that both partners bring" (p. 493). Additionally, in the clinical work with preteens and adolescents, there is value in not intellectualizing their experience, potentially taking them out of the experience and further disconnecting them from the self that is present in a particular moment in treatment. Though experiencing some hurt and anger, I am also a little grateful to Nicole for connecting me with my father of long ago (the father of my adolescence), and more than a little admiring, perhaps somewhat grudgingly, of her youthful spunk. Through this, Nicole is linked to a younger and more dependent self as well as her preadolescent self, partly ready and excited to make her own way into the world of boys and peers. In this interaction, I am linked to younger parts of myself and linked to Nicole, with a deeper understanding of Nicole at this stage in her life and in her relationship with me.

Conclusion

Throughout development girls come to inhabit many "new" bodies and experience a multiplicity of self-states in the process. Nicole is but one example of a preadolescent on the cusp of puberty. With puberty, the many physiological and cognitive changes that take place in the bodies of preadolescent and adolescent girls intermingle with changing familial, social, and cultural patterns and needs. Through a variety of interpersonal exchanges, both verbal and nonverbal, therapists can work with children and adolescents to negotiate these complex and evolving developmental stages, life changes and life experiences. Clinicians need to appreciate the depth and significance of the dramatic physiological and the accompanying psychological changes that are taking place in the maturational processes of puberty. This awareness can enhance interactions between therapists and their female patients and, perhaps, contribute to preventing the development of more problematic ways of coping with the many problems in living that confront preadolescent and adolescent girls. The potentially troubling waters of puberty need not be lasting.

Notes

1. Estrogen is a major player affecting a girl's body, mind, and behavior, but there are many other hormones that are involved, including progesterone, testosterone, oxytocin, etc.

2. This is not meant to be a complete summary; for a more detailed accounting of development in girls, you are referred to references on adrenarche, puberty and physiological development in girls.
3. There are other hormones at play in girls, including small amounts of testosterone, that affect how a girl sees, feels, and acts.
4. Consider the potential impact of the flat face from a mother's Botox injections on the female infant (Brizendine, 2006, p. 15).
5. The emphasis on interpersonal experience of all infants is highlighted in the developmental theories of attachment (Bowlby, 1969, 1973, 1980; Fonagy & Target, 1997; Fonagy, 2001) and attunement (Stern, 1977, 1984, 1985). Attachment draws our attention to the critical early connection between caregiver and infant—as well as the essential ties between human beings, including close friends, lovers, and many therapist–patient relationships. Stern highlights the importance of responsive care giving, affectively attuned to the physical and emotional needs of the infant.
6. Androgens are hormones "usually associated with aggression in both males and females." In females androgens, such as testosterone, are present and circulating in varying amounts and may contribute to aggressive impulses (Brizendine, 2006, p. 54).
7. Potential vulnerability may include such issues as childhood anxiety and perfectionism, shyness, and sensitivity to perceived criticism (Le Grange & Lock, 2011).

References

Aron, L., & Anderson, F. S. (1998). *Relational perspectives on the body.* Hillsdale, NJ: Analytic Press.
Bowlby, J. (1969). Attachment and loss: Vol. 1: Attachment. *The International Psycho-Analytical Library* (Vol. 79, pp. 1–401). London: Hogarth Press.
Bowlby, J. (1973). Attachment and loss: Vol. 2: Separation. *The International Psycho-Analytical Library* (Vol. 95, pp. 1–429). London: Hogarth Press.
Bowlby, J. (1980). Attachment and Loss: Vol. 3: Loss, sadness and depression. *The International Psycho-Analytical Library* (Vol. 109, pp. 1–462). London: Hogarth Press.
Brizendine, L. (2006). *The female brain.* New York: Three Rivers Press.
Bromberg, P. (1998). *Standing in the spaces.* Hillsdale, NJ: Analytic Press.
Buechler, S. (2008). *Making a difference in patients' lives: Emotional experience in the therapeutic setting.* New York: Routledge.
Campbell, B. (2011). Adrenarche and middle childhood. *Human Nature, 22,* 327–349.
Erikson, E. (1979). *Childhood and society.* New York: W. W. Norton.
Ferraro, J. (2013). It's never just about the food! Puberty, eating disorders and the self. *Contemporary Psychoanalysis in Action.* Retrieved from www.psychologytoday.com/blog/contemporary-psychoanalysis-in-action/201302/it-s-never-just-about-the-food
Fonagy, P. (2001). *Attachment Theory and Psychoanalysis.* New York: Other Press.
Fonagy, P., Gergely, G., Jurist, E., & Target, M. (2002). *Affect regulation, mentalization, and the development of the self.* New York: Other Press.
Fonagy, P., & Target, M. (1997). Attachment and reflective function: Their role in self-organization. *Development and Psychopathology, 9,* 679–700.
Freud, S. (1938). Three contributions to the theory of sex. In *The basic writings of Sigmund Freud.* New York: Random House.
Howell, E. F. (2005). *The dissociative mind.* New York: Routledge.
Howell, E. F. (2007). Inside and outside: "Trauma/dissociation/relationality" as a framework for understanding psychic structure and problems in living. *Psychoanalytic Perspectives, 5,* 47–67.

Keel, P. K., Klump, K. L., Miller, K. B., McGue, M., & Iacono, W. G. (2005). Shared transmission of eating disorders and anxiety disorders. *International Journal of Eating Disorders, 38,* 99–105.

Klump, K. L., McGue, M., & Iacono, W. G. (2003). Differential heritability of eating attitudes and behaviors in prepubertal versus pubertal twins. *International Journal of Eating Disorders, 33,* 287–292.

Klump, K. L., Perkins, P. S., Burt, S. A., McGue, M., & Iacono, W. G. (2007). Puberty moderates genetic influences on disordered eating. *Psychological Medicine, 37,* 627–634.

Klump, K. L., Wonderlich, S., Lehoux, P., Lilenfeld, L. R. R., & Bulik, C.M. (2002). Does environment matter? A review of nonshared environment and eating disorders. *International Journal of Eating Disorders, 31,* 118–135.

Kolod, S. (2010). The menstrual cycle as a subject of psychoanalytic inquiry. *Journal of The American Academy of Psychoanalysis and Dynamic Psychiatry, 38,* 77–98.

Lachmann, F., & Beebe, B. (1998). Co-constructing inner and relational processes: Self- and mutual regulation. *Psychoanalytic Psychology, 15,* 480–516.

Le Grange, D., & Lock, J. (2011). *Eating disorders in children and adolescents: A clinical handbook.* New York: Guilford Press.

Mahler, M., Pine, F., & Bergman, A. (1975). *The psychological birth of the human infant: Symbiosis and individuation.* New York: Basic Books.

Putnam, F. W. (1997). *Dissociation in children and adolescents.* New York: Guilford Press.

Rosenfeld, R. L. (2012). Normal adrenarche. *UpToDate.* Retrieved from www.uptodate.com/contents/normal-adrenarche#

Stern, D. (1977). *The first relationship: mother and infant.* Cambridge, MA: Harvard University Press.

Stern, D. (1984). Affect attunement. In J. D. Call, E. Galenson, & R. L. Tyson (Eds.), *Frontiers of infant psychiatry* (pp. 2, 3–14). New York: Basic Books.

Stern, D. (1985). *The interpersonal world of the infant: A view from psychoanalysis and developmental psychology.* New York: Basic Books.

Strober, M., & Peris, T. (2011). The role of family environment in etiology: A neuroscience perspective. In D. Le Grange & J. Lock (Eds.), *Eating disorders in children and adolescents: A clinical handbook* (pp. 34–60). New York: Guilford Press.

Sullivan, H. S. (1953). *The interpersonal theory of psychiatry.* New York: W. W. Norton.

Yurgelun-Todd, D. (2002). Inside the teenage brain [Interview]. *Frontline.* Program #2011. Retrieved from www.pbs.org/wgbh/pages/frontline/shows/teenbrain/interviews/todd.html

Yurgelun-Todd, D. (2007). Emotional and cognitive changes during adolescence. *Current Opinion in Neurobiology, 17,* 251–257.

11

'THE CIRCLE (CYCLE) GAME'

Ovarian Hormones, Self-States, and Appetites

Sue Kolod

It is quite common for a woman to experience several different self-states accompanying her menstrual cycle, as the production of ovarian hormones ebbs and flows. A self-state, as defined by Bromberg, is an "internally coherent aspect of the self . . . with its own narrative, its own memory configuration, its own perceptual reality, and its own style of relatedness to others" (1998, p. 245). These different self-states can be quite dissociated from each other (i.e., the premenstrual self loses contact with her postmenstrual self and vice versa).

Appetites, cravings, and body image can all vary in relation to the phases of the menstrual cycle and production of ovarian hormones. This can have implications for the treatment of eating disorders: Just as women with mood disorders are more prone to an increase in symptoms during the premenstrual phase, women who express anxiety and depression through disordered eating often show an increase in symptoms during the premenstrual phase. Likewise, when the production of ovarian hormones slows down and finally stops at perimenopause and menopause, the *loss* of cyclicy can affect appetites, mood, body image and sense of self.

Cyclic hormonal experience is basic to adult female life. It is an experience that has no male correlate. To a greater or lesser degree, all women are familiar with the fluctuations in mood and self-state that accompany the menstrual cycle. Each woman reacts to her hormonal cycle differently; some women go through life with very little reaction to hormonal shifts while others react dramatically. Across a woman's lifetime, there can be some times when she responds more powerfully to her hormonal body than others. The hormonal shifts that women experience can be used in the service of understanding and furthering therapeutic action.

I will begin with some general clinical observations about the role of ovarian hormones and cyclicity and then focus on specific areas of functioning that are affected by hormones, such as mood, affect, self-experience, sexuality, and appetite.

It has become the cultural norm to assume that the moods and perceptions occurring during the premenstrual phase are not something to take seriously or even to consider. Female patients frequently relate incidents in which they became anxious, angry, and upset and then negated or disavowed these thoughts, feelings, and perceptions by the statement, "I was just PMSing." Analyst and patient may collude to ignore or disqualify material reported while under the influence of what I term the "hormonal body." Thus, the question of how the hormonal body affects the psyche never gets addressed. The avoidance of this topic in psychoanalytic writing is a type of "selective inattention" (Sullivan, 1954) which serves to keep hormonal experience out of awareness.

Christiane Northrup is a gynecologist and popular author whose best selling books on the subject of the hormonal body and its impact on women have changed the ways that contemporary women think about their hormonal experience. Northrup questions the notion that the thoughts and perceptions of women during the premenstrual phase are distorted. To the contrary, she maintains that during this phase women tend to contact and articulate the aspects of their lives that are truly unsatisfying. "This is a reflective time, looking back . . . on the negative or difficult aspects of our lives that need to be changed or adjusted" (1994, p. 105).

Northrup states that the demands of daily life make it possible for a woman to dissociate from her own needs and care of herself—both physical and emotional. During the premenstrual phase she may turn her attention to her own needs and the ways in which those needs are not being met. This is the time when women are "more in tune with their inner knowing and with what isn't working in their lives" (p. 107). Northrup acknowledges the emotionality that often occurs during the premenstrual phase but insists that, "the tears are always related to something that holds meaning for us" (p. 108). She urges women to pay attention to the physical and emotional changes that occur during the pre-menstrual and menstrual phases and notes that many stress-related diseases could be lessened or avoided if women simply paid more attention to these hormonal shifts and reacted to them.

Avoidance of the Hormonal Body in Contemporary Psychoanalytic Literature

In contrast to the popular authors such as Northup, the impact of the hormonal body on the psyche is a subject that is virtually absent from contemporary psychoanalytic writing. It is seldom addressed in clinical case seminars and seems to be almost taboo. For example, several years ago at a psychoanalytic conference I presented a paper that raised the issue of how to use hormonal experience in clinical work. Two noted feminist psychoanalysts were also on the panel, both about 10 years older than I. Both were uncomfortable with the focus on female hormonal experience. Later, each voiced concerns that this was not a suitable topic for psychoanalytic inquiry and should probably be avoided.

The reason for the this concern and avoidance, I believe, is the stigmatization and sexism to which women have been subjected and the ways in which the female hormonal body has been used to support a negative view of women. Classical psychoanalytic theories of female development used the hormonal body to support a negative view of women (Freud, 1933; Deutsch, 1945). Although it is beyond the scope of this chapter to fully review the classical position on female development, some salient features of the classical psychoanalytic position on women include the following:

1. Anatomy is fate (i.e., the basic nature of woman is determined by her anatomy). Female anatomy was presumed to be inferior in comparison to the anatomy of men, which was taken as the universal standard.
2. Penis envy (i.e., the desire for a penis) is a universal fact of normal feminine psychology.
3. Masochism and passivity are outgrowths of normal feminine development.
4. Faulty superego development is a normal part of feminine development as a result of the castration complex (Marmor, 2004).

Karen Horney, a contemporary of Freud and Deutsch, moved away from the "anatomy is destiny" hypothesis (1924). She was critical of Freud's idea of penis envy and believed that although women might be jealous of men's power in the world it was not related to the penis, per se. Horney, who was influenced by Erich Fromm and Harry Stack Sullivan, was more attuned to the ways in which society and cultural factors affected women's views of themselves. This sets up the dichotomy—Deutsch on the one hand, focusing on the female body as the culprit for women's sense of inferiority, and Horney on the other, expressing the view that societal and cultural factors create a sense of inferiority in women. This split, which equates a focus on the body with sexism, is still evident in the avoidance of the body in psychoanalytic theories of female development.

Although many women analysts, in addition to Horney, have published original ideas about female development and sexuality that challenge the classical position (Thompson, 1937; Dinnerstein, 1976; Chodorow, 2003, 2004; Benjamin, 1996, 2004; Dimen, 1997; Goldner, 1991; Harris, 1991, 1997, to name a few), Freud's original notions about women persist today (Yonke & Barnett, 2001).

The second-wave feminists rightly took exception to the psychoanalytic view of female development and regression. Friedan (1963) questioned the axiom that "anatomy is destiny" and regarded concepts such as penis envy and the castration complex as ways of disempowering women. She and others noted that attention to the effect of hormonal shifts was used against women as a way of demonstrating instability; that women are unfit to serve in positions of power, particularly during their reproductive years. But what began as a challenge to the notion that women are slaves to their menstrual cycles became an avoidance of the hormonal body altogether. Laan and Everaerd noted, "Feminists have long criticized the notion that behavior and abilities of women are uniquely determined by their biology. This criticism led to an almost total rejection of the role of biology in the construction of gender. It also contributed, unfortunately, to an image of female sexuality devoid of the body" (Laan & Everaerd, 1995, p. 22).

Therese Benedek

One notable exception to the stigmatizing psychoanalytic theories on female development is the work of Theresa Benedek. Benedek was a psychoanalyst and a researcher who considered psychoanalysis a scientific discipline whose validity could be proven through scientific methods. In her pioneering work, Benedek considered female development on its own—not in comparison to male development.

Benedek (Benedek & Rubenstein, 1939) reportedly had an uncanny ability listen to a female patient's clinical material and to predict with accuracy the phase of her menstrual cycle. In 1939, she conducted research with Boris Rubenstein, a gynecologist, in which she studied the psychotherapy records of a group of female patients, while Rubenstein studied the ovarian hormonal cycles of the same women. The two investigators worked independently. Also, any references to menstruation or allusions that might provide clues to the patient's cycle phase were redacted from the transcripts.

By looking at the psychotherapy notes, especially of dreams, Benedek (Benedek & Rubenstein, 1939) was able to predict the phase of the patient's menstrual cycle. She found that just before ovulation, when estrogen levels were at their highest, women's emotions and behaviors were directed toward the outer world. At ovulation, women were more relaxed and content and receptive to being cared for and loved by others. During the premenstrual phase women were most likely to be focused on themselves and involved in inward-directed activity. Benedek (Benedek & Rubenstein, 1939) noted that during the premenstrual phase, women were much more prone to experience dysphoric emotions, including depression, anxiety, anger, and a feeling of tension. They were more likely to have diminished frustration tolerance and to be emotionally labile. These negative experiences were likely to dramatically improve with the onset of menstruation. Although the focus of Benedek's research was not eating disorders, her work is relevant. Patients with eating disorders seek external stimulation through bingeing and purging as a way of soothing their internal turmoil.

Benedek (Benedek & Rubenstein, 1939) observed that sexuality also had different meanings and functions during the different cycles. During the preovulatory phase, sexuality as expressed in associations, fantasies, and dreams was organized around pleasurable stimulation, novelty seeking, and romantic/erotic scenarios. During the luteal phase, however, sexual fantasies involved procreational themes, such as having babies, building a home, and needing to be cared for and protected.

The work of Benedek and Rubinstein (1939) presages the research from evolutionary biology that I will discuss later.

Cyclicity and Self-States

It can be useful to view cyclical hormonal experience in terms of self-states. The self, as described in the relational literature, is not a unitary entity but rather is composed of a multiplicity of "self-states" that are more or less integrated with one another. The mind, according to Bromberg, "is a configuration of discontinuous, shifting states, with varying degrees of access to perception and cognition." (1998, p. 225) As stated previously, it is quite common for a woman to experience several different self-states accompanying her menstrual cycle. These different self-states can be quite dissociated from each other (i.e., the premenstrual self loses contact with her postmenstrual self and vice versa). Patients who use dissociation as a way of coping with unpleasant affects, memories, and experiences are sometimes able to access and connect with dissociated self-states during the premenstrual phase. The following clinical example illustrates the ways in which a patient's premenstrual experience was used to connect with dissociated material.

Amy

Amy first consulted with me when she was in her early 30s. She was suffering from depression and had developed a severe eating disorder. Amy came from an abusive family background; both parents were alcoholics and she was alternately neglected and physically abused. When she was 19 she married a man 25 years her senior who took on the role of "protector" and "teacher." He had two children from a previous marriage who were only a few years younger than Amy. Amy took care of the children and worshiped and idealized her husband who was controlling, sexually demanding, and tight with money. In addition, her husband, who was a Vietnam veteran and suffered from post traumatic stress disorder, could become quite abusive with her, both verbally and physically.

At the time Amy first consulted with me, the children were grown and out of the house. Amy's husband had begun staying out late at night and when he came home gave her excuses that did not make sense to her. Accounts of her husband's explanations made it obvious to me that he was lying to her. For example, she once found a used condom in the waste basket. When she confronted her husband with the condom he told her he was "just trying on a new brand to see if it fit." He had become increasingly controlling with money and flew into a rage if Amy spent any money without first asking his permission.

Amy became severely depressed and developed bulimia. She reported to me that she was purging every morning and sometimes later in the day as well. She was still in a state of denial about her husband and his late-night activities and blamed herself and her emotional instability for their marital problems. After a year of psychotherapy in which I focused on her emotional life and her nutritionist focused on her food intake, Amy's depression had lifted and her bulimia was under control, but she still idealized her husband and made excuses for his behavior and his lying. However, I began to notice that when she was suffering with premenstrual tension she was able, for a few days, to view her marriage and her husband more realistically. She started to question his truthfulness and to complain about his controlling behavior. Her premenstrual self-state provided us with a window of opportunity to address issues that were not usually available for examination. For a few days the veil was lifted, and Amy was able to see things about her husband and her marriage that were usually dissociated. But as soon as she got her period, the problems and her unhappiness were trivialized as "just PMSing".

Over the course of several years, by discussing and referring back to her premenstrual experience, Amy started to give credence to these thoughts and feelings. By helping Amy to see that her PMS thoughts and feelings were valid, she was able, eventually, to come to the realization that she wanted to leave the relationship. Ultimately, Amy got a divorce.

This vignette demonstrates that in our clinical work we should ask questions and draw attention to hormonal experience and the impact of the hormonal body on the psyche. It is useful to conduct a detailed inquiry (Sullivan, 1954; Levenson, 1991) concerning menstrual history and current symptoms. Some women report that they do not experience premenstrual symptoms at all—particularly if they are on birth control pills. However, many women are very disturbed and confused by the thoughts, feelings, and perceptions that occur during the premenstrual phase and have not talked about this with anyone before. The feeling of "going crazy" for a few days or "not being myself" is very common and upsetting. As with any type of dissociated experience, we need to help patients to contact, articulate, and give credence to all aspects of the self.

Menopause and the Self

From a medical standpoint, menopause involves the attenuation and gradual cessation of the production of ovarian hormones. However, the combination of physical, emotional, and social factors that accompany the cessation of hormones can create a crisis in a woman's identity. Children are leaving home, parents are getting sick and dying, beauty is fading—all the elements that have defined a woman's identity for last 20 to 30 years begin in come apart. This crisis, as many crises do, also creates an opportunity for growth and expansion.

Menopause, like menstruation, is ignored in contemporary psychoanalytic literature. I have frequently attended case presentations where the discussion focused a woman in her late 40s or early 50s suffering from depression, mood swings, difficulty in her marriage, problems with sex drive, loss of self, feeling as if she's going crazy; and the issue of menopause never came up. In the standard edition of the *Collected Works of Sigmund Freud* there is a single entry for menopause or the "climacteric" and it has to do with male menopause. (Freud, 1937, vol. 3, pp. 101–112).

Why is this developmental milestone in the life of a woman ignored in the psychoanalytic literature? I will outline three factors that contribute to the lack of attention paid to menopause.

First, it is difficult to tease out effects of menopause from that of aging in general. Flabby bodies, memory problems, and the changing social roles are all part of aging and thus cannot be blamed on menopause per se. Which factors can be attributed to menopause alone?

Second, as stated previously, whenever there is a focus on female hormones there is a possibility of stigmatization. For example, the diagnosis of involutional melancholia grew out the theories of Helene Deutsch (1945), who hypothesized that menopause reactivated the castration complex in women, and, thus, women inevitably became depressed in menopause. She refers to it as "an incurable narcissistic wound."

And third, menopause is transitory. Like childbirth, it can be hellish while it's going on, but once it is finished it becomes a nonevent or a dissociated self-state. Daly (1997) reported the following:

> Anne is an older woman who dismissed menopause as "nothing at all." Her niece, who had suggested that we interview her, reminded her that she had prepared for death on her fiftieth birthday. She had tidied her life, including her linen cupboard, tying sheets and towels with blue ribbon so that her husband's next wife would think well of her as a housewife. Reminded of this, Anne shrugged and spoke of a day when her husband came home to lunch and she calmly asked him for his handgun because she thought she should shoot herself. Her husband was a doctor. He hid the gun and left the house to return an hour later with a colleague, the superintendent of the local "lunatic asylum." She was tranquilized, admitted, and spent the next six months there. At that stage they told her that she would have electro-convulsive therapy unless she "pulled herself together." She did, returned home, gradually recovered, and is now a hale and hearty seventy-six year-old. The worst part of her experience, she says, was her isolation. "We weren't supposed to talk about problems."
>
> (pp. 165–166)

The lack of attention in the literature parallels many women's sense that they have become invisible, "lost themselves," lost their bearings, are no longer who they once were. It can be a very isolating and confusing experience. Several menopausal women have reported to me, "I feel like I'm going crazy."

To summarize, the hormonal body has a profound impact on the psyche whether it be during the phases of the menstrual cycle or during the process of perimenopause/menopause. Different self-states can emerge and disappear depending on the production or cessation of ovarian hormones.

Hormones and Sexuality

Current research from the field of evolutionary biology and endocrinology demonstrate that estrogen, its presence and absence, has a profound impact on sexual desire and object choice.

"Dual sexuality" refers to the evidence from research that women do, in fact, have a "season" each month in which they are fertile, known as estrus, and that women's estrus sexual interests differ from their sexual interests during the non-fertile times of the cycle, resulting in a "dual sexuality."

Women's menstrual cycles link them with the animal world. It can be uncomfortable to think that hormones affect women in ways of which they are not aware. Since women are able to enjoy sex throughout their menstrual cycle, both when they are fertile and when they are not, the fact that a woman's sexuality may differ during these two phases has been easy to overlook. However, the menstrual cycle, fertility, sexuality, and reproduction are obviously intertwined and interdependent. In most nonhuman animals, copulation occurs only during the period of "heat," or estrus, although some animals do copulate out of season, as well. The question of whether women experience estrus and whether there are changes in women's sexuality and object choices accompanying the menstrual cycle is currently being debated in the fields of endocrinology and evolutionary biology. The results are fascinating and disturbing.

Evolution-minded research on women's sexuality began at the end of the 19th century and continues today. The question of woman's estrus and whether a woman's sexuality changes in response to her menstrual cycle are important contemporary research issues. Evidence of estrus and its impact is a crucial issue for clinicians working with women in psychoanalytic treatment.

Two issues significant for clinical work with woman have emerged from the evolutionary biology research. The first issue is whether and in what way the sex drive is affected by estrus. The second is the ways in which estrus may influence attraction to one's primary partner or to someone outside the couple (EPC, or extra pair copulations).

Thornhill and Gangestad (2008) and Gangestad, Thornhill, and Garver-Apgar (2008) conducted research testing the hypotheses that women would feel more willing to engage in sex outside of a committed pair bond during estrus and would feel more willing to engage in sex with someone with whom they do not feel close. They surveyed women in committed relationships and asked them to fill out questionnaires both at the fertile (ovulatory) phase and also at the luteal (premenstrual) phase. They focused on attitudes toward "sexual opportunism" and sought reaction to such items such as, "I believe in taking my sexual pleasures where I find them"; "The thought of an illicit sex affair excites me"; "Sometimes I'd rather have sex with someone I didn't care about"; and "If an attractive person (of my preferred sex) approached me sexually, it would be hard to resist, no matter how well I knew him/her." The results indicate that "at estrus, they endorsed approximately 25% more items than they did when in the luteal phase" (Gangestad, Thornhill, & Garver-Apgar, 2007, p. 253).

Similarly, Jones et al. (2005) found that women expressed less commitment to their relationship during estrus and a greater willingness to risk the loss of the relationship. During the premenstrual phase, the same women expressed a greater level of commitment to their primary relationship, which the researchers attributed to "selection for increased pursuit of long-term investment from the partner during pregnancy" (Thornhill & Gangestad, 2008, p. 254).

179

Evidence from research supports the idea that women's estrus sexual interests differ from their sexual interests during the nonfertile times of the cycle, resulting in a "dual sexuality." During estrus, women have increased motivation to have sex with a "good genes extra pair partner" for short-term mating, with a high desire for orgasm and sexual satisfaction. These findings indicate that women's estrus sexuality "is an adaptation that functions to achieve conception by a male of high genetic quality, including contingently through extra-pair mating" (Thornhill & Gangestad, 2008, p. 265).

Results of research in evolutionary biology suggest that women are more similar to nonhuman female animals than one would think. The hypothesis of dual sexuality demonstrates that when women are fertile during estrus, they are attracted to a partner perceived as having superior genes who will provide orgasm and sexual satisfaction but not long-term investment. During the premenstrual phase, women are attracted to long-term, committed partners who provide intimacy, investment, and support for offspring. If the woman's primary partner is also sexy, she is less likely to be attracted to someone outside the relationship during estrus.

The following vignette illustrates the concept of dual sexuality and intense attraction to extra-pair mating during estrus. Helen, a 32-year-old lawyer, reports, "It was the same thing every month. Two weeks before my period I'd become very combative with my boyfriend. My anger would build until I could say something mean enough to instigate a fight, and only after I knew he was in as much emotional pain as I was could I finally relax. I think this happened because I got very horny and wanted to sleep with everyone *but* my boyfriend. He has a baby face and I became very attracted to men with more masculine faces during this time. Once I got my period, I was satisfied with my boyfriend. This whole thing stopped when I went on birth control pills. But the down side is my libido has dropped. In retrospect, I think I was getting angry at my boyfriend in the times before my period because I wanted to have sex with other people and felt I couldn't because of the relationship."

Obviously, a major difference between human and nonhuman animals is that humans can reflect on their experience and make judgments and decisions. These findings can be useful in helping female patients understand how their thoughts and feelings, their attraction to one partner or another, may vacillate in response to the menstrual cycle.

As stated above, the different phases of the menstrual cycle can constitute distinct self-states in many woman. Research from evolutionary biology suggests that a woman can experience several different "sexual self-states" across her cycle, referred to as dual sexuality. Knowledge of dual sexuality can help female patients understand their sometimes perplexing and vacillating reactions to sex partners. The evidence for dual sexuality is not well known in the psychoanalytic world, but it should be.

Menopause and Sex Drive

One of the most troubling and least talked about aspects of menopause is a diminishing sex drive. For many women, as cyclicity declines, so does sex drive.

Several female patients have told me that if it weren't for their partner's objection, they would simply give up sex altogether. I have also heard complaints from male patients that their menopausal wives/girlfriends are not longer interested in sex.

This decrease in a woman's sex drive can lead to serious disruptions in the relationship. Problems with decrease in the menopausal woman's libido have been exacerbated by the popularity of Viagra. In the past, the menopausal woman's lessening interest in sex was matched by her husband's/boyfriend's decrease in sexual potency. Now it is possible for men in their middle age and even old age to maintain erections like teenagers.

The decline in sex drive can be addressed in a variety of ways. It can be addressed, for example, in psychotherapy and can provide an opportunity to tackle problems you never thought you could tackle—long-standing problems that have been swept under the rug. In my clinical work with menopausal women, I have found that in addition to the cessation of ovarian hormone production, the accumulation of resentment towards one's partner and other dissociated sexual trauma are two important psychological factors that can contribute to a decline of sexual interest and activity at menopause. I've described a two-part treatment approach that has been quite successful in helping women to reactivate their sex drive, even as ovarian hormones decline (Kolod, 2009).

In the first phase of the treatment, I do a very careful, detailed inquiry (Sullivan, 1954; Levenson, 1991) focusing on the patient's sexual history. In particular, I focus on experiences that may have seemed like adventures at the time but are now felt to be painful, traumatic, humiliating events. The second phase of the treatment focuses on contacting and articulating thoughts and feelings that are erotically compelling to the patient—to facilitate reconnection to her sexual desires. One could call this a detailed inquiry of eroticism. I have found that it requires some degree of courage in these situations, with women who have become anxious and phobic about sex and disconnected from sexual desire, to ask about their sexual fantasies, masturbation practices, and to inquire about details of the sexual experiences that have been arousing to the patient. The therapist may be worried about intrusiveness or afraid she will humiliate the patient further. However, if the therapist patiently and slowly persists, she creates a climate in the room where such things can be discussed openly.

It has been my experience that when a menopausal woman is interested in resuming or reinvigorating her sex life, there are ways to approach the issue. In fact, sometimes difficulties with sexual arousal at menopause can serve as a catalyst to reexamine relationships that have been problematic for a long time.

Estrogen and Appetite

It has often been noted that eating disorders are more prevalent among women and adolescent girls (see Ferraro, Chapter 10) than men, particularly anorexia, bulimia, and binge eating. The greater prevalence of eating disorders among women is usually attributed to cultural attitudes that equate female beauty with a particular body type. However, new research suggests that ovarian hormones and cyclicity may be important biological factors contributing to the increased risk factor for eating disorders in women. Women are more prone to eating disorders than men. Statistics indicate that 80% to 90% of all people who suffer from eating disorders are women. This is usually explained by "cultural" differences: In the fashion industry, media and cinema, female beauty is synonymous with a thin body; girls are brainwashed to believe they must have little or no body fat to be attractive. But this is not the whole story. New research[1] suggests that the menstrual cycle and the production of sex hormones are equal, or even more important, factors. Although both men and women produce sex hormones, women experience a monthly hormonal cycle from puberty to menopause. And the cyclical nature of sex hormone production has a powerful impact on appetite for both human and nonhuman female animals. Although very little has been written on this subject, many women know intuitively that their relation to food changes across the menstrual cycle. It is common in my psychotherapy practice to hear female patients comment, "I was PMSing and couldn't stop eating" or "I always binge on chocolate right before I get my period."

Theresa Kinsella, MS, RD, CDN, a nutritionist in New York City who specializes in work with eating-disordered women reports, "I have one client who is overweight and a binge eater. She calls her PMS phase 'the monster' and has cravings for chocolate, frozen yogurt, and candy. 'But it's over,' the client observes, 'the second I start to bleed.'"

Kelly Klump, PhD, a research psychologist and professor at Michigan State University, studies the etiology of eating disorders with an emphasis on genetic and neurobiological factors. Klump and associates (2008) have demonstrated empirically that certain hormones are implicated, not only with regard to changes in appetite during the menstrual cycle but in body image as well. In a recent issue of the *International Journal of Eating Disorders*, Klump and her associates (Racine, 2012) examined changes across the menstrual cycle in two independent samples of women and found a direct effect of sex hormones on both appetite and body image.

The researchers found that both binge eating and body dissatisfaction peaked during the premenstrual phase, when there is increased progesterone production. Estrogen, highest just before ovulation in the follicular phase, has been found to be an appetite suppressant. In a recent conversation, Klump told me (personal communication, 2013) that binge eating during the premenstrual phase and appetite suppression during the follicular phase is also found in nonhuman animals. Animals show the same pattern of binge eating during the premenstrual phase and appetite suppression during the follicular phase. So, in addition to cultural factors, biology clearly contributes to female eating behavior.

Klump et al. (2008) also found that during the premenstrual phase, when progesterone production is at its highest, women were less satisfied with their bodies. How do hormones affect body (dis)satisfaction? Klump et al. (2008) hypothesized that progesterone leads to binge eating, which then triggers body dissatisfaction.

In addition, progesterone contributes to premenstrual anxiety, a state that can make women feel more critical of their bodies.

What are the implications of this research for the treatment of eating disorders? Just as women with mood disorders are more prone to an increase in symptoms during the premenstrual phase, women who express anxiety and depression through disordered eating, particularly binge eating, would be expected to show an increase in symptoms during the premenstrual phase. This is exactly what Klump et al.'s (2008) research found.

Jean Petrucelli, PhD, director and co-founder of the Eating Disorders, Compulsions and Addictions Service at the William Alanson White Institute in New York, emphasizes the importance of creative treatment strategies. She asserts that eating disorder symptoms are not something to simply eradicate but rather part of a story about the patient's relational experience with caretakers. She stresses the importance of helping patients become aware of all that contributes to their disordered eating.

Petrucelli (2008; see Chapter 1) often recommends that patients keep a food journal as a vehicle for examining symptoms in analytic treatment. The journal is a record of eating times, locations, and food choices as well as associated feelings and eating-disorder "behaviors." She may suggest patients email a report of their weekly food intake and other ingested substances (alcohol, laxatives, diuretics, drugs, etc.) prior to meeting with her. Pictures of plates of food may also be included when portion sizes are in question. In this way, the eating behavior is engaged and experienced by both analyst and patient. Active documentation helps alert the patient to feelings and experiences that trigger disordered eating. Sharing this information on a real-time basis brings the analyst into a relationship with the patient and her eating disorders. Given the new research findings implicating sex hormones in eating behavior, it is useful to expand the journal to include notes about the timing of menstrual cycle phases.

Some Thoughts for Further Consideration

It is my hope that this chapter will stimulate psychotherapists to investigate the hormonal body and its impact on the psyche, particularly with female patients. The menstrual cycle, pregnancy, perimenopause, and menopause all have a profound impact on the mood, thought processes, self-concept, and appetites of many women, and this topic has been ignored and avoided in the psychoanalytic literature. Several questions have occurred to me while writing this chapter: How many psychotherapists actually know the menstrual histories of their patients or have asked anything about their patients' hormonal experience? How frequently do clinicians use symptoms that are only experienced and expressed during premenstrual states as evidence of psychiatric disorders, such as borderline personality disorder? How might hormonal experience influence transference/countertransference phenomena in any way? How do the various shifts in one's hormonal cycle affect the course of desire, appetite, and disordered eating over time? These questions are all worthy of further investigation and research. But in the meantime, it might be enough just to ask and think about these issues with one's patients.

Note

1. Bautista, Martinez-Samayoa, and Zambrano (2011); Eckel, (2011); Edler, Lipson, and Keel, (2007); Klump, Keel, Culbert, and Edler (2008); Racine et al. (2012).

References

Bautista, C. J., Martinez-Samayoa, P. M., & Zambrano, E. (2011). Sex steroids regulation of appetitive behavior. *Mini Rev. Med. Chem., 12*(11), 1107–1118.

Benedek, T., & Rubenstein, B. (1939). Correlations between ovarian activity and psychodynamic processes: The ovulatory phase. *Psychosomatic Medicine, 1*(2), 245–270.

Benjamin, J. (1996). In defense of gender ambiguity. *Gender and Psychoanalysis, 1*, 27–43.

——— (2004). Deconstructing femininity: Understanding "passivity" and the daughter position. *An. Psychoanal.,* 32, 45–57.

Bromberg, P. (1998). *Standing in the spaces.* Hillsdale, NJ: Analytic Press.

Chodorow, N. (2003). Too late: Ambivalence about motherhood, choice and time. *JAPA, 51,* 1181–1198.

——— (2004). Psychoanalysis and women: A personal 35 year retrospective. *An. Psychoanal. 32,* 101–129.

Daly, J. (1997). Facing change: Women speaking about menopause. In *Reinterpreting menopause* (pp. 165–166). New York: Routledge Press.

——— (1945). *The psychology of women.* New York: Grune & Stratton.

Deutsch, H. (1925). The psychology of women's sexual functions. In R. Fleiss (Ed.), *The psychoanalyst reader.* New York: International University Press 1948.

Dimen, M. (1997). The engagement between psychoanalysis and feminism. *Contemporary Psychoanalysis, 33,* 527–548.

Dinnerstein, D. (1976). *The mermaid and the minotaur.* New York: Harper & Row.

Eckel, L. A. (2011). The ovarian hormone estradiol plays a crucial role in the control of food intake in females. *Physiol Behav., 104*(4), 517–24.

Edler, C., Lipson, S. F., & Keel, P. K. (2007). Ovarian hormones and binge eating in bulimia nervosa. *Psychol Med., 37,* 131–141.

Freud, S. (1933). The psychology of women. In *New introductory lectures on psychoanalysis.* New York: W.W. Norton.

——— (1937). Analysis terminable and interminable. *Collected Works of Sigmund Freud: Standard Edition, 23,* 226.

Friedan, B. (1963). *The feminine mystique.* New York: W. W. Norton.

Gangestad, S., Thornhill, R., & Garver-Apgar, C. E. (2007). Fertility in the cycle predicts women's interest in sexual opportunism. Manuscript submitted for publication.

Gangestad, S., Thornhill, R., & Garver-Apgar, C. E. (2010). Fertility in the cycle predicts women's interest in sexual opportunism. *Evolution and Human Behavior, 31,* 400–410.

Goldner, V. (1991). Toward a critical relational theory of gender. *Psychoanal. Dial., 1,* 249–272.

Harris, A. (1991). Gender as contradiction. *Psychoanal. Dial., 1,* 197–224.

——— (1997). Aggression, envy and ambition: Circulating tensions in women's psychic life. *Gender and Psychoanalysis, 2,* 292–325.

Horney, K. (1924). On the genesis of the castration complex in women. *Int. J. Psycho-Anal., 5,* 50–65.

Jones, B. C., Little, A. C., Boothroyd, L., DeBrune, L. M., Feinberg, D. R., & LawSmith, M. J. (2005). Commitment to relationships and preferences for femininity and apparent health in faces are strongest on days of the menstrual cycle when progesterone level is high. *Hormones and Behavior, 48*, 283–290.

Klump, K. L., Keel, P. K., Culbert, K. M., & Edler, C. (2008). Ovarian hormones and binge eating: Exploring associations in community samples. *Psychol. Med., 38*, 1749–1757.

Kolod, S. (2009). Menopause and sexuality. *Contemp. Psychoanal., 45*, 26–43.

Laan, E., & Everaerd, W. (1995). Determinants of female sexual arousal: Psychophysiological theory and data. *Annual Review of Sex Research, 6*, 32–77.

Levenson, E. (1991). *The purloined self.* New York: Contemporary Psychoanalysis Books.

Marmor, J. (2004). Changing patterns of femininity: Psychoanalytic implications. *J. Amer. Acad. Psychoanal., 32*, 7–20.

Northrup, C. (1994). *Women's bodies, women's wisdom.* New York: Bantam Books.

Petrucelli, J. (2004). Treating eating disorders. In R. Coombs (Ed.), *Handbook of addictive disorders: A practical guide to diagnosis and treatment* (Chapter 10). Hillsdale, NJ: Wiley & Sons.

Racine, C., Culbert, K. M., Keel, P. K., Sisk, C. L., Burt, S. A., & Klump, K. L. (2012). Differential associations between ovarian hormones and disordered eating symptoms across the menstrual cycle in women. *International Journal of Eating Disorders, 45*, 333–344.

Sullivan, H. S. (1954). *The psychiatric interview.* New York: W. W. Norton.

Thompson, C. (1937). Sexuality: Karen Horney. The problem of female masochism. *Int. J. Psychoanal., 18*, 64–65.

Thornhill, R., & Gangestad, W. (2008). *The evolutionary biology of human female sexuality.* New York: Oxford University Press.

Yonke, A., & Barnett, M. (2001). Persistence of early psychoanalytic thought about women. *Gender and Psychoanalysis, 6*, 53–73.

12

'BODY AND SOUL'

Eating Disorders in the Orthodox Jewish Population

Caryn Gorden and Sharon Kofman

Eating Disorders: What's Orthodox Judaism Got to Do With It?

Caryn Gorden

Prevalence of Disordered Eating in the Orthodox Jewish Population

There is increasing concern over the emergent phenomenon of eating disorders in the Orthodox Jewish population. Because little formal research has been conducted to determine whether the proportionately high number of eating disorders in this population points to a rise in frequency of incidence or reporting, the data is inconclusive and the controversy continues. The same deliberation regarding the overrepresentation of eating disorders in the general Jewish population similarly remains ongoing. Some speculate that the high numbers are equivalent to those in all upwardly mobile groups (of which Jews are mostly members) and attributable to the same media messages of thinness, as well as the relentless pressures and conflicts regarding achievement and the heightened need for control.

The eating-disorder literature has identified cultural beliefs and attitudes as important contributors in the development of pathological eating issues (Katzman & Lee, 1997). Indeed, prevalence of eating disorders appears sensitive to both culture and time, as different racial and ethnic groups in the U.S. and abroad display varying rates of eating disorders across time as cultures evolve (Miller & Pumariega, 2001, p. 93). In considering eating disorders in both the general Jewish and Orthodox Jewish population, there are distinct sociocultural and historical factors that may synergistically contribute to putting this population at risk for disordered eating. Some of those factors include the paradoxical messages inherent in Judaism, the centrality of food, the significance of family, the *shidduch* phenomenon, and traumas of the Holocaust. Permeating all these factors is the issue of religious observance, which may for certain individuals potentiate a cascade of psychodynamic and social conflicts. This may be truer now because

186

the recent shift of orthodoxy to the right demands an increased, effortful negotiation of the tension between a traditional culture and a modern secular world.

Preliminary research findings illustrate the complexity inherent in examining the effects of religion on body image dissatisfaction and disordered eating (Feinson & Meir, 2012). Some findings suggest that any religious fundamentalism or high level of rigidity related to religiosity might correlate with body issues and disordered eating (Smith, Richards, & Maglio, 2004). However, these results are currently inconclusive and have not yet been consistently borne out in studies with Orthodox and ultra Orthodox Jewish women. Instead, religious adherence has been shown to have mixed effects, both insulating and protecting against eating disorders (Gluck & Geliebter, 2002; Latzer, Tzischinsky, & Gefen, 2007), as well as serving neither as a risk nor buffer regarding their development (Feinson & Meir, 2012). These inconsistent findings are understood in part to the way that clinical studies confound spirituality and organized religion, subsuming them under one entity referred to as religion, when indeed they are different constructs (Weinberger-Litman, 2007). Additionally, the characteristics of extrinsic and intrinsic religiosity intersect with spirituality and organized religion, each denoting a different attitude and experience of religion. For extrinsic individuals, religion provides a means to an end while for intrinsic individuals religion is an end in itself (Allport & Ross, 1967). Therefore, the dimensions of spirituality, religiosity, and intrinsic and extrinsic orientation must be unpacked when considering the role that religion plays (protecting against or facilitating) in the development of eating disorders.

We are not suggesting a causal relationship between Orthodox Judaism and eating disorders but rather are interested in any possible correlation and/or intersection. Specifically, we are considering which sociocultural, religious, and historical factors may contribute to heightening exposure to this pathology. We are also interested in helping clinicians understand and make use of the ways that these features can link up with psychodynamic conflicts and in suggesting possible directions for future research.

Forbidden Fruit: A Fundamental Paradox

The richness and complexity of Jewish culture and religion ensues in part from its intrinsic dialectic and paradoxical nature, where religious imperatives and rituals may in practice contradict their original intentionality. Indeed, the implicit cultural expectations of Judaism may be incongruous with their stated and prescribed social roles. These and other layered dualities and mixed messages are inextricably woven through many fundamental aspects of Judaism. While the ambiguous Talmudic meanings and arguments of "on the one hand . . . but on the other hand" are hallmark characteristics of Jewish exegesis, this spirit of inquiry and curiosity is oddly juxtaposed with exacting rules and regulations that may generate certainty, rigidity, and literality. This essential contradictory component is exemplified through countless paradigms of Orthodox Jewish observance. For instance, Jewish scripture celebrates the body and sexuality, yet the numerous corresponding regulations and hence propensity for asceticism (i.e., law of circumcision, cutting of hair and beards, covering hair, laws of family purity) communicate a mixed message and sanction ambivalence regarding physicality and desire. Women are taught *tzniut* (modesty) about how to dress, and which parts of the body may or may not be revealed. Yet today's modern *shetel* (hair covering) often enhances an Orthodox Jewish woman's attractiveness and sexual appeal, and the religious male's obligation and concern with female modesty may unwittingly contribute to a sexual preoccupation and arousal. Negotiating the various tensions while living fully in the liminal spaces between them is one of the many enduring challenges facing observant Jews.

The theoretical literature on the cultural determinants of eating disorders identifies how disordered eating may result from an individual's failed attempts to negotiate or straddle two conflicting cultural worlds, particularly when values about physical aesthetics are implicated (Miller & Pumariega, 2001). This notion has been similarly raised regarding the efforts to negotiate challenging social expectations, transitions, or generational disparities (Katzman & Lee, 1997). In this paradigm the eating disorder can be understood as a byproduct of the endeavor to resolve discordant demands. The theory suggests that cultural conflicts are projected onto the body, which serves as a canvas, symbolizing and communicating the unsolvable dilemma. The eating disorder, while expressed concretely, signifies the conflict (conscious or unconscious) and serves as an embodiment of a protest, wish for power, control, or even self-definition. We are proposing extending this idea to elucidate the challenges Orthodox Jews may confront as they try to negotiate the many contradictions and mixed messages inherent in living an observant life. While organizing one's life around Orthodox Judaism may be a source of joy and meaning for some, others may experience religious observance as a potential conflict—hence a risk for the development of an eating disorder.

Cultural Conflict: Lost in Transition

Orthodox Judaism's recent shift to the right and self-imposed segregation and separation from the modern world has reinforced the schism between observant Jewish existence and the ever-increasing demands of secular life reorganized by modern technology and globalization. The deepening of each of these opposing cultural realities has heightened the dilemma of negotiating the gulf between public and private life, religious ritual, and globalization, as well as traditional and postmodern feminist gender roles. Education, intellectual pursuit, and professional success have always been highly valued by the Jewish population. This intense pressure to achieve may often launch the striving individual into the vicissitudes of the secular world. Simultaneously, the rules that accompany orthodoxy demand and privilege spiritual values that may be felt as paradoxical. Many Orthodox men and women are encouraged to meet through a shidduch, marry young, abstain from birth control, and have large families. Women are expected to care for their numerous children and prepare many family meals. While doing so they may also be driven to stay thin (by the surrounding media and culture but also by the shidduch, culture which validates and mirrors the images and WASPy archetypes of the secular world). In the ultra Orthodox communities, wives are also expected to work and support their husbands while they study and pray. The pressures for achievement outside the home combined with all the religious and cultural expectations are not only inherently contradictory but often impossible to fulfill. The individual who consequently develops an eating disorder may be symbolically communicating through the body the (failed) attempts of living in these incongruous worlds. Her resulting eating disorder may function as a last-ditch attempt at perfectionism and an intensified need for control. However, the development of anorexia is also a frantic effort to silence these insurmountable pressures, as the consequential cessation of menstruation and hence diminished potential for childbearing halts the entire enterprise of fulfilling incompatible demands. Compulsive overeating or bulimia that results in obesity can alternatively serve to lessen one's chances of making a good shidduch, thereby also functioning as a desperate solution. Being aware of the potential incongruous demands accompanying an Orthodox Jewish life necessitates the clinician's attunement to these complex issues and mechanisms, so that the clinician keeps them alive and highlighted in treatment.

Body and Soul

Food, an organizing theme in Jewish life, is paramount in the lives of Orthodox Jews due to its role in religious practices and the demands of preparing for and feeding large families. As with other essential elements, however, food is layered and entwined with contradictory messages regarding eating, social and relational role expectations, and body image; food is a source of pleasure and celebration but also a cradle of restriction and denial. Many rituals are embedded in food. Shabbat and holidays are celebrated with family and communal repasts, consisting of special foods often comprising many large meals. Simultaneously there are many regulations surrounding food, including blessings related to specific food consumption and ritual hand washing. Laws of kashrut (keeping kosher) forbid certain foods, prohibit the mixing of dairy and meat, and restrict dairy products for 6 hours after consumption of meat. Besides Yom Kippur there are many other fast days that must be observed. Therefore, the vital role that food plays in Jewish life similarly elevates the likelihood of its role as a medium for symptom expression. Furthermore, as the communal observance of rituals, traditions, and holiday meals are mediated by family and their interactions, any family dynamics that may be contributing to the individual's conflicts can become enhanced and inextricably linked with food and eating issues. As such, the eating disorder can serve as a distraction or smoke screen for unspoken family stress. Food's ubiquity and accessibility in the Orthodox Jewish population makes it (like drug and alcohol use in the secular culture) a prime vehicle for acting out. In fact, the certainty surrounding the religious regulations of food serves for some as a breeding ground for the rigidity, control, and disordered desire characteristic of anorexia.

Family Ties

The paradoxical nature of Judaism is robustly conveyed through the mixed and contradictory familial obligations. Honoring one's parents is deemed so essential that it is considered a decree regarding an individual's relationship to G_d. Family is a central tenet in Jewish life, and the duty to preserve heritage and a strong connection to the legacy of previous generations is fundamental to Orthodox Jewish thinking. Simultaneously, the Old Testament states that a man should "leave his father and mother and cleave unto his wife," suggesting that the marital relationship is privileged over the parental one. This imperative is further enhanced through the commandment to "be fruitful and multiply," suggesting that to marry and create one's own family is the essence of life. Therefore staying connected and involved with one's family of origin while also individuating and separating so that one can fulfill the obligations of the marital relationship and establish one's own large family may sometimes feel irreconcilable.

The psychodynamic link regarding disordered eating and family enmeshment has long been established in the eating-disorders discourse. The symptom can function to create a boundary and separation, a demand for personal control, a plea for attention or a communication represented by the body of the psychic difficulty of managing the dialectic of being merged and separate at the same time. Jewish educators report on the high incidence of eating disorders among Orthodox high school students who leave their families to study abroad in Israel. This is similarly the case with going off to college. The abrupt transition and resulting separation creates strong feelings that are mediated by the eating disorder.

The Holocaust literature delineates a common element of enmeshment that often exists in survivor families whose traumatic history resulted in securing the family as a haven and refuge, although these conflicts regarding separation are also often present in families without a trauma history. During the Holocaust, physical separation between parents and children (healthy ones to work, sickly ones to die) frequently resulted in death. Consequently, children of survivors may unconsciously perceive their parents' fantasies of death as well as real memories of loss (Zeliznikow & Lang, 1989) and therefore attempt to protect them from further aggression, destructiveness, desertion and betrayal that the separation and independence symbolize. Additionally, the failures of humanity and consequently the enduring suspiciousness of a world that witnessed the genocide of millions of Jews produced and transmitted a deep distrust of anyone outside the family, rendering both intimacy and separation a fear-laden and guilt-ridden enterprise.

Shidduchim: "Matchmaker, Matchmaker, Make Me a Match"

Although historically a phenomena of ultra-Orthodoxy, *shidduchim* have become a more common occurrence for modern Orthodox Jews. For those pursuing a shidduch, the trend is toward a brief dating period prior to an engagement and quick marriage. There is general pressure to marry young, and immediately have children and a large family. Additionally, the common practice of underexposure to the opposite sex can create fear and avoidance of physical intimacy. As a result, the looming shidduch often generates conflict regarding the pressure to marry. The inexperience, regarding emotional or physical intimacy with the opposite sex can therefore function as a stimulus to develop an eating disorder, thereby dodging the more dreaded bullet.

What Size Does the Girl Wear?

The aesthetic of "thinness," combined with the value placed on achievement outside the home, can contradict the values that the shidduch was intended to promote and also creates what is frequently a tall and maybe impossible order. Furthermore, some Orthodox Jews have fallen prey to the "commoditization of marriage," where the shidduch process has morphed into a shopping expedition with a list of necessary "attributes" (Fishman, 2005), and the "shidduch resume" has become a common occurrence. It is quite common for the potential groom's mother to ask, "What size does the girl wear?" suggesting that anything larger that a size 6 might lower her marital value and viability. In addition to being objectified and possibly fostering body dissatisfaction, this process implicitly contradicts the laws of modesty and the intensified expectation to marry can spur the development of an eating disorder.

History of Persecution and Holocaust Trauma

There is little empirical research that explores the correlation between Holocaust exposure and disordered eating in the Jewish population, particularly among the children and grandchildren of survivors. The limited number of existing clinical and qualitative studies, however, that demonstrate a correlation between these two variables (Chesler, 2005; Zohar, Giladi, & Givati, 2007) are buttressed by many anecdotal examples and clinical case studies (Farber et al., 2007; Grubrich-Simitis, 1984; Rabinor, 2002). Although both the Holocaust literature on the offspring of survivors and the literature on eating disorders include some consideration and explication of these links, neither fully develops the connection between these factors. The aim here is to further elaborate on their relationship and phenomenology.

Notwithstanding the genocidal atrocities of the Holocaust, Jews have been subjected for ages to relentless anti-Semitic hatred and persecution. It has been suggested (Perlstein, 2010) that members of the (ultra) Orthodox Jewish community irrespective of their Holocaust exposure (but in part because of their self-imposed insularity and segregation) have a more potent desire to hold, memorialize, and consequently transmit these traumas intergenerationally. Yet the Holocaust traumas and present-day traumas, such as 9/11, which reactivate the past, appear to have imprinted culturally and collectively (Lazar, Litvak-Hirsch, & Chaitln, 2008; Volkan, 1997) on *all* Jewish psyches. Kogan (1995) stated, "It is therefore possible that the collective memory of past traumas, in a certain sense, turned us all into the second generation" (p. 145).

The unfathomable emotional and physical horrors visited on the survivors resulted in a dissociation of experience. The chaotic, unintegrated quality of the traumatic memories resulted in their being incomprehensible—unsymbolized, unspoken, and psychically delinked, though felt, remembered, and somatically held by the body. The survivor's inability to develop a coherent narrative may serve as fertile ground for transgenerational transmission, and for the offspring's (referring to children, grandchildren, and great grandchildren) reenactment, of this trauma history. The transmission occurred both through the attachment relationship and parenting as a result of the adaptive strains that accompanied the parents' survivorship (Kestenberg, 1982; Bar-On et al., 1998; Scharf, 2007; Scharf & Mayseless, 2011) as well as through the children's unconscious identification with the previous generation and their (known or unknown, spoken or unspoken) history (Auerhan & Laub, 1984; Faimberg, 2005). The unmourned persecutory and Holocaust traumas of previous generations can render future generations affectively dysregulated, psychically concrete, somatically encoded, relationally enmeshed, and unwittingly identified alternately with the helpless victim and/or unmerciful aggressor. These same psychodynamics and vulnerabilities are often identified as facilitating or underlying patterns of disordered eating.

Concretization

Trauma compromises reflective and symbolic thinking. The distinctions between internal and external experience and fantasy and reality collapse, and thoughts are delinked from each other and from their affective meanings. The impairment of the function of metaphorization, as seen in Holocaust survivors, is thought to be transmitted to their offspring who grow up in a "world beyond metaphor" (Herzog, 1982, p. 114), and who "concretistically act out the traumatic aspects of their parents' lives as if it were their own story" (Grubrich-Simitis, 1984, p. 311). This concretization may get realized in the form of an eating disorder where the actual body serves as a screen upon which a generational story or collective myth gets told about the fear and wish for death, and the guilt and euphoria over survival. Though concretism is viewed here as a sequelae of trauma, clinicians frequently report anecdotally on its common appearance in the Orthodox population regardless of family Holocaust trauma. We may speculate that this is due to the collective trauma suffered by all (Orthodox) Jews. Similarly we may hypothesize that it is linked to the tendency toward literal interpretation and the certainty with which religious imperatives are practiced, yielding perhaps an absence or underdevelopment of reflective and symbolic functioning, used defensively to avoid having to tolerate ambiguity and uncertainty. This is particularly interesting when considered in conjunction with eating disorders where the psychic conflicts get reified through concrete and physical expression by the body.

Starvation

Of the entire bodily trauma that Holocaust victims endured, the most ubiquitous was severe starvation. Subsequently many survivors were preoccupied with food and eating. Their offspring may then unconsciously identify with their ancestors' previous emaciated condition and enact the same physical and psychic state by starving themselves or by secret binge eating. Additionally, the survivor guilt experienced by those victims who lost family members yet survived may be lived out by the next generation(s) who silently tells this story through their wasted bodies (Farber et al., 2007; Jackson & Davidson, 1986). Their anorexia, which comprises a "deadened" state, is a compromise formation for the feelings of guilt over being alive. The survivors' history also often included experiences of desperate hiding, of having to either escape or retreat. The symptoms of anorexia can simulate this physical withdrawal. The hiding is enacted through the disappearance and invisibility the anorectic feels as she is shrinking as well as in the way she may conceal her body in baggy clothing. The bulimic or compulsive overeater may similarly obscure her shame and greediness by eating in secrecy and shrouding her unacceptable feelings in the layers of protective fat.

Identification With the Aggressor

Like their earlier ancestors, offspring of survivors often alternately act out the paradox of survivorship (special for surviving yet degraded for being victimized, Auerhan & Laub, 1984), as well as the oscillating and contradictory self-states of victim and aggressor. If anorectic, the offspring may play out this history by condensing both sides of the dyadic interaction. Through starvation (or bulimia) the offspring operates self-destructively, being both aggressor and victim to herself, and though she remains alive (survives) despite the starvation, in her profound loss and mourning she is lifeless and dead in life. Through this compromise formation, the offspring mimetically achieve the survivor's wish to die (reject life) as well as conquer (deny) death (Bachar et al., 2002; Kogan, 2002).

In identifying with the aggressor, the offspring may not only enact the sadism of her ancestors' persecutors but also introject their ethnic hatred and anti-Semitism. This is illustrated by the offspring's (often unconscious) self-hatred of her Jewishness, which among other genetically predisposed attributes is stereotypically represented through her "zaftig" Jewish body, which she wishes to transform and control into a thin, non-Jewish silhouette. Moreover, by striving for and achieving perfection, the Jewess unconsciously hopes to avoid criticism and anti-Semitism.

Through Parenting Relationship—Affective Dysregulation

The long-term biochemical shifts resulting from trauma may even be transmitted transgenerationally at the prenatal stage or during infancy and early childhood when maternal behavior influences a child's hormonal and metabolic processes

(Yehuda & Bierer, 2009). Early empathic failure has been delineated as disrupting the development of a stable, integrated, and continuous body image, for which the eating disorder compensates (Krueger, 1989). Because the child's affect tolerance is developed through exposure to and the internalization of the parent's regulatory capacity, the traumatized and affectively dysregulated parent's inability to organize and contain the child's affective experience often results in the child's failure to modulate and express strong affect: "One generation's trauma leads to the next generation's lack of affect tolerance" (Wilson, 1985, p. 69). The psychoanalytic literature, which clearly establishes a link between relational trauma and eating disorders (Bromberg, 2001; Sands, 2003; Ferguson & Mendelsohn, 2011), views the dysregulation of affect as the crucible for the development of disordered eating. Bromberg (2001) stated that the absence of the self-regulating experience of human relatedness and its potential for reparation results in the individual's necessary reliance on her own physiological and affective states. The outcome of this protracted self-reliance is the dissociation of psyche from soma, which is thought to be at the heart of eating problems (Bromberg, 2001; Farber et al., 2007). In the absence of the ability to self-regulate affect, the eating disorder functions as a self-regulatory Other, a failed attempt to ward off or control anxiety and an anesthetic, relieving the patient from her intense and overwhelming feelings. For example, compulsive overeating becomes a way for patients to "stuff down their feeling" while maintaining the imperative for verbal silence (Rashkin, 1999).

In sum, this brief psychoanalytically informed examination of the sociocultural and historical factors that are interlaced with religious attitudes elucidates some of the processes that may contribute to the development of the eating disorder as a symptom in the Orthodox Jewish community. However, by no means does this tell or account for the whole story. The following section explicates the psychodynamic determinants that can play a role in setting eating disorders in motion for this population.

"Awesomely, Wondrously Made"[1]

Sharon Kofman

This section addresses the pathway to eating and body-image disorders among Orthodox Jewish women from a psychodynamic, clinical perspective. Eating disorders are conceptualized here as psychodynamic solutions designed to address underlying tensions in self-identity development in vulnerable religious Jewish adolescents. From a clinical point of view, religious and cultural factors can only partially explain the incidence of eating disorders among Orthodox Jewish women. In the Orthodox community, although many women are exposed to the pressures of the shidduch system, young marriage and early motherhood, the ritual requirements of kashrut (dietary regulations) and the tradition of lavish meals on the Sabbath, only some develop eating disorders (Altmann, 2009). We now understand that multiple determinants contribute to development of eating disorders (i.e., temperamental, neurobiological, affective-cognitive, genetic, and personality factors), which emerge in the context of families with their own unique characteristics (e.g., affect tolerance, conflict avoidance, neglect, over protectiveness, psychological mindedness, flexibility, rigidity, authoritarianism, perfectionism, and shame avoidance), and within idiosyncratic social and religious contexts. Intrapsychic and temperamental factors that remap in interaction with familial, cultural contexts, and life events across development describe the complex and unpredictable processes that precipitate an eating disorder.

Within the category of eating disorders there is a wide spectrum of symptomatic manifestations ranging in severity from mild and episodic to the more severe and chronic. Although more serious disorders of anorexia and bulimia have dominated the literature, Feinson (2012) commented on the wide range of eating and body issues (e.g. addictive food attachments, anxious overeating, body shame, body image dissatisfaction) among Jewish women of all ages. In large and over-extended families excessive dieting may operate under the radar and go undetected until the situation worsens (Altmann, 2009). In the clinical setting, one may encounter the situation of treating a chronic or unrecovered eating-disordered woman who feels desirous or pressured to become pregnant.

It is important to highlight that clinically, Jewish females with eating symptoms and syndromes present with signature features and symptom manifestations (i.e., the way food and the body are employed) that characterize all eating-disordered patients (Kadish, 2012). Often, these young women show weaknesses in the domains of separateness, robustness of self-development, and in self-and-other differentiation, among other features. In the absence of evidence to the contrary, it is fair to say that Jewish women's' eating disorders resemble eating disorders in other populations. In other words, there is no evidence of a biological basis of Jewish eating disorders, or a unique or "essential" "Jewish" etiological cause or clinical presentation. This is important to underline because, as is well-known, representations and stereotypic distortions of Jewish "difference" and "otherness" have been employed for malevolent and prejudicial purposes in many contexts.

"Rejoice in Thy Youth": *Religious Jewish Adolescence*

Psychoanalytic theorists of self-identity development in adolescence have described the consolidation of identity (in late adolescence) as involving processes relevant to ownership of an adult body and sense of self, the integration of sexuality, gender identification, intimate partner relations, and the realization of autonomy and competence (Levy-Warren, 1995). Growing up Orthodox can present challenges in any of these domains. The struggle to build an "I," the gradual defining of who am I, and who and what do I wish to be?, is a universal personal struggle shaped within established patterns of behavior, communal expectations, and prohibitions (Heilman, 2006). In the case of Orthodox Jews, this struggle is additionally played out within the religious Jewish hierarchy and discourse. The developmental transition from adolescence to adulthood requires the young person to engage in an unconscious "sorting-out" process: What from the past do I dispose of, and what do I keep? Who should I be like, and who should I be different from (Goldman, 2010)? How shall I "be" Orthodox (Heilman, 2006)? Anxious, immature, or sheltered Orthodox girls who have tentative capacities for independent thinking and reality testing or who lack adequate "holding" may feel threatened by novelty, exploration, and questions of choice that are part and parcel of this process. In Orthodox families in which individuality and subjectivity are underrecognized and in families where parental models are limited—when "recipe knowledge" substitutes for guidance and wisdom—it can be harder for vulnerable girls to separate while staying connected. Brisman (1992) detailed how the vulnerable eating-disordered adolescent defensively reverts to early adolescent modes of perceiving and thinking, including idealization and imitation as a solution. Examples of this include carbon copying of peer behavior and/or the Jewish mother's gender role behavior, or aspiring to illusory images of the "perfect" slender girl with the perfect life script and perfect husband (Altmann, 2010) as well as practicing rigid black-and-white thinking. One can see how absolutist, good and bad categories of thinking might lend themselves as sources of certainty and regulation of stimulation in vulnerable Orthodox Jewish girls.

Theorists of adolescence suggest that successful navigation of this developmental phase involves the integration of strivings, affects, and fantasies from previous phases of development. With the advent of puberty a new reintegration of the body-self, including its sensual–sexual and reproductive capacities come into play with its transforming implications for sexual subjectivity and desire. Based on a review of the literature and observations from clinical practice, we suggest some lines for further exploration about the internal world of the religious Jewish eating-disordered adolescent. In particular, we highlight developmental psychodynamics that may be relevant to understanding hidden vulnerabilities of the religious Jewish adolescent and linked dynamically to her eating and body issues. These dynamics are not necessarily unique to the Jewish population and may be descriptive of women from any culture. We only propose that these issues may resonate clinically for this group. Parenthetically, these dynamics are more likely to be accessible in the recovery phase when the patient has progressed to a higher level of psychological organization.

In view of the powerful idealization of the fertile, abundant mother and her pregnant body in Jewish femininity, oedipal rivalry strivings at adolescence that are associated with aggression, envy, and guilt in relation to the early mother may be threatening to some girls, particularly those with narcissistically fragile mothers. For needy and dependent young women still overly involved with mother and family, the individuation process of investing in oneself, articulating self-derived opinions and preferences, and tolerating differences may be compromised (Levy-Warren, 1995). Zehavah, a Russian Modern Orthodox adolescent, was insecure about living up to her mother's demanding standards of performance and appearance. She enlisted her mother in editing her papers, scheduling her violin lessons, and intervening for her when she missed appointments. Her mother was overidentified with her daughter's neediness and anxiety. Wishing to relieve and ease her anxiety, the mother inadvertently exacerbated Zehavah's feelings of ineffectiveness and inferiority, which were also manifest in body shame and self-consciousness. Zehavah was highly critical of her body shape and weight, which was fuller and curvier than her mother's leaner body type. She created an identification and intimate bond with her mother through becoming a dieter, like her mother. Zehavah reveled in the attention she received when she lost weight. Her control over appetite seemed to offer an illusory sense of personal authorship, power, and independence. With the therapist, Zehavah was able to relive resentful, subordinated feelings, while acknowledging her longings to be close and acknowledged by her mother. The treatment process addressed Zehavah's need to transform and perfect herself in order to feel acceptable, and to be able to inhabit her own, separate body and person more comfortably.

In some parentified patients or in girls from large families, it appears that repressed preoedipal wishes and longings to be "babied" may be experienced as greedy or devouring and require continuous suppression and monitoring. The "hunger" for a close and intimate relation with a containing mother, especially in teens with histories of maternal disappointment, is projected onto food preoccupation and restriction. The driven pursuit of the thin, youthful body may reflect the hidden wish of the pseudomature teen to reveal and preserve her "lost childhood" (Zerbe, 1993) in the fantasized hope of a second chance with a disappointing or absent mother. Dare and Crowther (1995) linked the anorectic's self-denial and negativism to an enactment of the anal struggle of autonomy revived at adolescence and symbolized in the internal and interpersonal struggles around eating. Entering the mind of the eating-disordered adolescent, these writers articulate the experience as follows; "Who's in charge? For whom do I exist, myself or others? Do I have a right to a life based on my own self-derived needs?" (1994, p. 134). The Jewish eating-disordered adolescent who feels she has always done what she's been told to do appears to be insisting on "making her own rules" in the narrow sphere of her food behaviors.

The connection between orality and sexuality in Jewish collective thought—and its association with transgression—harkens back to the ancient Biblical story of the Garden of Eden (Lefkovitz, 2008; Weinberger-Litman, Latzer, & Stein, 2011) and its construction of womanhood around the body. A number of researchers, including Weinberger-Litman, et al. (2011), link the role of asceticism and sexuality as relevant to the development of eating and body disorders in some Jewish religious girls from strict or rigidly observant environments. In these women, she theorizes, perfection coalesces with ideals of purity, innocence, and control; dissociated anxieties about permissible versus nonpermissible physical urges are "oralized." From the perspective of the dyadic mother–daughter relationship, the mother's access to pleasure, joy, and desire can shape a positive affective climate within her early caregiving and her gendered relation to her daughter, or—alternatively—a tense, stifled, affectless relation, entangling the daughter in connections interwoven with suffering or pain.

Unnamed fears of sexuality as mindlessly out of control, and unformulated expectations of sexual relations involving loss of boundary or submission to a coercive, invasive "other" (Dare & Crowther, 1994) may be relevant to this population. Weight loss or gain may be a way to disavow desire and avoid the anxieties associated with the consequence of becoming the desirable female object of the male gaze. "Bad" or "not-me" attributions may apply to the self-states and affects that are traditionally inhibited in male-dominated traditional societies among women: separateness, assertion and agency, and "me" feelings—I want, I claim, I desire, I am important. Sands (1989) submitted that eating-disordered symptoms can become an arena to enact frustrated and conflicted exhibitionistic longings, infantile grandiose strivings (e.g., channeled into the omnipotent thrill of controlling hunger, becoming skilled in purging), and urgent wishes for attention, albeit in a self-punitive way. In the construction of gender in Western society, she observes, girls learn to subordinate their exhibitionistic strivings if they are seen to be in conflict with the needs of others, and they are also taught to put a lid on their excitement. Eating-disordered patients are noted to be hyperattuned to the needs of others, to endorse "selflessness," and to have difficulties "taking up space" and having their presence known (Bachar & Samet, 2011; Sered, 2000). In the extreme, this can extend to an anxious avoidance of eating in public. Jewish feminist scholars (Sered, 2000; Szotkman, 2005) see the alignment of unconscious historical, religious constructions of the ultra-orthodox ideal, "modest," and "hidden" female in the modern cultural symbol of the anorectic body—unobtrusive, nonimposing, desire-absent, her virtues lived interiorly.

Unconscious ambivalent feelings about the female gender and body, as well as the revival or resolution of bigendered wishes in adolescence may play a part in eating-disorder symptomatology in some patients. The anorectic fascination with the thinnest body can both reflect the desire for male approval and an unconscious identification with stereotypic and privileged ideal male characteristics, such as control and detachment, self-sufficiency, and moral superiority. These identifications can also exist alongside her unconscious rejection or disavowal of the female body perceived as "soft," inferior, or passive. Consider the impacts of the modern reenvisioning of the Jewish body in terms of the Zionist ideal of the physically strong, masterly, "muscular" Jew(ess) and this ideal's role in shaping the contemporary body image ideal for young Jewish women. Equally important is the history of the female adolescent daughter's relational position and father identification, as in the achieving daughter who is secretly the father's son. This may play an unconscious dynamic role. In some girls, the eating disorder may also contain and counter feelings about her father's excesses, such as anxious overeating, temper, or bossiness.

"Behold Thou Art Beautiful": The Jewish Body

As is the case in any culture, the young woman's emerging ability to connect and care for her evolving body is understood psychoanalytically to reflect the transmission of her mother's procedures, feelings, and attitudes towards her daughter's and her own female body. The earliest experience of touch, handling, and gaze in the maternal relationship shape the daughter's sense of self as a person (Orbach, 2009). In a familial context that is unattuned, awkward, or ambivalent about the body—or, alternatively, preoccupied with it and/or misattuned—the daughter's ability to inhabit her changing body with confidence and pleasure will be affected (Sands, 1989). The mother's feelings about her gender, including unconscious feelings of unworthiness, devaluation, or inferiority may be transmitted unconsciously (Harris, 2005) and contribute to the pervasive unsymbolized body shame experienced by so many Jewish women. Negative representations of the Jewish female have also been traced by scholars, exemplified by the images of the exotic and/or contaminating Other, the demanding and self-indulgent Jewish Princess, or the devouring Jewish mother (Lefkovitz, 2008). The girl's spontaneity and comfort with observing and thinking about her body and observing her mother's body may be affected, as is the valuation and naturalness with which the mother talks about the body with her daughter. In view of the gender divisions in orthodox families, there is also the question of the father's distance and avoidance of things "female." This may be one of the reasons the female identification is often amorphous and vague in some eating-disordered patients; they are lacking internalizations and forms of self-holding and self-soothing that would allow them to feel at home within their bodies.

Blending therapeutic techniques that enhance body awareness and bodymind integration sensitive to orthodox patients can facilitate connection, vitality, and reflectiveness (Ressler, 2012). Many advocates endorse the need for education and communication about healthy sexual attitudes in the community and during the adolescent years when gender beliefs and ideas about male and female sexuality are becoming established. We wonder whether the rise in eating disorders may reflect an unconscious collective attempt to unsettle the unspeakability and marginalization of the body to allow a space for it in direct talk (see Eilberg-Schwartz, 1992). In this light, Sered noted how "biblical tradition lauds heroines who attained their own goals or who saved the Jewish people through their *words*" (emphasis mine, Sered, 2000, p. 170).

Clinical Management

In two-person psychotherapy, feelings and fantasies about cultural difference and "otherness" are inevitable aspects of the transference/countertransference and can create distance and inhibition. Information about the patient's culture and religion (Goldwasser, 2010) helps the therapist elicit trust, be more attuned, and offers the patient a feeling of being seen and known, which is often profoundly missing in the development of these patients. Individual, familial factors, the age and psychological maturity of the patient most relevantly determine a therapeutic approach (e.g., individual, family treatment, or some combination) and often shape the recovery process and outcome. The families of patients I have treated often initiate with requests for family-based treatment (Loeb & Le Grange, 2010), even for young adult patients. "You don't understand," they say, "we are different, we are very close as a family. We can make this work." The orthodox patient often requires a process of education to inaugurate the team approach to treatment: She relies upon tact and sensitivity by the therapist to invite curiosity about themes of her life and dysfunctional family processes that underpin and maintain her eating disorder.

Earlier, we emphasized the meanings of separation in Jewish culture and its psychic elaborations with dilemmas of self-definition and conflicts of merger or isolation, outcasting, and annihilation anxieties. Some ultra-orthodox eating-disordered patients experience the stigma of their eating disorders with shame, guilt (sometimes for feared religious transgression), and fears of not belonging; this brings an added dimension of anguish to their condition and preoccupation. They may be secretive about their symptoms to avoid exposure. Even within the privacy of the treatment relationship, issues of trust, exposure, and safety are in play. Fears of stigmatization and subtle complications relevant to Jewish ethical principles regarding disclosure of medical or psychological vulnerability to the prospective suitor may also affect discussions and decisions around medication. In contrast to conflicted, shame-ridden patients are eating-disordered patients who are surprisingly blasé and normalize their condition and its risks. Their own communities seem to discount the reality and consequences of the disorder, and they require a different engagement.

Managing Holiday Eating and Religious Observance[2]

Girls in the throes of a serious eating disorder usually have difficulty with any sort of family or communal meal. Since the long-range goal is normal eating, patients need to be encouraged to eat family meals as much as possible. Many girls with severe disorders may need to eat separately until their eating has normalized. This needs to be approached on a case-by-case basis. Since the eating-disordered condition can magnify the perception of large family meals as overwhelming, it is useful for the therapist to remember that the patient may wish to resume family and holiday meals after she recovers. Also, while exploring the experience of family meals, the therapist must not join in a literal externalization of the meals itself as the source of the problem.

Within the process of individuation, it may be that the daughter may wish to practice religiously in ways that are different from her parents and the community. This might, for example, come up with respect to matters of clothing and dress. This is a delicate matter to navigate for the treatment, as encouraging independent decision making may be threatening to the parents who could perceive it as defiance and blame the treatment. Esther Altmann (personal communication) advises that parents be included in the conversation so as not to lose the therapeutic alliance. She recommends that emphasis be given to the overarching goal of the daughter's health, even if her skirts are shorter or the parents don't like the color of her nail polish. She further observes that healthier, more flexible families are usually able to tolerate these accommodations, whereas authoritarian families can tolerate them to a lesser extent.

Conclusion

Courtney Martin (2007) asserted that the current young adult generation's preoccupation with food and thin perfection needs to be framed within the broader context of their loss of personal meaning, balance, and wholeness in body and mind. Perhaps this is applicable to Orthodox Jewish eating and body-image disordered girls and women as well. Martin recommends (2007, pp. 314–315) that the contemporary generation learn to develop faith in experience and people over ideas, confidence in process over short-term solutions, and discover wonder in the diversity of human bodies and the struggles of an engaged life. The psychoanalytic treatment relationship uniquely offers these possibilities, and more.

Notes

1. Psalms 139:13–14, cited by Miriyam Glazer (2008).
2. The author would like to thank Esther Altmann, PhD, for her contributions to this section.

References

Allport, G., & Ross, M. (1967). Personal religious orientation and prejudice. *Journal of Personality and Social Psychology, 5*(4), 432–443.

Altmann, E. (2009, June). *Food, body image and eating disorders in the Jewish community.* Paper presented at Renfrew Center Foundation Conference.

Altmann, E. (2010, October). *Paper on eating disorders.* Paper presented at the Fifth Annual Medical Ethics conference, a Beautiful mind—Jewish approaches to mental health.

Auerhan, N., & Laub, D. (1984). Annihilation and restoration. *International Review of Psycho-Analysis, 11,* 327–344.

Bachar, E., Latzer, Y., Canetti, L., Gur, E., Berry, E., & Bonne, O. (2002). Rejection of life in anorexic and bulimic patients. *International Journal of Eating Disorders, 31,* 43–48.

Bachar, E., & Samet, Y. (2011). *Self-psychology in the treatment of anorexia nervosa and bulimia nervosa.* In Y. Latzer, J. Merrick, & D. Stein (Eds.), *Understanding eating disorders: Integrating culture, psychology, and biology* (pp. 181–196). New York: Nova Science Publishers.

Bar-On, D., Eland, J., Kleber, R.J., Krell, R., Moore, Y., Sagi, A., . . . Van Ijzendoorn, M. (1998). Multigenerational perspective on coping with the Holocaust experience: An attachment perspective for understanding the developmental sequelae of trauma across generations. *International Journal of Behavioral Development, 22,* 315–338.

Brisman, J. (1992). *Bulimia in the older adolescent: An analytic perspective to a behavioral problem.* In J. O'Brien, D. Pilowsky, & O. Lewis (Eds.), *Psychotherapies with children and adolescents: Adapting the psychodynamic process* (pp. 171–187). Washington: American Psychiatric Press.

Bromberg, P. (2001). Treating patients with symptoms and symptoms with patience: Reflections on shame, dissociation, and eating disorders. *Psychoanalytic Dialogues, 11,* 891–912.

Chesler, B. (2005). Implications of the Holocaust for eating and weight problems among survivor's offspring: An exploratory study. *European Eating Disorders Review, 13*(1), 38–47.

Dare, C., & Crowther, C. (1995). *Psychodynamic models of eating disorders.* In G. Szmukler, C. Dare, & J. Treasure (Eds.), *Handbook of eating disorders* (pp. 125–139). Chichester: John Wiley.

Eilberg-Schwartz, H. (1992). *People of the body: Jews and Judaism from an embodied perspective.* Albany: State University of New York Press.

Faimberg, H. (2005). *The telescoping of generations.* New York: Routledge.

Farber, S., Jackson, C., Taabin, J., & Bachar, E. (2007). Death and annihilation anxieties in anorexia nervosa, bulimia, and self-mutilation. *Psychoanalytic Psychology, 24*(2), 289–305.

Feinson, M. (2012, May). *Eating problems in the Jewish community: An overview.* Paper presented at a conference, in pursuit of perfection: body image and eating issues in the Jewish community at the Renfrew Center Foundation Seminar, New York, NY.

Feinson, M., & Meir, A. (2012). Disordered eating and religious observance: A focus on ultra-orthodox Jews in an adult community study. *International Journal of Eating Disorders, 45*(1), 101–109.

Ferguson, H., & Mendelsohn, S. (2011). Full of yourself: How eating disorder symptoms encode a relational history. *International Journal of Psychoanalytic Self Psychology, 6*(3), 352–376.

Fishman, S. (2005). *Perfect person singular: Unmarried adults in contemporary orthodox American Jewish communities.* In R. Blau (Ed.), *Gender relations in marriage in and out.* New York: Yeshiva University Press.

Glazer, M. (2008). *Reclaiming dignity, freedom, health: The Jewish body in America.* In E. Dorff & L. Newman (Eds.), *Jewish choices, Jewish voices. Vol. 1. The body* (pp. 32–39). Philadelphia: Publication Society.

Gluck, M., & Geliebter, A. (2002). Body image and eating behaviors in orthodox and secular Jewish women. *Journal of Gender Specific Medicine, 5,* 19–24.

Goldman, D. (2010). As generations speak. *Psychoanalytic Psychology, 27,* 475–491.

Goldwasser, D. (2010). *Starving souls.* Jersey City: Ktav Publishing House.

Grubrich-Simitis, I. (1984). From concretism to metaphor—Thoughts on some theoretical and technical aspects of the psychoanalytic work with children of holocaust survivors. *Psychoanalytic Study of the Child, 39,* 301–319.

Harris, A. (2005). *Gender as soft assembly.* Hillsdale, NJ: Analytic Press.

Heilman, S. (2006) *Sliding to the right: The contest for the future of American Jewish orthodoxy.* Berkeley: University of California Press.

Herzog, J. (1982). *World beyond metaphor.* In M. Bergmann & M. Jucovy (Eds.), *Generations of the Holocaust* (pp. 103–119). New York: Basic Books.

Jackson, C., & Davidson, G. (1986). The anorexic patient as a survivor: The denial of death and death themes in the literature on anorexia nervosa. *International Journal of Eating Disorders, 5,* 821–835.

Kadish, Y.A. (2012). Pathological organizations and psychic retreats in eating disorders. *Psychoanalytic Review, 99*(2), 230–252.

Katzman, M.A., & Lee, S. (1997). Beyond body image: The integration of feminist and transcultural theories in the understanding of self-starvation. *International Journal of Eating Disorders, 22,* 385–394.

Kestenberg, J. (1982). A metapsychological assessment based on an analysis of a survivor's child. In M. Bergmann & M. Jucovy (Eds.), *Generations of the Holocaust* (pp. 137–158). New York: Basic Books.

Kogan, I. (1995). Love and the heritage of the past. *International Journal of Psychoanalysis, 76,* 805–824.

Kogan, I. (2002). Enactment in the lives and treatment of holocaust survivors' offspring. *The Psychoanalytic Quarterly, 71,* 251–272.

Krueger, D. (1989). *The parent loss of empathic failures and the model symbolic restitution of eating disorders.* In D. Dietrich & P. Shabad (Eds.), *The problem of loss and mourning* (pp. 213–231). Madison: International Universities Press.

Latzer, Y., Tzischinsky, O., & Gefen, S. (2007). Level of religiosity and disordered eating psychopathology among modern-orthodox Jewish adolescent girls in Israel. *International Journal of Adolescent Medicine and Health, 19*(4), 511–521.

Lazar, A., Litvak-Hirsch, T., & Chaitlin, J. (2008). Between culture and family: Jewish-Israeli young adults' relations to the Holocaust as a cultural trauma. *Traumatology, 14*(3), 10–119.

Lefkovitz, L. (2008). *Judaism, body image and food.* In E. Dorff & L. Newman (Eds.), *Jewish choices, Jewish voices. Volume 1. The body* (pp. 67–73). Philadelphia: The Jewish Publication Society.

Levy-Warren, M. (1995). A Freudian perspective on Rachel's struggle. *Psychoanalytic Review, 82,* 515–520.

Loeb, K., & Le Grange, D. (2010). Family-based treatment for adolescent eating disorders: Current status, new applications and future directions. *International Journal of Child and Adolescent Health. 1: 2*(2), 243–254.

Martin, C. (2007). *Perfect girls, starving daughters.* New York: Berkley Books.

Miller, M., & Pumariega, A. (2001). Culture and eating disorders: A historical and cross-cultural review. *Psychiatry, 64*(2), 93–110.

Orbach, S. (2009). *Bodies.* New York: Picador.

Perlstein, P. (2010). *An evaluation of potential transgenerational transmission of Holocaust trauma in the third generation.* Doctoral dissertation submitted to Hofstra University.

Rabinor, J. (2002). *A starving madness: Tales of hunger, hope and healing in psychotherapy.* Carlsbad: Gurze Books.

Rashkin, E. (1999). The haunted child: Social catastrophe, phantom transmissions, and the aftermath of collective trauma. *The Psychoanalytic Review, 86,* 433–453.

Ressler, A. (2012, May). *Jewish mothers and daughters: Honoring our bodies.* Paper presented at a conference, in pursuit of perfection: body image and eating issues in the Jewish community at the Renfrew Center Foundation Seminar, New York, NY.

Sands, S. (1989). Eating disorders and female development. *Progress in Self Psychology, 5,* 75–103.

Sands, S. (2003). The subjugation of the body in eating disorders: A particularly female solution. *Psychoanalytic Psychology, 20*(1), 103–116.

Scharf, M. (2007). Long-term effects of trauma: Psychosocial functioning of the second and third generation of Holocaust survivors. *Development and Psychopathology, 19,* 603–622.

Scharf, M., & Mayseless, O. (2011). Disorganizing experiences in second and third generation Holocaust survivors. *Qualitative Health Research, 21*(11), 1539–1553.

Sered, S. (2000). *What makes women sick: Maternity, modesty, and militarism in Israeli society.* Hanover: Brandeis University Press.

Smith, M., Richards, P., & Maglio, C. (2004). Examining the relationship between religious orientation and eating disturbances. *Eating Behavior, 5,* 171–180.

Szotkman, E. (2005). *Gender, ethnicity and class in state religious education for girls in Israel: The story of Levy Junior High School (1999–2002).* Thesis for the degree of Doctor of Philosophy, Hebrew University, Jerusalem, Israel.

Volkan, V. (1981). *Linking objects and linking phenomena: a study of the forms, symptoms, metapsychology, and therapy of complicated mourning.* New York: International Universities Press.

Volkan, V. (1997). *Bloodlines: From ethnic pride to ethnic terrorism.* Boulder: Westview Press.

Weinberger-Litman, S. (2007). *Influence of religious orientation, spiritual well-being, educational setting and social comparison on body image and eating disturbance in Jewish women* (Dissertation prepared for City College of NY.) Ann Arbor: Proquest.

Weinberger-Litman, S., Latzer, Y., & Stein, D. (2011). *Historical, cultural, and empirical look at eating disorders and religiosity among Jewish women.* In Y. Latzer, J. Merrick, & D. Stein (Eds.), *Understanding eating disorders: Integrating culture, psychology, and biology* (pp. 109–122). New York: Nova Science Publishers.

Wilson, A. (1985). On silence and the Holocaust: A contribution to clinical theory. *Psychoanalytic Inquiry, 5,* 63–84.

Yehuda, R., & Bierer, L. M. (2009). The relevance of epigenetics to PTSD: Implications for the DSM-V. *Journal of Traumatic Stress, 22,* 427–434.

Zeliznikow, J., & Lang, M. (1989). Separation crises and the Holocaust. *Australian and New Zealand Journal of Family Therapy, 10,* 31–32.

Zerbe, K. (1993). *The body betrayed.* Washington: American Psychiatric Press.

Zohar, A., Giladi, L., & Givati, T. (2007). Holocaust exposure and disordered eating: A study of multi-generational transmission. *European Eating Disorders Review, 15,* 50–57.

Part IV

APPETITE REGULATION IN AN INTERPERSONAL AND CULTURAL CONTEXT

'THESE BOOTS *AREN'T* MADE FOR WALKING, BUT THAT'S JUST WHAT THEY'LL DO'

The Use of the Detailed Inquiry in the Treatment of Obesity

Janet Tintner

Introduction: The Loop

For those New Yorkers too sedentary to use their boots for walking, and for those non–New Yorkers among you, I want to tell you about the loop in Central Park. I lived and worked blocks from the Park for twenty years before I had a stroke and discovered a drive to push myself to walk longer, walk further, and walk faster. After I left the hospital I started by walking five frightening, icy city blocks with a cane. Gradually, I built up my strength and was able to walk to the Park and begin to explore it. I didn't know the loop existed. I happened on the loop at 79th Street, where I entered and kept going, on the road, which is like an inner circumference of the Park. I went upwards and west to 110th St., then across, then downwards and east back to 79th and sometimes all the way to 59th Street, and across again. If, like me, you're out of shape, it can be hard to make it. Unlike the cyclists and runners who pass through at all hours, I had to build up to it, especially the hillier sections. Before my illness I hadn't wanted to walk, but after I knew I had to. Then I started to appreciate it. As it became easier, the rhythmic pace and a little exertion provided a soothing mental bubble to mull over residues of the week I didn't know were bothering me, including my interactions with patients.

Relaxed and cool around 6 a.m. one late August morning, breathing mildly labored as I approached an incline on the way uptown, I noticed my mind drift back to my last session with a patient I shall call Perdita. I had started working with Perdita about six months before. As with all obese patients, I had from the word go inquired into food, eating, and size as well as her experience of movement in her body. I find overweight (and other) people can be squeamish or inhibited about walking, exercising, and moving, so I encourage them to explore their discomfort. As I will discuss, this process didn't happen with Perdita. Thus, after

207

a long while, at the end of that last session, I offered a futile "homework" assignment of walking twelve blocks on three days that week.

Maybe it was the glorious quiet and the blissful caress of the 6:30 a.m. breeze, gentle enough to allow me to revisit my ignominious "homework" moment. Maybe my body was freed enough by exertion to jolt my thinking out of its unaware haze. Anyway, around 105th Street, in the area known as "the Great Hill," the absurdity of it all hit me: "What was I thinking?" I said to myself, "Twelve blocks? She's a sedentary 300 pounds. She can't walk twelve blocks!" I had ignored her avoidance and my impatience. I had replaced words and feeling by action. It couldn't and didn't work. I was ignoring what was obvious. She was too heavy to walk twelve blocks, even one day a week!

In our next session, I told Perdita about my walk, mainly my chat with myself about her, or maybe my chat with her in her absence. I asked her how many blocks she could walk. She was taken aback, thought for a minute, and said she didn't know. She thought it was an interesting question. She said she'd try it out, and we'd see.

My question created more movement than my homework assignment had. Her curiosity galvanized, Perdita's boots came out of her closet. By the next session she had tried walking. She had hoped to make it to the library and back, around six blocks each way, but by the end of two blocks she was so out of breath she had to sit down and take a rest. She hadn't realized, she said, shaken. She was only thirty-six, she said, crestfallen. She should be able to walk more than two blocks without needing a rest. It was shocking to her. It was shocking to me—one of those mind-blowing "how could I miss it" moments. It was the sudden ascendance of the unconscious in all its simple, complex glory, rising above my daily grind of doubt, cynicism, and questioning the efficacy of what I do, which felt especially acute at a time when I had been facing Perdita's intractable obesity.

You might wonder how all of this—Central Park, amazement, boots walking— relates to the interpersonal treatment of obesity. There is one more element to add before turning to that central question. Back in my office, which was several blocks, a museum, and a dog walk away from the Park, during months of recovery, I was reading Levenson's (1991) incisive writing about the detailed inquiry— at the time it informed my thinking on my walks as well as when working with patients. It is to his writing I now turn.

The Detailed Inquiry

Levenson (1991) invites us to question the very notion of where we, as psychoanalysts, direct our gaze. His vision is not pretzel-like, not classically inwards and intersubjectively roundabout. He takes us on another route, mercifully away from plumbing those much-idealized relational depths. He encourages us to keep our eyes wide open for an interpersonal view, facing straight ahead. To discuss the clinical material on obesity I will draw upon three theoretical points Levenson (1991) makes about the detailed inquiry: "collection of data," "holes in Swiss cheese," and "the quintessential analytic event."

Collection of Data

For the classicists among you, data collection does not use free association. You are not listening for the latent, but actively and collaboratively pursuing what you meet directly. Levenson (1991) comments:

> I have said that the data of psychoanalysis are often so obvious, so in the open, that we do not look for them. . . . Let me define more specifically what I mean by "data." The data of psychoanalysis are acquired through the detailed inquiry, again H. S. Sullivan's phrase. . . . The therapist collects information from the patient: history, early experience, present difficulties, dreams, fantasies, loose associations. . . . The detailed inquiry is a kind of deconstructionism: I mean simply that when one breaks down the surface of an inquiry, and pursues the details, an entirely new level of meaning emerges.
>
> (p. 181)

Here the analyst is an active participant, not an authority. The analyst questions rather than interprets. This means that the analyst's feelings and experiences about the taboo subjects (here, eating and moving) are crucial, real, and influential in the unfolding of the process, in what the analyst does and does not think of asking.

Lost into Found: Holes in Swiss Cheese

Data collection sounds easy enough, but talking about bodies can evoke powerful and disturbing feelings one might rather avoid. The entry point is clear enough, it is in the specific, but how do we know what questions will elucidate what cannot be thought or talked about. How do we find the data, which has been lost because they are too painful to find? Brilliantly, Levenson conjures up the idea of holes in Swiss cheese to help us think about this. He writes the following:

> Assuming that the patient's account is, like a Swiss cheese, full of holes produced by anxiety and dissociation. The patient does not dare to see what is there to be seen, because, as I said earlier, in his or her experience great anxiety and discordance was called out in the significant parenting person and still is called out. So the inquiry puts its foot into these holes.
>
> (1991, p. 181)

Our conundrum, therefore, is how to find what is known but has been lost—what I will call the "lost-known." The onus of discovering the "holes in Swiss cheese" during the detailed inquiry is on the therapist. Levenson (1991) commented that therapists may have difficulty because they are too immersed in their own theory:

I would suggest that most of the trouble in psychoanalysis arises because the therapist listens to the patient's account and then, instead of looking for holes in the story, tries to make sense of it as presented, tries to formulate, in the mode of his or her metapsychology, some rational framework for understanding.

(p. 181)

As I understand this, it is the analyst's job not to be seduced by the quest for hidden meaning but rather to keep her lenses clear so she can see what is straight ahead. But analysts have anxiety too. It is hard not to rely on an idealized theoretical crutch. This may make analysts more anxious, which is difficult when you are dealing with potentially powerful feelings evoked by obesity. The degree to which analysts can tolerate their own anxiety is crucial.

Finding Holes in Swiss Cheese and the Quintessential Analytic Event

If analysts cannot face themselves, it will be hard to see what is happening to and with their patients. If they can think freely, identify their own issues; ask freer and more direct questions, this will crucially influence the course of the detailed inquiry, which in turn impacts the evolving relationship, the unfolding treatment, and what Levenson (1991) called the quintessential analytic event:

The first face of the data of psychoanalysis is the inquiry. The second face is what happens between patient and therapist in the process of this inquiry. Bear in mind again that I am defining this as real, an actual mutual experience, not a projected fantasy. It is the correspondence of the data elicited from the inquiry and the data elicited from the relationship which constitutes the quintessential psychoanalytic event. It is what is *done* about what is *said* that matters.

(p. 182)

Detailed Inquiry in Practice

I will now explore the way these three aspects of the detailed inquiry: data collection, finding holes in Swiss cheese, and the inquiry with the context of this therapeutic relationship lead up to this quintessential analytic event as it developed in this treatment. I will conclude by discussing ramifications for the treatment of obesity.

Lost and Found: What's in a Name?

Perdita was not a random choice. While writing this material, I conjured up in my mind's eye pastoral scenes from a glorious production of my favorite Shakespearean play, *The Winter's Tale*. Perdita is the orphan princess heroine of the play, who was banished (lost) and found, bringing redemption with her. *Perdita* means "lost one" in Latin, and *perdre* is French for "lost."

Perdita weighed over 300 pounds when I first met her. She was enormously appealing in demeanor, manner, and intelligence. She had such a wonderfully articulate, thoughtful, and evocative way of putting things. I immediately liked her a lot.

Shamefully, at first I found her painful to look at. She was so lumpy, her shape so obscured. Yet with her pure complexion and blondish locks, it was achingly obvious she could be a glorious "English rose." Writing, I imagined her with rosy, rugged cheeks among the frolicking shepherdesses dancing round a maypole in *The Winter's Tale.* This pastoral scene is in the middle of the play, which opens with crazy, paranoid rage that results in expulsion, banishment, and destruction, followed by abject grief and loss. Here then was a 300-pound woman who I associated to pure beauty and lightness as well as loss and redemption (that is recovery and redemption at the end of the play)! This was the backdrop I want you to have in mind: heavy and light, lost-known, and maybe, lost-found. Now, back to those boots that didn't want to walk.

It is my practice to take a history of the family and prior therapy with the eating disorder center stage. It is my impression that most interpersonal analysts do this (at the White Institute, at least), though they may differ in the persistence, pervasiveness, and scope of their questions. With Perdita, the history-taking piece—that is also used by more classical analysts—occurred primarily in the initial stages of treatment. But, as I will show, it kept on going on, though the way the material evolved alongside and in interaction with the developing therapeutic relationship.

Perdita was the youngest in a family of eight. Money, supplies, clothes, time, and guidance were all in short supply in the face of huge demand. Mother was young and needed help. She was alone. She didn't know how to manage in life and acquired too many children before she had a chance to grow up herself. Her husband was absent and recalcitrant.

Mother was petite, and no one else in the family overate or was overweight. In the midst of this chaos and deprivation, Perdita was ravenous, starving emotionally and physically. She coped by bulking up on food as a distinct way to get attention and communicate inner turmoil. She viewed this concretely as an actual way to get something from her mother that her other siblings did not get. She said it best.

> Inquiring about her size, *I asked, "If you were bigger, then what?"*
> She responded, *"It felt that I had presence."*
> I asked, *"And if you were smaller you couldn't have as much presence?"*
> She answered, *"As a child it was a way to get attention. My mom had to go to special stores. She couldn't give me hand me downs. Kids teased me. It was some level of attention I didn't get otherwise. It was negative attention, especially when I was teased. But it was better than no attention at all. In every other way I was raised to be a child who needed very little."*

Technically, I did very little here. I didn't interpret. I didn't come up with anything deep or meaningful. All I did was to inquire, "If you were bigger then . . . and if you were smaller then. . . . "

I don't know if these were the correct questions. I don't think there is a correct question. These were my questions. They came from my thinking and experience. Like other analysts who have written about their patient's responses to their size (Burka, 1966), I wrote about my patient's responses to my weight loss and the meaning of my size (Tintner, 2009, 2010). It was something I came to understand as taboo and important. Levenson (1991) wrote that a question is an invitation, a sign that the analyst is willing to allow a subject to be addressed. I knew and learned more that size, especially large size, was forbidden even though it was constantly seen. I used that reading and that understanding in a conscious experiment in which I asked about size, mine or hers, or her families. From the word go, therefore, with my questions I let people know that size matters. With my questions I communicated my understanding that talking about size was forbidden, that I was most interested in what was forbidden and believed it could addressed by invitation only.

Perdita felt a need for understanding and insight that would draw upon her natural intelligence and capacity for introspection, which had been absent in her prior behavioral therapy. However, talking about the feelings of deprivation alone was not sufficient, and it was also important to attend to what was actually eaten.

Talking About Food: Bonding, Keeping on Going, and Building the Therapeutic Relationship

Of course, talking about eating as an analyst, I ask about the actual food and listen for, or inquire into, the emotional meaning of food. I wanted to know what made her feel she had to have chocolate chip cookies, and, maybe more importantly, what feelings emerged if she did not have said cookie.

The one component of her behavioral therapy Perdita missed was tracking, so, early on, we incorporated this. We started out with the regular food logs she knew from days of behavioral yore. About two years in, she discovered online tracking, which performed an analysis of the different components of food being eaten (carbohydrates, salt, sugar, protein, etc.) and allowed for input on type, duration, and intensity of activity. Those programs automatically calculated calories expended versus calories taken in. They would also indicate what was left to eat for the rest of the day to meet the stated goals based on the reported activity level and the calories consumed. In this way, tracking brings together the natural physiological connection between eating and moving. But eating and moving both relate to a person's experience of the body as well as an awareness of what bothers her most, or makes her so anxious she cannot even think about it. It is these holes in the cheese, the lacunae in reporting eating and moving, that are most important and most difficult to explore.

Even without explorations of how a person feels moving in her body, tracking occurs in an interpersonal context. Knowing I am not especially tech savvy, Perdita brought in various programs to show me. She pulled her iPhone out of her bag and demoed that day's tracking for me. She saw I was impressed and upped my amazement at the device by describing how she scanned products at the supermarket. I was so blown away by this technology, so enthused at the prospect of the quickly imagined marriage between technology and psychology it proffered, that I remember squealing in delight during the session. Amusedly, she joined me, smiling wryly in response.

Our interrelating during the tracking was an integral part of our actual relationship. There we were: two girls struggling with our bigness giggling together over how to cope with it. She, a tech and research wiz, educating technically dense me on a subject (obesity) with which I was trying to help her. It helped that I was endlessly enthralled talking about food. Perdita loved to cook. I wanted to know what spices she experimented with, what layers of flavor she discovered, and how people responded to her meals.

Lest you think that this was merely some recipe-sharing love fest, let me set the record straight. What was important in this phase of treatment was that food talk was a way to connect. This bonding may be of particular import for a problem in which, as sky rocketing recidivism rates indicate, change is so hard to come by and the whole arena of food and eating can feel toxic.

As treatment progressed, I began to follow what was going on when the hiccups in the process of controlling or structuring eating become more pronounced, or how it felt when there was little outward progress, or when there was a downward turn and weight was regained. In an interpersonal version of food tracking, it is most crucial that feelings around the intractability of weight loss are verbalized in the relationship. Perdita, as usual the best teacher and commentator, said it best on one of those days she had regained weight lost, as she noted:

> "Mostly I feel frustrated that for as long as I've spent thinking about things and trying to change, I haven't gotten very far. Also I feel how far I have to go yet, and it makes me very sad, and I have tears in my eyes when I think about it."

In addition to the tracking of the actual food ("data collection"), what evolved was an observing of the relationship and the therapy around the tracking. I began to become aware of a pattern in which there were periods when Perdita displayed a heightened enthusiasm about tracking. She was pleased by her weight loss, and talked about her food choices and the feelings associated with them, as well as about her size. These periods then evaporated and all these concerns were seemingly lost. During these sessions I became aware that I felt tense about whether to bring up the food/size issues. Noting my own associations to what she was saying, I waited for her. But after observing several rounds of this lost-and-found pattern, I began to itch to say something. I didn't want to feel I was in the role

213

of a disciplinarian or food monitor. However, I also didn't want to (and frankly couldn't) ignore my own reactions to what I saw. Eventually, I voiced my tension, telling her what I observed, telling her I wondered about whether to bring it up, and that I wondered about how to deal with it.

Increasingly, almost imperceptibly, the focus of the detailed inquiry shifted away from food towards what was being kept out of awareness. She lost 20 pounds, and then didn't talk about putting it back on. Typical for a patient with a problem with recidivism rates in the high 90s, she embarked upon the clichéd yo-yo pattern. However, she did not go over the weight at which she had started treatment. Overall, she stayed at a high, but relatively maintained weight

The Lost Known: Holes in Cheese, or Boots Walking

From the word go, when I work with someone struggling with eating I ask details about how they eat and how they move. When I ask about moving, I am never asking about calories expended, even if the online tracking tackles it that way. Rather, I have in mind the degree of a person's awareness of being in her body and what moving entails emotionally for her.

As I have noted, one of the fascinating dimensions of tracking is that it brings together, or concretizes, awareness of the experiences of eating and moving. If one is talking about the feelings not only around food but also about size, shape, and mobility, then an awareness of weight loss and the apparent encouragement such a perception brings may also bring about an awareness of a changing (and lighter) body. Talking during a period of enthusiastic weight loss, and therefore feeling less anxious about observing the impact of her size, Perdita commented:

> "I also feel better physically when I can do more. Like bending down by the cupboard to pick things up and walking up subway stairs. I am able to say to myself not so much 'you're bad for eating,' but I am more able to realize it's an emotional reaction."
>
> I responded by saying, "When you are more present with people, you are able to be more present around food."
>
> She concurred, "Yes, that's how I've coped, with withdrawal. I feel like when life gets too much I tend to "bubble myself out."

Tracking, automatically linked calories consumed and calories expended, therefore providing a frame through which to ask more persistently about movement. My inquiries were not vague. I asked Perdita about classes. I asked what kind of movement she liked, what, what was convenient for her given her current life circumstances. Intermittently, we talked about what classes she was thinking of. She told me about yoga and Pilates, what she liked about each, and how they had been enjoyable and helpful to her. She named specific gym chains, specific identified locations, either near home or work. She considered which classes she might want to attend and when she could take them so she could slip out of work with ease. She thought about how she could manage to take three of four classes a week. All this took place over an extended period of time, months, if not a year or two, including the eating.

Eventually—and I don't know how we got there—she said, or more likely intimated, that she needed to go her way. She didn't want anything organized. She didn't want to do any classes. She wanted to do it her way. She said she was going to go to the gym on her own. Perdita again planned specifically what she would do. Based on past experience she would do the elliptical and not the treadmill and build up to a concurrent weight-lifting regimen. But she would do it her way.

Here was a hole in the cheese: I never actually asked if she had been to a class, or how it was, or what feelings came up when she started moving. I never formulated for myself the thought I am forced to think by writing this chapter—namely that the plan didn't translate into action or attempt. Thus, the underlying anxiety-provoking issue, of how limited her movement was, could be kept out of awareness.

Interestingly, there was a difference here between the way the detailed inquiry occurred around eating and moving. This is a question I address in the discussion.

Discussion: Understanding the Quintessential Analytic Event, or Back to the Loop and Boots Walking

Levenson (1991) explicitly comments upon the importance of the relationship in interaction with the unfolding detailed inquiry:

> The first face of the data of psychoanalysis is the inquiry. The second face is what happens between patient and therapist in the process of this inquiry. Bear in mind again that I am defining this as real, an actual mutual experience, not a projected fantasy. And it is the correspondence of the data elicited from the inquiry and the data elicited from the relationship which constitutes the quintessential psychoanalytic event. It is what is *done* about what is *said* that matters.
>
> (p. 182)

As I have described, there had been a buildup of what I experienced as tension on and off for several years, first around the weight loss and gain not being talked about, and then around tracking and not tracking. These issues were addressed. When it came to movement (boots walking) we got more stuck, and there was a clearer enactment—the process of avoidance in the therapeutic relationship paralleling the avoidance in real life. Perdita and I were talking about her feelings about her larger size and ways she could start moving more. Yet, in reality, she was avoiding moving. Between us, just as in her actual life, it was all talk and avoidance of action. And, I would add, an avoidance of the really anxiety-provoking material (the limitations in her movement). I conclude that movement (boots walking), and especially the constriction of movement (boots not walking), may be the more anxiety-provoking issue.

In the arena of food, the enactment (the not talking) was more contained because there was an easier actual connection. Perdita knew I shared her passions for food and admired her culinary talents. I could share with her and learn from her. Movement was harder for both of us. No shared passion there, possibly more shared anxiety—all too difficult to touch.

In retrospect, the way the tension around what was not getting talked about (boots *not* walking) emerged was in that homework assignment. I am not averse to homework assignments, but this one made no sense because it addressed a problem that could not be identified. In retrospect, the fact that we got to the place of a homework assignment indicates to me that I understood something was stuck that I couldn't verbalize. I turned to words and actions. But actions were useless without the awareness to go with them.

Levenson (1991) noted that the relationship is an actual, real relationship. I have struggled with obesity myself, although by the time I started seeing Perdita I had lost a lot of weight. My work was also informed by my patient's reaction as well as my patients' battles with themselves and sometimes with family members. I knew from experiences with dance classes I first feared and then loved that movement could be an arena fraught with intense emotions. Everyone's experience is different, but my experience taught me that movement could bring intense anxiety and also pleasure.

However, something else happened after I had been seeing Perdita for a few years. I had a stroke! Luckily, the damage my brain sustained was very limited. As my neurologist said, I was "young enough" to be able to recover fully. I returned to work three weeks later. However, the one arena where I had residual damage was in the area of balance. In the hospital I used a walker. I needed a walking stick when I came home, and then I had to start working at it to get better. I had to walk to fully recover my functioning. For the next six months I pushed myself, until the issues with balance were almost completely resolved. That was how I discovered the loop.

Perdita knew I had struggled with weight, but she did not know I had suffered a stroke because she had ankle surgery during the time I was ill and was therefore one of the few patients on whom I did not have to cancel when I was in the hospital and then briefly used a walking stick when I first returned to work. So, interestingly, she could not react to the actual stroke, which meant the change between us can be more clearly identified as coming from shifts within me.

It is hard to admit that what may have helped here was that a stroke forced me to face my own anxiety and allowed me to be better able to address what she was avoiding. Even though I was very lucky in sustaining so little damage, a stroke is a terrifying experience. I was terrified for a long time. Walking was a way to recover. It was a way to face and remedy the problem (I was not in good shape). That awareness allowed me to think more freely and clearly.

The Use of the Detailed Inquiry in
the Treatment of Obesity

As an interpersonal analyst, I view obesity as a problem that offers particular challenges as well as possibility for greater understanding of how to work more creatively, effectively, and honestly. In this work, there is the potential for us to state, and maybe clarify, our potential contribution to real social and emotional issues.

Part of what distinguishes an interpersonal approach from a classical approach is the interest in what is kept out of awareness, due to anxiety, and most centrally, how this plays out within the therapeutic relationship. Such an approach may be particularly relevant to a problem, which is so palpably obvious on the surface yet so painful to address directly. One way of viewing obesity is as private agony on public display. As therapists we need to find ways to talk about this with our patients, hopefully with sympathy for unfair judgment, but also with curiosity about the meaning and the experience. An interpersonal approach, which emphasizes the importance of questions over interpretations, alongside the importance of the relationship, may be better equipped for this difficult task than classical approaches.

As with other eating disorders, it is clear that with a problem so frustrating and recalcitrant to change it is crucial to be open to other therapies and aides. Sometimes, surprisingly, technology can help us as long as we remain open, questioning, thinking, feeling, and talking about the bumps and hiccups on the road.

Data collection, which is the focus for food diaries, food logs, or food plans, is so pervasively in use by behaviorists, commercial weight-loss programs, as well as interpersonal analysts and online tracking programs, that it is virtually ubiquitous. Analysts distinguish themselves from this pack by adding a layer of meaning in relationship, as they also link past to present. Not insignificantly, this need to add meaning may have also entered the cultural domain, as analysts are not alone in asking not only about food eaten but also about the emotional experience accompanying eating. This may be an area where the importance of an analytic view could be clarified and highlighted. In this paper, I have added the dimension of movement to the inquiry, adding to it the dimension of meaning, not otherwise present. From this point of view the focus is not calories expended but a person's sense of being in their body and the accompanying emotional experience.

Applying an interpersonal point of view to the tracking, there are two central points I emphasize. One is that tracking occurs in the context of a relationship, and the second is that what may be most important is not the moment when a person is successfully tracking, but what goes on when a person stops tracking.

A central aspect of the detailed inquiry is identifying what Levenson (1991) called "holes in Swiss cheese," or finding out what is obscured from awareness, or what is not happening. With recognition for the themes of loss and gain so intricately connected to obesity, I have termed this the lost-known.

In conclusion, dealing with obesity one wants to identify the areas of functioning or experience causing the greatest anxiety and help them emerge into awareness. Working with obesity it may be as important, or maybe more important, to pay attention to when material gets lost as when material is found. Periods of weight gain may be more important than periods of weight loss, though they are much more difficult to tolerate emotionally. We live in a society that talks about mindfulness, but as analysts we are most equipped to understand the intense pull not to be mindful, and maybe that is more important. Indeed, and this merits a paper of its own, in my work I think and talk of mindlessness, thus hoping to recognize the strength of the pull not to feel. As analysts, I think this is where we can offer most. We can understand that some experiences, past and present, can be too painful and too frightening to address. With this understanding, along with approaches for facing what makes us most afraid, we have much to offer.

Maintenance is now recognized as a vicious and ubiquitous problem. This approach allows us to shift focus away from how knowledge is implemented to observing how people struggle, maybe "fail," or do not pay attention, and then most importantly how they literally and figuratively pick themselves up.

References

Burka, J. (1996). The therapist's body in reality and fantasy: A perspective from an overweight therapist. In B. Gerson (Ed.), *The therapist as a person* (pp. 255–276). New York: Routledge.

Levenson, E. (1991). The purloined self. In *The purloined self: Interpersonal perspective in psychoanalysis* (pp. 175–185). New York: White Institute.

Tintner, J. (2009). Getting real: From inquiry to enactment and beyond, courtesy the analyst's physical self. *Contemporary Psychoanalysis, 45*, 530–544.

Tintner, J. (2010). The incredible shrinking shrink. In J. Petrucelli (Ed.), *Knowing, notknowing and sort-of knowing: Psychoanalysis and the experience of uncertainty* (pp. 281–293). London: Karnac.

14

'NO SELF-CONTROL'

Working in the Binge Eating Spectrum

Anne F. Malavé

> Got to get some food
> I'm so hungry all the time
> I don't know how to stop
> I don't know how to stop . . .
> Peter Gabriel,
> "No Self-Control"[1]

I met Susie[2] two weeks after the 9/11 New York City World Trade Center trag-edy. In her initial interview, as she presented her history of "serious problems with drugs, alcohol, binge eating, and shoplifting." I felt there was something significant left unsaid. So I asked and she confessed that, following our consulta-tion, she was going to see a judge for court sentencing relating to a drug-related crime. Forced to attend a drug and alcohol rehabilitation program, Susie now had 10 months sobriety from alcohol and drugs, but her bingeing and purging had escalated. I asked her something like,

> *"Well it seems very clear that you are feeling great distress, and that you need help for very many problems, not the least being the bulimia. It is equally clear that you have a way of getting people to go out on a limb for you, but what is not clear to me is whether or not you are here only because you want to use this interview as part of your argument before the judge, or whether, in fact, you want to participate in therapy."*

Susie burst into tears, the atmosphere suddenly felt raw, and I felt quite moved. She expressed relief, gratitude, and shame, admitting that her appearance in my office was intended exactly for that purpose. She told me that she felt I "got her number" and that perhaps I was the first person who might really be able to help her.

Susie's initial interview captures clearly the central elements of people who have problems with binge eating: The binger feeling out of control, their inter-personal impact, and an attempt on the part of the therapist to resist the invitation

219

to "take over" and instead help the person contact his or her sense of *personal agency*. I believe that the reason I was able to engage Susie in what has now been an intense and transformative long-term treatment is because of my training as an interpersonal psychoanalyst.

This chapter describes an interpersonal psychoanalytic treatment approach to help patients with binge eating problems and find the sense of personal agency and self-authority that allows them to become fully alive. Although the term *binge* as applied to eating is relatively new (Stunkard, 1959), binge eating is the original and earliest recorded eating disorder (Stunkard, 1993). It is also a common experience found across the eating-disorder spectrum (Fairburn & Wilson, 1993), all levels of psychopathology (Tobin, 1993), and in nonclinical populations. Definitions of a binge vary greatly. The layperson's understanding of a binge is "unrestrained indulgence" while the conventional, clinical definition of bingeing pairs "loss of control" of eating with "consumption of a large amount of food." Research has focused strongly on observable, objective criteria, while little is known, for example, about the "subjective" binges of people with anorexic problems (where a loss of control accompanies the ingestion of a small amount of food) or the phenomenological experience of bingeing. What remains consistent, however, is the common description of a "loss of control" (Beglin & Fairburn, 1992), which is a central focus of this chapter.

The most common psychotherapy treatment for eating disorders is a cognitive-behavioral (CBT) approach. It is well known that CBT treatments suffer from high rates of relapse and problems with long-term maintenance (Herzog et al., 1991). From an interpersonal perspective, these treatments may work only in the short term for some, because a patient feels temporarily controlled "from the outside." Although some patients may benefit from such programs, others will find greater benefit from a psychoanalytically informed psychotherapy treatment that might also combine some action-oriented behavioral techniques. This type of treatment provides a deeper, long-term approach to help patients develop an internal locus of control in which they gain personal agency and the ability to manage choices and uncertainty in life. This is especially important for patients for whom this bingeing behavior becomes chronic, who have a "bingeing style," similar to the "neurotic styles" described by Shapiro (1965; see especially Chapters 5 and 6 on "Impulsive Styles"). Furthermore, people who have relied on bingeing as a major coping style are vulnerable to regressing to bingeing throughout their lives at predictable periods, such as during times of great stress or crisis.

In the binge, the experience of the "loss of control" has many layers of meanings—only a few of which will be considered here. Precipitants of binge eating include restricting food and an adverse event or mood (Polivy & Herman, 1993). Food restriction creates a sense of deprivation, usually referred to by patients as "being good," which cannot be sustained and is followed by "being bad" and the binge. Binge eaters often have problems in self-regulation and self-soothing (Beebe & Lachmann, 1998; Krueger, 1989; Schore, 1994). Often, these are lives marked by histories of chaos, trauma, disorder, and neglect. Binge eating may therefore be considered an attempt to self-regulate and self-soothe (Polivy & Herman, 1993, p. 193). From an interpersonal perspective, binge eating is not only a problem but also an adaptive security operation (Sullivan, 1940, 1954) and coping tool, a vital function of the person's survival.

In bingeing, the person tries to get rid of inner tensions, affects, and responsibilities. The binger has not yet achieved self-regulatory mechanisms such as mentalization and symbolization, which are crucial for the safe experiencing of affects that would otherwise be overwhelming and dangerous. Self-regulation and self-soothing are learned in relationship with another person (Beebe & Lachmann, 1998). Without these capabilities, people remain stuck in a default position where they feel entirely dependent upon others.

Bingeing behavior is an experience that is not only personal and private but also fundamentally interpersonal. The interpersonal psychoanalyst is interested in how the binge affects the patient's relationships with the people in his or her world. The person who binges on food also binges as a way of being in the world, and this includes how this individual interacts with people. The binge is therefore also a *lived experience between people.* In the consulting room, the analyst looks for how this experience enters the interpersonal field between therapist and patient (Brisman, 1992, 1995), and then by using an awareness of transference–countertransference phenomena and an understanding of what is needed, works with the patient to change that field. Recognizing common interpersonal dynamics with people with binge eating problems can be a much needed guide in this process.

The binger enters the consulting room with their loss of control and (unconsciously) extends an invitation to a dance with the therapist around power and control. For the binge eater the answer to the felt problem of the loss of control lies outside, and the binger puts pressures on the therapist to take control and responsibility for her life instead of relying on her own resources. Brisman (1995) described this experience: "The addiction is an enactment of an interpersonal affair in which there is an insistence on granting an external agent control (albeit temporarily) over one's life" (p. 546). The patient's binge or loss of control creates an interpersonal field in the form of a split between two persons, each holding part of the whole experience. With a patient who is out of control, the therapist responds by feeling an urge to control the patient. With a patient who is restricting, the therapist responds by feeling out of control. This polarization is also two sided. For example, the therapist who is trying to control her patient is unable to gain access and also feels controlled by the patient. Likewise, the therapist with the restricting patient sees how this patient is out of control with her restricting and attempts to control the patient.

I am arguing here that from an interpersonal perspective the experiences of the binge (being "out of control") and of restriction (being "in control") are complementary—mirror images of each other, figure-ground in the same gestalt, two sides of the same coin—and present in all eating disorders. Along the eating-disordered spectrum, the shape of the interactions may "tilt" in one direction or the other, towards restriction (and anorexia) at one end of the spectrum and loss of control (and obesity) at the other end—with a wide variety of experiences and movements in between (including bulimia). Nonetheless, there is *common ground.* An attunement to these dynamics is not only a useful part of conducting a psychotherapy treatment, but also may be helpful in detecting the presence of such disorders, which are often hidden and not a part of the presenting problem.

For patients with binge-eating problems, the struggle for control with the people in their lives is partly an attempt to outsource the painful experience of feeling out of control. However, in the process of this "getting out of" one kind of experience patients also deprive themselves of another, richer experience (Phillips, 2010). The "getting out of" is a way to avoid feeling the loss that is part of choosing. Not surprisingly, many who struggle with these difficulties have suffered traumatic loss. However, this attempt to avoid loss brings about other losses, such as the loss of the joy of being fully engaged in life.

The challenge for the therapist is to allow herself to lose her personal inner stability, equilibrium, and spend long periods of time fluctuating between being out of control and controlling. Inevitably, in the beginning of the treatment the treatment feels shallow. Talking often feels like being on a walkie-talkie radio, without the other person saying "over." The therapist enters a world of messiness, chaos, and disorder. Boundaries are collapsed, and walls are built. Saying yes and saying no become confused. Challenges to the boundaries of the treatment frame abound. Interpretations can feel like—can *become*—power plays. The treatment frame may feel distorted into a wall. Bodily experiences become magnified and dysphoric. The therapist feels grandiose, special and relevant one moment, and completely ashamed, a silly amateur the next.

Before change can occur in interpersonal treatment, the experience must be lived by both patient and therapist. The interpersonal psychoanalyst must enter the patient's world to experience firsthand "what is going on around here" (Levenson, 1983).

Returning to Susie . . .

The impact of the first session, combined with, as she put it, "a brutal honesty born out of desperation," provided a window of opportunity and hope for the possibility of change. This initial session contains a pattern of interaction that has been continually repeated since, in ever-expanding ripples; with Susie's propensity for self-sabotage and creating messes, the absence of personal responsibility and conscience, the need for protection, fears and wishes around concealing and being seen, the need to deceive, and turning to people for help only in the nick of time. I have repeatedly found myself in the precarious position of trying to protect the treatment while clearly falling into her messes and confusion, hoping she will change. Susie has moved forward, retreated, has never been so vulnerable to self-destruction (and undoing) as after she has moved ahead. Often she has experienced me as caring for her most when I call her on her manipulations and maneuvers.

After her visit to the judge, Susie was sentenced to probation instead of prison. She credited her initial session as "for the first time," her experience felt real and she was able to show feelings of remorse in front of the judge. In turn, I found myself being transformed into a judge of sorts, an authority figure sentencing her to take responsibility. Later in treatment, she talked about how she had also longed to be imprisoned by that judge so someone else could take over her life.

Susie is an immigrant from India, the second in a family of five daughters who came to the United States when Susie was 5 years old. She describes herself as "the boy my father never had," the interpreter for the family's experience in the United States. As a child she got attention "for being bad" and "for being just like a boy." Her father encouraged her precocity and defiance. Her special position in the family brought immunity from her father's violence and verbal abuse, most of which was aimed at her mother. Being a substitute son also brought a damaged sense of female identity, exacerbated by Susie's body being larger in height and bone structure than other female family members and other Indian women.

Susie recounted a childhood in which her parents worked "all the time" while the children were left to fend for themselves. She described how the family failed to achieve the "American Dream" in a childhood dominated by poverty, deprivation, neglect, violence, and chaos. In her fantasy life, she remained attached to her early life in India, remembered as luxurious and rich in food and attention. She showed contempt for her father's arrogance and her mother's submissiveness, and her internalized racial prejudice produced contempt for other Indians.

Susie started restricting her eating after she left for college, and this soon led to bulimia. She gradually descended into a destructive world of food, drugs, and promiscuity after being raped by a close friend's boyfriend. She became irresponsible and rebellious, embracing recklessness and self-objectification as an attempt at mastery over being abused, and as a way of feeling special. She consistently defeated attempts from others to help, even after she given second and third chances at different jobs. She sabotaged two previous psychotherapy treatments. Of the first therapist, she described how "(she) talked about herself . . . (and) did not address core issues," while, with the second, "I felt I could talk circles around her."

The beginning of treatment was about having a treatment. There was bravado and defiance alongside hunger for contact. Susie was not accustomed to sharing a space with another person: In fact, for Susie, sharing and mutuality did not exist. Rather, contact was about subjugation, exploitation, contamination, and getting needs met at the other's expense in a dog-eat-dog world, where the struggle for survival prevailed.

Food retained a dominant space from the start. Susie described the stashes of clothes and food in her closet in her parents' bedroom, where she was installed while her parents slept in the living room—perhaps more of an attempt to contain her messes than of self-sacrifice. The felt experience that she could never be satisfied, that she was always greedily hungry, driving her to binge and purge five or six times in one sitting repeated her childhood experience of inadequate supplies and attention. She felt that she was constantly consuming or being consumed by others' needs. Susie was scared not to get better and scared to give up bingeing. Getting better meant abandonment, having supplies cut off, being expected to do too much by herself, and sacrificing her own needs in order to take care of others. Choosing meant losing. Being responsible only meant more responsibility. Getting better meant giving up the dream world—her alternate universe in India.

Early dreams were mostly devoid of people in empty rooms and corridors with substances like dirt, food, rats, and bugs. Her first dream included me:

She's Such a Problem Child . . .

S: You were in my dream . . . it was a school setting . . . there was a long bench, table, and there were some counselors on one side. . . . I went to one. . . I was going to start talking with her . . . I see someone sitting next to me in my peripheral vision, and it was you and you looked a little disheveled—hair messy, you sat down, you started talking about your daughter and saying, "I don't know what to do about her—she's such a problem child," and I remember turning my body away so you wouldn't recognize me. . . . I was telling my counselor, whispering, "Don't tell my name," and my counselor said, "Speak up! What?" I feel anxious and uncomfortable. . . . I was trying to have you not see me so we could work together and not have to go through this unpleasantness.

Some of Susie's associations included the following:

> *"I see you as unflappable, very together . . . maybe I was your daughter. . . . I fear that you might be flappable too. . . . I feel like you're the first person who's kind of cut through a lot of smoke screens. . . . I fear you would recognize me. . . . I would've preferred not seeing you that way."*

Susie's bingeing and purging remitted as she became more dependent on me. The majority of early sessions consisted of tracking affect ("What are you feeling? . . . What are you feeling now?"), and making connections between feeling states and triggers for bingeing. As Susie went to and fro with the tides of the bulimia, so did I: alternating between being pulled in to fight for the treatment and then disengaging to talk about what was going on in her life and between us ("What do you want to do? What do you want to do now"?") Susie told me later in treatment that she had no idea what I was talking about: "What I want has been irrelevant."

As treatment progressed, I found myself veering between extremes. I often felt in a double bind: if I told her what to do, I became her dominating father; If I did not, I became the neglectful mother. In the transference I (a white woman from England) also became the "other": "Just because you are an immigrant in this country, do not *dream* that you have had the same experience as me, or that you have any idea of what it is like to be a minority member in this country!"

While recognizing the importance of being culturally sensitive, I also felt both exploited and guilty for my class and for my white privilege. I had both low and great expectations of Susie and of the treatment. I felt hopeful and hopeless. I felt overly responsible and helpless. I constantly found myself "waiting for the other shoe to drop." My body developed symptoms: neck pain (Susie or the treatment as "a pain in the neck"?), restless legs (to escape?), gnawing at the pit of my stomach (dread? hunger?), and I often found myself rubbing my temples (trying to think?). I did my best to stay present and to find a way of working: of calling Susie on her deceptions, and simultaneously being a helpless witness to her dangerous behaviors. The image I had of the treatment at this time was of Susie clinging to me as I clung to an *unmoored buoy* in choppy seas.

Gradually, with repetition, reliability, and the constancies of the frame, we started to form a collaboration. It involved recognizing both sides of Susie's experience: the part of her that wanted to become whole and the part of her that wanted to destroy, to obliterate. I gradually found a way of working between tensions, for example, of witnessing (Stern, 2010), letting her claim her treatment, calling her on her deceptions, and also talking to her about what she was doing and what we were doing together. I remained curious: Being so, slowed her down and helped her gradually tolerate the intolerable.

I talked with Susie about how the bingeing and purging were an adaptation, a short-term solution with longer term negative side effects. We started to look at what was going on between us. The interpersonal detailed inquiry method (Sullivan, 1940, 1954) of asking questions allowed us to explore, develop complexity, and seek multiple meanings and multiple layers of meanings. It also helped Susie learn how to reflect. With time, there developed a potential space where Susie started to trust me, and I began to trust myself.

After working with Susie for several years I discovered that she treated her reproductive capability the same way she treated her digestive system, with multiple pregnancies and abortions. As we explored the multiple meanings of this, Susie talked about her feelings of guilt and remorse for this extreme behavior. She spoke about the rape and her past sexual experiences: reflecting on her sexual experience, she said, "I could have been an inflatable doll." During the treatment, she aborted a pregnancy that she wished to continue. She felt a strong desire to have the baby, but felt incapable of caring for a child. This was reflected in another dream:

Snapshots of My Past . . .

S: This tiny helpless thing . . . I got to see snapshots of my past . . . in one I was holding a baby and the baby was really banged up . . . bruised . . . this tiny helpless thing . . . I had even a name for this baby . . . an Indian name starting with "A" . . . I was holding this baby and I was dreaming about my aborted body . . . I actually had the baby . . . the baby died shortly after I had it, and I was feeling so sad about it . . . I put it . . . him? . . . through so much trauma . . .

I was profoundly moved by her sorrow, and my witnessing and acceptance of her choice seemed to help Susie be more accepting of her dreadfully difficult decision. She has taken precautions not to get pregnant since.

A primary goal of Susie's treatment is for her to live a more "ordinary" life without "the drama." As treatment has progressed, Susie has experienced increasingly long fallow periods in which she feels dissociated and, increasingly, periods when she is more in touch with depressive affects and dysphoric memories. We both understand these as experiences that she has been trying to avoid. During these times I try to be present but also stay out of her way to let her work things out in my presence rather than trying to figure problems out for her. Recently, however, Susie was talking about a work promotion, and hearing she was about to sabotage it, I jumped in to point this out. Her response was immediate:

A Glimmer of Glee . . .

S: I feel as though you get a kick out of proving me wrong . . . you catch me out and I feel as though there's a glimmer of glee in there? Rather than be helpful . . .

AM: What would being helpful look like?

S: You'd tell me what to do!

AM: So I'm either getting a kick out of catching you out or telling you what to do?

S: Well, sometimes you do tell me what to do . . .

AM: Yes, that's true.

I acknowledged that she was quite correct about the "glimmer of glee," of my excitement about pointing out the sabotaging. We talked about this enactment, which illustrates challenges to the therapist's own "drama": As therapists, we, too, like variety and sometimes enjoy finding opportunities to interpret. We are, after all, people who strive—and need—to "be helpful." Yet, in doing so, we can easily rob the patient of her struggle to discover and own her real experience.

Susie and I also talked about how she had a parallel glimmer of her own in challenging me. By doing so, she demonstrated her growing independence and personal agency. As Susie individuates, becomes increasingly self-authorized, and finds new ways to self-regulate and self-soothe, my interaction with her has become more relaxed.

Susie's life has significantly improved during this treatment. She has finished her education and maintains a successful career; she gets on well with her coworkers; she has an enriching marriage; she has reconnected with college friends; and she is much closer to her family. She is now more compassionate towards others and towards herself. She has been able to develop healthy boundaries with others and within her family. In a recent session she exclaimed: "I have just realized, my *whole family* has a case of PTSD!" She no longer looks down on her parents for their failures, but admires them for their perseverance. She is now thinking of having a baby. She told me recently she feels she has "turned a corner." Below is our interaction around a recent dream.

A Fish the Size of a Chihuahua . . .

S: I had a dream last night . . . I moved into a new apartment when it was already furnished . . . somehow I ended up with a bag—a giant sac . . . of the most ugly fish in the world—the size of a Chihuahua . . . ugly! It's the world's ugliest fish . . . bumps, scales, crazy things sticking out of it . . . (like) deep sea nature shows of fish that live thousands of feet under the ocean and are absolutely alarming looking . . . this was one hideous fish. . . three eye balls . . . absolutely revolting! I don't know what to do with this thing . . . almost too big to kill! And then somehow a dog . . . packed in a giant bag, in a tote bag . . . packed along with the fish . . . not in the same water . . . somehow I brought home a fish and a dog . . . so I come home to this new home . . . I don't know what to do and whoever I was with said "the fish tank" . . . this whole time there was this giant fish tank already there, with a giant fish in it . . . about this big (stretches arms wide) . . . the size of a barracuda! Long, also absolutely hideous . . . looks like the fish I already had . . . with a giant mouth . . . you know how some fish have giant mouths and travel with their mouths open, capturing food, and plankton . . . so this giant fish was living there the whole time. I can't remember if I talked it over . . . must have been Dave (husband) . . . well I guess I'll put this fish in the tank with the giant fish . . . a baby fish I guess. . . . So this person helped . . . hard to lift the cover off . . . a lot of water spilled, but I managed to slip the fish in . . . the water level went down, and leaked more . . . and oh no, suppose the giant fish eats the smaller fish . . . a mess . . . worried they were too crowded . . . but they didn't attack each other . . . and the fish was blinking at me with three eyeballs . . . they were swimming around really fast—but not attacking each other . . . seemed like they were enjoying themselves . . . huge bugs around . . . came out of the tank . . . must have been what they were eating . . . my companion put them back in the tank . . . one of those dreams so vivid I didn't want to get up. . . . Isn't that crazy?

AM: What do you make of it?

S: I remember feeling . . . less revulsion for the fish because I was taking care of it . . . thinking I have to take care of them . . . figure out a way . . . what if they die . . . what do I do with their giant fish carcasses . . . I started feeling responsible for them and got a sense of accomplishment for not having killed them through this process. I had to replenish the water carefully and I did it . . .

AM: . . . what about this dream as having something to do with this treatment?

S: Obvious symbol . . . thinking of having a child . . . ambivalence . . . creating messes . . . I don't know . . .

227

AM: Anything else . . . about in here . . . or about me?

S: I forgot to tell you I lost my phone over the weekend . . . I'm creating chaos in my life . . . I need to get out of my way . . .

AM: Well you may be creating chaos . . . (but) also taking care of the fish . . . new space already furnished . . . fish and a dog . . . you got help . . . but you made it on your own . . .

S: Pretty powerful. . . . There's a bit of a mess . . . the water levels went down . . . I thought fish would fight or one would eat the other . . . but they didn't . . . I put some water in the tank so they'd have more room but worried it wasn't good kind of saltwater . . . it was (OK) for the time being . . . but I wondered in the long run what would happen to them . . .

AM: How does it make you feel now?

S: A little weird . . . makes me feel so out of touch with my feelings . . . hard to say . . . but already a sense of recognition . . . The uncertainty of dealing with . . . it makes me feel a little sad maybe . . . these fish were so ugly . . . but I didn't hate them . . . I was semi-revolted, well half-revolted, but I didn't hate them . . .

AM: Makes me think of the expression "warts and all" . . . accepting a person for who they are . . .

S: That's absolutely a good point . . . I feel at a point in my life where I just have to accept who I am . . .

AM: Well it does sound like you are accepting of your faults and so on . . .

S: Catch 22, but makes you complacent, right?

AM: I don't know . . . but the giant fish is not alone . . .

S: Are you the fish? You must be the little fish! One way to think about . . . I am the giant fish and you're the little fish . . . I might have eaten you but I did not . . . we played together in the tank. . . . Many ways of looking at it . . . I see it as very powerful symptomatology . . .

AM: Symptomatology?

S: Oh my god, I meant powerful symbolism!

There are many meaningful things to say about this dream and what it suggests about the treatment. The images of "a big fish in a small pond," "a small fish in a big pond," and being "a fish out of water" are, for example, familiar themes in our work together. However, I would like to emphasize here the elements of nurture and caring, acceptance, and *play*. In this dream and in its discussion between us, nothing awful is happening: "no one (as they say) *died.*" There is hope.

Although Susie still overeats at times, she is now more fully alive, more fully present with me and others, and there is a significant and qualitative difference from the way she used to be so out of control. She is gradually becoming aware of her impact on other people, and of her own sense of personal agency. Nevertheless the bingeing has not completely disappeared. For example, from a recent session:

The Truth Is It Was About Me . . .

S: I was giving myself time the night before (to get ready for an important business trip) . . . thought ahead . . . so far so good . . . had hair cut, on way home . . . decided to shop for shoes . . . for 60 minutes . . . still ok . . . on my way to the subway slipped into another store . . . another 45 minutes . . . up to that point I was myself—even now I'm trying to not take responsibility . . . started getting back to old habits . . . I decide to do what I want . . . like when I was bulimic . . . going through the motions as I started shopping for food . . . being a zombie or something . . .

AM: It sounds as though you see the shape of it, slow motion . . .

S: That's exactly it . . .

AM: Have you been able to think about why . . .

S: I was anxious . . . something I'm doing wrong . . . I revert back to the familiar . . . sort of a binge . . . different to other times I go shopping . . . I can do what I want . . . (instead of being home at the stated time) . . .

AM: Pushing the limits, moving the goalpost . . .

S: Exactly . . .

This was followed by a discussion of how being home late had upset her husband, and about me waiting for her to return a telephone call.

AM: What was it like knowing I was waiting to hear from you?

S: It didn't . . . it felt OK . . . in the past it would've felt like a demand . . . because of your help I am so at peace with my parents . . . in Matrix the bullets come slow motion . . . I am dodging them . . . I see it's about them, not about me . . . I can get frustrated . . . but not huge resentment . . . before I made it always about you . . . when the truth is, it was about me.

Susie and I are doing something *together*. With the "slow motion" of the *Matrix* bullets following my description of the "slow motion" shopping binge, I see the developing links between us. She is better, yet there's more to do.

The work continues.

Notes

1. Written by Peter Gabriel. Published by Real World Music Ltd./EMI Music Publishing. Reprinted by permission. Courtesy of petergabriel.com.
2. All identifying details have been changed for reasons of confidentiality.

References

Beebe, B., & Lachmann, F. (1998). Co-constructing inner and relational processes: Self and mutual regulation in infant response and adult treatment. *Psychoanalytic Psychology, 15*(4), 480–516.

Beglin, S. J., & Fairburn, C. G. (1992). What is meant by the term binge? *American Journal of Psychiatry, 149,* 123–124.

Brisman, J. (1992). Bulimia in the late adolescent: An analytic perspective to a behavior problem. In J. O'Brien, D. Pilowsky, & O. Lewis (Eds.), *Psychotherapies with children* (pp. 171–188). Washington DC: American Psychiatric Press.

Brisman, J. (1995). Addictions. In M. Lionells, J. Fiscalini, C. Mann, & D. Stern (Eds.), *Handbook of interpersonal psychoanalysis* (pp. 301–316). New York: Analytic Press.

Fairburn, C. G., & Wilson, G. T. (1993). Binge eating: Definition and classification. In C. G. Fairburn & G. T. Wilson (Eds.), *Binge eating: Nature, assessment, and treatment* (pp. 3–14). New York: Guilford Press.

Herzog, T., Hartmann, A., Sandholz, A., & Stammer, H. (1991). Prognostic factors outpatient psychotherapy of bulimia. *Psychotherapy & Psychosomatics, 56,* 44–48.

Krueger, D. W. (1989). *Body self and psychological self.* New York: Brunner Mazel.

Levenson, E. (1983). *The ambiguity of change.* New York: Basic Books.

Phillips, A. (2010). On getting away with it: On experiences we don't have. In J. Petrucelli (Ed.), *Knowing, not-knowing, and sort-of-knowing* (pp. 165–173). London: Karnac Books.

Polivy, J., & Herman, C. P. (1993). Etiology of binge eating: Psychological mechanisms. In C.G. Fairburn & G. T. Wilson (Eds.), *Binge eating: Nature, assessment, and treatment* (pp. 173–224). New York: Guilford Press.

Schore, A. (1994). *Affect regulation and the repair of the self.* New York: W. W. Norton.

Shapiro, D. (1965). *Neurotic styles.* New York: Basic Books.

Stern, D. B. (2010). *Partners in thought: Working with unformulated experience, dissociation, and enactment.* New York: Routledge.

Stunkard, A. J. (1959). Eating patterns and obesity. *Psychiatry Quarterly, 33,* 284–295.

Stunkard, A. J. (1993). A history of binge eating. In C. G. Fairburn & G. T. Wilson (Eds.), *Binge eating: Nature, assessment, and treatment* (pp. 15–34). New York: Guilford Press.

Sullivan, H. S. (1940). *Conceptions of modern psychiatry.* New York: Basic Books.

Sullivan, H. S. (1954). *The psychiatric interview.* New York: Norton.

Tobin, D. L. (1993). Psychodynamic psychotherapy and binge eating. In C. G. Fairburn & G. T. Wilson (Eds.), *Binge eating: Nature, assessment, and treatment* (pp. 287–313). New York: Guilford Press.

15

'SWEET THING'

Racially Charged Transferences and Desire in the Interpersonal Treatment of a Black American Woman With Binge Eating Disorder—Who Needs Chocolate Cake When You Can Have Chocolate Men?

Andrea Hamilton

Historically, sociocultural factors render the female image and construct meanings that define ideal beauty based on a complicated mixture of politics, art, fashion, historical events, and individual choice. While icons of beauty are ever shifting depending on the social climate, the enduring image of a woman with an eating disorder is that of a white woman or girl who is emaciated, frail, and with a vacant expression. The woman of color has not been seen by culture as having eating problems or problems with body image. To the contrary, the stereotype of a black woman is that she is comfortable with her larger size and that for her both food and sex are taken with uncomplicated pleasure. Only in the last twenty years has science included black women in studies of eating and body-image problems. While black women may not have been considered to suffer with eating disorders, per se, I believe that their ideas about food and their bodies are impacted in unique and challenging ways by the racially charged historical and sociocultural atmosphere in which they exist and grow. Black women are not immune to the pressures that stem from the white beauty ideal of excessive thinness, either. While, at the same time, they are impacted by equally unrealistic black beauty ideals, destructive racial and sexual stereotyping, and the social pressure to use their bodies to express allegiances to both black and white culture.

In this chapter, I will explore the cultural factors informing stereotypes of the black female body and sexuality, and provide a clinical example that hopefully demonstrates how these elements of culture become part of the psychoanalytic conversation in the case of a black American woman with a binge eating disorder. In this case, it is particularly interesting to see how the symptom of binge eating is replaced by a symptom of intense sexual need over the course of the treatment. Looking at this transitional space in the treatment, I will highlight the importance

231

of understanding this transition from a psychoanalytic point of view as well as in terms of how her racial identity and racially informed sexuality played a role in how the transition became an important moment of therapeutic connection and, I believe, a transformative moment in her recovery.

Race as Part of the Body

Because I will be discussing race, racial dynamics in the analysis, and racial identity, I think it is apt for me to clarify my own background (and appearance) as it pertains to the material I am about to present. I am an American woman, and I identify myself as mixed race. My mother is Caucasian from European ancestry and my father is African American. I am slender, and my skin color is light brown. I have long, dark brown hair that I sometimes wear curly and sometimes wear straight. Based on my appearance, my cultural heritage has frequently been misidentified. *Because* my racial identity is not always apparent to my patients, so I disclose my race or inquire as to their thoughts about my race as patients begin to express a curiosity about it.

Patients with eating disorders often have a powerful reaction to the therapist's image, and some therapists have written about how their size, weight, and fitness have impacted their patient's treatment (Burka, 1996; Kahn, 2003; Pizer, 1998; Tinter, 2007; Petrucelli, 2008). I would add that the therapist's color and the patient's perceptions of race and racial identity also have a powerful impact on patients, and discussions about how my patients perceive me and interpret my appearance often have a profoundly therapeutic impact. Discussions of how race impacts their sense of their own bodies and minds are often facilitated by expressions of curiosity in the therapist and patient in the context of an atmosphere of acceptance of racial and body related content.

In the case I present here, the patient specifically requested a black therapist and immediately inquired about my racial identity during our initial phone contact. At the time she expressed no obvious negative or positive reactions to my racial identity, and we were able to schedule an appointment. Before I give further details about the case, I will discuss some background pertaining to it on the subjects of black female body image and eating disorders. The discussion of black women that follows pertains most closely, I believe, to the black American female and the specific experiences of growing up with brown skin and African heritage in the United States. At the same time, I fully acknowledge the multiplicity of points of view among black women, and want to express my strong understanding that experiences of "blackness" in women vary greatly between individuals and subcultures of people of color both nationally and internationally.

Black Women, Body Image, and Eating Disorders

Historically, studies of women and eating disorders have excluded black women. Though there seems to be a trend in the past decade toward inclusiveness of multiple ethnicities and genders in the field, much remains undiscovered about eating disorders and black women.

Studies have shown that black women receive diagnoses of eating disorders at a lower prevalence than white women (Striegel-Moore et al., 2003). Among black women who are diagnosed with eating disorders, binge eating disorder is by far the most common diagnosis, followed by bulimia and then anorexia. There is some evidence to suggest that black women who binge tend to do so more recurrently and use fasting, laxatives, and diuretics at higher rates that white women (Striegel-Moore et al., 2000). Furthermore, black women may seek treatment less for their binge eating and may have a higher tolerance for the weight gain associated with the binge-eating behavior (Pike et al., 2001). Some research has shown that white women and girls (primarily from college samples) are more influenced by the over idealization of thinness in our culture than women and girls of other races (Abrams & Cook-Stromer, 2002; Altabe, 1998; Chamorro & Flores-Ortiz, 2000; Demarest & Allen, 2000; Goodman, 2002; Lopez, Blix, & Gray, 1995) and that black American women are generally more satisfied with their bodies than whites (Greenberg & LaPorte, 1996; Harris, 1995; Powell & Kahn, 1995). However, one study has shown black prepubescent girls to have higher degrees of striving for thinness than white girls (Striegel-Moore, 1995) and the protective factors related to black cultural stereotypes depicting black women as comfortable with larger size have been challenged (Williamson, 1998). For example, research has shown that some black women do suffer with depression and, to a lesser degree, anxiety as a result of their disordered eating and its sequelae, including weight gain (Pike et al., 2001). Although, family dynamics and the particular eating practices experienced in one's family of origin, including the presence of a childhood diagnosis of obesity, appear to be more powerful predictors of binge eating disorder than race when black and white women with binge eating disorder are compared (Striegel-Moore et al., 2005).

Most studies that have evaluated cultural differences and eating disorders, however, have not articulated specific culture based body image preoccupations, racial identity factors, and body image concerns. One exceptional study based on extensive qualitative interviews of black adolescent females (Hesse-Biber et al., 2004) found that black girls used the following adjectives to describe their body ideal: "thick . . . sturdy thighs . . . not too thin, not humongous . . . big butt, big chest . . . not too flabby" (p. 55). The girls also expressed a concern about their skin and hair, parts of the body not frequently addressed in assessment of body image. Hair—the way hair is styled, the products used, and the hairstyle's racial affiliation were a source of distress, preoccupation, and self-consciousness. This study also highlights the problematic relationships girls and women can have with food and body image that may not call for a specific diagnosis but, nevertheless, may cause significant distress and detract from quality of life. Furthermore, disordered eating in minority women that may fall below the threshold for diagnosis and yet still present cause for concern has received little attention. While more information about how black women experience their bodies and their relationship with food is emerging in a clinical sense, much remains left to be discovered.

As a result, there appears to be the potential for black women's maladaptive eating patterns and body image concerns to be under diagnosed, under treated, and disregarded even when present in psychological treatment settings. There is limited study of the unique familial, social, historical, and cultural experiences of black women and how these may symbolically inform their relationships to their bodies and eating (Tyler, 2003).

Cultural Stereotypes of Black Women and Black Female Sexuality: A Psychoanalytic Point of View

Race is typically understood in concrete terms. Greene (1993) suggested that racial content in conversation is best understood as a concrete expression of racial experience and racial identity that usually, but not always, pertains to racism. When race comes into the psychoanalytic conversation, for example, this way of thinking about race emphasizes that the analyst hold a primary appreciation for how being black has a major impact on the life experience of the black person. Being black involves experiences of racially charged traumas and deep emotional wounds related to slavery (and the atrocities that accompanied it) that have been transmitted across generations and through cultural stereotypes. This idea calls for a validation of the black person's experience of racism and its powerful impact on shaping the individual's identity. Leary (1997a) wrote about this concept as the "really real" aspect of race in the psychoanalytic space.

An alternative thought about race and its role in the analytic space offers race *and racism* as symbolic of broader meaning. Conversations involving race, racial identity, and racial differences, for example, may hold transference/countertransference dynamics that include emotional undertones of dominance and submission, desire and longing, and aggression. Holding this concept in mind moves the analytic focus toward emotional experiences common to us all rather than unique to the person of color. The analyst recognizes what is held in common rather than what sets us apart.

I believe it is useful to think of these attitudes simultaneously, allowing the emphasis of both to ebb and flow. The experience of race *is* tangible, but I believe it is also fluid. For example, racial identity can be in the foreground, background, or held completely out of one's awareness. Race is also not necessarily black and white. White people can experience blackness, and black people can experience whiteness on a symbolic level. Race, as with other aspects of our images, when held symbolically, can transform and move between us. Through this process, I believe, we can begin to understand each other and understand more completely the experiences women have of their bodies, and the complicated experiences of being in a black body.

I think it is also helpful to think of trying to position oneself somewhere in between blackness, whiteness, and what they represent while allowing the meanings to emerge without relying too much on what is known about race to define the moment. This brings to mind Bromberg's (1996) concept of standing in the spaces between mind states that may be vulnerable to dissociation as a means of decreasing the intensity of affect associated with them. In describing this phenomenon, he states, "Standing in the spaces is a shorthand way of describing a person's relative capacity to make room at any given moment for subjective reality that is not readily containable by the self he experiences as 'me' at that moment" (1996, p. 515). He writes when describing the concepts of multiplicity of self, self-states, and transference as the ability to "maintain dual citizenship in two domains of reality with passports to the multiple self-states of the patient" (p. 528). In some cases where race is a central theme, I find it useful to imagine these states as containing degrees of blackness or whiteness. In doing so it is crucial to register the degree to which there is a racially charged energy or intensity, which may indicate an important transference shift or coming to awareness of the patient's need to use race unconsciously to communicate. The communication may be about race itself, but is not always or exclusively about race or racism.

I want to address now what I believe are some of the "really real" components of race that may become central to black women who experience eating disorders and disturbances in body image. The concept of the female body containing cultural ideation is not new, and much has been written about it from a feminist perspective (Hesse-Biber, 1991; Wolf, 1992). This concept is also widely recognized as a major contributing factor in the development of eating disorders and excessive dieting (Bloom et al., 1994). The overvaluation of thinness, for example, can be viewed as a modern cultural ideal of beauty, constructed by a society that fears female power and control, and therefore renders her frail, childlike in appearance, and unable to think about anything but food. How then does this waif-like image impact the experience of black women? Can black women be truly immune to this characterization of beauty that is so pervasive and insidiously acculturated? Are there other cultural factors at play for the black woman that in a "really real" way impact her, how she experiences herself in her body and mind? I believe that the black woman, in addition to coping with the demands of the white ideal, also struggles to manage cultural projections that are placed on her (and experienced in her body) based on race and the history of racism.

What cultural meanings are attributed uniquely to the black female body? I believe there are vast differences between how we as a culture see black and white women. The iconic references to the black female body are highly sexualized, in stark contrast to the white ideal, which deflates secondary sex characteristics. Black women are often invisible, but when *seen,* they are sexualized. Why?

Cornel West (1994), in *Race Matters*, argued that the historical devaluation of black Americans was, in fact, an attack on the black body and black sexuality, and that culturally held ideations about race and sexuality are so closely linked that it is impossible to fully address race without appreciating the sexual undertones of historically held prejudicial ideas about black people. He emphasizes that the attack on black people during slavery and the systematic terrorization of black people through white supremacy was aimed at the black form in order to denigrate the very essence of the self and irradiate its future promise. The images that are ingrained in the minds of black Americans: black people being lynched, raped, brutal separation of mother and child, branding, charred and castrated bodies hanging from trees, whipping posts, and hosings, are all experienced viscerally as a hatred of the body and an attack on the skin one lives in.

West (1994, pp. 122–123) wrote, "White supremacist ideology is based first and foremost on the degradation of black bodies in order to control them . . . one of the best ways to instill fear in people is to terrorize them. Yet this fear is best sustained by convincing them that their bodies are ugly, their intellect is inherently underdeveloped, their culture is less civilized, and their future warrants less concern." Out of this hatred grew stereotypes of the black woman and accompanying body types and sexual personas. There is Jezebel, a promiscuous, thin, light skinned schemer who uses sex to get what she wants from men and then discards them. The large-sized, large-breasted, always smiling, ubermaternal Mammy and Aunt Jemima are sexless yet eager to please at the expense of their own needs and desires, which are few. They are jovial house slaves who will side with the white man to maintain their privileged yet martyr-like status. There is Sapphire, who is a lean and plain angry bitch, standing with one hand on her hip, the other waving a finger in the face of whoever has crossed her. She is desperate for male attention yet drives them away with her fits of rage and disappointment. There is the Welfare Queen, the modern day, stressed out Mammy (or Nanny). She is tense, plump, and disheveled, but she is the matriarch who sacrifices all to take care of her multiple children, most of whom she had out of wedlock and by multiple "baby daddies." Then there is the Tragic Mulatto, or Peola, who is very light skinned and beautiful but hides (and hates) her blackness and attempts to pass for white, desiring only white men, and remains consumed by wishes to be white. She is ultimately found out, and it is the discovery of her blackness that proves to be her downfall. The stereotypes of black female sexuality (all equally dysfunctional) range from insatiable and immodest (Jezebel), to evil seductiveness (Sapphire), to selfless and sexless supermaternal (Mammy and Aunt Jemima).

These images are far from ideals, *and represent* a projection of feared libidinal experience. Black women do not aspire to these stereotypes but are powerfully influenced, I believe, by the understanding that they exist. Awareness of these stereotypes breeds self-consciousness in black women about their bodies and their expression of sexual desire and longing, which in an extreme form may preoccupy the black woman's consciousness in the same way a white woman may long to look like a supermodel. Additionally, there is the image of the white female ideal that looms somewhere in the consciousness of the black woman as well, along with its connotations of chastity and waifish sexual naiveté. *Black women* can feel a sense of invisibility, that her unique self is unknown and her reality is interpreted by these mythical anti heroines.

In addition to the images of beauty that are related to body mass and proportion that black women may aspire to, there are also concerns about skin color and hair that are uniquely important to women of color, with meanings deeply rooted in powerful historically prejudicial ideation. Various types of hair (fine, straight) and skin tones (lighter) symbolize strength and superiority, particularly in terms of sexual desirability but also in areas of overall achievement, including professional success. Black women are uniquely vulnerable to feeling evaluated and judged on the texture of their hair and their skin color and have expressed a preoccupation with hair texture and style and skin color, reporting that maintaining hair and not being too dark skinned are more important to them than their weight (Hesse-Biber et al., 2004).

Throughout history and across cultures, black women with lighter skin and straighter hair have been considered more beautiful, more sexually desirable, and more powerful economically (Tummala-Narra, 2007). These characteristics, however, can bring negative attention (envy, hatred) from women who feel they are unable to achieve these culturally based stereotypical ideals. There have been movements in modern society that have encouraged women to reject these stereo-types. Many have called for women to stop straightening their hair with chemicals and boycott expensive extensions or hair weaves (see Melissa Harris-Perry, 2012; see also www.curlynikki.com). These movements often call for women to view their hairstyles as expressions of their political beliefs and to reject the ideal image of white female beauty that causes black women to diminish the value of their black heritage. Studies have shown that even when racial identity is positive and the white ideal for thinness has been rejected, a desire to conform to white ideals of hair and skin color remain high (Hesse-Biber et al., 2004).

In psychoanalysis, racial content may concretely express sameness or difference, observations about appearances, consequences of appearance (for example, racism) or, positively, racial bonding, desirability, and pride. Racial content *may*, however, be viewed, as many other subjects are viewed in psychoanalysis, as conduits to deeper meaning and pathways to exploring transference, countertransference, or cultural transferences (Bonovitz, 2005). Racially charged processes may be explored by understanding the projections that underlie them, particularly when the analyst is keenly aware of their own racial prejudices that naturally occur (Altman, 2000). I will explore some of these concepts in the clinical case discussion below, and highlight how the analyst's open and curious attitude towards racial themes played a role in achieving healthy body image, regulated eating patterns, and a patient's appreciation *for* and greater understanding *of* her uniqueness.

Clinical Illustration

Ms. T, an African American woman with longstanding binge eating disorder, morbid obesity, and a history of childhood neglect began treatment with me in her late 30s. She requested that she see a black, female therapist who was experienced in treating African American women with eating disorders. During our initial phone conversation I felt strong feelings of inadequacy, and I thought, *I am not black enough for her.* I told her over the phone that I was biracial, something I do not ordinarily do during the initial contact with a patient, because I had a sense, that upon seeing me she might be disappointed by my ambiguous racial appearance.

From the start of treatment, she identified her eating behavior as reckless and life threatening. Her binges, starting at age 8, were daily and accompanied by feelings of deep loneliness. Though isolated and depressed, she developed a "life of the party" persona which was prone, also, to overindulge in food and alcohol. Though she seemed to enjoy this part of herself, in reflective moments she admitted that pleasurable feelings felt "funny," to her, and should be limited.

Detailed descriptions of her binges and longing for food consumed our sessions for the initial months of treatment. Cake was above all her favorite binge food, especially chocolate cake. As she described the deliberate process by which she sought out and savored this cake, it became apparent to me that this may be her only way of safely experiencing pleasure and excitement. Whenever she spoke of this chocolate cake, my appetite for it was also aroused, sometimes to the point of distraction.

Several months into treatment, she mentioned, "There is a restaurant around the corner that has the most amazing chocolate cake," and asked me if I had ever tried it. When I said no, she said, "That's too bad, you should." I then became vaguely aware of a desire to avoid talking about it. There was something about our conversation about the cake that made my blackness feel unwanted and undesirable. Did she (or I) wish I were as dark and lovely as this cake? My thoughts were too unformulated to put words to at the time, but I identified a racially charged transference process.

In the weeks that followed, she disclosed that she was bingeing on the cake before coming to sessions, and on weekends driving to the restaurant from her boyfriend's house (a considerable distance) just to buy this cake. I was prompted to ask her about what it was like to stay at his house. She described an atmosphere of deprivation, rejection, and unsatisfied longing. They sat together, but did not speak. It was often dark, and despite its vapidity she felt comfort there and dreaded leaving. She wanted to be held, but he angrily rejected her, demanding weight loss before marriage. She described her boyfriend as a large, muscular, dark-skinned black man who relied on her financially. She added, that despite his dark skin, he was "too white." His friends were white, and he attended all white schools.

Reflecting upon this moment, I put more explicit words to the anxiety I had experienced during our initial phone conversation and my "gut feeling" when she encouraged me to taste the chocolate cake. The anxious thought I was having was about how she did not want my kind of blackness, and that *she hates me for it.* Upon further thought, I extended this idea to include hatred for not only my skin color but for my body as a whole: my hair, my shape, my facial features, and my style of dress. I was experiencing, while hearing her talk about her unrequited desire and hatred of her boyfriend's whiteness, a complete hatred of my self located in the concrete physical form. I believe this was an experience of hers that we both came to know unconsciously through enactment with the cake. I was able to understand her through this enacted process, and know the tenacity with which this hatred (of her self and unmet desires) occupied her mind and body.

As Ms. T became more aware of the intensity of her longing and disappointment about being rejected (and how this was enacted with food), she slowly disclosed an early life of deprivation with very limited amounts of physical affection from either parent. She said she could not remember being physically held by her parents, though she had a sense she was loved. Her mother, she said, often encouraged her to eat large portions of "comfort food" and her mother joined her in these medicinal binges. In her disclosures of the painful and deep longing for affection, I felt that the racial aspects of our experience receded. The chocolate cake became a symbol of desire and love related to her wish to excite and be excited.

After several years of treatment, Ms. T was able to manage her impulsive eating to the point of minimal bingeing and infrequent overeating. She lost weight. She married her boyfriend. Though her anger toward him did not lessen in intensity, she was able to broaden its meaning to the extent that she moved away from being angry at his whiteness, to acknowledging that she was disappointed by his passivity and limited ability to partner with her. Her body shape transformed into a more curvaceous form, and she began regularly receiving (and seeking out) flirtatious attention from men for the first time in her adult life. She found this irresistible, and began a series of extramarital affairs with black men whom she described as the "crème de la crème."

She experienced these encounters with intense excitement followed by a kind of shock and deep sense of grief. I thought of it like the sadness that occupied her finishing the chocolate cake. It was so rare, she said, for her to feel satisfied, that as soon as she felt satisfied by him, she felt the longing, again, as if it could not be held, savored, or even reflected upon. Then she longed for his attention again, often ending the relationship to cut off this feeling of longing, which she despised. As she immersed herself in discovering her desire and accompanying grief, we recognized that her food bingeing stopped completely. She had begun to allow herself to relate to people in an emotional way that had previously been reserved only for food.

After several sessions during which she had exclusively focused on her sexual experiences with various men, she came in and asked me "what are *you* thinking about all this?" The thoughts I was having were multiple, layered and complicated. I was struck in the moment how important that question was and felt that the idea that I might be judging her was implied. I was aware in the moment that I had, in fact, been monitoring her ability to protect herself. I had a concern for her safety and had asked in a previous session whether she had been having safe sex. I also had asked if she was worried about getting caught by her husband. The reckless abandon with which she was pursuing these relationships left her vulnerable to being harshly rejected, as well. We had discussed these thoughts in previous sessions, so I was aware that she knew I was evaluating her ability to care for herself, and, with her (though this is not the case with all my patients) I felt this evoked a very white-dominant role in me. I was the doctor observing the symptom. It also occurred to me upon reflection that I had been judging what seemed to me to be an objectification of black male sexuality. The stereotyped manner in which she described "these men" did make me uncomfortable and suspicious (that she was idealizing them even more than she was putting forth). I felt a deeper level of discomfort, however, like I had become her white male superior: the exploitive voyeur, as she described him, who sat back, watched, and scrutinized her achievements.

In the moments after she asked this question, however, I felt a shift in my attitude towards her sexuality. I saw her expression of sexuality in the session less as a part of her "sickness" and more as a developing healthy part of herself, a broadening of her ability to feel her own excitement and take pride in it. I recalled how painful it was in the beginning of our work together for her to speak of her desire for excitement let alone experience it with another human being. A crucial feeling I had in this moment was one of excitement for her. And, so I said, "I have been noticing your enjoyment, and though I am curious about my own reaction . . . ordinarily I might be a little worried . . . instead I'm feeling really happy for you, and really curious about this new phase of your life, and (I added tentatively), well, more than a little envious, too." She then said, "I know, isn't it great. I used to binge on chocolate cake and now I binge on chocolate men. That's quite an improvement!" We both laughed, and I agreed, that for her, at this moment, it meant she had come a long way.

I see this as a powerful moment of connectedness between us but also a pivotal moment toward her understanding herself and enjoying her excitement. We came together in a spontaneous, genuine, and enjoyable moment ourselves. There was a feeling of collaboration and pride in our shared experience. It was an exciting moment, too. I believed, also, that our mutual enjoyment of the black men she was talking about represented a safe, albeit objectifying inroad to explore her own deliciousness and desirability which was so new and frightening to her. I believe that it was important to her that I received this communication of her sexual experience (excitement) without reservation, digest it, and reflect it back to her in a nonjudgmental way that allowed her to continue to be curious.

Discussion

I hope that the presentation of Ms. T illustrated some of the complex cultural, racial and sexual issues at play in the psychoanalytic treatment of disordered eating and body image in women of color. Ms. T was particularly articulate regarding her racial identity and experience and readily brought race into the analytic space, inviting discussion of race even during the initial phone encounter. Most patients will not be so forthcoming, as race is often considered forbidden territory (West, 1994; Leary, 1997b). Even when racial content is subtly expressed, however, I believe it is useful to think symbolically about race and observe racially charged experience in the analyst and patient, understanding there may be a strong tendency to want to avoid it.

Race in psychoanalytic space holds ideas about human psychic experience and relatedness that run deeper than the image, but focusing on racial concerns may, at times, helps us to speak about the body in ways that are useful, I believe, for black women who are suffering with complicated, culturally informed body image concerns. I think with patients with eating disorders, race may be power-fully charged in sessions, because the work with our patients is often focused on aspects of bodily form to begin with. One could argue, when considering body image and states of bodily experience, that it is hard to ignore and negligent to overlook something so basic and crucial a part of the body as the skin that enfolds us. After all, the skin is what protects the body. It is the barrier between outside and in. It is also the tool, if you will, with which we feel and experience touch. So much of the focus of treatment is concerned with managing the perceived image of the patient and helping the patient attain a more realistic and authentic view of herself in the shadow of the cultural ideals that call for radical alteration of her natural form. For women of color, this includes often the call to radically alter their natural selves to conform (or reject) unrealistic white or black ideals and stereotypes related to shape, size, sexuality, hair, and skin.

I believe that the myth that black women like their bodies more than other women may serve to exclude the complicated body image and sexual concerns that black women do experience (symbolized in some ways by the complicated relationship women have to their hair and skin color). Experiences of racial trauma and the stereotyping of black femaleness may damage and diminish a black woman's ability to experience her own uniqueness. In the case of Ms. T, this was profoundly experienced at the level of disassociating her own feelings of longing, desire, and sexual excitement. The extent to which this process occurs is, of course, unique to each individual's experience, and there is some evidence that a strong racial identity (positive associations to ones' blackness and black heritage) protects girls and women from low self-esteem and body image distur-bances (Hesse-Biber et al., 2004).

It takes time and patience to fully explore and make sense of internalized rac-ism and how it has fractured the self and injured the body. In the case of Ms. T, race-based rejections that were both her own and inherited from previous gen-erations, left her with painful unfulfilled longing and desire, which I believe she had primarily allowed herself to experience only completely with food. I found it necessary to stay closely attuned to my own intrapsychic shifts between states of blackness and whiteness, paying careful attention to signals of internally held prejudices and self-loathing. In her case, it was often through my experience of self-hatred in the countertransference and a feeling that she was attacking my whiteness that I became aware of projected aspects of Ms. T's experience: her desire for acceptance from white culture, for example, that was projected, I believe, when she demanded that I (and her boyfriend) conform to a certain type of blackness, a deeper and darker blackness that represented not only her racial identity but also her sexual desires and desirability.

It was when I recognized the full extent of the racialized hatred in the room—that I felt hated by her and was hating myself for not being as black as she wanted me to be—that we were able to begin to explore experiences of her body that were off limits to her before. As Altman (2000) and Bonovitz (2005) illustrated in their explorations of racial concepts in psychoanalytic work, experiences of racial

hatred are bound to surface in the minds of the analyst. Rather than (or in addition to) being feared, it is useful to see them as part of what could be defined as a
historical cultural phenomenon entering the analytic field.

The analyst may become the oppressor (whether white or black) to the patient's
oppressed aspects of self experience. Recognition of these dynamics often opens
up to understanding of other taboo emotional states central to conflicts in the dyad
and patient (Leary, 1997b; Bonovitz, 2005; Altman, 2000). As Bonovitz stated,

> race and culture cannot be separated from the internal objects that reside
> in our unconscious. Nor can race and culture be weeded out from our web
> of interpersonal relations. Neither the inner world nor the outer world is
> more primary than the other. The cultural dimension is not a layer to
> be peeled away in order to get at the "deeper" unconscious roots of the
> transference . . . we must . . . critically examine the unfolding of the cul-
> tural transference/countertransference within the analytic relationship.
>
> (p. 70)

In doing so, the historical nature of what it means to experience black and white
and for differences to be negotiated becomes known and explored. For Ms. T, her
sexuality with its complicated cultural meanings was able to be explored first
safely (excluding race) in the context of her appetite for food and the chocolate
cake she so loved. Then, in a racially informed transference relationship with me,
she was able to acknowledge her object of desire shifting to men, specifically
black men, and then explore her relationship to her own sense of disempowerment
that was also racially charged and projected. I believe it was an understanding
and willingness to hear her experiences of blackness and whiteness (held in mind
and body) that allowed for the transition to a greater shared known experience
of her longing, desire, and the fear of it that was maintaining her food and body
preoccupations.

References

Abrams, L. S., & Cook-Stromer, C. (2002). Sociocultural variations in the body image perceptions of urban adolescent females. *Journal of Youth and Adolescence, 31,* 443–451.
Altabe, M. (1998). Ethnicity and body image: Quantitative and qualitative analysis. *Inter-
national Journal of Eating Disorders, 23,* 153–159.
Altman, N. (2000). Black and white thinking: A psychoanalyst reconsiders race. *Psycho-
anal. Dial., 10,* 589–605.
Bonovitz, C. (2005). Locating culture in the psychic field. *Contemp. Psychoanal., 41,*
55–76.
Bloom, C., Gitter, A., Gutwill, S., Kogel, L., & Zaphiropoulos, L. (1994). *Eating problems:
A feminist psychoanalytic treatment model.* New York: Basic Books.
Bromberg, P. M. (1996). Standing in the spaces: The multiplicity of self and the psychoana-
lytic relationship. *Contemp. Psychoanal., 32,* 509–535.
Burka, J. B. (1996). The therapist's body in reality and fantasy. A perspective from an
overweight therapist. In B. Gerson (Ed.), *The therapist as a person: Life crises, life*

choices, life experiences and their effects on treatment (pp. 255–275). Hillsdale, NJ: Analytic Press.

Chamorro, J., & Flores-Ortiz, Y. (2000). Acculturation and disordered eating patterns among Mexican American women. *International Journal of Eating Disorders, 28*, 125–129.

Demarest, J., & Allen, R. (2000). Body image: Gender, ethnic, and age differences. *The Journal of Social Psychology, 140*, 465.

Greenberg, D. R., & LaPorte, D. J. (1996). Racial differences in body type preference of men for women. *International Journal of Eating Disorders, 19*, 275–278.

Greene, B. (1993). Psychotherapy with African-American women: Integrating feminist and psychodynamic models. *Journal of Training and Practice in Professional Psychology, 7*, 49–66.

Goodman, J. R. (2002). Flabless is fabulous: How Latina and Anglo women read and incorporate the excessively thin body image ideal into every day experience. *Journalism and Mass Communication, 79*, 712–727.

Harris, S. M. (1995). Family, self, and sociocultural contributions to body image attitudes of African-American women. *Psychology of Women Quarterly, 19*, 129–145.

Hesse-Biber, S. J. (1991). Women, weight, and eating disorders: A socio-cultural and political-economic analysis. *Women's Studies International Forum, 14*, 173–191.

Hesse-Biber, S. J., Howling, S., Leavy, P., & Lovejoy, M. (2004). Racial identity and the development of body image issues among African American adolescent girls. *The Qualitative Report, 9*, 49–79.

Kahn, N. (2003). Self-disclosure of serious illness: The impact of boundary disruptions for patient and analyst. *Contemporary Psychoanalysis, 39*, 51–74.

Leary, K. (1997a). Race in psychoanalytic space. *Gender and Psychoanalysis, 2*, 157–172.

Leary, K. (1997b). Race, self-disclosure, and "forbidden talk": Race and ethnicity in contemporary clinical practice. *The Psychoanalytic Quarterly, 66*, 163–189.

Lopez, E., Blix, G. G., & Gray, A. (1995). Body image of Latinas compared to body image of non-Latina white women. *Health Values, 19*, 3–10.

Melissa Harris-Perry Show. (2012, June). Why black hair matters [Television broadcast]. New York: MSNBC.

Petrucelli, J. (2008). When a body meets a body: The impact of the therapist's body on eating disordered patients. In F. Anderson (Ed.), *Bodies in treatment: The unspoken dimension* (pp. 237–254). New York: Analytic Press.

Pike, K. M., Dohm, F. A., Striegel-Moore, R. H., Wilfley, D. E., Fairburn, C. G. (2001). A comparison of black and white women with binge eating disorder. *American Journal of Psychiatry, 159*, 1455–60.

Pizer, B. (1998). Breast cancer in the analyst: Body lessons. In L. Aron & F. S. Anderson (Eds.), *Relational perspectives on the body* (pp. 191–214). Hillsdale, NJ: Analytic Press.

Powell, A. D., & Kahn, A. S. (1995). Racial differences in women's desires to be thin. *International Journal of Eating Disorders, 17*, 191–195.

Striegel-Moore, R. H., Dohm, F. A., Kraemer, H. C., Taylor, C. B., Daniels, S., Crawford, P. B., & Schreiber, G. B. (2003). Eating disorders in white and black women. *American Journal of Psychiatry. 7*, 1326–1331.

Striegel-Moore, R. H., Fairburn, C. G., Wilfley, D. E., Pike, K. M., Dohm, F. A., & Kraemer, H. C. (2005). Toward an understanding of risk factors for binge-eating disorder in black and white women: A community-based case control study. *Psychol. Med., 35*, 907–917.

Striegel-Moore, R. H., Schreiber, G. B., Pike, K. M., Wilfley, D. E., & Rodin, J. (1995). Drive for thinness in black and white preadolescent girls. *International Journal of Eating Disorders, 18*, 59–69.

Striegel-Moore, R. H., Wilfley, D. E., Pike, K. M., Dohm, F. A., & Fairburn, C. G. (2000). Recurrent binge eating in black American women. *Archives of Family Medicine, 9*, 83–87.

Tinter, J. (2007). Bypassing the barriers to change: Bariatric surgery, case material. *Contemporary Psychoanalysis*, *43*, 121–134.

Tummala-Narra, P. (2007). Skin color and the therapeutic relationship. *Psychoanal. Psychol.*, *24*, 255–270.

Tyler, I. D. (2003). A true picture of eating disorders among African American women: A review of the literature. *Association of Black Nursing Faculty Journal*, *14*, 73–74.

West, C. (1994). *Race matters.* New York: Vintage Books.

Williamson, L. (1998). Eating disorders and the cultural forces behind the drive for thinness: Are African American women really protected? *Social Work Health Care*, *28*, 61–73.

Wolf, N. (1992). *The beauty myth.* New York: Anchor Books.

16

'BEWITCHED, BOTHERED, AND BEWILDERED'

Sharing the Dream

Iris Ackerman

> If I am asked how one can become a psychoanalyst, I reply: By studying one's own dreams.
>
> (Freud, 1910, p. 33)

One night, approximately two years into a three-times weekly treatment with Kate, a 23-year-old patient with bulimia, I had the following dream: I was en route to a night club in New York City. I knew Kate was celebrating her birthday there, and she asked me to "come through" (her term for stopping by). I think I was alone. I walked into a dimly lit club with modern décor. I liked the music playing and felt uplifted by it. Kate appeared and handed me two shots of Patron. I don't know if I drank them or not. Kate seemed glad to see me, although I sensed a strange awkwardness hanging in the air that may have been the result of seeing each other in "life" rather than in the familiar setting of my office. People were dancing, chatting, and having fun. At some point (not sure how much later), I saw Kate again. She was dressed in a long, white, flowing dress and she was dancing with little inhibition. She "danced" up to me and raising her voice above the music said, "I realized something big." As she said this, her large brown eyes lit up. She said, "Words are just words—that's all they are." I felt very happy that she had this revelation . . . then I woke up.

Although this was not the first time that I have had dreams about patients, this dream left me unusually startled, unsettled, and deeply curious about what this was all about. I tried to go back to sleep in an attempt to reenter the dream, but was unsuccessful. Questions began flooding my thoughts. What was I doing accepting an invitation to Kate's party? Why did she invite me to begin with? And how did I imagine she would experience my actually showing up? I wondered whether "my dream" could be interpreted as just that: *my dream* that she fulfill a wish or a vision of what I imagined was possible for her. Perhaps it expressed some narcissistic "underlying craving" (Coen, 2007, p. 1169) that conveyed more about what I needed from her than what she may have needed or desired at all. Did I wish Kate to make peace with her body and experience joy more than she? Had I manifested this wish in my dream? Maybe, but in addition I felt strongly that it had captured something real about Kate and the relationship we shared that needed to be understood. The more I resonated with this dream, the more curious I became. I wanted to understand who I was in the dream, who Kate was, and who we were together. I wanted to explore the storyline that showed up around our relationship, the part I was not privy to in the many analytic hours spent talking together in my office. I felt that sharing my dream with Kate would most directly help us to know the "Kate" that appeared in my dream. My intention was to facilitate a process whereby the meaning of my dream would help us learn something new and revise our experiences of what we thought we knew for many sessions to come.

Bewitched

What struck me about this dream, in addition to my behavior, was Kate's behavior. Specifically, she was free from thinking that something was wrong with her body. In my dream, she exhibited a joie de vivre that always seemed a stone's throw away from her possession. Her social ease and ability to "work the room" stood in high contrast to more typical experiences of intense social clumsiness, lack of self confidence, and the sexual inhibitions that plagued her. In the dream Kate was a "free-spirit," flowing across the dance floor with grace and purpose. There were no traces of her obsessive, measured, and sarcastic style. I watched her eat, drink, and "digest" the fullness of the experience without scoping out the nearest route to the bathroom so that she could purge her food and her anxiety. Kate danced and played, accepting her appetite (Orbach, 2009), with no visible sign of the "body hatred" (Orbach, 2009, p. 66) or tyrannical food control that stalked her life like a predator on a daily basis. In my dream, Kate was free from the hold that food, weight, bulimia, and "living in a hated body" (Orbach, 2009, p. 67) had claimed over her life since she was eight years old.

About Kate

Kate would say that she was "fat" by the time she was eight. By 13, she weighed around 275 pounds, and by age 15 she began a rigid dieting regime that morphed into very strict food control and bulimia. It was not uncommon for Kate to binge and purge as much as five times a day. She abused laxatives and exercised excessively. Kate described being a prisoner to the gym, not being able to pull herself off the treadmill until the desired number of calories burned appeared on the digital panel. At one point, Kate was spending four-and-a-half hours a day working out. By 18, she had lost about 125 pounds and began a series of plastic surgeries to remove sagging skin and fat deposits. She described each surgery as triggering a need to have another as she launched venomous attacks on parts of her body that disgusted and embarrassed her. She particularly loathed the appearance of surgical scars that seemed to be an indelible reminder of a war that was waged on her body.

Kate stopped attending high school regularly because of paralyzing anxiety, depression, and self-consciousness. She thought that peers were talking about her due to the dramatic changes in her appearance from the weight loss and consequent surgeries. When she did go to school, getting there on time for classes was nearly impossible. Although not a favorite among teachers, she did well for the little time she spent in class. She spoke with great appreciation and affection for an English teacher who supported her through this difficult time.

Kate smoked a good deal of pot and hung out with a crowd known as the "stoners." She explained that pot "calmed her craziness" more effectively that any of the medications prescribed. At the beginning of treatment, Kate was taking an antidepressant and a minor tranquilizer, which according to her "did absolutely nothing." Kate also reported five unsuccessful forays into therapy, describing the therapists as "on crack," and complaining that they "asked stupid questions" and "didn't get" her. Kate did remarkably well in school, indicative of her sharp intellect despite her irregular attendance and emotional upheavals. When I inquired about her stellar academic record, she said, "I may be crazy but I'm not stupid." Kate told me her family was "messed up." She was disappointed in her father, whom she describes as a wealthy, volatile, and disengaged man. She believed he cared more for the employees of his company than for his family. In contrast to this relationship, Kate was very connected and dependent on her mother, who shared some of Kate's resentment towards the father. Kate's mom appeared to overcompensate for her husband's surly behavior by indulging Kate's every whim. "My mom would never say no to me," said Kate. "Anything I ever wanted she would get me. I wish she would have been able to say no to me like other parents did." Kate's parents were at odds with each other most of the time and resided in separate wings of their large home. Kate repeatedly questioned why her parents stayed married. In that question I heard her confusion about her own existence. She described herself as a "misplaced old soul."

Kate came to me with diagnoses of bulimia nervosa, obsessive–compulsive disorder, major depression, and generalized anxiety disorder. At the time that Kate and I met, she was feeling lost and hopeless. She could not stay in college. Her bulimia was more and more out of control, and she felt she had little hope of ever finding a romantic relationship. She described herself as a "hot mess."

In our first session, Kate sat down on my couch and—before I said anything—blurted out, "You better not ask me something stupid like the rest of those idiot therapists . . . like what do you fantasize about when you have sex?" I remember laughing. Kate is funny, endearing, sarcastic, witty, entitled, tough, fragile, smart, lost, scared, stubborn, warm, and much, much wiser than her years. She really wants a chance at a better life. After about 30 minutes into the first session, Kate got up and said, "I'll be back. This will work for me!" That was 350 sessions ago.

Boundaries Shared

Working with dreams has long been recognized as a powerful tool to add more depth to understanding the psychic lives of patients and analysts. Like everything else, how one understands and utilizes dream material correlates with a clinician's perspective, sensibilities, and what the goals of the dream analysis are.

Broadly speaking, from a classical position, the main focus of dream analysis is to sharpen the clarity of the patient's psychodynamics, neurotic conflicts or dilemmas, and to discover the unconscious wish or fantasy disguised in the content and/or symbolism of the dream (Freud, 1957).

From an interpersonal perspective, the purpose and usefulness of the dream in clinical practice shifts to interest in how the dream highlights interactive and relational issues between the patient and analyst (Watson, 1994). Interpersonal analysts are concerned with what is "really going on" in the dream, what is implied in the dream (Levenson, 1983), and how the dream translates into some recognizable aspect of the treatment relationship (Watson, 1994). Interpersonal dream analysis revolves around these parameters and questions. Tauber and Green (1959) focused on the usefulness of analysts' dreams and suggest that an analyst's dream about a particular patient can be shared with the patient. They believed that when an analyst shares a dream with a patient in which the patient appears, the result can be educative for both members of the dyad and yield greater depth, contact, and expansiveness in the treatment. Watson (1994) cautioned, however, that while there is a valid rationale for analysts sharing of dreams, the decision to do so must be judicial and is best served by patients in treatment for several years and/or in instances of entrenched treatment impasses.

I want to state clearly that my decision to share my dream with Kate was made after careful consideration of the possible ramifications to her treatment. As such, a decision to intentionally self-disclose raises issues of boundaries and the analytic frame. Since Freud proposed an explicit structure for psychoanalysis with clear, specific rules and techniques of operation (Freud, 1913), the analytic frame has undergone many transformations. Today, the frame still retains its status as being an "essential reference point throughout any analysis" (Bass, 2007 p. 6). Its main utility, regardless of its shape, reference points, or theoretical underpinnings is to create and uphold a practical and symbolic structure where safe and clear boundaries enable the therapeutic process to occur (Bass, 2007; Goldberg, 2008). Historically, it stands to reason that the analytic frame Freud conceived was very much influenced by the staunch Victorian culture of his time and reflected a more rigid, fixed set of "framing principles" (Bass, 2007, p. 8). Reverence to this classical frame constituted the hallmark of a proper analysis, while deviations were regarded as technical mistakes, which could potentially threaten the integrity of the analysis.

More contemporary conceptions of the analytic frame, however, reflect "frame construction" (Bass, 2007, p. 14) that places more emphasis on the importance of meeting unique needs and goals of the analytic dyad within the specific context of that treatment. Understood this way, more contemporary views of the frame support the idea that as the patient/analysts' relationship evolves in the treatment, the analytic frame will also reflect these changes in form, function, and utility. Newer conceptions also appear to provide analysts with more creative freedom and flexibility to subjectively define the form of the frame that makes sense for the task and objectives of a particular treatment. These newer ideas are significant, for example, with regard to the concept of self-disclosure.

With the advent of more flexible frames of reference, the inevitability and applicability of self-disclosure or self-revelation, as part and parcel of the daily activity of doing psychoanalysis, is recognized. Aron (1996) made the point that it is virtually impossible to prevent communication about the analyst's inner states to the patient. He suggests that "communication about the therapist's internal states is continuously conveyed to the patient. All our interventions are behaviors, including our decisions not to intervene; our silences, too, are behaviors, and all behaviors are communications" (Aron, 1996. p. 229).

The issue becomes more complicated however, when the distinction is made between those disclosures that are inadvertent and those that are intentional or deliberate (Abend, 1995; Aron, 1996). As such, the decision to deliberately reveal something about an analyst's thoughts, feelings, and dreams (in this case) are the subject of considerable controversy and debate in psychoanalytic practice. Fundamentally, the debate revolves around the question of whether intentional self-revelation enhances and expands the "analytic space" (Aron, 1996, p. 230) or actually serves to constrict or shut it down. This begs an interesting question of whether deliberate self-disclosure somehow interferes with the patient's "job" to "be whatever," "project whatever," "invent whatever," and interact in whatever way he or she chooses. Although a detailed discussion of this topic is beyond the scope of this paper, I will highlight some of the pros and cons concerning this issue. Analysts who support the use of deliberate self-disclosure generally feel that with careful use, countertransferential experiences can enliven and enhance therapeutic action as well as encourage mutuality and collaboration in the analytic dyad (Chrzanowski, 1980). Gorkin (1987) took the position in favor of the judicial use of self-disclosure by suggesting that it helps to establish the therapist as real, with feelings and experiences not so dissimilar to those of the patient's. In this sense, the patient may feel as if he or she really "matters" to the therapist in an authentic way. This can have the effect of loosening and transforming negative behavioral patterns and interactions.

It strikes me that the more important question is not whether to use deliberate self disclosure or not, but whether the analyst has tried as best as possible to consider how this might impact the patient and the goals of the analysis. This said I believe that ultimately all analytic technique and discourse must fall upon the trusted shoulders of each analyst to intervene in a way that seems to be right for him or her at the moment for that particular patient (Mitchell, 1993).

Boundaries Denied

The concept of boundaries, as defined by traditional theorists, held firm to the notion that boundaries served to define the parameters of analytic discourse in a clear, particular manner, citing the shortcomings that transgressions from the prescribed template had for patients, analysts, and the treatment as a whole. Evolving viewpoints define boundaries as the "structural characteristics of the therapeutic relationship that allow the therapist to create a climate of safety" (Goldberg, 2008, p. 861). Boundaries are also considered to be the borders at which analytic conversation is constructed and organized as well as the site where the potential for change reaches its potential. Goldberg (1999, 2008) takes the position that there needs to be a distinction made between the concept of "boundary crossings" and "boundary violations" because they exist as two separate conditions that confuse moral issues with technical ones. This creates confusion and lack of clarity in the process. Boundary crossings are character- ized by their inevitability and applicability in the treatment setting. When an analyst crosses a boundary, it is thought to be unpreventable and potentially useful. Goldberg (2008) conceptualized boundary crossings as behaviors or incidents that can be processed, discussed, and analyzed as informative experi- ences. "Boundary violations," on the other hand, are evidence that something wrong or immoral has occurred. Yet, even with this being the case, the issue of "violation" becomes murky at times. Goldberg (2008) summed up the dilemma that arises in grappling with the idea of boundaries in that there is nothing clear- cut or definitive about them. He says:

> Before we can possibly detail the violations, it seems a wise course to describe the proper dimensions of a boundary, and these would seem to vary by the nature of the intervention being entertained. A therapist who, for example, believes in optimal gratification of a patient might well assume a different position than one who supports optimal frustra- tion. . . . Without in any way supporting or discouraging these particular stances, we must examine them more carefully before we can consider any particular action as a violation of a boundary. In this sense, one dis- tinguishes between boundary crossings and boundary violations (Gab- bard and Lester, 1996), in that, one necessarily crosses boundaries in treatment but need not thereby commit a violation.
>
> (p. 251)

Coming from an interpersonal/relational orientation, I am naturally drawn to the process of interaction, its meaning, and what unfolds thereafter. I can never really "prepare" (technically or emotionally) for a session, even when it seems like a good idea. For me, that kind of preparation detracts from the aliveness and power of the moment. Similarly, as I consider my take on the frame, boundaries, and self-disclosure, my tendency is to be far less focused on what the nature of the particular intervention is (with the exception of gross violations) than on the meaning of the event and what happens between the dyad thereafter. So when I came across Mitchell's (1993) description of how he thinks about and manages the frame, I felt that his understanding resonated most closely with mine. Mitchell suggested that:

> What is most important is not what the analyst does, as long as he struggles to do what seems, at the moment, to be the right thing; what is most important is the way in which an analyst and analysand come to understand what has happened. What is most crucial, is that whatever the analyst does, whether acting flexibly or standing firm, he does so with considerable self-reflection and openness to question and reconsider, and most important with the patient's best interests at heart. . . . In short the process itself is more important than the decision we arrive at.
>
> (1993, p. 196)

Sharing the Dream

Kate comes to the session and I tell her that I had a dream about her. With what seems like a combination of shock and horror, she says, "I'm so sorry to have bothered you in your dream. I'm such a pain. . . . I mean the last thing you want is me intruding on your sleep!" Kate goes on like this until the end of the session. When the session was over, I sat there, dazed. She didn't even ask about the dream! And I didn't press her. The discussion never progressed beyond the issue of her sense that she was such a "bother" to me.

I found Kate's response to the dream almost as interesting as the dream itself. I was confused about who was intruding upon whom, who crossed whose boundaries, and what was conveyed in this enactment? In the next session, I asked her again about her reaction to telling her that I had a dream about her. Like an instant replay of the previous session she looked at me with what I thought was a hint of a smile and said, "So sorry to have bothered you." When I repeated my inquiry as to why she felt like a "bother" and what a bother felt like, this usually verbal and articulate young woman would not or could not respond to the question. As the session continued, she laughed at one point and said "You see me enough, and, lucky you, I am now showing up in your dreams!" When I asked her if she felt I was "lucky" (even though it was said in her usual sarcastic manner), she only responded by chuckling a little and repeating, "I'm so sorry to have bothered you."

I have to say that I actually felt glad (and maybe a little lucky) that I got to "compose" such a rich, uncensored piece about a part of our work that I consciously knew very little about. It was also becoming more apparent to me that Kate and I were not going to talk about this dream in the manner that I usually did with other patients: exploring, questioning, and playing together. Kate simply would not have it. I found my thoughts drifting to her family, where the borders between parent and child were confusing and painful for her. Kate described often feeling like the parent and forever wished to feel like the child. She wistfully longed for parents who knew the "right things" to do, reporting that her parents were too involved in an unhappy marriage to pay "the right" kind of attention to her. I wondered whether her verbal apologies about "bothering" were symbolic efforts to "purge" or stave off the insurgence of my dream and its boundary intrusion upon her. Did she feel that I, as her "analytic parent," was—like her parents—not doing the right thing or paying the right kind of attention to her? I thought about her need to control the intrusion of her hunger and need with bulimic obsessions. Inasmuch as an enactment was unfolding, Kate and I appeared to be living the dream.

About a week later, Kate began to uncharacteristically call me between sessions, either claiming to need to change appointment times or with "minor situations" that could not wait until the next session. Now, all of her contacts were prefaced by, "I'm so sorry to bother you, but. . . ." She then would proceed with her particular concern at the moment. Was this an outgrowth of my bothering her or crossing into her borders? Was she reciprocating in kind by bothering me between sessions in this unusual manner? Interestingly, I never felt bothered or annoyed at having to field multiple phone calls around incidents that I knew Kate was capable of handling or, at least, holding until the next session. This behavior continued until, finally, the enactment became clearer to me. Kate called one day, and said yet again, "Sorry to bother you," and then explained that she needed a "suggestion" to quell her anxiety. She was "suddenly" getting a lot of male attention that was making her feel like she wanted to purge, an activity she was diligently trying to stop. Again, I wondered whether sharing my dream was the "sudden" attention she could not digest and needed to get rid of. Historically, Kate had a failproof method for alienating any male who pursued her. In short, she would barrage them with endless text messages and demands to get together. When they ran away, "screaming" from her relentless pursuits, she would dissolve into despair, self-debasement, and a confirmation that she would never have a romantic relationship. Was she playing out this scenario with me? Had I shown too much interest that she had to "get rid of it" fast and efficiently—words she used to describe her expertise at throwing up at will? Yet, as Kate's "bothering me" continued, it seemed to be having the effect of helping her to find more ability to self-regulate. In a very general sense, it was possible that Kate's improved regulatory skills were simply the result of my being able to stay connected to her through her bothering. I believe however, there is more operating here. I think that as Kate was able to experience me "digesting" her bothering me, she was better able to normalize and manage her own internal bother—to herself and to others—in a more balanced manner. Specifically, as she bothered me, we noted a reduction in her purging and exercise regime. For the first time, she was also able to go on two dates. The dates opened a discussion between us that she had previously dismissed: her self-defeating behaviors around men. She also started to show up on time more regularly for classes and her sessions.

Bewildered

The question of why I needed to "write" this dream in this particular way is an interesting one. Wilner (1996) has postulated that dreams are metaphoric descriptions of things that are happening in the treatment that are not necessarily distorted and need to be understood. There I was (as I experienced it), an ambivalent "guest" at Kate's spirited birthday celebration in a New York club. Not much of a club enthusiast, I believe my dream placed me *outside* my borders in order to see a version of Kate *inside* hers. I saw Kate own her body and her mind in a way that precluded any need for her to scope out the nearest bathroom for purging. In the dream, I seemed to understand the power of Kate's insight, "words are just words," and the personal meaning it had for us. Yet, right after the dream, its meaning was less clear to me. Still later, however, it occurred to me that this phrase had more than one meaning. For one, I think that "words" could be understood as the most basic symbol in the dream for our analytic work together, as well as the tools that make communication and connection possible. She may have also been telling me that although I was working with her to put feelings into words, words may not be that useful without the addition of purposeful action. Finally, I think that the phrase "words are just words" conveyed my recognition of Kate's keen ability to neutralize the power that "words" or feelings had claimed over her life. The partial phrase "are just" (in the phrase "words are just words") implied a conscious diminution in words' power and danger for Kate. It seemed that she was celebrating her newfound ability to use and understand "words" as helpful ways to express and connect, rather than a means of hurting and humiliating her and others. The two shots of "Patron" Kate handed me when I entered the club could have multiple meanings. It might suggest our shared "patronage" or support of one another that we were celebrating together. Because it was unclear in the dream whether Kate was also drinking Patron, was our celebrating shared or was she specifically acknowledging my role as guardian/protector and supporter in her life? Was it also possible that the Patron was expressing a feeling of being "patronized" or condescended to? Did some part of Kate, feel like I took a "shot" at her in our work together by somehow making her feel inferior in our relationship? Similarly, did I feel patronized by Kate as I struggled in the awkwardness of her nightclub environment? Indeed, my ambivalence about being Kate's "benefactor" was represented by my not knowing whether I drank (took in) the "Patron" or not. It seemed to me that, my dream suggested that I longed for closer involvement with Kate, yet struggled with just how much "dancing together in the night club," celebrating her, might open up the analytic process or serve to close it down. In an evocative way, the dream illustrated the tightrope that I walked with Kate as we tiptoed around her feelings and experience.

Bothered

So what do I think took place when I shared my dream with Kate? To be sure, there are things that I may never know: in fact, I am left with more thoughts, questions, and curiosity than I have answers for. What I can say is that since I shared the dream, the severity of Kate's bulimic behavior has steadily declined and her ability to sustain the changes has improved. It certainly seems feasible that Kate's improved functioning could simply be the evidence that intensive treatment and effort can yield an improved life (Buechler, 2008). Yet, although our sessions are still filled with Kate's considerable struggles with her body, weight, fears of food, and her "bulimic craziness" (as she calls it), I think she would say that her life "on the outside" feels more "normal," purposeful, and hopeful.

In addition, I believe that something transformative took place in the treatment as the direct result of my having the dream, disclosing the dream, and engaging in the process of exploring the meaning it had in the context of my relationship with Kate. Specifically, what became clear from looking at this dream experience together and individually was our joint ambivalence about the boundaries we share, the boundaries we want to share, and the boundaries we deny we share. More specifically, I understand this to be a co-created struggle to come to terms with our mutual desire and need to be involved in each other's lives, while feeling conflicted about how acceptable and productive such involvement will be.

About boundaries between me and Kate: Who did what to whom? Did I "bother" her by crossing a boundary into her celebration, or did Kate "bother" me by "creating" the need for me to have such a dream about her? I wondered what the meaning was of our reciprocal bothering of one another within the context of the relationship and the goals of the analysis? What was clear was that Kate's struggle with bother, boundary crossing, and involvement was also mine. It was also no coincidence that the details of the dream highlighted an enactment that Kate and I were involved in.

Clinically, the issue of "bother" and "mutual bother" has captured my curiosity and interest. In the absence of anything that I have been able to find about the word *bother* in relationship to the treatment of eating-disordered patients, I will offer some of my preliminary thoughts and feelings on the subject. To the degree that eating-disordered patients fundamentally struggle with deficient self-regulatory functions, being a bother, apologizing for being a bother, or mutual bothering between patient and analyst may represent the patient's best attempt to communicate the degree to which developmental needs and deprivations may have been denied or dissociated. With this in mind, my bothering of Kate with my dream may have sanctioned a level of acceptability or permission to "wander," "bother," and "intrude." It seems as if the necessary bothering for parental attention and concern was absent in her childhood. She had no words for her despair for this neglect. As such, in the analytic situation, it found symbolic expression through a transference-countertransference enactment. By sharing my dream, I gave Kate tacit "permission to bother," which functioned as an essential precursor to discussions about hunger, fullness, and need. Understood this way, it might be the case that we *must* "bother" each other and engage in "mutual bothering" in any treatment, or risk the possibility that crucial pieces of our patients' experiences will stay sequestered and silent forever.

In the case of Kate, I have little doubt that my decision to disclose my dream has changed the feel of our relationship and the way in which we collaborate. Specifically, our work together has intensified in power, authenticity, and connection. My sense is that Kate views me as a more genuine, accessible, and honest person whom she can trust with her deeper vulnerabilities because I trusted her with mine, albeit in the form of a dream (Ehrenberg, 1992; Gorkin, 1987). It also seems as if Kate's level of motivation and interest in the treatment has increased as she makes a concerted effort to get to the sessions on time and works with more determination and desire for greater understanding. This may be so because she has been able to experience herself as "important" and capable of having an impact on me and the treatment (Gorkin, 1987). After all, I took the time to dream about her! Finally, months after I disclosed my dream to Kate, scenes, images, and feelings from the dream continue to be referred to and shared in the sessions. Sometimes these "dream discussions" highlight something that is now understood more clearly, and sometimes it leads us to discover something new and surprising about Kate, myself, and the relationship. For example, beyond the specific dream itself, the act of my dreaming about Kate has confirmed for her the fact that I think about her when I'm off-duty and not working. This has made her feel favored, special, and cared about. The undeniableness of these feelings has forced her to challenge entrenched beliefs about feeling unloved and unwanted. We also have had many conversations about my showing up at her party, what I thought of her at the party, who would leave the party first, and what it would be like if she came to a party of mine. While the disclosure of my dream perhaps imposed a level of intrusion upon Kate, it has also introduced something unique between us that we have been able to share on many levels. This has allowed us entry into psychic possibilities that have been meaningful, challenging, and deeply personal (Ehrenberg, 1992). It is at these moments that I feel as if "the dream is still dreaming."

In closing, it is now eight months since I disclosed my dream about Kate to her. Here is what I can report. The severity and chronicity of her bulimic behaviors (bingeing, purging, laxative use, and excessive exercise) have declined, and more importantly she has maintained this reduction fairly consistently. Kate has reduced her exercise regime by more than half and now wonders why she "just didn't do this in the first place." She has tried "new foods" that were forever on her "bad list." Nothing has really changed on the parent front, except that she has some greater empathy for her mother's struggle. She volunteers in the community, has a part time job, and aspires to be therapist. She's back in college, tries very hard to get to her classes on time, and does not sleep all day. Her social interactions feel less frenetic. She is a little less terrified of human touch. She still wants a boyfriend and isn't sure whether that will ever happen. She can tolerate sunny days. She can't tolerate dishonesty. She can still tolerate me. She is on speaking terms with her body and, "Sorry to bother you" at this point, feels more like "I am so glad you can bother me, and I can bother you."

References

Abend, S. (1995). Discussion of Jay Greenberg's paper on self-disclosure. *Contemporary Psychoanalysis, 87,* 61–79.

Aron, L. (1996). *A meeting of minds mutuality in psychoanalysis.* Hillsdale: NJ: Analytic Press.

Bass, A. (2007). When the frame doesn't fit the picture. *Psychoanalytic Dialogues, 17,* 1–27.

Buechler, S. (2008). *Making a difference in patients' lives emotional experience in the therapeutic setting.* New York: Routledge.

Chrzanowski, G. (1980). Collaborative inquiry, affirmation and neutrality in the psychoanalytic situation. *Contemporary Psychoanalysis, 16,* 348–366.

Coen, S. J. (2007). Narcissistic temptations to cross boundaries and how to manage them. *Journal of the American Psychoanalytic Association, 55,* 1169–1190.

Ehrenberg, D. B. (1992). *The intimate edge.* New York: Norton.

Freud, S. (1910). Five lectures on psycho-analysis. *Standard Edition, 11,* 1–56. London: Hogarth Press.

Freud, S. (1913). Further recommendations in the technique of psychoanalysis. In *Collected Papers, Vol. 2, The international psychoanalytical library* (No. 8, 1959). New York: Basic Books.

Freud, S. (1957). The interpretation of dreams. *Standard Edition,* 4 & 5. London: Hogarth Press.

Goldberg, A. (1999). Boundaries as pre-conditions. *Psychoanalytic Quarterly, 68,* 248–263.

Goldberg, A. (2008). Some limits of the boundary concept. *The Psychoanalytic Quarterly, 3,* 861–875.

Gorkin, M. (1987). *The uses of countertransference.* Northvale, NJ: Aronson.

Levenson, E. (1983). *The ambiguity of change.* New York: Basic Books.

Mitchell, S. A. (1993). *Hope and dread in psychoanalysis.* New York: Basic Books.

Orbach, S. (2009). *Bodies.* New York: Picador.

Tauber, E. S., & Green, M. R. (1959). *Pre-logical experience.* New York: Basic Books.

Watson Jr., R. I. (1994). The clinical use of the analyst's dreams of the patient. *Contemporary Psychoanalysis, 30,* 510–521.

Wilner, W. (1996). Dream and the holistic nature interpersonal psychoanalytic experience. *Psychoanalytic Dialogues, 6,* 813–829.

17

'HOOKED ON A FEELING'

Emotions That Facilitate the Movement From Compulsion to Choice—Three Bodies. . . . Patient, Analyst, and Supervisor

Sandra Buechler

Ellen will talk about anything, except her problems with eating. That is forbidden. However, there is no shortage of approved topics. The deaths of her parents, her marital problems, her bouts of depression, her sibling relationships—these all make the acceptable list. But the fact that she is so heavy that she has trouble getting up to leave her session is taboo.

Ellen is the thirty-one-year-old patient of someone I supervise. I can only "see" her in my mind's eye. I imagine an extremely overweight woman, who frequently seems unaware that she is bulging out of her clothing. Although it is clear to her analyst and to me that her health is greatly endangered by her weight, Ellen has proclaimed that this issue cannot be broached.

In this chapter I will discuss my situation as the supervisor of this treatment, including the following issues:

1. What feelings are stirred in me, as I listen to the work with Ellen? How might they be affecting the supervision, and Ellen's treatment?
2. Since I believe that all emotions exist in a system, with the intensity of any one emotion modulating the intensity of all the others, what feelings in Ellen could help detoxify her relationship to food, and to her body?
3. Who does Ellen's analyst need to be in order to help her? That is, aside from being a trained clinician, what are the qualities as a human being that he or she needs to have?

Each of these questions leads me to consider the power of shame, the avoidance of shame, the contagion of shame, and the effect of being terrified of shame. I believe that the fear of shame rules Ellen. It determines what she can know about herself, what she can say, and what she can allow to be said to her. In other words, I suggest that a terror of shame rules Ellen's life—shapes her treatment and the supervision. Ellen is, in a sense, hooked on the *absence* of a feeling of shame. I am working on the hypothesis that she can't focus on her eating because this would bring her too near shame. My guess is that compulsively eating blanks her mind of potential shame. I am sure it is much more complicated than that, but what I am suggesting is that Ellen is haunted by shame, bullied by it into an absence of self-awareness. I think that when Ellen says she won't talk about her eating, it would be more accurate to say that she can't talk about it, because it exists in an island of experience, cordoned off by dissociation, to protect Ellen from shame. Paradoxically, this perpetuates a cycle of shame, since Ellen cannot be totally unaware of the negative ways in which her body is seen by others. In short, I will argue that Ellen is hooked on absenting herself from feeling shame, and this dislocates her from her eating, her body, and other aspects of her experience. My concern in this chapter is not solely to argue for this theory about Ellen's psychological functioning. I also want to address how my hypotheses affect my supervisory behavior.

What Is the Supervisor Hooked On?

While Ellen is hooked on the absence of shame, I am hooked on the presence of hope. To be more specific, my character and life experience have shaped me into someone who needs to fight for psychological and physical health, in myself and in others. Particularly when it comes to threats to physical health, I am a fighter. How does this affect my supervision of the treatment of a patient who will not or cannot address the impact of her eating on the health of her body?

Before I try to answer this question, I would like to briefly describe some of my ideas about the supervisory process. This is addressed much more fully in the issue of *Contemporary Psychoanalysis* (Buechler, 2009), in which I asked seventeen analysts to describe their notions of an "ideal" psychoanalytic training. But, briefly, to my way of thinking, "ideal" supervisory behavior closely approximates the "ideal" behavior of the patient in a classical analysis. For the purposes of this discussion, I am assuming that the clinician being supervised is experienced enough to need no instruction about how to set a frame, maintain adequate boundaries, and other basics.

In that situation, my "ideal" supervisor would free associate, just as the patient is instructed to do in a classical analysis. Self-censorship, if present, would be examined as it occurs. That is, if I, as a supervisor, find myself reluctant to say something, I would comment on this, as soon as I am aware of it. I believe that some of the best supervisors (like freely associating patients) verbalize the flow of their thoughts and feelings as they occur, so that the supervisee can hear their *sequence,* and not just the content. The sequence of the patient's thoughts is considered meaningful. If the patient remembered her father's favorite joke just after she spoke of her husband, most analysts would make note of this sequence, whether or not they would comment on it. This enables the *structure* of the patient's thinking/feeling processes to be explored. Similarly, I would say it is vital for the supervisee to experience the *structure* of the supervisor's thinking/feeling process, and not merely the content. The only way I know how to convey this, as a supervisor, is by freely associating.

I am not ignoring the vast differences between supervision and treatment, and, most especially, between the responsibilities of a patient in analysis versus a supervisor in supervision. But I am suggesting that a talent for transparency is an advantage for both. So, when I supervise, I try to think out loud. Sometimes the content of these thoughts proves useful, but, I think, more importantly, it provides a model of one viable way of thinking/feeling clinically. I hope I convey that I don't think of it as *the* way, but only as *a* way.

I would like to spell out some of how I think/feel when listening to the presentation of the treatment of Ellen. In many ways it is no different from hearing about the work with any other patient. I will mention the similarities but emphasize how I think this work differs from my usual supervisory experience. In brief, I would say that Ellen's body is unusually present for me, and my feelings about it are unusually vivid, sometimes rendering me acutely conscious of the three bodies of the patient, analyst, and supervisor.

While it is obvious that our three bodies differ greatly (I am a petite older woman, the supervisee is a much taller, younger man, and Ellen is a very heavy-set younger woman) I am thinking about their health, as well as their sizes. I would say that, perhaps more than most supervisors would be; I am very definitely hooked on feelings about our bodies. I think it is relevant that, at times, I have had to fight hard for my own health. I don't take my body's ongoing existence for granted. I work hard for it. I am "hooked" on the feeling that hard work can make a difference. I am very conscious of the strong pull in me to encourage others to fight for better health and more life.

I realize that this has a cost, for the supervision and the treatment. Exploring this cost is the main focus of this chapter. Of course, my attitude conflicts with "neutrality" as it is usually understood. As an aside, I don't feel that our literature has adequately grappled with how much supervisors should adhere to any particular version of neutrality. Like many other issues (such as supervisory abstinence, the operation of the supervisor's defenses, and the supervisor's transferences and countertransferences), whether or not any form of neutrality makes sense in supervision is not generally addressed. Those who see supervision as mostly an educative process, in which the supervisor imparts information to the supervisee, are less likely to be troubled by its nonneutral aspects. But for those who see supervision as very similar to treatment, in that it deals with the supervisee's defenses against the clinical material, the issue of supervisory neutrality may be very relevant. For example, would I be a better supervisor, in this case (and in general) if my feelings about fighting for health were in better check? Should I aim for this?

Another way to address this question is, what is the line between a supervisor's *conveying* passionately held beliefs versus a supervisor's attempts to *indoctrinate?* For example, in 2004, I wrote a book called *Clinical Values* (Buechler, 2004), in which I discussed the clinician's hope, curiosity, courage, integrity, and love of truth, among other attributes that I consider part of our basic equipment. Where is the line between my conveying my beliefs about the importance of clinical values versus my pressuring candidates to become my acolytes?

So, when I listen to Ellen's treatment I am not "without memory or desire," as Bion (1988) recommended the *analyst* be. I don't know if many analysts would suggest that the *supervisor* should have this stance. At first it seems like an absurd idea, but there might be something useful in being able to bring that open a mind to each supervision session.

In any case, I know I bring memories and desires to this work. I frequently remember that Ellen's weight endangers her health, and I definitely desire for her to do something about it. For me, this brings up some of the same issues I explored in my paper "Searching for a Passionate Neutrality" (Buechler, 1999). In that paper I was exploring the meaning of neutrality to me as an interpersonal analyst. Briefly, I was responding to the idea that the analyst should maintain an even focus on material coming from the patient's id, ego, and superego (Freud, 1936). According to this thinking, the analyst should hold countertransferential passions in check, to create an atmosphere that is conducive to the observation of *all* the patient's ways of functioning. The analyst should not attempt to sway the patient toward certain kinds of change, or impose his or her own values. The analyst follows, rather than directs, the flow of material. All this facilitates the patient's fullest expression, even of feelings, thoughts, and impulses of which the analyst might not approve. This still makes a great deal of sense to me. If I express my passion for health when I am working with a patient, is it likely that he or she will feel able to fully explore death wishes? More specifically, given these tendencies in me, as the supervisor, will Ellen's analyst be fully free to register everything self-destructive about Ellen that he could potentially know? Will he be fully free to formulate it all with me? I come back to these questions shortly.

In sum, the dangers of strong biases in supervision may be similar, in some senses, to the dangers of biases in treatment. But I think supervision has added elements that augment these dangers. I deal with this much more fully in my book *Still Practicing* (Buechler, 2012), where I explore some problems that frequently hamper analytic training. In many situations the supervisor has actual, real-world power to affect the career of the supervisee. To the extent that I have this power, how does that affect how my supervisee experiences my values, slants, biases, and passions?

The Vivid Presence of the Absent Body

Ellen had entered treatment about six months before the supervision began. When she began this treatment she had just emerged from a brief hospitalization due to a suicide attempt. While there were many reasons why she might be depressed (the fairly recent death of her mother, her father's ongoing serious health problems, her troubled marriage, her obesity), the triggers for the suicide attempt were not entirely clear to me. What did seem striking, however, was how much her body inhabited my mind. Ellen felt both "invisible" and "on display" because of her weight. She deeply resented that when people looked at her, her obesity was all they seemed to see. In my mind's eye, I saw a young woman who was deeply ambivalent about being seen. She wore clothing and tattoos that appeared to deliberately call attention to her body, and yet she would not let it be the focus of any attention in the treatment.

Here is where my own thinking about shame comes into play. I think of her as aggressively demanding to be seen, without ever consciously asking for it. Her shame makes her want to hide, but that wish evokes intense rage in her, so she provocatively thrusts her body in our faces, as she dares us to mention it. She sometimes neglects hygiene or the "propriety" of which body parts are appropriate to expose, by wearing clothing that is too small to contain her, or skimping on underwear. But her provocations are so casual, so seemingly inadvert, that the viewer is likely to take responsibility for them. That is, since she doesn't own the hunger to be seen, but seems to display herself by mistake. When I "look" at her I feel ashamed of how I see her. I create a grotesque image, feel some revulsion, and then guilt and shame. Her analyst has reported some similar reactions. Thus *we* are left with the shame about how she looks, to us.

Much about Ellen speaks of shame: her social anxiety, "inappropriate" blushing (according to her own standards), and feelings of being the family's "weak link." I think of her as dogged by shame and constantly trying to avoid it. It would be shameful to care how people see her and want their attention, especially if it isn't forthcoming, so she aggressively demands to be noticed, but outside her awareness.

In the interests of confidentiality and brevity I am leaving out a great deal about this treatment, the supervision, and all three of the participants, but one incident especially stands out for me. Just a few weeks into the supervision, Ellen seemed to her analyst to be barely holding herself together. Again, the triggers were not entirely clear for me, but one factor was her terror that her friends would see that during their visit she had been sobbing. She told her analyst that she had only two options: to hurt herself or go back into the hospital. In consultation with her psychiatrist, her analyst felt she should be hospitalized, and she had another brief hospitalization. When she was discharged she was extremely angry at her analyst.

These events leave me with many questions. I feel that her analyst made a good, though very difficult, judgment call. It is the kind of moment we all dread. Should we, perhaps, err on the side of caution, or take the risk that the patient "doesn't really mean it," but is "only" looking for attention, in yet another (aggressive) way? I feel that, at these moments, the clinician often has to follow a gut instinct, knowing that there may be negative consequences no matter what action is chosen.

What is most fascinating to me, as I reflect on this moment, is the question of my part in it. It is just a few weeks after I enter the scene. I am supervising the treatment of a woman who compromises her health with her weight but won't talk about this. I am particularly fierce about health. She threatens to kill herself. Her analyst decides to be cautious and hospitalize her, taking no chances with her life. Have I influenced him in some way we both may not consciously understand? *Did I (somehow) bring out the issue of life and death for this patient and her analyst?* Would anything have been different if he were not in supervision with me? In my opinion, this is, ultimately, something we can never know.

261

Hooked on a Theory?

I assume that when I enter a supervisory session I bring my character, my theories, and my own clinical experience, as well as my particular defensive proclivities. My theories may be serving defensive needs in ways I am unaware of. For example, how much do I *need* to see Ellen as ashamed? Is this a way for me to focus away from some of her aggression? Can I, then, like her more?

But, regardless of my motives, I do believe that a fear of shame, and feelings of acute shame, play roles in Ellen's inner life. I bring to this work a belief that the emotions form a system, with any strong feeling affecting the level of intensity of all the others. I have discussed the clinical implications of this in most of my previous work (Buechler, 2004, 2008, 2012) so I will only address how these ideas may be influencing my thinking about Ellen. My theoretical understanding and clinical experience tell me that the feeling that most often helps to modulate shame is pride. One of my formulations is that the clinician's task includes helping the patient derive some pride from the courage it takes to look at herself (figuratively and literally) no matter what she sees when she looks. That *pride* may make the *shame* bearable. One emotion modulates another, more powerfully than any verbal formulation, although verbal interpretation plays a role in the process. I trust a shift in the balance of feelings to provide most of the "therapeutic action."

But treatment itself can be shame inducing for the highly vulnerable person, since it requires him to face all of himself. We must *embody* the attitude that, no matter what any one of us sees when he looks in the mirror, he deserves credit for looking. That is, the courageous integrity it takes to be a patient must be seen by both patient and analyst. In a departure, perhaps, from the patient's earlier life experience, in the treatment the patient must feel respected for the act of self-confrontation, even though some of what is confronted may evoke shame. This "credit" may enable the patient to keep digging, to value the pursuit of self-knowledge over the pursuit of all-positive self-reflections. Instead of needing each session to feel good because he looks good to himself, he will become able to feel good because he looks *at* himself. Shame sensitive patients often enter treatment unable to extend themselves this credit. In every possible way the analyst must embody the inherent value of insight, treatment, and, more generally, the fully explored and experienced life.

Of course, a mechanistic application of this idea is absurd. Ellen's analyst can't hand her some pride. This was the fallacy of Alexander's (1961) idea of the "corrective emotional experience." We can't just decide that a patient needs some joy, or pride, or love, and manufacture it. That would be stilted, inauthentic, and ineffectual. But, as the supervisor, when I think the analyst might help Ellen take pride in herself, I am likely to point this out. In other words, my focus on this will not be neutral.

This work is based on my own understanding of empathic processes. Briefly, I don't believe that I can feel Ellen's feelings, or my supervisee's feelings, without their being shaped by my own. That is, if my supervisee is feeling sad, for example, this may evoke a similar feeling in me, but, once it enters me, it is shaped by my whole history of sad feelings. Thus, I can't, strictly speaking, feel "his" sadness, because it is changed once inside my emotional milieu, so to speak. I can only feel "my" sadness. It may be similar to his, and it certainly may be triggered by his, but it is also my own brand. Perhaps, for me, sadness has always evoked some anxiety. In that case, anxiety will be part of my experience as I listen to the material. But if sadness generally recruits anger in me, I am likely to feel that feeling as I listen.

Given that we are human beings, when supervisors hear about a treatment; our efforts at empathy with the supervisee and his or her patient are inevitably affected by who we are. Our characters, life, and clinical experience play roles in what we focus on, forget, and feel intensely, and so on. All this would apply no matter what issues Ellen brought to treatment. But, shame poses unique problems in treatment and, I would suggest, in supervision. In shame, human beings want to hide. This wish runs counter to the fundamental nature of all psychological treatment, which is, in a sense, a process of self-exposure, *as is supervision.* All three of us have to reveal something about ourselves in order to do our best work. If any one of us is too motivated to hide, some part of the exploration will be truncated.

Ellen both mandates and prohibits her own self-exposure. Her analyst, trying to be sensitive to her needs, will inevitably serve some of them more than others. He wants to be able to see her as she says she wants to be seen. She is Ellen, and not her obesity. She is Ellen, and not her tattoos. She is Ellen, and not the flesh bulging out of her short skirt and skimpy blouse. She is Ellen, and not her provocations (e.g., daring her analyst to take her literally when she says she has only two options). But her analyst and I, given our own characters and analytic upbringing, see all these as *aspects* of Ellen. Ellen's shame and fear of shame set up the *possibility* that we will each feel that seeing her is equivalent to hurting her. Some analysts, and some supervisors, would be more likely to feel this than others. Said in another way, Ellen's issues make certain aspects of the characters of her analyst and his supervisor most salient. How much can he, and I, bear feeling we are causing someone shame, or, at least, not doing all we can to prevent it?

As a human being, I want everyone (including myself) to prioritize life over pride. This shapes the extent and the limits of my empathy with each of the participants in the treatment. I wish Ellen would wake up one morning, look in the mirror, have the courage to see her body as it is, and decide to do anything necessary to lose weight, so she will have a longer, healthier life. Inevitably, I wish my supervisee would magically make this happen. I know that my impact is limited, as is his. But I can't help what I feel. I guess that is a way of saying that I am hooked.

Clinicians as Fools for Love

I believe that an important aspect of therapeutic work with shame is the clinician's willingness at times to risk shame. I call this being able to be a "fool for love." That is, in front of the patient we must cope with our own self-esteem needs without allowing them to dominate us. We have to embody a way of valuing life over image. Sometimes we must be willing to look like fools.

On the concrete level this is played out in the analyst's handling of his or her own potentially shame-inducing moments in the treatment. For example, when I am the analyst, how do I react to my mistakes? What do I do with my own slips of the tongue? When the patient accuses me of not helping, questions the value of our work, or, more generally, of psychoanalysis, do I respond defensively? Must I uphold my own image, at all costs? Must I look smart, right, well-intentioned, intuitive, emotionally responsive, self-contained? Must I emerge from every conflict "smelling like a rose?" Am I willing to take interpersonal risks in the name of the treatment? Will I say what can sound foolish if I think it is right, and risk the patient's scorn, dismissal, and contempt? On a more subtle level, how much do I need credit for the treatment's accomplishments? More generally, do I take credit for the *patient's* accomplishments?

How easily can I allow myself to cry in front of the patient, or ask potentially foolish-sounding questions? Can I be "childishly" eager, openly curious? Can I need help? In areas where the patient is more expert can I ask for information? What is the feel of moments when I am the one who asks, or needs, or is more emotional?

It often seems to me, when analysts' credit self-disclosure as having helped a patient, that what helped was not the disclosure itself but the values embodied in the act of choosing to disclose. The analyst is saying, in effect, "I am willing to give you information you could use to shame me. I am willing to do whatever it takes to reach you." The analyst is behaviorally expressing valuing the treatment more than her own pride and, more generally, life more than image. I view the treatment of empathic failures similarly. What I believe the patient often derives from this work has mainly to do with how the analyst relates to his or her own self-esteem. I see the value of work on empathic failures as deriving from the patient providing an opportunity for the analyst to fail, acknowledge the shortcoming, react without undue shame, guilt, or denial, and move on.

Here are the essential offers I believe the analyst must make to the patient, especially when the patient is prone to shame.

1. I will go first, in exposing my foibles, in the service of our work. When I have to choose between protecting my own image versus serving the treatment, I will choose the treatment.
2. I will make myself psychologically available, knowable, enough for the patient to see how I manage my own self-esteem requirements.
3. In how I work I will embody my values, live out my belief that treatment (and life) has purpose.

In addition, I feel the analyst must embody a value I have already described— that there is much pride to be gained from honest self-confrontation. Another way to say this is that if we are willing to brave the narcissistic injuries inherent in seeing ourselves clearly, we can develop self-respect for having integrity. It takes courage to face one's shortcomings. The analyst must model having respect for oneself for facing oneself.

The first offer, the analyst's willingness to "go first" in valuing the treatment more than his own pride, is another way to express the concept of being a "fool for love." This "fool" is a wise innocent. He speaks when most would be silent. He asks questions that may reveal his ignorance and innocence, as well as his abiding curiosity.

The second offer involves giving the patient access to how we manage our own self-esteem. Sometimes this takes the form of self-disclosure. I believe we can provide something useful, at times, when we directly tell the patient something about our own emotional self-management.

The third offer is to embody a sense of purpose that may contrast with the patient's deadened capacity. The shame prone patient turns away from reality when it isn't complimentary. He is a true cynic, seeing his own self-absorption everywhere he looks. The only aims worth striving for are those that enhance him. This robs the self of transcendence. He can never lose himself. Even in his most creative or playful or generous acts his self-concern ties him down. He is an isolationist—only really caring about what lies within his own borders. Around him he sees only other isolationists. In the world he creates it is difficult to have any abiding purpose. He just doesn't see the point of anything, unless it makes him look good to himself.

The challenge for the analyst is to communicate a strong sense of purpose. The treatment and, more generally, life itself, must be inherently important. Nothing in the culture's negating attitudes toward analysis, or in the neutrality and abstinence requirements of his traditional role, or in the postmodern turn away from singular truths, must keep the analyst from a passionate, steadfast expression of purpose.

Without inspiration from the analyst's sense of purpose, the patient will not feel sufficiently called upon to deal with the crucial issue of time. Time can feel like an enemy, since it pressures us to accept reality's limitations. But unless life has purpose, how does the passage of time matter? Unless it is important to have a life, what difference does it make if the patient lets his only chance at life go by? Without purpose, it doesn't matter if life is squandered in the hope that someday a truly impressive role will come along. The analyst must capitalize on the pressure of time, but that can only happen if he conveys that life has purpose.

The analyst has a vast array of opportunities to embody purpose and risk being a fool for love. Will she take a stand, for example, about the need to maintain the frequency of sessions, even at the risk of the patient's objection and rejection? How hard does she fight for the life of the treatment? Does she (obviously) work hard in its interest, even if she is the only one who seems committed to it? In our own willingness to invest in the treatment we contrast with the shame avoidant patient's conservative isolationism.

Treatment is, often, a profound fight for life. In our passion we convey how much we feel it matters whether or not a life is fully lived. The analyst's tempo, pitch, and tone provide a kind of background music that can rouse the patient toward a more intense experience of her life.

In treating profoundly vulnerable people we encounter our deepest priorities, as human beings. What really matters? When am I willing to be a fool for love? Each of us has to come to our own conclusion about what we will fight for. Somehow we must embrace the paradoxes essential to our role. We need the humility born of recognizing our limitations, but also, passion born of fierce conviction. I must know that I can only see subjectively, yet I must believe in my vision with all my heart. In her book *Sacred Therapy,* Estelle Frankel (2003) quotes a Hasidic master, Reb Zusia, who once told a disciple, "I'm not worried that I'll be asked why I wasn't Moses when I die and enter the heavenly realm, but why I wasn't Zusia" (p. 85). Remarkably similarly, Erich Fromm wrote, "Joy, then, is what we experience in the process of growing nearer to the goal of becoming ourselves" (1976, p. 106). We are always trying to rise to the challenge of being ourselves with our patients, but, I suggest, our own and our patients' needs to avoid shame make this task especially daunting.

To close, I borrow a quote that Frankel takes from the Talmud: "One should not appoint anyone as a leader of a community unless he carries a basket of impure reptiles on his back, so that if he becomes arrogant, one could tell him: 'Turn around and look behind you'" (2003, p. 186). As analysts we must be acutely aware of the reptiles on our own backs, willing to reexperience and expose them, and yet centered in a profound confidence in our essential, life-affirming capacity to heal.

References

Alexander, F. (1961). *The scope of psychoanalysis, 1921–1961.* New York: Basic Books.
Bion, W. (1988). Notes on memory and desire. In E. Bott-Spillius (Ed.), *Melanie Klein Today* (Vol. 2, pp. 17–21). London: Routledge.
Buechler, S. (1999). Searching for a passionate neutrality. *Contemporary Psychoanalysis, 35,* 213–237.
Buechler, S. (2004). *Clinical values: Emotions that guide psychoanalytic treatment.* Hillsdale, NJ: Analytic Press.
Buechler, S. (2008). *Making a difference in patients' lives: Emotional experience in the therapeutic setting.* New York: Routledge.
Buechler, S. (Ed.). (2009). Special issue on the ideal psychoanalytic institute. *Contemporary Psychoanalysis, 45.*
Buechler, S. (2012). *Still practicing: The heartaches and joys of a clinical career.* New York: Routledge.
Frankel, E. (2003). *Sacred therapy.* Boston, MA: Shambhala Publications.
Freud, A. (1936). *The ego and the mechanisms of defense.* New York: International Universities Press.
Fromm, E. (1976). *To have or to be?* New York: Harper & Row.

Part V

BEYOND THE INTERPERSONAL
Clinical and Assessment Tools Across Modalities

18

'COME TOGETHER'

Blending CBT/DBT and Interpersonal Psychotherapy in the Treatment of Eating Disorders

Carrie D. Gottlieb

My early training as a therapist was almost solely in CBT and DBT models. I had no formal exposure to interpersonal psychotherapy, but was beginning to catch glimpses of how operating within a strictly CBT/DBT context could leave me feeling limited as a therapist. While the practical, problem solving nature of CBT and DBT still made sense to me, I began to feel somewhat stuck with patients. Even though we would make progress initially, I felt like I was 'running out of things to talk about' as treatment progressed. I knew that I could provide more for patients in helping them work through their relationship issues and interpersonal conflicts as well as the ways in which they sabotaged both themselves and their treatment. Over time I found myself asking questions such as 'how do I take this patient deeper?'—something my former CBT self would not have paid much consideration to. I was hungry for something more.

Core differences exist between interpersonal therapy and CBT/DBT in terms of theory, technique, and therapeutic stance. Interpersonal therapy focuses on themes such as affect and emotional expression, exploration of resistance, identification and exploration of patterns within a patient's relationships, past experiences, and a focus on the therapeutic relationship (Blagys & Hilsenroth, 2002; Connors, 2010). The goal of interpersonal treatment is to bring about change in an individual's entire system of relating to themselves and to others.

By contrast, CBT and DBT therapists tend to focus more directly on symptom reduction and work with patients to change the way they approach their thoughts, feelings, and behaviors. While the therapeutic relationship is important to a CBT/DBT therapist, it is seen as way to enhance patient retention and keep them in treatment long enough to complete treatment protocols and bring about symptom reduction. This stands in contrast to the interpersonal perspective, which views the relationship as so central to the therapeutic process and the means by which change is made possible.

The differences in therapeutic approaches lie in the goals of treatment, with CBT/DBT focusing on making changes to the symptoms while interpersonal psychotherapy targets changes to the system in which a symptom exists. However, despite such differences, these therapeutic approaches can intuitively make sense together. Why would you not work towards symptoms reduction while at the same time trying to understand its context?

Mary Connors (2010) speaks of 'symptom focused *dynamic* psychotherapy,' by which she refers to using action-oriented CBT and DBT techniques within the context of relational or analytic therapy. According to Connors (2010), action-oriented CBT and DBT approaches are often effective at targeting symptoms and therefore result in significant levels of symptom reduction. However, symptom-focused approaches are often not enough to bring about lasting changes, and an understanding of an individual's personal history, defenses, and interpersonal style is necessary. By targeting symptoms and their context, therapists are able to work with patients on making more lasting, meaningful changes.

It is possible for interpersonal case formulations and interventions to blend seamlessly with more action-oriented strategies, especially in the treatment of eating-disordered patients. The term *integrative,* for me, implies that there is no one good or best approach. By drawing on theories and techniques from multiple schools of thought, it is possible to create a rich, full treatment approach.

Why Use an Integrative Approach With Eating-Disordered Patients?

Treating eating-disordered patients presents with many unique challenges. While on one hand this work is particularly interesting and engrossing; at the same time therapists are managing patients who are dealing with a myriad of complicated emotional, behavioral, and physical issues. Given the fact that eating disorders are associated with a variety of medical complications, some of which may be life threatening, an integrative approach can be especially useful (Johnson, Conners, & Tobin, 1987; Conners, 2001). The potential for physical danger necessitates that therapists move patients towards stability quickly, instead of waiting for symptoms to slowly changing over time. Additionally, the malnutrition associated with eating disorders may result in cognitive impairments that make more insight-oriented or relational work more difficult. Skills training can aid patients in the management of factors that maintain an eating disorder in their day-to-day life. Early symptom abatement can become a meaningful way to join with patients, fostering the therapeutic relationship and setting the stage for more relational work in the future.

Often, at the onset of therapy with eating-disordered patients, there is little ability to see beyond food and their physical bodies, leaving little room for insight, introspection, and a relationship with a therapist (Petrucelli, 2004). Patients substitute food for relationships and use eating-disorder behaviors, like purging or restriction, instead of words (Brisman, 2001; Petrucelli, 2004). Given this, traditional interpersonal psychotherapy, with its reliance on the 'verbally loaded therapy setting' (Brisman, 2001), can be difficult with eating-disordered patients who lack the ability to express themselves verbally. Both Brisman and Petrucelli argue for starting with more direct behavior interventions as well as weaving these strategies throughout relational psychotherapy. In this type of integrative approach, behavior change goals continue to be important, but the incorporation of an interpersonal perspective calls for a deeper curiosity and opportunities to explore the emotional and historic underpinnings of these symptoms (Conners, 2010).

Before moving on to discuss how such an integrated approach might work, I will briefly introduce CBT and DBT theory and applications and how it is applied to work with patients with eating disorders.

Cognitive Behavior Theory and Therapy

According to the cognitive behavior therapy (CBT) model, human functioning is based on the interplay of thoughts, feelings, and behaviors (Walen, DiGiuseppe, & Dryden, 1992). The emotions and behaviors experienced and displayed by an individual are largely determined by their thoughts and interpretations (Beck, Rush, Shaw, & Emery, 1979). Psychopathology is thought to result from repeated, rigid patterns of distortions in cognitions and dysfunctional beliefs. Therefore, treatment in a cognitive behavior model targets symptom relief by focusing on an individual's misinterpretations, dysfunctional attitudes, and self-defeating behaviors (Beck et al.). Since all three factors (thoughts, feelings, and behaviors) are interrelated, a change in one will likely result in a change in the others (Walen et al., 1992).

Fairburn is credited with the creation of enhanced cognitive behavior therapy, CBT-E, for the treatment of eating disorders. According to Fairburn, Cooper, and Shafran (2003), "people with eating disorders judge themselves largely, or even exclusively, in terms of their eating habits, shape, or weight (often all three) and their ability to control them" (p. 510). The central psychopathology of eating disorders according to CBT-E theory stems from this faulty means of self-evaluation with its overemphasis on weight and shape.

As a treatment, CBT-E is focused on the processes that maintain an eating disorder, not those that are responsible for its development in the first place (Fairburn et al., 2003), a stance consistent with CBT in general. In this way, treatment is geared towards making changes in thought patterns, or cognitively restructuring, so that food, weight, and shape are no longer as paramount. The cognitive and behavior targets of CBT-E include eating patterns, cognitive distortions around food and body shape, perfectionism, low self-esteem, mood intolerance (or the inability to cope with intense mood/affective states), and interpersonal difficulties. Such targets are clearly very symptom focused and stand in contrast to a more interpersonal perspective, which would consider both the eating-disorder symptoms and the systemic factors contributing to its maintenance and development.

Dialectic Behavior Therapy

Dialectic behavior therapy (DBT) was first developed by Marsha Linehan for the treatment of borderline personality disorder (BPD). However, since that time it has been used to treat a wide array of conditions such as chronic depression, substance abuse, and eating disorders (Lynch, Chapman, Rosenthal, Kuo, & Linehan, 2006). While DBT does share some of the skill-focused strategies of traditional CBT, there are some key features that make DBT unique.

DBT is rooted in the biopsychosocial theory of psychopathology, which assumes that deficits in affect regulation underlie BPD as well as other mental illnesses. Such dysregulation is a result of the interplay between a heightened sensitivity and reactivity to emotional stimuli (biological) and an invalidating environment (social). Typically, this invalidating environment is described as one in which an individual's attempts to express emotions are punished, ignored, or trivialized (Lynch et al., 2006). Therefore, DBT skills aim to compensate for these deficits, helping patients to better regulate their affect.

The biopsychosocial model of DBT takes note of the environment in which a symptom has developed. However, the symptom is still the target of treatment and interventions are largely skills focused. In contrast, interpersonal psychotherapists consider both the symptom and its context and therefore work to help a patient understand and explore the symptoms as well as its historical and contextual underpinnings.

As applied to eating disorders, dialectic behavior theorists conceptualize eating-disordered behaviors as a mechanism by which an individual seeks affect regulation or modulation (Wiser & Telch, 1999; Wisniewski & Kelly, 2003). In this way, behaviors such as binge eating, purging, and/or food restriction are used as a means to escape from or regulate emotional distress. The term *dialectic* refers to the tension between two opposing or interacting forces. As a treatment, DBT holds the dialectic of both acceptance and change (Lynch et al., 2006), whereby patients are taught how to both bring about meaningful changes in their lives while at the same time acknowledging an acceptance of emotions, which can be both painful and intense. In the treatment of eating disorders specifically, the concept of a dialectic is used to describe the under- and overcontrolled eating patterns of food restriction and binge eating (Wisniewski & Kelly, 2003). Patients are encouraged to take the 'middle road' approach to food, thereby helping them gain more flexibility in both the variety and quantity of food eaten.

Treatment in the DBT model includes the following modules: mindfulness skills, interpersonal effectiveness, emotional regulation, and distress tolerance.

Eating Disorders and Affect Regulation

Regardless of theoretical orientation, it is proposed that individuals with eating disorders struggle to appropriately manage their affects (Conners, 2010). Because emotions can often be felt as unmanageable, the eating-disordered behaviors become the means by which an individual avoids painful or intense affects (Wiser & Telch, 1999). A cognitive narrowing, whereby an individual can shift focus from a distressing emotion or event to something related to food, weight, shape, and so on, effectively finding a way to alleviate their initial distress. In this way, eating-disordered behaviors 'work' in that they lessen or alleviate distressing emotions, yet clearly in a dysfunctional way.

CBT/DBT and interpersonal therapists use the term *dissociation* when talking about the shifting of cognitive focus occurring in eating-disordered patients and describe ways in which patients are split off from uncomfortable feelings states and/or parts of themselves. However, the term takes distinctly different meanings in each theoretical orientation. In CBT/DBT, dissociation is discussed as difficulties in behavioral and affective awareness, emotional expression, and emotional avoidance (Wisniewski & Kelly, 2003). In this way, patients are cut off (or dissociated) from their emotional lives. Therefore, treatment, from the CBT/DBT perspective, targets dissociation by didactically teaching patients how to identify and manage affective states, a symptom-focused treatment approach.

Interpersonal psychotherapists talk about dissociation in a more intricate and complicated way. From the interpersonal perspective, dissociation is seen as a means to prevent or modulate anxiety (Howell, 2005). According to Philip Bromberg (1998), dissociation serves to protect against "shock: the real or perceived threat of being overwhelmingly incapacitated by aspects of reality that cannot be processed by existing cognitive schemata without doing violence to one's experience of selfhood and sometimes sanity itself" (p. 184). In the face of extreme anxiety or dysregulation, 'substitutive behaviors', such as eating-disorder behaviors, are enacted to refocus attention away from anxiety causing stimuli and serve to 'bolster' the dissociative process (Bromberg, 1998; Howell, 2005).

Regardless of the theoretical stance, the message is the same. Individuals with eating disorders have difficulty regulating their emotions and use the symptoms of their disorder (restricting, bingeing, purging, etc.) to help them gain more control over their emotional lives. Given this, affect regulation becomes a primary target of treatment. However, how and why affect regulation is addressed is radically different. In CBT/DBT a therapist's main task is to teach direct skills that target the mismanaging of affect regulation, thereby creating more emotional stability and lessening the need an individual has for the use of the eating-disordered thoughts and behaviors. From an interpersonal perspective, the secure relationship with the therapist provides a foundation in which it becomes safe to verbalize what had previously been dissociated. Such verbalization and mentalizations lessen one's need for a 'substitutive behavior.' thereby reducing pathologic dissociation and, consequently, increasing affect regulation.

Integration of therapy provides a forum in which a patient is able to acquire affect regulatory skills that they are lacking while simultaneously working through the relational underpinnings of such deficits. In this way, patients not only learns how to better manage their mood and affect but also why and how such affect came about in the first place.

Integrative Treatment for Eating Disorders

When treating eating-disordered patients, I focus on two key issues: the eating-disordered behaviors themselves (the symptoms) and self- or affect regulation (the function of the symptom).

For the purposes of this chapter, I will not attempt to provide a detailed description of either CBT or DBT. Instead, what I will attempt to accomplish is to demonstrate how specific skills and strategies can be pulled from these therapies to provide an integrative approach.

Treating Eating-Disordered Behaviors: Treating the Symptoms

Self-Monitoring via Food Journals. In describing his protocol for CBT-E, Fairburn (2008) discussed the use of detailed food journals. This is often how I begin with eating-disorder patients. Self-monitoring of this kind involves detailed recording of what was eaten, time of the day, level of hunger/fullness, compensatory behaviors such as purging, laxative use, over exercise, and so on, and thoughts/feelings associated with this eating episode. Fairburn encouraged patients to complete food journals in the moment, when possible, indicating that 'real time' monitoring will allow for the capturing what is happening 'moment to moment.'

Food journals allow for observations of mood, affect, bodily sensation, and thought patterns as well as when they eat or don't eat, when they use eating-disorder symptoms, and when they follow their meal plan. As eating patterns become more regulated, I move away from the use of such structured food journals and planning yet make sure that patients are aware that this is a foundation piece that they will always hold on to, especially given that eating-disordered symptoms tend to fluctuate throughout the course of treatment.

While food journaling is critical in traditional CBT, journaling exercises such as these can be used as tool for patients to gain a better connection to their internal world and processes (Petrucelli, 2004). The act of putting their food, thoughts, and feelings on paper provides a space for patients to be self-reflective and aware of the parts of themselves that had historically been unaware of (Petrucelli, 2004).

Other Types of Monitoring. In addition to food journals, CBT-E also addresses the importance of monitoring body 'checking behaviors,' such as feeling for bones, looking in the mirror, comparing themselves to the shape of others around them, which are often occurring beyond a patient's awareness. Helping the patient to gain awareness over these behaviors is often helped by the use of self-monitoring logs to track their occurrence. While this is not a behavior pattern that that every patient will exhibit, I find it is useful to monitor, should it occur, as it often serves to maintain eating-disordered behaviors and overemphasis on body image.

Mindfulness. Mindfulness is a DBT module described as "cognitive and behavioral versions of meditation skills taught in eastern spiritual practices" (Linehan, 1993a, p. 144). From a DBT perspective, mindfulness involves attending to an internal state or emotion without actively trying to change, alter, fix, or avoid it, thereby allowing the emotion to be just experienced (Lynch et al., 2006). By 'just experiencing' an emotion, DBT teaches patients that emotions are temporary states that will pass and 'will not last forever,' as well as how to take a nonjudgmental stance so that patients are able to avoid the secondary experience of emotions such as shame and guilt that are often associated with negative emotional experiences (Wiser & Telch, 1999).

In traditional DBT, mindfulness is the first module taught and its concepts flow through the other core elements of DBT. Mindfulness skills are reviewed throughout the course of structured DBT therapy, and mindfulness 'diary cards' are assigned weekly. It is helpful to talk about mindfulness early on in treatment as the skills can be applied to a variety of contexts and is a skill that will be referred back to through the course of treatment.

A hallmark feature of most eating disorders is significant difficulty in viewing one's body without shame or judgment as well as an inability to attend to bodily signals of hunger fullness in an appropriate manner (Wisniewski & Kelly, 2003). DBT offers to patient's a new way to eat that encourages "full, present-oriented, moment-to-moment, single-minded, nonjudgmental awareness to eating" (Wiser & Telch, 1999, p. 761). Such a style of eating is often in contrast to the impulsive, dissociative, dysregulated, and/or overcontrolled manner in which eating-disordered patients tend to approach food.

It is helpful to teach self-monitoring techniques alongside mindfulness skills, as both involve ways in which patients are taught to raise their levels of awareness and attention. In addition, the nonjudgment qualities stressed in DBT mindfulness skills are of particular importance when monitoring both food and eating-disorder behaviors, such as bingeing, purging, and overexercising, as these actions are often experienced with some degree of shame or guilt. Wiser and Telch (1999) referred to these feelings as 'secondary emotional reactions' and warned that they often add to the level of distress an individual is experiencing. By teaching patients to approach such experiences with less judgment, some of this distress is reduced.

Competing Activities/Alternative Activities. Self-monitoring and food logs often help patients identify what sets them up for eating-disorder symptom use. Given this, it is useful to help patients generate lists of alternative behaviors that they can engage in order to avoid or distract from these precipitating events (Johnson et al., 1987). When faced with either an intense emotion or an urge to engage in eating-disordered symptoms, patients often describe a 'deer, in headlights' moment, in that they feel so overwhelmed and frozen that they are unable to think of what else they can do. Patients often turn to activities that are either distracting or self-soothing, such as calling a supportive friend, taking a walk or a bath, listening to music—it is difficult to binge or purge with wet nails.

Cognitive Restructuring. CBT theory posits that at the root of eating disorders lies an overevaluation of weight and shape, 'clinical perfectionism,' and low core self-esteem (Fairburn et al., 2003). Because these standards often fuel or underlie eating-disordered behaviors, it is often important to target these thought patterns directly.

Restructuring or changing distorted thoughts is central to CBT (Walen et al., 1992; Beck et al., 1979) and involves identifying illogical thought patterns, challenging or disputing them, and, consequently, helping the patient reach new, more realistic patterns of thinking. In this case, thoughts related to clinical perfectionism and low self-esteem are the targeting thought distortions.

In working with eating-disordered patients, it is useful to challenge their beliefs about food groups, importance of the thin, 'ideal' body shape, and expectations of body and weight (Johnson, et al., 1987; Fairburn, 2008), thereby correcting unrealistic standards and setting more reasonable/realistic goals.

Self/Affect Regulation: The Function of the Symptoms

Emotional Regulation Skills. Emotional regulation skills is one the core targets of DBT and are rooted in the understanding that individuals experience difficulty with emotional regulation when they attempt to control what they are feeling or, more simply, try to not feel it (Linehan, 1993a). Emotional regulation skills include things such as instruction in how to observe and describe emotions. In DBT this involves identifying prompting events (who, what, where, when), bodily sensations and body language, labeling behavioral urges, and the function of an emotion (Linehan, 1993a).

In working with eating-disordered patients, a vacillation between over- and undercontrolled emotional expressions is observed, where there is either too much or too little emotion expressed. Both extremes are problematic for patients. Drawing on the skills that encompass the DBT emotional regulation modules, work with patients can begin to understand how to identify not only emotions themselves, but also their prompting events and consequences. In addition, helping patients to become aware of the utility of emotions and emotional expression is necessary, especially for those eating-disordered cases where there is restricted emotional expression.

Emotional Acceptance/Distress Tolerance. Linehan (1993a) contended that "the ability to tolerate and accept distress is essential for mental health" (p. 96). DBT uses the term *radical acceptance*, which translates to mean a complete acceptance from within. Patients are taught that painful emotions are part of life. While these experiences are difficult, radical acceptance speaks to an understanding that they are a normal and expected part of life. Central to these skills is acceptance strategies, teaching patients to stop fighting both emotionally and behaviorally against the unavoidable distressing situation but rather to embrace/ accept this situation.

Conclusion: Opportunities and Challenges for Therapy Integration

For me, integrative therapy fits nicely with who I am as a therapist. I gravitate to the ease and practicality of CBT and DBT skills, yet simultaneously feeling drawn towards the importance of a patient's attachment and relational histories and an appreciation for the power of the therapeutic relationship.

One of the hardest things to reconcile when practicing from an integrative perspective is the core difference in therapist–patient stance between CBT/DBT and interpersonal psychotherapies. CBT/DBT is a one-person model of psychotherapy in which the patient is asked to explore thoughts, feelings, and behaviors with the therapist serving as an observer, facilitator, and/or guide in this process. While the relationship between the therapist and patient is acknowledged, there is a still a distinct 'separateness' between the two. The therapy relationship is not explored or seen as the source of therapeutic action. Interpersonal psychotherapy is rooted in a two-person model of therapy, in which the therapist is engaged intimately with the patient so that the patient is able to feel the 'presence and involvement' of the therapist (Bromberg, 1998). The therapy relationship is seen as integral to the therapeutic process. This is what is so interesting and complicated about integrative therapy. It becomes a process of engaging didactically with patients while at the same time appreciating the more relational aspects of such interactions.

As an integrative therapist, I am more thoughtful with how and why I ask patients to complete more goal-oriented CBT/DBT tasks. My perspective is broader in considering how a coping strategy might work for a patient. I fully explore what it is like for a patient to engage in these strategies and exercises as well as what is like for them to have me ask them to do so. I am less likely to get into a power struggle with my patient for not completing homework assignments or being 'noncompliant with therapy.'

Terms such as awareness and mindfulness take on new meanings when viewed through the interpersonal lens. While I want my patients to know better how they think, feel, and behave, it is important to appreciate how these thoughts, feelings, and behaviors are rooted in their current and historic history. Additionally, how they feel about their relationship with me is always of relevance. The need to consider such things is something a strictly CBT/DBT therapist would give little thought to, yet is intrinsically important to deepening work with patients. As Brisman (2001), eloquently stated (p. 58), "The ways in which food and bodily obsessions are used to strangulate the therapy relationship are now alive in the room, available to be more directly experienced by both therapist and patient." While I may be engaged in a very concrete exercise with a patient, the therapy relationship is always relevant and part of what is being worked on and explored.

Cohesively weaving CBT and DBT skills with interpersonal themes and interpretations allows therapists to not only concretely focus on symptom reduction and skill building but also explore meaningful relational themes and attachment patterns. I have found that this combined treatment approach is not only effective for the treatment of eating disorders but is also engaging to my patients. It promotes patients to take on an active and reflective simultaneously in sessions, something that I encourage them to carry with them out of the therapy room.

Bringing Things Together: A Case Illustration

When S first entered my office, she reported that she struggled with a long history of bulimia nervosa. At the time she initiated therapy, S was in her late 20s. She indicated that her eating disorder first emerged around age 16, and by and the time she entered college S had a well-established restrict, binge, purge cycle. Over the years, S had attempted therapy several times but had not participated in long-term treatment and made little to no gains. At the onset of our treatment together, S indicated that she felt out of control and reported engaging in severe binge/purge episodes, typically multiple times per day. Any food that she kept down was described as inconsistent and often restrictive.

Background and Family History. S is oldest of three living children. Her parents are married and reside in S's childhood home. When talking about her history, S reported an early childhood loss of her brother who died during infancy due to a congenital heart defect when S was about 3 years old. S's parents went on to have two additional children following this loss and S notes that her mother got pregnant quickly following the death of her brother. S has some vague memories from the time of her brother's death, indicating that mostly she remembers feeling a need to be 'OK' for her parents and recalled her parents frequently making remarks to other people about being OK in reference to how the family, including S, was coping following the loss. She later added that she grew up thinking and feeling that she needed to be enough of a child to fill in the gap left by her brother. From this desire to be good enough for two children started S's strive for perfectionism and high achievement.

S's family resides in the Bible Belt, and religion plays a large role in their lives. They attend church services regularly and are actively involved in the church community. According to S, her parents relied heavily on this church community following the death of her brother. They often speak of "God's will" as a means by which to seek comfort. S is a religious and spiritual person herself but does not feel as connected to organized religion as her parents do.

Early Treatment. When S first entered into treatment, I was concerned about her high level of symptom use and worried about my ability to be helpful to her given how emotionally and behaviorally dyresgulated she appeared. However, S seemed eager to work and appeared motivated for treatment. She indicated that she had never been in a long-term, ongoing treatment before and that she felt ready to do so. S was immediately referred to a nutritionist and a medical doctor, knowing that she needed a team-treatment approach and to have her medical status followed closely. She began with weekly therapy and nutrition sessions.

The beginning of our work together was symptom focused. This felt like the natural place to start with S as her life was so consumed by her eating disorder that little other content was brought into the therapy room. S had limited capacity to think beyond her binges, purges, and body-image concerns.

S was taught to keep detailed food journals to begin to identify her patterns with food and eating-disordered symptoms. For S, who described being so emotionally and cognitively 'checked out' during her binge-eating episodes, journaling exercises were particularly important as a means to identify her thoughts and feelings both before and after engaging in these behaviors. Initially, this proved difficult and embarrassing for S. She had trouble at times detailing her binge-eating episodes, which were often very deliberate, premeditated, and included a significant amount of food. The process of writing down what she consumed often raised feelings of shame, guilt, and embarrassment for her. At times, just the word 'binge' would appear in her food journal, a sign that providing more detail would have just been too overwhelming for her and a signal to me just how painful the examining or 'taking ownership' over her symptoms was for her. I used this kind of information as a way to pace S and our work together. I did not want to move too quickly or flood her emotionally, especially in the early phase of treatment when I knew that I needed to build a more stable therapeutic relationship before she could trust me with what she felt were the most shameful elements of her life and behaviors.

Before beginning therapy, S had kept a journal of her thoughts and feelings, having historically found this useful. I encouraged her to continue to journal as much as possible. Journaling became an interesting theme in sessions with S. We noticed how helpful this was for her in terms of providing a designated space for emotional awareness and processing.

In addition to food journaling, S found other more directive treatment interventions helpful. Given that S has an interest in yoga, mindfulness skills felt natural to her. We worked on mindfulness and increasing emotional and behavioral awareness. Radical acceptance, encourages patient to accept, as opposed to avoid, painful emotional experiences. For S, she was able to acknowledge not remembering a time in which pain and loss did not exist in her life, having had such a significant loss in early childhood. However, her parents' intense need for her to be 'OK' gave her little room for emotional expression of such painful affects. Instead, S learned how to dissociate these affective experiences as she strived to be the perfect daughter, throwing herself into school, dance, and, by the time she was in high school, her eating disorder. Acknowledging and tolerating emotional experiences in therapy was, in many ways, a new experience for S. At first, most of these affects centered around her eating disorder, and S began to talk about how intolerable eating without purging felt, how out of control she often felt when asked to eat real meals during her work day, and how uncomfortable she felt physically in her body and terrified of body changes she truly was. Learning to 'sit with' instead of dissociate these feeling states laid the ground work for tolerating other emotional experiences S would have through the course of therapy.

Therapy with S felt very easy initially. She was ready for treatment and wanted very much to be better. Within the first two years of working together, S's symptoms decreased dramatically. She went from bingeing and purging daily to engaging in these symptoms approximately one time per week. She seemed engaged and motivated in both her therapy and nutrition appointments. Her eating patterns were more normalized, she reported less symptoms of depression and anxiety, she was more engaged with her friends, and she even started a romantic relationship, her first significant relationship in several years. In many ways, S had achieved stability, her eating-disorder symptoms no longer felt out of control, her life had more balance, and she reported feeling better both physically and emotionally. However, despite such progress, S's eating disorder still lingered—things were better but she was not free from her eating disorder.

My work with S acutely reflects the need for therapy integration. Initially working with S more concretely on her food plans, coping strategies, and journaling exercises was extremely useful in bringing about changes initially. However, this was not enough to facilitate the systemic changes that S would need for complete symptom abatement.

Interpersonal Themes. The third year of S's treatment felt stale, and S hit a plateau. Her symptoms ebbed and flowed; some weeks S reported being a-symptomatic and others she would engage in binge/purge behaviors several times per week. While S expressed a desire to be completely free from her eating disorder, with it interfering significantly less in her daily functioning, it proved difficult for S to make the needed changes. She talked often about clinging to the 'remnants' of her eating disorder and expressed fear about letting go entirely of something that had been part of her life for such a long time.

During the fourth year of my work with S, she ended her relationship with her boyfriend. This was a difficult break up for S, and she became more depressed. Historically, when faced with an emotional crisis, S would turn to her eating disorder, finding relief from emotional pain in the behaviors and rhythms of her symptoms. However, this break-up was a new experience for S, who described being able to feel her emotional states in a more raw, acute way than she had before. While her eating-disorder symptoms worsened somewhat, she was still able to maintain a state of overall stability.

One of the most salient emotions for S during this time was anger. In the aftermath of her break-up, S turned to her parents for support. Unfortunately, the kind of support S's parents were able to offer her came in the form of spiritual guidance, with statements such as 'God has a husband out there for you.' S found this not only unhelpful but also invalidating of her pain and suffering. Feelings such as these were reminiscent of early misattunement of her needs by her parents following the death of her brother. S's parents had relied heavily on the church at that time, believing that there was a spiritual purpose for the loss of their baby son. Additionally, the family mantra of being 'OK' was thrust upon S. Once again, she felt forced to be OK even when she wasn't, feeling that her parents were forcing her to feel fine before she was ready to.

In addition, S was able to access anger at her parents for the way in which they currently and historically dealt with her eating disorder. S's parents first learned about her eating disorder in high school. While they were very concerned, S felt that they did little for her. She indicated that her mother would read books and go to conferences about eating disorders, but they had trouble speaking directly to her about it and never forced her to therapy. In the present day, S's parents will ask her vague questions about her food or her therapy sessions, but they are not able to be direct and tend to dance around the issues. While this angers S, she is vague in her responses to them, answering them curtly and in ways that tend to shut down communication quickly, while simultaneously wanting them to be more empathic and concerned. S is aware of her role in this dance that she is in with her parents and admittedly wants to do little to alter the interactions. My work with her has been largely focused on identifying and expressing her anger tying to events occurring in the present day, such as her break up, and those more historical. S is actively working on accepting her parents more and anticipating their likely reliance on religion to manage difficulties, even though this still feels highly uncomfortable to her. While these are largely relational themes, S and I use DBT skills, such as radical acceptance and other distress tolerance skills to aide in 'sitting with' her feelings of anger. While S can still fall into dissociative patterns with her feelings of anger, she has shown dramatic improvements in both understanding and tolerating this feeling.

Relapse Prevention. S's treatment with me, currently still ongoing, has spanned the course of about four years. During that time, she has made tremendous strides with regard to eating-disorder symptoms as well as her symptoms of depression. S has experienced periods of time when she was not engaging in any eating disorder-symptoms as well as times when her depressive symptoms have significantly abated. As is the course of many treatments, this has fluctuated so that following a period of remission, her symptoms would return, although never to the extent that they did early on treatment. Currently, S's symptoms are variable, with times during which she reports engaging in binge/purge one to three times per week and then weeks during which she is more stable. Her eating overall is less restrictive, although she still works with her nutritionist and reports some difficulty tolerating feeling full.

Since S and I have built a strong CBT/DBT foundation, often when her behaviors are less stable we talk about relying more on those skills of self-monitoring and mindfulness/emotional awareness. While S no longer consistently does so, she finds that it is helpful to go back to these skills at times to feel more in control of her behaviors and eating as well as to enhance her awareness of her thoughts and feelings.

Summary

In working with S, an integrative approach felt particularly useful. S presented in my office with such a high level of symptom use that it was clear that stabilizing her behaviorally was of paramount concern. While S is a psychologically minded individual, her engagement in her eating disorder prevented her from thinking reflectively about herself or her emotions. By first working with S to decrease her symptom use, her psychic space became more available and was evident in her therapy sessions and in her relationship with me. There was also a growing shift in her personal life and the ways in which she related to herself and others. S was now more open and willing to meaningfully reflect on the function of her eating-disordered behavior in her present life, as well as, in the role this served for her historically. The potential for further progress and growth is foreseeable.

Acknowledgement

I wish to thank Elizabeth Halsted for her valuable insights, help, and support in the writing and editing of this chapter.

References

Beck, A. T., Rush, A. J., Shaw, B. F., & Emery, G. (1979). *Cognitive therapy depression.* New York, NY: Guilford Press.

Blagys, M. D., & Hilsenroth, M. J., (2002). Distinctive activities of cognitive behavioral therapy: A review of the comparative psychotherapy process literature. *Clinical Psychology Review, 22,* 671–706.

Brisman, J. (2001). The instigation of dare: Broadening therapeutic horizons. In J. Petrucelli & C. Stuart (Eds.), *Hungers and compulsions: The psychodynamic treatment of eating disorders and addictions.* Northvale, NJ: Jason Aronson.

Bromberg, P. M. (1998). *Standing in the spaces: Essays on clinical process, trauma, and dissociation.* New York, NY: Psychology Press.

Conners, M. E. (2001). Integrative treatment of symptomatic disorders. *Psychoanalytic Psychology, 18,* 74–91.

Connors, M. E. (2010). Symptom-focused dynamic psychotherapy. *Journal of Psychotherapy Integration, 20,* 37–45.

Fairburn, C. G. (2008). Eating disorders: The transdiagnostic view and the cognitive behavioral theory. In. C. G. Fairburn (Ed.), *Cognitive behavior therapy and eating disorders* (pp. 7–22). New York, NY: Guilford Press.

Fairburn, C. G., Cooper, Z., & Shafran, R. (2003). Cognitive behavior therapy for eating disorders: A 'transdiagnostic' theory and treatment. *Behavior Research and Therapy, 41,* 509–528.

Howell, E. F. (2005). *The dissociative mind.* New York, NY: Taylor & Francis Group.

Johnson, C., Conners, M. E., & Tobin, D. L. (1987). Symptom management of bulimia. *Journal of Consulting and Clinical Psychology, 55,* 668–676.

Linehan, M. M., (1993a). *Cognitive-behavioral treatment of borderline personality disorder.* New York, NY: Guilford Press.

Linehan, M. M. (1993b). *Skills training manual for treating borderline personality disorder.* New York, NY: Guilford Press.

Lynch, T. R., Chapman, A. L., Rosenthal, M. Z., Kuo, J. R., & Linehan, M. M. (2006). Mechanisms of change in dialectic behavior therapy: Theoretical and empirical observations. *Journal of Clinical Psychology, 62,* 459–480.

Petrucelli, J. (2004). Treating eating disorders. In R. Coombs (Ed.), *Handbook of addictive disorders: A practical guide to diagnosis and treatment* (Chapter 10). New Jersey: Wiley & Sons.

Walen, S. R., DiGiuseppe, R., & Dryden, W. (1992). *A practitioner's guide to rational-emotive therapy.* New York, NY: Oxford University Press.

Wiser, S., & Telch, C. F. (1999). Dialectic behavior therapy for binge eating disorder. *Psychotherapy in Practice, 55,* 755–768.

Wisniewski, L., & Kelly, E. (2003). The application of dialectic behavior therapy to the treatment of eating disorders. *Cognitive and Behavioral Practice, 10,* 131–138.

19

'ONE PILL MAKES YOU LARGER, AND ONE PILL MAKES YOU SMALL' . . . AND THE ONES THAT DOCTOR GIVES YOU MAY OR MAY NOT DO ANYTHING AT ALL

A Brief Summary of Pharmacological Approaches in the Treatment of Eating Disorders

A. Mittsi Crossman and Zev Labins

Introduction

Eating disorders as defined by the DSM-IV (anorexia nervosa, bulimia nervosa, and binge-eating disorder) comprise a complex constellation of biological, psychological, and social factors that contribute to their usual complex clinical presentation, diagnostic challenges, unpredictable course, and need for a multifaceted therapeutic approach (American Psychiatric Association [APA], 2006). Although in nearly half of the cases a psychotropic agent will be prescribed (Moore et al., 2013), the data and research to support this practice continue to be limited. The use of psychopharmacological agents is mostly recommended as adjunctive treatment to psychosocial interventions (i.e., psychotherapy) or to complement the treatment of other comorbid conditions, such as mood, anxiety, and substance and personality disorders (Hudson et al., 2007).

Anorexia Nervosa

The relatively low prevalence rates of anorexia nervosa (AN) among US adults, estimated to be 0.6% by the National Institute of Mental Health (NIH, 2011), may partially explain the limited availability of studies addressing the use of psychotropic agents in this condition (Gabbard, 2007). Antidepressant agents, monoamine oxidase inhibitors (MAOIs) and tricyclics (TCAs), and, more recently, selective serotoninergic agents (SSRIs) as well other various agents have consistently failed to demonstrate a robust effect in ameliorating the core symptoms

283

that constitute AN (Aigner et al., 2011; Claudino et al., 2006). Antidepressants, nevertheless, seem to offer a beneficial role when used to treat comorbid depressive and/or anxiety spectrum symptoms, which, left untreated, would certainly exacerbate or complicate the ultimate prognosis of the illness.

Typical (dopamine D_2 receptor blockers) and atypical or second-generation antipsychotics agents (dopamine/serotonin 5-HT$_2$ receptor blockers or SGAs) have been used to treat body-image symptoms of delusional proportions in AN. More frequently, they are used as an augmentation strategy in the treatment of comorbid mood, anxiety, or obsessional symptoms. Although it is not uncommon for practitioners to capitalize on the weight gain side effects of SGAs, a recent meta-analysis (Kishi et al., 2012) did not support this practice due to the lack of weight gain coupled with the heightened risk of severe adverse effects associated with this class of agents (such as tardive dyskinesia, cardiovascular disease, and metabolic disturbances). On the other hand, the antidepressant mirtazapine has been reported in case studies to be useful in AN. Mirtazapine may be helpful due to its associated weight gain, antidepressant and anxiolytic activity, and less risky side effect profile compared to the SGAs (Safer et al., 2010).

Bulimia Nervosa and Binge-Eating Disorder

Bulimia nervosa (BN) and binge-eating disorder (BED) have traditionally shared common psychopharmacological approaches. As with AN, TCAs and MAOIs have been used for treatment of BN and BED. Today, TCAs may be considered as a second-line treatment in patients presenting with comorbid mood or anxiety disorders who have failed trials of the newer antidepressants that typically have more benign side effects. MAOIs are not recommended given their numerous side effects and the strict dietary restrictions (tyrosine-free diet in order to minimize hypertensive crisis) required with their use (Shapiro et al., 2007; Aigner et al., 2011).

In the United States, the only Food and Drug Administration (FDA)–approved medication for BN is the SSRI fluoxetine (Fluoxetine Bulimia Nervosa Collaborative Study Group, 1992). As expected, other SSRIs also have shown positive results in a few randomized controlled studies for BD and BED, although the weight loss in BED may be variable (McCann & Agras, 1990; Appolinario & McElroy, 2004; Agras et al., 1994). Other agents that exert their effect on serotoninergic, norepinephric, or dopaminergic systems (venlafaxine, duloxetine, atomoxetine, trazodone, and bupropion) have shown some promise in treating BN or BED. Bupropion, however, is contraindicated due to a significant seizure risk (Aigner et al., 2011; APA, 2006; Mitchell et al., 2013).

There is accumulating evidence that new anticonvulsants agents such as topiramate and zonisamide, notwithstanding the high rates of discontinuation due to poor tolerability, are superior to placebo in reducing binge eating and purging (McElroy et al., 2009). Given the predominant comorbid mood and personality disorders, other anticonvulsants (such as lamotrigine or oxcarbazepine) may be considered in some cases of BN or BED.

Promising areas of research focus on the shared genetic and/or neurobiological pathways associated with substance use and eating disorders (particularly with BN and BED). Medications considered include acamprosate, a NMDA antagonist used in alcohol dependence, as well as agents that target the endocannabinoid and endogenous opioid systems (McElroy et al., 2011; Scherma et al., 2014; McElroy et al., 2013). Other agents that are under recent investigation in BED include memantine (a noncompetitive NMDA receptor agonist), orlistat (a lipase inhibitor), and chromium picolinate (Brennan et al., 2008; Grilo & White, 2013; Brownley et al., 2013). Medications such as sibutramine (a SNRI) and fenfluramine (a serotonergic medication) have shown positive effect in treatment of BED and/or obesity but have been removed from the US market due to safety concerns (Appolinario et al., 2003; FDA, 2010; Weintraub et al., 1984; FDA, 1997).

Summary

Eating disorders present a complex clinical scenario that require multifaceted treatment modalities in which pharmacological agents may be indicated, particularly when the treatment of comorbid mood or anxiety symptoms and/or augmentation strategies are sought. Antidepressants, particularly SSRIs, seem to offer the best benefit with an overall safe and tolerable side-effect profile in treatment of BN or BED. Bupropion should be avoided in BN due to the associated increased risk for seizures. MAOIs should also be avoided due to the strict dietary restrictions required.

Antipsychotics (particularly SGAs) are commonly prescribed in AN but have not shown benefit in weight gain and carry the risk of increased metabolic risks. Unless comorbid symptoms (e.g., psychotic, manic, refractory depression or obsessive compulsive disorder) are present, they should be avoided.

Anticonvulsant medication, particularly topiramate and zonisamide, with their associated weight loss side effects, have shown positive effects in some studies. Given the high correlation of mood, anxiety, personality, and substance abuse disorders, anticonvulsants may be particularly helpful given the multitude of off-label uses for these associated disorders with high comorbidity eating disorders.

In summary, a comprehensive therapeutic approach that combines psychosocial interventions with a skillful use of psychopharmacological agents, particularly if co-occurring psychiatric disorders are present, has shown to be the most effective therapeutic approach to eating disorders.

References

Agras, W. S., Telch, C. F., Arnow, B., et al. (1994). Weight loss, cognitive-behavioral, and desipramine treatments in binge-eating disorder: An additive design. *Behavior Therapy, 25,* 225–238.

Aigner, M., Treasure, J., Kaye, W., et al. (2011). World Federation of Societies of Biological Psychiatry (WFSBP) Guidelines for the pharmacological treatment of eating disorders. *The World Journal of Biological Psychiatry 12,* 400–443.

American Psychiatric Association. (2006). *Guideline watch: Practice guideline for the treatment of patients with eating disorders* (3rd ed.). Washington: Author.

Appolinario, J. C., Bacaltchuk, J., Sichieri, R., et al. (2003). A randomized double-blind, placebo-controlled study of sibutramine in the treatment of binge eating disorder. *Arch Gen Psychiatry, 60,* 1109–1116.

Appolinario, J. C., & McElroy, S. L. (2004). Pharmacologic approaches to the treatment of binge eating disorder. *Current Drug Targets, 5,* 301–307.

Brennan, B. P., Roberts, J. A., Fogarty, K. V., et al. (2008). Memantine in the treatment of binge eating disorder: An open-label, prospective trial. *Int J of Eat Disord, 41,* 520–526.

Brownley, K. A., Von Holle, A., Hamer, R. M., et al. (2013). A double-blind, randomized pilot trial of chromium picolinate for binge eating disorder: Results of the Binge Eating and Chromium (BEACh) study. *Journal of Psychosomatic Research, 75*(1), 36–42.

Claudino, A. M., Silva de Lima, M., Hay, P. P. J., et al. (2006). Antidepressants for anorexia nervosa. *Cochrane Database of Systemic Reviews, 1,* CD004365. doi:10.1002/14651858. CD004365.pub2

FDA. (1997). *FDA announces withdrawal fenfluramine and dexfenfluramine (Fen-Phen).* Available from www.fda.gov/Drugs/DrugSafety/PostmarketDrugSafetyInformationfor PatientsandProviders/ucm179871.htm

FDA. (2010). *Meridia (sibutramine): Market withdrawal due to risk of serious cardiovascular events, 2010.* Available from www.fda.gov/Safety/MedWatch/SafetyInformation/ SafetyAlertsforHumanMedicalProducts/ucm228830.htm

Fluoxetine Bulimia Nervosa Collaborative Study Group. (1992). Fluoxetine in the treatment of bulimia nervosa: A multicenter, placebo-controlled, double-blind trial. *Arch Gen Psychiatry, 49,* 139–147.

Gabbard, G. O. (2007). *Treatments of psychiatric disorders* (4th ed.). Arlington, VA: American Psychiatric Publishing.

Grilo, C. M., & White, M. A. (2013). Orlistat with behavioral weight loss for obesity with versus without binge eating disorder: Randomized placebo-controlled trial at a community mental health center serving educationally and economically disadvantaged Latino/ as. *Behaviour Research and Therapy, 51*(3), 167–175.

Hudson, J. I., Hiripi, E., Pope, H. G., Jr., et al. (2007). The prevalence and correlates of eating disorders in the National Comorbidity Survey Replication. *Biol Psychiatry, 61,* 348–358.

Kishi, T., Kafantaris, V., Sunday, S., et al. (2012). Are antipsychotics effective for the treatment of anorexia nervosa? Results from a systematic review and meta-analysis. *J Clin Psychiatry, 73*(6), e757–e766.

McCann, U. D., & Agras, W. S. (1990). Successful treatment of compulsive binge-eating with desipramine: A double-blind placebo-controlled study. *Am J Psychiatry, 147,* 1509–1513.

McElroy, S. L., Guerdjikova, A. I., Blom, T. H., et al. (2013). A placebo-controlled pilot study of the novel opioid receptor antagonist ALKS-33 in binge eating disorder. *Int J Eat Disord, 46*(3), 239–245.

McElroy, S. L., Guerdjikova, A. I., Martens, B., et al. (2009). Role of antiepileptic drugs in the management of eating disorders. *CNS Drugs, 23*(2), 139–156.

McElroy, S. L., Guerdjikova, A. I., Winstanley, E. L., et al. (2011). Acamprosate in the treatment of binge eating disorder: A placebo-controlled trial. *Int J Eat Disord, 44,* 81–90.

Mitchell, J. E., Roerig, J., & Steffan, K. (2013). Biological therapies for eating disorders. *Int J Eat Disord, 46,* 470–477.

Moore, J. K., Watson, H. J., Harper, E., McCormack, J., & Nguyen, T. (2013). Psychotropic drug prescribing in an Australian specialist child and adolescent eating disorder service: A retrospective study. *J Eat Disord, 1*(27), 1–13.

National Institute of Mental Health. (2011). *Eating disorders.* NIH Publication No. 11–4901.

Safer, D. L., Darcy, A. M., & Lock, J. (2011). Use of mirtazapine in an adult with refractory anorexia nervosa and comorbid depression: A case report. *Int J Eat Disord, 44*(2), 178–181.

Scherma, M., Fattore, L., Castelli, M. P., et al. (2014). The role of the endocannabinioid system in eating disorders: Neurochemical and behavioural preclinical evidence. *Current Pharmaceutical Design, 20.* Available from www.ncbi.nlm.nih.gov/pubmed/23829365

Shapiro, J. R., Berkman, N. D., Brownley, K. A., et al. (2007). Bulimia nervosa treatment: A systematic review of randomized controlled trials. *Int J Eat Disord, 40,* 321–336.

Weintraub, M., Hasday, J. D., Mushlin, A. I., et al. (1984). A double-blind clinical trial in weight control: Use of fenfluramine and phentermine alone and in combination. *Arch Intern Med, 144*(6), 1143–1148.

20

BODY OR MIND

A Discontinuous Model of
Neural Emotional Processing

Barbara Pearlman

Internal Language Enhancement (ILE)—A Novel
Treatment for Eating Disorders based on Research
into the Neuroscience of Emotional Processing

We all know that eating disorders are a puzzle. Why do people who in all other respects think and talk rationally, suddenly, for supposedly no apparent reason, begin to talk about their weight and shape or how many calories they can or will eat?

If we pay close attention to how our patient sitting opposite us is talking, we begin to realize that she[1] has changed state from thinking and talking symbolically about her feeling state, to suddenly talking about her body or the number of calories contained in food. As practitioners we might think the patient is offering us a concrete symbol to explain a troubling thought, for example, by beginning to talk about how heavy she feels. But if we try to shift the conversation to the symbolic emotional realm—perhaps we might begin to talk about how heavy hearted she might feel—we find that the patient steadfastly refuses (or is unable) to follow us and instead continues to talk about her weight.

Communication between patient and therapist is of the utmost importance in treating any psychiatric illness but is perhaps even more crucial in eating disorders precisely because the patient is at times unable to focus on anything except her concrete bodily experience. This causes a disruption in the therapy where the therapist and patient are no longer in communication. The therapist is trained and wishes to help his or her patient talk about their emotional world in symbolic language. This allows the patient to understand the meaning of why she does what she does, and therefore can have a choice to change what she does, which is the reason the patient has gone to the therapist in the first place. Whichever therapy is employed, this bumping into miscommunication frequently happens and leaves the therapeutic couple struggling to find one another again.

The impetus for this theoretical work and the subsequent development of a new treatment for eating disorders, Internal Language Enhancement (ILE), was that as a clinical psychologist specializing in treating eating-disordered patients for 28 years, I frequently noticed how at times patients spoke symbolically about their lives. Yet suddenly, at others, there was no route to communication, other than talking concretely about the body and food. At times the professional and the patient were speaking a different language.

As patients became well, they spoke of how they were no longer capable of starving or bingeing and vomiting, and several, quite independently, described feeling as if a switch had been 'flipped' in their brain. The previous eating-disordered act, that had seemed so natural, now appeared as bizarre in the extreme. The patient and therapist started to consistently speak the same language about conscious feelings of emotions and emotional relationships, quite in contrast with the early conversations that mainly involved weight, food, and bodies. This work follows Damasio's (2000) distinction between emotions and feelings of emotions. He proposes that "the term feeling should be reserved for the private, mental experience of an emotion, while the term emotion should be used to designate the collection of responses, many of which are publicly observable" (p. 42).

Thus I began to concentrate on the content of my patients' symbolic utterances, just prior to their collapse into the concrete state. This became the focus of our therapeutic discourse. Rather than an incremental improvement in the ability to understand emotions, my patients suddenly stopped, or dramatically reduced, their eating-disordered behavior within as little as three sessions, and spoke of how their brains, as one woman described it, had experienced a 'tsunami.' Patients were able to think symbolically about emotions, recognize reality, and plan how they wanted to solve emotional demands and problems. Eating-disordered behavior suddenly seemed bizarre and as if it belonged to another altered state. One patient spoke of 'waking up' after 35 years. Patients expressed increased anxiety, but this anxiety remained in the realm of feelings and emotions, not acted-out behavior.

Learning theory could not account for such rapid change, and my patients' responses seemed to have a neurological flavor. So I began to explore the neurological underpinnings of this patient group. The resulting clinical approach, ILE, crosses the divide between different theoretical approaches. It is based on neurological understanding and borrows techniques from both psychoanalysis and cognitive behavioral therapy with some input from the field of linguistics. ILE might prove to be a treatment that benefits our patients especially because of its collaborative, multidisciplinary origins.

The aim of ILE is to repair or reconnect the neural pathway that allows us to think symbolically about our emotions; for example, "I have a lot on my plate this week, and I am not sure how I am going to manage it all." When we cannot think symbolically about our feelings, we get trapped in our 'bodyminds.' For example, we might think "there is too much food on my plate, and I cannot eat it all." All symbolism is lost and the sufferers are trapped. They are trying to say something to themselves about their feeling state, but all that appears in the mind is about the body or things, with no way of expanding the thought to 'stretch' it to include deeper meaning. If the 'problem' is that the body is too big, then the answer is to make it smaller, rather than articulate "I am not mature enough and feel too young to deal with the demands of grown-up life."

Until recently, professionals who treat eating disorders have viewed their patients as being on the concrete end of a spectrum with fully symbolic thought at the 'desired' end can be 'moved along' the spectrum via the application of treatment. However, if we take a look at the neuroscience of emotional processing, we understand that it functions as an on/off switch. Under neutral conditions we process our emotions via our higher executive functions that include symbolic language, reality testing, planning, and memory in language. However, when excessive levels of anxiety are experienced by the brain as a danger signal, the symbolic pathway closes, and we are left only with bodily sensations and concrete language. Under such circumstances our internal emotional world becomes our 'insides' (i.e., our stomach), and we get rid of uncomfortable feelings by emptying our 'insides' (i.e., our bodies) and not by thinking about and resolving difficult emotional challenges.

We gain a clearer understanding of what happens during an eating-disorder episode when our patient suddenly 'goes concrete' when we consider both how we process feelings in the present, and how emotional processing and language develop from birth, especially in the brains of (mainly) girls and young women who go on to develop an eating disorder.

When patients are in the concrete state, the ILE theory suggests they cannot just gradually increase their symbolic capacity. Instead, the 'concrete' body pathway must be switched off in order for the symbolic pathway to be reconnected. To achieve this we need to discover the emotional trigger that caused the brain to become overwhelmed and to disconnect the symbolic emotional processing pathway. Then we can begin to reverse the process and open up the symbolic pathway by understanding why the emotional thought was so distressing. The moment the therapist and patient begin to think about the emotional challenge in symbolic language there is the opportunity to find real solutions to the very problem that tripped the patient into the concrete state. This is the aim of the ILE treatment.

The following traces the development of the brain from birth and describes the risk factors that can predispose individuals to developing an eating disorder.

Risk Factors for Eating-Disordered Thought and Behavior

It seems that the brains of sufferers of eating disorders share certain characteristics that predispose them to develop an eating disorder. In the first place, they appear to be ill equipped for reducing their anxiety or self-soothing (Oskis et al., 2011). It is this excess of anxiety that can trigger the shutting down of the symbolic higher functions. These patients also have significantly more difficulty putting their feelings into language (alexithymia; Corcos et al., 2000) and are more likely to have experienced an insecure attachment to a primary caregiver (Beckendam, 1997; Fonagy & Target, 1997). They also seem less able to understand complex emotional metaphor and irony (Amanzio et al., 2008). Their ability to process emotions in language can be easily overwhelmed by complex and negative emotional challenges

(Seeley et al., 2007). This can result in a compromised ability to comprehend a complex emotional environment (Vrticka et al., 2008; Zeitlin et al., 1989).

The Vital Function of Maternal Care and the Development of Language

In the field of eating disorders, mothers are often given a hard time. Just because in this illness the mother–child relationship often looks quite fraught, it does not necessarily follow that parents, and mothers in particular, are responsible for caus-ing the problem. Eating disorders generally appear in adolescence when the tasks of individuation and separation from parents (for girls, separating from mothers in particular) are the order of the day. But if a young girl has difficulty in processing and understanding the very complex adolescent emotional world, these tasks are not easily addressed and completed, possibly leaving her both angry that she can-not separate and yet be very dependent. When faced with a daughter who on the one hand says she wants to be independent and on the other shows herself to be incapable of feeding herself properly and putting her health at risk, parents are in a double bind. The call from their child is both come here and go away. So we often see parents who become paralyzed, knowing that their child needs to develop independence yet unable to step away for fear that their child might not survive.

There are some maternal tasks that are important in very early life that help to build the baby's brain that are not really addressed by childcare books and are largely dependent on both the kind of nervous system the baby brings to the mother–child relationship and the ability of the mother to contain her own and her child's anxieties.

Maternal preoccupation determines that after giving birth a mother will be hyper-aware of the needs of her child for food and comfort. If all goes well, the mother deciphers her baby's primitive cries by identifying with her baby and using her own feelings to help her understand her baby's communication. By con-tinually monitoring her baby's state and offering accurate and timely responses, she contains her baby's primitive anxiety and encourages the beginnings of com-munication and language. She mirrors back to her child what she understands her child's feelings to be, and in this way the baby begins to feel a sense of agency. If the mother and baby are not attuned to one another, the connection between the baby's arousal and the beginnings of language—the symbolic representation of mental states—the building blocks of the sense of self and understanding the 'other' can be disrupted (Fonagy & Target, 1997).

The capacity to undertake the work of maternal pre-occupation is dependent on what is happening in the mother's life around the time of giving birth. Does she have support? Has she been recently bereaved? Is she suffering from postnatal depression? Has her own experience of being mothered been compromised by losing her own mother in childhood? Is she preoccupied with difficult events in her life? On the other hand, babies have to join the 'communication dance' and make their needs known to the mother. (For many decades mothers of children with autism were described as 'refrigerator mothers' who did not respond to their child's communications, until it was discovered that the babies' lack of response to their mothers' attempts at communication had demoralized the mothers. Nowadays mothers of autistic children are encouraged to persevere in the absence of emotional response that characterizes this condition.)

The result of this 'communication dance' is often described in terms of attunement of mother and baby. If this attunement and subsequent attachment goes awry, the baby has difficulty in containing anxiety or being able to self-soothe. Too little emotional arousal or excessively high levels of negative emotional arousal may result in permanent alterations in the development of the orbitofrontal cortex, which affects activity in the amygdala, vital to the process of emotions (Schore, 1994, 1996).

It is important to state that it is not only the external environment (i.e., mothering) and all that it entails, but also the internal environment (i.e., the genetic makeup) of the child along with personality factors that can affect the attunement or 'the fit' between mother and child. Mothers who may have postnatal depression, who are in mourning, who are unsupported or who function in a narcissistic manner may be unavailable to fulfill the requirements of maternal preoccupation. Alternatively, a child who is unable to demand mother's attention may allow poor mothering to continue, whereas a more forceful child might draw out of her mother appropriate attention. It may also be that the child may have neurobiological deficits that militate against joining in the 'dance' between mother and child. In addition, some children may be less affected by their mother's anxiety than others.

Whatever the causes, the possible result may be fragility in the baby's ability to tolerate anxiety, which in turn affects how the brain processes emotional information. As mentioned earlier, anxiety is a trigger to shut down the symbolic emotional processing pathway. We all know that the right amount of anxiety helps us perform well in exams, but too much anxiety will cause us to have difficulty remembering our names!

The next task that a mother does naturally is to help develop her baby's beginnings of language by imprinting the baby's right hemisphere (responsible for the nonverbal aspect of language) with the building blocks of language via her facial expression, how she handles her baby and her tone of voice (Stuss & Alexander, 1999). In this way the mother lets her baby know that her communications have been understood, such as with hunger or discomfort. Again, if this period of development is less than optimal, the process of the baby understanding its internal world begins to be weaker than optimal. Later on, if less able to make sense of their internal emotional world in language, these children may naturally turn to others to do their emotional processing for them and their parents may naturally fill in the gaps. This then looks to the world as if the children are not allowed to think for themselves. On closer examination, however, it may emerge that the child is inviting the parent to help her by processing emotions and thinking about the world, activities that the child finds quite difficult and would rather avoid. If this mode of communication beds in, the parent–child relationship may settle down to there being one mind and two bodies, as it were, and given the anxieties around, this may be hard to change.

How Language Develops

It is generally accepted that the 'language' hemisphere is the left hemisphere while the right hemisphere is responsible for the processing of emotional words, including being alert to hearing one's first name, humor, laughter, social meaning, and, importantly, metaphor (Damasio, 1994). When body responses become accessible to conscious awareness, affects are differentiated from bodily feelings. But if this information cannot reach the symbolic functions, thinking about what is distressing is not possible. The only language available is located in the 'body-mind' and the only solution is to do something to the body to get rid of the discomfort.

Dealing with emotional stress through body responses interferes with emotional learning. Past experiences are then of no help when solving present difficulties. The right hemisphere has the task of retrieving past emotional experiences which, if sent over to the left hemisphere via the corpus callosum (the bundle of fibers connecting the two sides of the brain), are able to influence reasoning (Shuren & Grafman, 2002). It is precisely these right-hemisphere functions, of differentiating a body state from a feeling state and dealing with negative emotions, which seem to be operating suboptimally in the eating-disordered population.

The Importance of Communication Between Our Right and Left Hemispheres in Understanding Our Emotions

Identifying, evaluating, and communicating feeling states within oneself and others, requires a well-functioning interaction between right-hemisphere emotional perception and left-hemisphere linguistic processing and reasoning (Teicher et al., 1996). This function is compromised in alexithymic individuals (including eating-disordered patients) who often misinterpret body sensations of emotional arousal as disease (Taylor et al., 1997).

As mentioned above, the left hemisphere has the important role of interpreting in conscious language the emotional events that are experienced via the right hemisphere. The right hemisphere is responsible for the metaphorical or figurative meanings of words, as well as the meaning of nonverbal cues and comprehension of alternative meanings to words. When this process is impaired it becomes difficult to understand the emotional world and, most importantly, to reduce anxiety.

The Development of the Frontal Lobes and Their Role in Emotional Processing

The frontal lobes are where our executive functions live. They extract reality from the environment, allow planning for the future in real time, allow access to memory in language, and, crucially, enable us to think symbolically.

When a child gets to the second year of life, what is often called the terrible twos, the frontal lobes of the brain pare down. This means that the connections that might serve a baby well in asking for food or a toy need to change. The child has to get ready to explore its environment and make deductions and so needs new connections in reality testing and memory in language, as well as the ability to plan ahead in time. Tantrums occur because the old pathways deteriorate and suddenly end in a cul-de-sac, and the ability to solve a problem is stymied. The same thing happens in adolescence when the frontal lobes pare down and the co-operative ten-year-old suddenly gives way to a tantruming teenager when the connections needed for latency fade away and the demands of adult life begin to shape the adolescent brain. When this process occurs in an average adolescent, where the processing of emotions is somewhat less efficient than at an earlier age, there is a preoccupation with the body and how one is seen by the world. Typically, the adolescent weathers the storm and comes through intact and with maturing frontal lobes, which settle down into adult form around the age of 23 to 24. However, when the paring down process occurs in someone who is already poor at putting their feelings into words (alexithymic) and has relied on others to process the emotional world for them, the reduction in the ability of the frontal lobes to function can have a devastating effect. This is the group that is at risk of developing an eating disorder.

This 'at risk' group is also less able to produce and use imaginative solutions to problems, and has reduced REM sleep (rapid eye movement–a measure of the time we spend dreaming and processing the events of the day; Macquet et al., 1996). This at-risk group also has difficulty being flexible and often reuses the same solution to an old task even when given a new task (Tchanturia et al., 2003). In fact, Oskis et al. (2011) found that those preadolescent girls at greater risk of developing an eating disorder displayed abnormal levels of the stress hormone cortisol throughout the day. Rather than follow the normal pattern of high cortisol in the morning slowly reducing towards the evening, the at-risk girls had their levels stay high all day.

When this group of adolescents, who are less able to perform the underlying tasks required for efficient emotional processing, is faced with all the hormonal, emotional, and physiological challenges inherent in adolescence, their brains become very sensitive to surges of anxiety.

Adolescence itself is a time of high stress. Hormone levels rise, sexual attractions develop, friendships can become volatile, and young people are also having to decide what it is they want to study and what career they may want to follow. As mentioned above, they are also in the phase when they feel the need to separate from parents and form their own opinions. The background emotional field is therefore one of quite complex, contradictory, and often negative emotions that need to be processed by the symbolic frontal functions in order to be fully comprehended.

The Two Pathways for Emotional Processing

Neural processes are highly complex, and the following explanations refer to general processes. The ILE approach follows Goleman's (1995) description of the two pathways available for emotional processing: one where the information from the amygdala has been perused by the symbolic functions and one where it has not.

A broader and deeper discussion of how brains develop and function can be found in Siegel (1999), *The Developing Mind: How Relationships and the Brain Interact to Shape Who We Are.* The following is his description of the workings of the amygdala, which will set the scene for later discussions:

> The amygdala is a cluster of neurons that serves as a receiving and sending station between input from the outer world and emotional response. As a co-ordinating centre within the brain, the amygdala along with related areas such as the orbitofrontal cortex and anterior cingulate plays a crucial role in co-ordinating perceptions with memory and behavior. These regions are especially sensitive to social interactions. They nonconsciously assign significance to stimuli; their actions influence a wide range of mental processes with the involvement of conscious awareness. These circuits are widely connected to other regions that directly influence the functioning of the entire brain as a whole system. . . .
>
> In fact, the limbic system also registers the state of the body and directly influences the body's state of activation via regulation of the autonomic nervous system. In this manner the limbic system serves as a source of social processing, stimulus appraisal and brain/body ("emotional") arousal. . . .
>
> Nonconsciously, the brain is wired, at least with regard to the fear response, to create a "self-fulfilling prophecy." If the amygdala is excessively sensitive and fires off a "Danger!" signal, it will automatically alter ongoing perceptions to appear to the individual as threatening. This may be a basis for phobias and other anxiety disorders.
>
> (pp. 132–133)

Optimally, the use of the symbolic emotional processing pathway begins with information gathered by the amygdala, and via the 'junction box' function of the insula engages the higher functions (see Figure 20.1). This route employs symbolic language and frontal function (involved in extracting information from the environment and in planning functions) and allows for a more abstract understanding of the emotional environment in context, having, as it does, access to memory in language. Emotions that pass through this system create a store of learned experiences that can be pressed into service when confronting similar events. The symbolic pathway, after engaging the language, memory and planning functions, finally returns to the amygdala, the area of the brain that also involves bodily action. Behavior is then guided by the symbolic functions in line with reality. It is this pathway that would normally be employed in a healthy subject and is the culmination of healthy development.

The second pathway is designed to be brought into service under conditions of extreme stress when the luxury of deciding exactly what kind of predator one

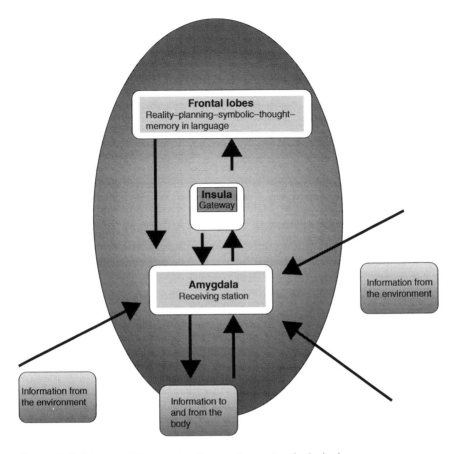

Figure 20.1 Diagram of the emotional processing system in the brain

is faced with might prove fatal. This pathway is usually only employed on occasion. All stimuli are routinely examined by the 'fast and dirty' amygdala route for potential risk but the memory systems triggered by this crude pattern-matching are not representationally encoded in language. This crude information is then sent to the insula (which acts as a 'junction box') where, if there is no danger, it is 'sent up' to the symbolic language and frontal reality functions for perusal, or, if there is danger, sent back down, unexamined, to the amygdala which then triggers the anxiety response experienced in the body (see Figure 20.1). This process, it has been suggested (Craig, 2009), can become self-fulfilling in that the incoming information is repeatedly pattern-matched for danger and returned to the amygdala, never touching symbolic language.

Thus under stress conditions there is no perusing of the experience, only a body response. There is some access to language but it is of a concrete nature allied to the body experience. In this state there is limited or no ability to use symbol and metaphor and thus no way of 'thinking' one's way through a challenging emotional problem.

Once the two routes are 'reconnected,' there is a new sense of integrated consciousness and an experience of a sense of self (Seeley et al., 2007).

Nunn et al. (2008) have suggested that the clinical symptoms of anorexia nervosa may be explained by the dysfunction of the insula, which has been described by Damasio (1994) as mapping the emotional state of the body. There is a fast and unconscious processing of sensory information from the peripheral senses and the internal organs. This process requires the insula to function efficiently and to balance the part of the brain that deals with adapting to the environment and the part that deals with the body state.

The more frequently the body pathway in the brain is engaged, the more easily it will be triggered. This follows from the principle spelled out by Hebb's axiom that neurons that fire together wire together (Hebb, 1949; Brown & Milner, 2003). This is a possibility for two reasons. First, there will be reduced opportunity to learn how to solve or come to terms with complex emotion and, as a consequence, to reduce anxiety. Second, when a pathway is triggered it becomes reinforced, making it more likely to be employed than a less frequently used pathway that over time will deteriorate, much in the way that concert pianists will find playing more difficult when they have not practiced.

When one's mind can only conceive of the world in concrete form, where the body takes the place of the mind, understanding the emotional and symbolic world is rather like deciding to eat this book to gain an understanding of it rather than to take in the contents with one's mind. Eating-disorder patients are occasionally, or, perhaps in some cases constantly, trapped in such a world where the only thing that makes sense is to manipulate the body or to count and measure it in calories.

For people with eating disorders, intellectual functions can remain intact and, if of considerable power, can be favored over emotional processing as a style of coping when the optimal emotional processing is unavailable. However, by definition, an intellectual understanding is unable to guide an emotional response and cannot reflect the feeling state.

The ILE Program

The ILE program has been formulated to address the overuse of the body pathway and the shutting down of the symbolic pathway. It follows the logic of how the brain develops and the difficulties in processing emotions experienced in patients who develop an eating disorder. The aim is to identify the complex emotional triggers (usually emotional challenges that incite both positive and negative feelings) that precede an eating disorder event (i.e., bingeing or vomiting or, in the case of anorexia, restricting).

The theory underlying the ILE treatment suggests that in vulnerable people it may be lack of comprehension of complex emotional language, and of metaphor and irony in particular, that might be a particular stressor that triggers the

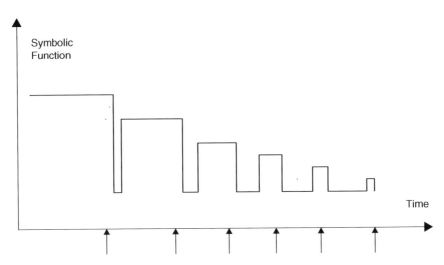

Figure 20.2 State change in eating-disordered patients from symbolic to concrete processing following a complex emotional trigger

amygdala to label the incoming information as a threat and causes the insula to close access to the symbolic functions. The result of this is the change in internal language function from symbolic to concrete thought and speech.

Figure 20.2 describes eating-disordered patients being generally low in their ability to process emotions symbolically. When a complex emotional trigger (bottom arrows) occurs, the fragile symbolic emotional processing pathway collapses to the concrete as the insula closes the symbolic pathway. With each emotional challenge the symbolic pathway weakens and the concrete body pathway strengthens. Thus with a reduced store of successful solutions to challenging emotional events, and a diminished capacity for reality checking, the patient becomes increasingly reactive to ever more minor triggers leading to the typical presentation of a worsening eating disorder. More time is spent in concrete thought and action, emotional learning is stopped in its tracks, and background anxiety increases. The eating-disordered behavior reduces the anxiety by attempting to solve the 'problem' of feeling too full by, for example, emptying the stomach. If we think of the mind as trying to tell itself that it is full of painful feelings, but the attempt at symbolic thought collapses into the concrete, we might expect to see an 'emptying' of the painful discomfort. Unfortunately, the concrete bodymind response cannot resolve the problem, and instead it stores up more anxiety.

The Nature of Trigger Material

The nature of trigger material, according to ILE theory, is of crucial importance in understanding how and why eating-disordered patients react to complex emotional stimuli.

To make sense of the swirling and complicated emotional information around at the time when vulnerable individuals are at risk of an eating disorder, we have to make use of the concept of theory of mind. To communicate with other minds we need second-order theory of mind, where we not only understand what is in someone's mind but also what that person is thinking about a third party. We also need to understand not just the literal words but what the speaker is 'really saying' (Steen, 2007). When faced with all the adolescent tasks outlined above, coupled with impaired comprehension of feeling states and poor comprehension of metaphoric and ironic language, we begin to understand the nature of complex and negative emotional triggers, why they create a 'danger' signal, and how the process of emotional maturation of the frontal lobes is impeded.

The trigger itself would have to be of a certain complexity, containing novel figurative material that requires rapid interhemispheric transfer. This transfer is between the ongoing self- state located in the right hemisphere and symbolic language processing skills in the left hemisphere that give access to stored memories.

The ILE Protocol

The first two sessions of ILE are devoted to taking a detailed history of family and social relationships as well as the standard physical information essential for this group of illnesses. This is in order to gauge possible difficult emotional triggers. The patient is given an explanation of how emotional processing in the brain functions and how and why this can go awry. In our clinic we have found that explaining to patients why they think the way they do has vastly reduced their anxiety. Patients have reported that the explanation makes sense and that they recognize the change of state, but most importantly they do not feel blamed. Once the patient has agreed to begin the therapy, the search for the 'lost' trigger thoughts begins. The role of the therapist in ILE is one of an amanuensis, leading the patient in the search for her own mind and opinions—the building blocks of the self. The therapist does not offer interpretations, which require quite a sophisticated understanding of nuanced, symbolic language in order to be understood.

The trigger material for an eating disorder event, ILE theory suggests, contains valuable information. It is suggested that when the processing of emotions breaks down, there is a signature residue of the trigger. Finding this residue will allow the stimulus thought to be resymbolized. It is this attempt at processing that falls back or collapses. The resultant concrete state, it is suggested, contains elements of the symbolic attempts, and it is this residue of the symbolic/metaphoric language that is expressed in the bodily symptom, where the body becomes the symbol. At this point the patient becomes totally unaware of the lost meaning and is trapped in the behavior.

Thus, what the ILE method aims to do is to systematically work back with the patient to discover the trigger thought just prior to the collapse into the concrete state. Once identified, the trigger becomes the focus of the therapy. At the very beginning of therapy it is quite difficult for the patient to identify the trigger thought, as they are so frequent, and a binge may last several days. The process is quite painstaking and needs to be pinpoint-accurate to be effective. If not accurate, the affect-laden trigger gives way to a guess that may not have emotional salience and is therefore not transformative. The process of clarifying the trigger employs dream analysis techniques borrowed from psychoanalytic practice. The patient is gradually taken back to the moment of state change and has to describe the scene in detail, as if reporting a dream. The aim is to find the AHA! moment of emotional recognition—which is symbolized and expanded by introducing metaphoric meanings. By this method, according to the ILE theory, the symbolic emotional processing pathway is exercised.

As mentioned above, in my practice I have found that initially patients reported a rapid loss of symptoms in the first three or four sessions, followed by some fluctuation in symptoms, but by sessions eight to ten, midway through the 18-session model, symptoms were rarely present and the therapy proceeded much as any therapy might—with the therapist and patient speaking the same symbolic emotional language. Occasionally, the patient and therapist may need to hunt for the trigger when there is an experience of state change, but the content of the therapeutic sessions, in my experience, has tended to be about the patients' lack of emotionally maturing experiences owing to their overuse of body solutions to complex emotional challenges. Whilst the symptoms may have receded and the patient is able to learn to catch moments of state change and reverse them, the underlying neurological deficits usually, to some extent, remain. Following treatment, the brain has had a chance to mature the frontal lobes by facing difficult reality and brings to a close the turmoil of the adolescent brain.

It remains to be seen if we can research whether changes in the brain pre- and posttreatment can be measured using fMRI techniques. ILE is now undergoing clinical trials.

Note

1. In this chapter the patient is always referred to as she, as this reflects the ten-to-one ratio of female to male sufferers. There is no theoretical reason why male sufferers would not respond in a similar manner to their female counterparts.

References

Amanzio, M., Geminiani, G., Leotta, D., & Cappa, S. (2008). Metaphor comprehension in Alzheimer's disease: Novelty matters. *Brain & Language, 107*(1) 1–10.

Beckendam, C. C. (1997). *Dimensions of emotional intelligence: Attachment, affect regulation, alexithymia and empathy.* Doctoral dissertation, Fielding Institute, Santa Barbara, CA.

Brown, R. E., & Milner, P. M. (2003). The legacy of Donald O. Hebb: More than the Hebb Synapse. *Nature Reviews Neuroscience, 4,* 1013–1019.

Corcos, M., Guilbaud, O., Speranza, M., Paterniti, S., Loas, G., Stephan, P., & Jeammet, P. (2000). Alexithymia and depression in eating disorders. *Psychiatry Research, 93,* 263–266.

Craig, A. D. (2009, January). How do you feel—now? The anterior insula and human awareness. *Nature, 10,* 59–60.

Damasio, A. R. (1994). *Descartes' error.* New York: Grosset Putnam.

Fonagy, P., & Target, M. (1997). Attachment and reflective function: Their role in self-organization. *Developmental Psychopathology, 9,* 679–700.

Goleman, D. (1995). *Emotional intelligence.* New York: Bantam Books.

Hebb, O. D. (1949). *The organization of behavior.* New York: Wiley.

Macquet, P., Péters, J-M., Aerts, J., Delfiore, G., Degueldre, C., Luxen, A., & Franck, G. (1996). Functional neuroanatomy of human rapid-eye-movement sleep and dreaming. *Nature, 383,* 163–66.

Nunn, K., Frampton, I., Gordon, I., & Lask, B. (2008). The fault is not in her parents but in her insula—A neurobiological hypothesis of anorexia nervosa. *European Eating Disorders Review, 16,* 355–360.

Oskis, A., Loveday, C., Hucklebridge, F., Thorn, L., & Clow, A. (2011). Anxious attachment style and salivary cortisol dysregulation in healthy female children and adolescents. *Journal of Child Psychology & Psychiatry, 52,* 111–118.

Schore, A. N. (1994). *Affect regulation and the origin of the self: The neurobiology of emotional development.* Hillsdale, NJ: Erlbaum.

Schore, A. N. (1996). The experience-dependent maturation of a regulatory system in the orbital prefrontal cortex and the origin of developmental psychopathology. *Developmental Psychopathology, 8,* 59–87.

Seeley, W. W., Menon, V., Schatzberg, A. F., Keller, J., Glover, G. H., Kenna, H., Reiss, A. L., & Greicius, M. D. (2007). Dissociable intrinsic connectivity networks for salience processing and executive control. *Journal of Neuroscience, 27,* 2349–2356.

Shuren, J. E., & Grafman, J. (2002). The neurology of reasoning. *Archives of Neurology, 59,* 916–919.

Siegel, D. (1999). *The developing mind: How relationships and the brain interact to shape who we are.* New York: Guildford Press.

Steen, G. J. (2007). *Finding metaphor in grammar and usage: A methodological analysis of theory and research.* Amsterdam: John Benjamins.

Stuss, D. T., & Alexander, M. P. (1999). Affectively burnt in: A proposed role of the right frontal lobe. In E. Tulving (Ed.), *Memory, consciousness and the brain: The Tallinn Conference* (pp. 215–227). Philadelphia: Psychology Press.

Taylor, G. J., Bagby, R. M., & Parker, J. D. A. (1997). *Disorders of affect regulation: Alexithymia in medical and psychiatric illness.* Cambridge: Cambridge University Press.

Tchanturia, K., Morris, R., Surguladze, S., & Treasure, J. (2003). Perceptual and cognitive set shifting tasks in acute anorexia nervosa and following recovery. *Eating & Weight Disorders, 7*(4) 312–316.

Teicher, M. H., Ito, Y., Glod, C. A., Schiffer, F., & Gelbard, H. A. (1996). Neuro-physiological mechanisms of stress response in children. In C. R. Pfeffer (Ed.), *Severe stress and mental disturbance in children* (pp. 59–84). Washington, DC: American Psychiatric Press.

Vrticka, P., Andersson, F., Grandjean, D., Sander, D., & Vuilleumier, P. (2008). Individual attachment style modulates human amygdala and striatum activation during social appraisal. *Public Library of Science, 3,* e2868.

Zeitlin, S. B., Lane, R. D., O'Leary, D. S., & Schrift, M. J. (1989). Interhemispheric transfer deficit and alexithymia. *American Journal of Psychiatry, 146,* 1434–1439.

21

THE ACQUISITION OF A BODY

Establishing a New Paradigm and Introducing a Clinical Tool to Explore the Intergenerational Transmission of Embodiment

The BODI—The Body Observational Diagnostic Interview

The BODI GROUP Members: Catherine Baker-Pitts, Carol Bloom, Luise Eichenbaum, Linda Garofallou, Susie Orbach, Jean Petrucelli, Victoria Sliva, Suzi Tortora

Introduction

In 2005, our multidisciplinary group was convened by London psychoanalyst Susie Orbach and attachment researcher Miriam Steele from the New School to investigate the intergenerational transmission of gendered embodiment[1]—how in the first body-to-body relationship between a mother and her child, 'body-states' are passed on. Borrowing from the abundance of attachment work focused on the co-construction of the psyche (Beebe & Lachmann,[2] 2002; Steele & Steele, 2008a, 2008b, 2008c), we set out to collaborate on a series of instruments[3] to look at the developmental trajectory of the body, culminating in the Body Observational Diagnostic Interview (BODI, see Appendix)[4].

The BODI probes key historical relationships, critical junctures in the making of femininity and gender, body development, pregnancy, and sexuality. This tool identifies developmental challenges, boundary confusion and transgressions, disruptions in going-on-being, telling gaps in a body narrative memory, emotional wounds, self-attack, and body insecurity. In the clinical and research settings using the BODI, the task of describing embodiment through an analytic lens relies upon observation of (a) self-report, (b) gestural and nonverbal movements, (c) anomalous statements and affect expressions, and (d) somatic countertransference.

The female body can be read and understood as the sine qua non of female experience. The BODI offers the therapist and patient a bridge to what is often hidden, forbidden, and unformulated. Just as the AAI (Adult Attachment Interview)[5] has been used as a tool for assessing attachment styles and the capacity for self-reflection, the BODI opens a portal to unsymbolized and dissociative experience as well as reflective thinking on the body. In our trial interviews with ten mothers of toddler daughters, we engaged in a dialectical process to harvest the arena of the body—the wealth of information which pours forth when women reflect on and speak about how they live in their bodies.

The aims of our project are manifold: to account for the growth in body-based difficulties; to understand in detail the intergenerational transmission of body-states; and, to reposition the gendered body in analytic thought and in clinical work. Our collective clinical impressions corroborate our preliminary research findings, in which we identify a spectrum of embodiment. At one end, bodies are *lived in,* able to connect with and move between fluid multiple body-states, which we call, following Winnicott (1965, 1975), 'indwelling.' At the other end of the spectrum, dissociated bodies are experienced as separate from the self, untamable, disappointing, adversarial, alienated, disorganized, or hated. We see borderline bodies, false bodies, neurotic bodies, disorganized bodies, psychotic bodies, alexithymic bodies. We see bodies with impaired boundaries and confusion about where they begin and end. We see bodies with a lack of understanding of what they feel, a paucity of knowledge about what they need, and a 'not-knowing' about what hungers emanate from them and at the same time an obsessive relation to the body punctured with critical internal body talk.

Embodying Gender

Recent work (Orbach, 1986, 1993, 2004, 2009, 2012; Bloom et al., 1994; Namir, 2006; Krueger, 2002; Stern, 2000; Tronick, 2003; Aron & Anderson, 1998; Anderson, 2008) has proposed that in order to work with body disturbances, the body as a body—not limited to a container or canvas for projections and displacements—needs to be understood within its own developmental trajectory. Secure attachments, empathic resonance, affect regulation, and attuned handling and touch are crucial ingredients in the development of interoceptive awareness and the acquisition of a secure body. Conversely, problematic attachment, trauma, a lack of mirroring, and the imposition of misattuned parental and cultural expectations impede the integration of psyche and soma and undermine the possibility for secure embodiment.

Bodies develop and come alive within a relational matrix, against the backdrop of a cultural holding environment. The caregiver's face is the baby's first mirror, which interacts with the baby's temperaments and endowments (Winnicott, 1971). In our theorizing, we elaborate this notion of mental gazing to the mother's physical relationship to her baby's body. Mother's skin, touch, and holding, as well as her own experience of embodiment, communicate to her baby what is possible in the most vital and emergent sense from within a mutually influencing, regulating, body-to-body environment. How the mother reads the baby's physicality prompts her responses to feed, wean, change, soothe, embrace, tickle, stimulate or set the baby the down; interactions imbued with relational meanings and constitutive of making the body. In addition, how the mother lives in her body, from confident to obsessive-preoccupied or tentative, will be brought to the body interaction and form an implicit substrata of embodiment. This is a corporeal version of the Implicit Relational Knowing as expressed by the Boston Change Process Study Group[6] (BCPSG, 2008).

The mother's embodiment of the psychological shape and possibilities of gender is the child's initial access to the world. From her culturally imbued body, the mother consciously and unconsciously, materially and imaginatively, engages with her daughter's developing body, just as she engages with her daughter's developing emotional life. The mother projects unconscious longings, hesitancies, and fears onto her baby's body, which further complicates the making of the baby's body.

Mothers and daughters often inhabit troubled bodies, vulnerable to internal, intersubjective, and external persecution, emblematic in the alarming bodily symptoms (i.e., restrictive dieting, picking, compulsive and compulsory body modifications), self-loathing, insecurity, body instability, and widespread alienation of the body and self. Increasingly, women we see in our consulting rooms experience their bodies as objects to be worked on and controlled, to be available for medications and surgical interventions—bodies susceptible to somatic enactments of all kinds. Under a magnifying glass, a woman's flesh is relentlessly scrutinized against a cultural ideal while simultaneously denigrated. In consumer capitalism, women's bodies and vulnerable self-states are exploited for profit. Girls are encouraged by the visual and commercial exigencies of our times to size up their bodies, contributing to an atmosphere of vigilance and ubiquitous self-criticism.

From one generation to the next, shared body difficulties are accepted as status quo within family systems and thus are not readily interrogated as problematic. Unconsciously enacted and culturally encouraged, unformulated and internalized, the embodiment of gender inequality and psychic femininity is passed through the mother daughter relationship (Chodorow, 1978; Orbach, 1978; Eichenbaum & Orbach, 1982). The baby enters a world shaped by psychic, cultural, class, gendered, ethnic, sexual, and social markers in the familial environment. Mothers (or those doing mothering) do not so much instruct their offspring. Rather, babies become part of the milieu in which the rules of culture are enacted as much as they are explicated. The mother does not stand apart from culture; she embodies it. What she does is culture. How she relates at a psychological and physical level is her idiomatic honing of the varied contexts that have shaped her. As the mother shapes the baby's psyche, so the mother shapes the baby's body. Winnicott says 'there is no such thing as a baby' to indicate the intricate interdependency of the mother–infant relationship; so too 'there is no such thing as a body' (Orbach, 2004, 2009). We need to understand the developing body as the outcome of relationship too.

To the extent that a mother is aware of her suffering in her own body, we observed a desire amongst the mothers of toddlers in our interviews to interrupt a negative body legacy. The mother's ability to reflect upon and critique the cultural view of femininity and to offer alternatives from a place of secure embodiment allows greater potential for her daughter's stable embodiment. In Western culture, secure embodiment, rather than being implicit, must often be earned. It develops in spite of persistent and insidious visual images in the mediascape that impinge on and attack female body integrity, and it relies on the mother's role as mediator. As the daughter's bid for independence mounts, the balance tilts in the sphere of influence from mother to direct digestion of culture by the daughter (Gutwill, 1994). Culture becomes explicitly sought rather than implicitly corporeally ingested. To feel alive in and connected to one's own body is an achievement that goes against the cultural grain.

Interpretative Phenomenological Analysis

Interpretative Phenomenological Analysis (IPA) uses a rich description of the semantic data that emerges from the participant's narrative (Smith, Flowers, & Larkin, 2009). As a two-pronged qualitative approach to data collection and analysis, IPA relies on both grounded, lived meanings of experiences and an interpretation of phenomenon through an analytic lens. Thus, meaning is made by the participant and interpreted through the investigators' theoretical perspectives, a stance emphasizing co-construction that resonates with our research team's experience in a two-person model of psychoanalysis. The different self-states (Bromberg, 1998), or facets of a person that come alive in a narrative, and the emphasis on the co-creation of new stories, or 'restorying,' parallels the psychoanalytic process (White & Epston, 1990).

After transcribing the ten interviews for the verbal analysis, each member of our verbal research group did a 'deep reading' of each transcript, working to gain an understanding of the participant's subjective voice. We read each interview line by line to identify emergent patterns and themes, looking at commonalities and nuances. We began with a single case and employed the two-column approach of citing the standout themes in the participant's own words in one column; the first column is descriptive at face value, highlighting key words, phrases, or important explanations offered by the participant. In column two, we captured analytic interpretations, conceptual comments, and self-reflections by the researcher. Our line by line study of the text made use of the hermeneutic circle, as we recorded our collective thoughts, feelings, images, and physiological responses until the list of themes reached a point of saturation, when we had exhausted all of the recurrent themes.

Through reading and rereading the transcripts, particular experiences created a tapestry of shared experiences across interviews, moving our analysis from rich description to interpretation. We then grouped themes together into meta-themes, informed by interpersonal, relational, cultural, and feminist psychoanalytic theories. Additionally, we noted initial reactions to the participant, and any 'body' feelings evoked during the interviews. Our team engaged in ongoing self-observation and reflection with the explicit acknowledgement of co-construction.

Nonverbal Analysis

Alongside the verbal narrative, the BODI taps what is embodied and detectable on a nonverbal level, paying close attention to the body-to-body interplay. Like the AAI, the BODI is interested in more than the content of the words. The narrative reveals subtle communications, such as hesitation or interruptions by the participant of her own thoughts, affects, self-criticism, and pauses.

Adding a nonverbal analysis to the BODI[7] here supports both our experience of the clinical body (Orbach, 2009, 2012; Petrucelli, 2008) as well as the growing interest in analyzing embodied experience in the fields of philosophy (Johnson, 2007; Koch, & Fischman, 2011; Merleau-Ponty, 1962), psychoanalysis, psychotherapy (Sletvold, 2011; Knoblauch, 2000, 2005; Anderson, 2008), neuroscience (Carr, Iacoboni, Dubeau, Mazziotta, & Lenzi, 2003; Damasio, 1994/2005, 1999; Gallese, 2009; Gallese, Eagle, & Migone, 2007) and infant mental health (Boston Change Process Study Group, 2008; Fonagy & Target, 2007; Stern, 2010; Tortora, 2010, 2012, 2013; Tronick, 1989, 2007).

The nonverbal analysis offers a window into the unconscious expression of the embodiment of the mother. The daughter's embodiment style emerges through her engagement verbally and nonverbally with her mother's body-states. The daughter's gestures, postures and actions, affects, and energy level mirror and mimicked versions of the mother's internalized body-states in a positive identification, or as a defense against the mother.

A dual approach of verbal and nonverbal analysis enables a comparison of the degree of continuity or discontinuity between the two. A high degree of incongruity for a particular individual raises questions about how aware she is of her own body-states, body actions, as well as her degree of defensiveness and dissociation. Her behavior may appear disorganized or it may reflect indifference and disconnection to what is being verbalized. The specific ways these incongruities manifest provide additional information about how the daughter sees and treats her own body. In the BODI nonverbal analysis, the clear articulation of this congruence or discrepancy will help clinician's appreciate the unconscious countertransferential experiences.

The BODI, which follows, promotes a subjectifying experience, or what Bloom calls a *bodiography*. It includes the questions posed by the investigator/clinician and those she reflects on post-interview, to account for the meeting of two bodies in the intersubjective field. The BODI invites body states to the foreground and enables a practitioner to address the body directly with gender and culture in mind.

Notes

1. The group worked in consortium with the initial group that was put together by Susie Orbach and Miriam Steele, with psychotherapists Carol Bloom; Luise Eichenbaum; Catherine Baker-Pitts; Jean Petrucelli; Tiffany Haik, a PhD student; dance/movement therapist Suzi Tortora and Infant Massage therapist Linda Garofallou; and graduate students to form the Body Attachment Group. The development of the BODI was created

by Catherine Baker-Pitts, Carol Bloom, Luise Eichenbaum, Linda Garofallou, Susie Orbach, Jean Petrucelli, Victoria Silva, and Suzi Tortora.

2. Beebe's work examines the emotional physical interchanges between mothers and babies and then translates these gestural exchanges into the building blocks of psychic functioning. Steele and Steele look at early attachment patterns to assess and predict the attachment capacities of children. In addition they investigate the link between parent and child attachment styles.

3. We developed addendum questions to the *Mirror Interview Paradigm* (Kernberg, Buhl-Nielsen, & Normandin, 2006) designed to elicit feelings about one's body, important others, and the relationship between the two. Further, we collaborated on a *Child Mirror Task* wherein toddler girls played in the interactional space between their mother and their own mirror image. Our research analysis using the BODI continues and is forthcoming.

Students at the New School have administered and coded these two tasks, in the context of a larger battery, and made important findings, such as demonstrating a negative relationship between reflective functioning and objectified body consciousness as well as a negative relationship between attachment security and mirror image preoccupation (McBirney & Tosi, 2010). The *body group* at the New School continues to employ these paradigms; the *BODI group* has forged forward to understand the intergenerational transmission of embodiment.

4. The first presentation of the Mirror Instrument was at the American Psychological Association Division 39 NY meeting in 2008, followed by presentations at The William Alanson White Institute, NY in 2008 and 2011.

5. Main and Hesse (1990).

6. Boston Change Process Study Group was created in 1995. It consists of a group of practicing analysts, developmentalists, and analytic theorists who shared the view that knowledge from the field of recent developmental studies as well as dynamic systems theory can be used to understand and model change processes in psychodynamic therapeutic interaction.

7. It is adapted from the nonverbal analysis tool Dyadic Attachment-Based Nonverbal Communicative Expressions (D.A.N.C.E.), developed by Tortora (2010, 2011, 2012a, 2012b), which analyzes the nonverbal elements that comprise the qualities of an infant/child–parent attachment relationship.

References

Anderson, F. S. (Ed.). (2008). *Bodies in treatment: The unspoken dimension.* New York: Analytic Press.

Aron, L., & Anderson, F. S. (1998). *Relational perspectives on the body.* London: Analytic Press.

Beebe, B., & Lachman, F. (2002). *Infant research and adult treatment: Co-constructing interactions.* Hillsdale, NJ: Analytic Press.

Bloom, C., Gitter, A., Gutwill, S., Kogel, L., & Zaphiropoulos, L. (1994). *Eating problems: A feminist psychoanalytic treatment model.* New York: Basic Books.

Boston Change Process Study Group. (2008). Forms of relational meaning: Issues in the relations between the implicit and reflective-verbal domains. *Psychoanalytic Dialogues, 18,* 125–148.

Bromberg, P. M. (1998). *Standing in the spaces: Essays on clinical process, trauma and dissociation.* Hillsdale, NJ: Analytic Press.

Carr, L., Iacoboni, M., Dubeau, M., Mazziotta, J., & Lenzi, G. L. (2003). Neural mechanisms of empathy in humans: A relay from neural systems for imitation to limbic areas. *Proceedings of the National Academy of Sciences of the United States of America, 100–109,* 5497–5502.

Chodorow, N. (1978, 1999). *The reproduction of mothering: Psychoanalysis and the sociology of gender.* Berkeley: University of California Press.

Damasio, A. (2005). *Descartes' error: Emotion, reason, and the human brain.* New York: Penguin. (Original work published 1994)

Damasio, A. R. (1999). *The feeling of what happens.* London: William Heinemann.

Eichenbaum, L., & Orbach, S. (1982). *Understanding women: A feminist psychoanalytic approach.* New York: Basic Books.

Fonagy, P., & Target, M. (2007). The rooting of the mind in the body: New links between attachment theory and psychoanalytic thought. *Journal of the American Psychoanalytic Association, 55*(2), 411–456.

Gallese., V. (2009). Mirror neurons, embodied simulation, and the neuronal basis of social identification. *Psychoanalytic Dialogues, 19,* 519–536.

Gallese, V., Eagle, M. N., & Migone, P. (2007). Intentional attunement: Mirror neurons and the neural underpinnings of interpersonal relations. *Journal of the American Psychoanalytic Association, 55,* 131–176.

Gutwill, S. (1994). Women's eating problems: Social context and the internalization of culture. In C. Bloom, A. Gitter, S. Gutwill, L. Kogel, & L. Zaphiropoulos (Eds.), *Eating problems: A feminist psychoanalytic treatment model.* New York: Basic Books.

Johnson, M. (2007). *The meaning of the body.* Chicago: University of Chicago Press.

Kernberg, P. F., Buhl-Nielsen, B., & Normandin, L. (2006). *Beyond the reflection: The role of the mirror paradigm in clinical practice.* New York: Other Press.

Koch, S., & Fischman, D. (2011). Embodied enactive dance/movement therapy. *American Journal of Dance Movement Therapy, 33,* 57–72.

Knoblauch, S. H. (2000). *The musical edge of therapeutic dialogue.* Hillsdale, NJ: Analytic Press.

Knoblauch, S. H. (2005). Body rhythms and the unconscious: Toward an expanding of clinical attention. *Psychoanalytic Dialogues, 15,* 807–827.

Krueger, D. W. (2002). *Integrating body self and psychological self: Creating a new story in psychoanalysis and psychotherapy.* New York: Bruner-Routledge.

McBirney, E., & Tosi, K. (2010). The mirror interview: Exploring the influences of parents and culture on disordered eating behaviors. Unpublished doctoral dissertation, New School for Social Research, NY.

Merleau-Ponty, M. (1962). *Phenomenology of perception.* London: Routledge.

Orbach, S. (1978). *Fat is a feminist issue.* London: Paddington.

Orbach, S. (1986). *Hunger strike: The anorectic struggle as a metaphor for our age.* London: Faber & Faber.

Orbach, S. (1993). Working with the false body. In A. Erskine & D. Judd (Eds.), *The imaginative body.* London: Whurr.

Orbach, S. (2004). There's no such thing as a body. In K. White (Ed.), *Touch: Attachment and the body.* London: Karnac.

Orbach, S. (2009). *Bodies.* Profile Books: London.

Orbach, S. (2012). Towards a nosology of body development. In V. Sinason (Ed.), *Trauma, dissociation and multiplicity.* London: Routledge.

Main, M., & Hesse, E. (1990). Parents' unresolved traumatic experiences are related to infant disorganized attachment status: Is frightened and/or frightening parental behavior the linking mechanism? In M. Greenberg, D. Cicchetti, & E. Cummings (Eds.), *Attachment in the preschool years: Theory, research, and intervention* (pp. 161–182). Chicago, IL: University of Chicago Press.

Namir, S. (2006). Embodiments and disembodiments: The relation of body modifications in two psychoanalytic treatments. *Psychoanalysis, Culture and Society, 11*(2), 217–223.

Petrucelli, J. (2008). When a body meets a body: The impact of a therapist's body on eating-disordered patients. In F. Anderson (Ed.), *Bodies in treatment: The unspoken dimension.* New York: Analytic Press.

Sletvold, (2011). The reading of emotional expression: Wilhelm Reich and the history of embodied analysis. *Psychoanalytic Dialogues, 21*(4), 453–467.

Smith, J. A., Flowers, P., & Larkin, M. (2009). *Interpretative Phenomenological Analysis: Theory, method and research.* London: Sage.

Steele, H., & Steele, M. (2008a). Early attachment predicts emotion recognition at 6 and 11 years. *Attachment and Human Development, 10,* 379–393.

Steele, H., & Steele, M. (2008b). On the origins of reflective functioning. In F. Busch (Ed.), *Mentalization: Theoretical considerations, research findings, and clinical implications* (Psychoanalytic Inquiry Book Series, *29,* pp. 133–158). New York: Analytic Books.

Steele, H., & Steele, M. (2008c). 10 clinical uses of the Adult Attachment Interview. In H. Steele & M. Steele (Eds.), *Clinical applications of the Adult Attachment Interview* (pp. 3–30). New York: Guilford Press.

Stern, D. (2010). *Forms of vitality: Exploring dynamic experiences in psychology, the arts, psychotherapy, and development.* Oxford, UK: Oxford University Press.

Stern, D. N. (2000). *The interpersonal world of the infant: A view from psychoanalysis and developmental psychology.* New York: Basic Books.

Tortora, S. (2010). Ways of seeing: An early childhood integrated therapeutic approach for parents and babies. *Clinical Social Work Journal, 38,* 37–50.

Tortora, S. (2012). Beyond the face and words: How the body speaks. In B. Beebe, P. Cohen, K. M. Sossin, & S. Markese (Eds.), *Mothers, infants and young children of September 11, 2001: A primary prevention project* (pp. 97–109). London: Routledge.

Tortora, S. (2013). The essential role of the body in the parent-infant relationship: Non-verbal analysis of attachment. In J. Bettmann & D. Friedman (Eds.) *Attachment-based clinical work with children and adolescents, essential clinical social work series* (pp. 141–164). New York: Springer.

Tronick, E. (1989). Emotions and emotional communication in infants. *American Psychologist, 44,* 112–119.

Tronick, E. Z. (2003). "Of course all relationships are unique": How co-created processes generate unique mother-infant and patient-therapist relationships and change other relationships. *Psychoanalytic Inquiry, 23,* 473–491.

Tronick, E. (2007). *The neurobehavioral and social-emotional development of infants and children.* New York: Norton.

White, M., & Epston, D. (1990). *Narrative means to therapeutic ends.* New York: W. W. Norton.

Winnicott, D. (1965). *Maturational processes and the facilitating environment.* New York, NY: International Universities Press.

——— (1971). *Playing and reality.* London: Tavistock.

——— (1975). *Through paediatrics to psycho-analysis* (The Inter. Psycho-Analytical Library). *100,* 1–325. London: The Hogarth Press and the Institute of Psycho-Analysis.

APPENDIX

THE BODI (BODY OBSERVATIONAL DIAGNOSTIC INTERVIEW)

NAME or ID #: _____

DATE: _____

The BODI provides a bodiography, an intergenerational narrative of bodily history and experience around the transmission of body states.

INSTRUCTIONS:

Preparation for the interviewer: *Allow one to two hours to complete the interview. As you proceed through the interview, make notes of how you feel emotionally and physically. Make a note of the questions or answers that create a body arousal or a particular awareness of your body. This might include excitement, contentment, revulsion, discomfort and so on. Leave pauses for the interviewee to reflect and elaborate. Don't rush to the next question.*

Please note—All prompts are in *italics.*

Preparation for the interviewee: I am going to ask you to tell me about significant experiences from the present and past in order to understand how you experience your body. There are no wrong answers. Take your time.

I. Family history

I'd like to start with your family. I am going to ask you to tell me about the household in which you grew up and what feelings, memories, associations come to mind when you think about specific family members' bodies?

I-1. Let's start with the people who raised you. (*List them*)
Primary caregivers? Mother? Father? Grandmother? Nanny?
And other significant family members? Sisters or brothers?

I-2. How would you say your mother felt about her body?
And your father, how did he feel about his body?
How about other significant family member?

I-3. What's the strongest image you have of your mother?
Can you imitate her? What do you feel when you do that?

I-4. What are your earliest memories of your mother's touch?

I-5. How did your mother connect with you physically?
How did you feel about that?
Prompts: hugged, tickled, spanked, hit?

I-6. How was your body regarded by your family when you were young? What memories come to mind?

II. Early Development

These next questions focus on your early life. Although you might not have explicit memories of this time, you might have been told certain stories, shown photographs, or retained physical memories from your infancy and early childhood.

II-1. What are the family stories about your birth and about you as a baby?

II-2. Were there any significant events that might have influenced how you have come to feel about your body?
Prompt: Was there a move, a long separation, a divorce, an illness, or a trauma event?

II-3. What kind of eater were you?
Prompt: Were you breast fed and for how long?

III. Adolescence and Experiences of Gender and Sexuality

These next questions focus on your adolescence, your experiences of being a girl, and your sexuality.

III-1. How would you describe the kind of girl you were?
What is your earliest memory of being a girl?

III-2. How did you learn about menstruation and from whom?

III-3. Describe your reactions to starting your period, growing breasts, and getting pubic hair? What age were you?

III-4. How did your mother, family members, and others react to your bodily changes? Are there any specific reactions that come to mind?

III-5. What was your first awareness of your sexuality?

III-6. What words or memories come to mind to describe your early sexual experiences?

IV. Eating Behaviors

Now I am going to ask you more specific questions about your memories, experiences and interactions around eating.

IV-1. What were family mealtimes like in your house growing up? What was the emotional atmosphere?
Tell me about the food?
Prompt: Pleasurable, anxious, too little food, too much food?

IV-2. How was food regarded and talked about?

IV-3. Were there any rules about food and eating?
Prompt: Good and bad foods, foods off-limits, differing rules for girl versus boys?
Comments on eating too much or too little?

IV-4. Who was responsible for shopping and preparing food? How do you imagine he/she (or you) felt about this role?

IV-5. What do you remember about your mother's eating behaviors and attitudes towards food? Did it change over time?

IV-6. And your father's? Did it change over time?

IV-7. How do you imagine your grandparents' influenced each of your parent's relationship with food?

IV-8. In the present, how do you know when to eat, how much to eat, and when to stop eating?

IV-9. Have you ever felt a need to control your food?
When did it start? Has it always been the same or has your eating changed over the years? Do you know what goes on for you emotionally around your eating?

V. Body Awareness

Now I am going to ask you about your perception and awareness of your body.

V-1. How do you view your body today?

V-2. Whose body in your family of origin is yours most like?

V-3. Are there ways in which you currently nurture or take care of your body?

V-4. Are there ways in which you punish or hurt your body?
Are you aware of the triggers?

V-5. How much do you think about your body?

V-6. What is your inner dialogue or chatter about your body? Where else have you heard these messages?
Does any person come to mind?

V-7. Walking down the street, do you imagine that other people are looking at you. If yes, what do you imagine they are thinking?

V-8. How do you feel when people comment on your body?

V-9. Would you like to change your body in any particular way? If yes, have you ever had a cosmetic surgery alteration?

V-10. Are you aware of areas in your body where you hold tension or stress?

V-11. What were the messages specific to your cultural background that you received about your body growing up? Today, what are the cultural messages influencing how you feel in your body?

Now I will ask you about your perceptions and awareness of other women's bodies.

V-1a. When you enter a room filled with people, to what extent are you aware of other women's bodies?
What are your thoughts?

V-2a. How do you and your friends talk about women's bodies? How about celebrities' bodies and bodies in the visual media?

VI. Experience of Pregnancy, Postpartum, and Early Motherhood

Now I am going to ask you about your experience of pregnancy, postpartum and early motherhood.

VI-1. What was your pregnancy like for you?
Prompt: Describe your level of comfort or discomfort with your growing body, nausea, eating behaviour, mood.

VI-2. How did you feel about your body after childbirth?

VI-3. What was your experience of feeding your baby?

VI-4. How do you feel about your child's body?
How would you describe your baby's looks?
Sounds? Smells? Touch? Taste?

VI-5. What kinds of messages might you send your baby about her or his body?

VI-6. What body did you hope your baby would have?
Did it matter if it was a boy or girl?

VI-7. Does tending to your baby's body evoke memories, even on a physical level, of the care you received?

INTERVIEWEE REFLECTIONS

VII-1. How have you felt talking with me today?
Did any of your responses surprise you?

VII-2. Have you been aware of any distinct feelings in your body during this interview?

VII-3. Is there anything I haven't asked that you feel is important and would like to share before we end?

INTERVIEWER RESPONSES TO BODIOGRAPHY: REFLECTIONS ABOUT HOW YOU FELT IN YOUR BODY DURING AND AFTER THE INTERVIEW

1. How aware are you of bodily experiences in yourself?
    Please check the appropriate word to describe.
    Sometimes _____, often _____, never _____
2. How aware are you of others' bodies in general?
    Please check the appropriate word to describe.
    Sometimes _____, often _____, never _____
3. How much do you monitor your eating?
    Please check the appropriate word to describe.
    Sometimes _____, often _____, never _____
4. Do you think people are better off (medically or emotionally) if they are thin?
    Please check the appropriate word to describe.
    Sometimes _____, often _____, never _____

I. Thoughts/Images

1. What kinds of thoughts and images went through your mind about the interviewee's body?
2. Did you find the interviewee's bodily expression at odds with what she was saying?
3. What were your most powerful thoughts/images that came up while the interviewee was discussing eating?
4. What were your most powerful thoughts/images that came up while the interviewee was discussing sexuality?
5. What were your most powerful thoughts/images that came up while the interviewee was discussing her changing body?

II. Feelings/Emotional Reactions

1. Did you have any feelings about the interviewee's body or something she said about her body?
2. Do you think any of your bodily responses could be a mirror or reflection of how the interviewee felt in her body?
3. Did you have any feelings that came up while the participant was discussing eating?

4. Did you have any feelings that came up while the participant was discussing sexuality?
5. Did you have any feelings that came up while the participant was discussing her changing body?
6. Did you have any feelings that came up while the participant was discussing her perception of her body?

III. Body Arousal/Body Awareness

Instructions: Please include at what point in the interview that you had a response, if you had one, for each of the questions in all the sections below.

1. If you were uncomfortable in your body during any part of the interview is this a known or usual feeling for you?
2. Did you have any visceral feelings about the interviewee's body?
3. What kind of thoughts went through your mind about the interviewee's body?
4. What were your most powerful bodily feelings that came up while the interviewee was discussing eating?
5. What were your most powerful bodily feelings that came up while the interviewee was discussing sexuality?
6. What were your most powerful bodily feelings that came up while the interviewee was discussing her changing body?

MEMBERS of the BODI GROUP:

Catherine Baker-Pitts, Ph.D., LCSW—The Women's Therapy Centre Institute, NYC

Carol Bloom, LCSW—The Women's Therapy Centre Institute, NYC

Luise Eichenbaum, LCSW—The Women's Therapy Centre Institute, NYC

Linda Garofallou, MS—Center for Autism & Early Childhood Mental Health, Montclair State University

Susie Orbach, Ph.D.—The Women's Therapy Centre Institute, London & NYC

Jean Petrucelli, Ph.D. —The William Alanson White Institute; NYU Post Doctoral Program in Psychoanalysis &Psychotherapy, NYC

Victoria Sliva, MA—The New School for Social Research, NYC

Suzi Tortora, Ed.D., BC-DMT—New School for Continuing Studies; NYC; Pratt Institute, Brooklyn, NY

22

'ACROSS THE UNIVERSE'

Christians, Patients, Women With Anorexia Nervosa, Then and Now

Emily A. Kuriloff

In her study of theory and praxis, sociologist Edith Kurzweil (1989, p. 1) determines that "Every country creates the psychoanalysis it needs." Confirming today's well–worn wisdom that there is, indeed, no transcendent truth, Kurzweil implies something more regarding place and psychoanalytic sensibilities. What needs, what desires, what hungers, she prompts us to consider, has psychoanalysis fulfilled in the global north from era to era? Then consider the very problem of desire itself, well expressed in the syndrome of Anorexia Nervosa or food refusal, a behavior women, for the most part, have engaged throughout history, and certainly from the beginning of the psychoanalytic era. Besides a means to manage an individual's symptoms and pain, I suggest that psychoanalytic designs regarding volitional hunger and wasting are both responsive to, and responsible for the shifting positions and identities of women in and out of the treatment room, in both modern and postmodern times.

While there is no direct mention of Anorexia Nervosa in the Bible, (Sours, 1980, p. 205) historian Joan Jacobs Brumberg notes that "female fasting is assuredly not a new behavior," (1988, p. 5) and begins her discussion with Europe's High Middle Ages (13th–16th century), a period during which large numbers of self-starving women laid claim to a transcendent connection to God, freeing them from earthly desire. Thus were they afforded status beyond what the ruling church hierarchy would otherwise allow a woman, if at a cost to body and mind. A psychoanalyst might perceive these avowed Christians enacting the perfect symptom—needless and emaciated as an expression of, but also protection against powerlessness. Or, as Sands (2003, p. 106) puts it, referring in this case to today's world, "Eating disorders have also been seen both as exaggerations of and rebellions against the female role." During the reformation (p. 49) other women would "hide" their food refusal with notions of diabolical possession, or the work of the anti-Christ upon their souls, perhaps also avoiding and enacting a devilish defiance—victims but also perpetrators, relinquishing and exerting control. But these are modern, psychoanalytic perspectives upon fasting women, based on mind theorized as private, layered and conflicted, rather than a vessel for God. What Heidegger calls the "clearing," or that place and time in which meaning is made and valued, was not the same in Freud's Vienna as it had been in Europe's hill towns of the 1500s.

By the end of the seventeenth century, Anorexia Nervosa was neither a divine virtue from God nor a curse from the Devil, but instead a medical and/or mental disorder, first catalogued by the British physician Richard Morton, in 1694 (Brumberg, 1988, p. 298n). Around this time a new merchant class enjoyed personal ownership, wealth and leisure time, allowing for the power of the individual, previously in thrall to church or monarchy as super ordinate, regulating forces. The European enlightenment then valorized man's, but not women's mindfulness, his reason above his faith and feeling—the antidote to the misery of the all too mortal condition.

Psychoanalysis arose from this positivism. The new deity was critical thinking, but a woman's identity, once again, was not entirely new. Freud's famous cases of hysteria, central to his theory before 1923, describe repressed genital urges displaced to the mouth and throat, to the nose, all reflecting women's tendency towards the corporeal rather than the cortical. In one Technical Paper (1915, p. 166) in which Freud instructs readers regarding the handling of Transference Love, he opines that some women may even render therapeutic interpretation of meaning useless, for they are possessed, as he puts it, "of an elemental passionateness. They refuse, "Freud continues, "to accept the spiritual instead of the material; to use the poet's words they are amenable only to the logic of gruel and the argument of dumplings." Gruel and dumplings indeed, for what desire is more elemental than the body's hunger? That women might cogitate and modulate their activity was Freud's challenge to socially reified notions of inferior feminine, vs. idealized masculine tendencies.

Other of Freud's hopes were much more revolutionary. In fact, the radical feminist Shulamith Fierstone (1970, p. 45) writes that Feminism and Freudianism emerge from "the same stuff." Freud's normalization of women's sexual arousal and need for satisfaction were in direct opposition to previous cultural norms. Still, the Freudian body is, as Harris (2005, p. 1087) describes it, "raw." Freud's 1923 dynamic, structural model of mind may allow for its sexuality, but leans on the socially molded Ego to "cook" it.

Fairbairn's (1962) notion that the goal of the libido is the object itself—not simply gratification of an urge—was widely embraced later in this post war era, yet Fairbairn's emphasis on this more nuanced motivation did not pose a significant challenge to the primacy of reason over desire, particularly regarding notions of psychoanalytic technique and therapeutic action. The mark of the empowered analyst's professionalism, that is, remained his (male) "work ego," a perch from where he would apply his ideas to the swirling mess of the interactive moment. The sufferer would benefit from her analyst's mind, revealing, and helping her to know heretofore repressed conflicts around her desire for a baby, and/or for a penis.

Even if he did not embrace such metapsychological formulations, the father of the interpersonal psychoanalytic school, psychiatrist Harry Stack Sullivan, also remained the "expert" in his consulting room, similarly above the fray. He assumed this mantle despite a prescient awareness that the quality of relatedness—a two person field in the case of the consulting room—greatly determines individual experience. Ironically, he experienced himself as the healer in the context of mid twentieth century paternalistic Western medicine. If an unstudied immediacy in Sullivan's connections with his patients shines through in the few clinical transcripts to which we are privy, we encounter his "expert" voice in his published lectures and essays. The reactive patient and the reflective doctor, therefore, were scripted, regardless of the theoretical innovations of the clinician. Indeed, borrowing from Chodorow's (2004, p. 209) characterization, I, too, would refer to Sullivan and his followers of the time as "cultural ego psychologists."

Hilde Bruch, a pioneer in the study and treatment of eating disorders, who credits Harry Stack Sullivan as contributing to her sensibilities, did not necessarily concede her expert role in the consulting room either. Yet she was among the first to question Freud's focus on so called insight in his method of "cure." She observed behaviors among mothers, for instance, who assumed their daughter's feelings in advance. For instance, these parents would give up their seats to their eating-disordered youngsters during clinic visits in anticipation of the child's discomfort. As a result, any opportunity for offspring to *experience* moments of subjectivity in relation—much less manage their feelings and soothe themselves—was deprived them. Bruch's empirical findings confirm her observations that without opportunities to feel and manage their own discomfort, many of her patients could not accurately identify primal sensations of hunger, nor did they know how much to feed themselves.

This research propelled Bruch's therapeutic work forward. She realized that interpreting her patient's behavior according to what she referred to as "psychiatric dribble," (Hatch-Bruch, p. 254) would only perpetuate impositions on the sufferer's beleaguered, unformulated subjectivity. Words, ironically, would inhibit, rather than promote mindfulness for these individuals. As Bruch puts it (1973, p. 336).

The "traditional psychoanalytic setting where the patient expresses his secret thoughts and the analyst interprets their unconscious meanings . . . represents in a painful way a repetition of the significant interaction between patient and parents, where "mother always knew how I felt," with the implication that they themselves do not know how they feel.

With the benefit of the psychoanalytic dialogue that came after her, I also read Bruch's recognition of, and responsiveness towards the patient's subjectivity as an implicit challenge to the gender based hierarchy in the consulting room, one in which the reasonable, acculturated man manages—indeed reinterprets— the unreasonable, rebellious anorexic woman. Still, Bruch remains, ironically enough, identified with the (male) expert, part and parcel of her membership in what was then very much a boy's club, prescribing her empirically tested, universally applicable "technique" to be deliberately applied.

It was the interpersonal analyst Edgar Levenson (1972) who first suggested that this, or any sort of rule for the analyst's engagement is but a conceit. Therapeutic process, he has shown us, is less formally structured and deliberate, and indeed more experiential, more visceral. The self reflective analyst is instead always acting and reacting in a relational matrix, often outside his or her awareness, even with his silence, even with her words. Levenson is thus among the first post Cartesian, post modern thinkers within the positivist "faith" of psychoanalysis. It would take time, however, before his rather irreverent views reached center stage in the community.

Women from the albeit marginalized interpersonal psychoanalytic school from which Levenson also emerged—particularly Clara Thompson and Ruth Moulton (1972)—did question the so called phallocentricity of metapsychology, sensitive as they were to the impact of culture and society on psychic life. Yet it was the highly politicized and much more widespread feminist turn in the 1970s (See also Dimen, 1995, who elaborates on this distinction) that finally popularized Levenson's prescient, radical deconstruction of the psychoanalytic situation, one that questions the very nature of truth and authority.

In response to the fight for civil rights and the student protests against government and the university during the 1960s, the so called women's liberation movement spread far and wide the 1970s, largely via consciousness raising groups, where women met together in their homes. Soon they were emphatic about distinguishing these gatherings from traditional therapy. Why? In 1969, Carol Hanisch (2012, personal website), a founding member of the influential New York Radical Women's group, felt the need to write a memo clarifying exactly why clinical work ran counter to consciousness raising groups in which she participated in New York and in Florida: "Women are messed over, not messed up! We need to change the objective conditions, not adjust to them. Therapy is adjusting to your bad personal alternative."

Instead, she and her cohorts reckoned that the "personal is political This is part of the backdrop for a new breed of psychoanalysts who began to insist the opposite as well—that the political is also personal. Among others social theorists, they were inspired by French philosopher Michel Foucault, who deconstructed views and practices regarding mental illness to reveal institutional and theoretical tropes of inequity."

Where does Anorexia Nervosa fit into this picture? Recall Bruch's, and also my hypotheses that food refusal, the subject of this essay, is indeed about power. The self starving woman, is, once again, expressing her sense of powerlessness, but is also empowering herself, for she is out of reach of her doctor's mainstream, unembodied theory that employs symbolism, not action, to promote his version of health. Embodied—hysterical or emaciated or both—the "patient" remains immune from the constraints of a gendered psychiatric/psychoanalytic canon. In this way the starving patient is the fly in the ointment, the one who renders the logical theory and the praxis questionable. It is she, perhaps more so than other women who are less abjectly ambivalent and self destructive in their methods, who comes into the consulting room and prompts the psychoanalyst to reconsider an intellectual and socio cultural tradition.

Not surprisingly, the psychoanalysts who took up this challenge to analytic theory and technique came not only from the more male dominated, hierarchical medicine and related health professions, but also from the other social sciences. Nancy Chodorow, (2005, p. 1106) for instance, applied her formal sociological training to her feminist sensibility and early psychoanalytic work. As she explains, "I wrote "Being and Doing" (1972), which located the origins of male dominance in men's dread of women and fear of their own internal femininity."

Psychiatrist Jean Baker Miller (1976) and her colleagues at the Stone Center in Wellesley, Mass, similarly suggested that the accepted psychoanalytic separation–individuation developmental line—largely based on Margaret Mahler's work—reflects the socio political bias towards traditionally "masculine," autonomous assertiveness. Rugged individualism well represented in the iconic lonesome cowboy/hero is an example of such rejection of vulnerability via dependency. Instead Miller et al. introduced the notion of a mature interdependency or as Dimen (1995, p. 306) sums it up:

> Miller is fond of pointing out that behind every "autonomous" man stands a support staff of women—wives, mothers, secretaries, nurses, and so on (as well as, we should add, lower-status men, whose subordinate status feminizes them). "Relatedness," in other words, is as psychologically and socially salient as autonomy.

Relatedness is prompted by a hunger, by Fairbairn's primal yearning for the other. The lonesome cowboy, on the other hand, has somehow disposed of such needs and receptivity, or perhaps is made from different "stuff." As author Carole Spitzack (1990) claims, women who eschew hunger and eating are indeed rejecting their roles as emotionally excessive, striving instead for the cowboy ideal (Allison, Kuriloff, B.A., personal communication). Spitzack evokes Foucault here, who reminds that social power relations "become material in conceptions of the body itself." Consider, then, another twist on starvation as the perfect compromise: A defense against the shame and blame of devalued femininity, the identification with empowered masculine autonomy, but also, finally, the signal to the family, to the doctor, en masse to the culture that something is inherently amiss in our preferences, our values, our thinned out identities.

Dorothy Dinnerstein's (1976) psychoanalytically informed, now classic *The Mermaid and the Minotaur,* also examines gender binaries via women's shame ridden excesses—bodily and otherwise—as men's characterization, a defense against *their* conflicted yearning for the mother-breast of infancy from whom they must separate. Benjamin (1988) has elaborated the process by which "the boy "splits" the oedipal mother, preserving the more agentic, desiring aspects in his own consciousness and projecting the helpless dependency onto a feminine object (Sands, 2003, p. 107).

Consider in this regard Bruch's earlier understanding of her anorexic patient's enmeshment with their mothers. Many of today's feminist psychoanalysis would suggest that mothers are not merely—or not only—depriving their female children of their minds. In feeling and speaking for them, in anticipating their needs before they emerge, these mothers are perhaps also teaching their female children to "perform" (Butler, 1990) inculcated scripts of "femininity," to disavow, or at least to temper the bodily, primal affects and expressions that tempt, and thus threaten male supremacy. If Freud helped women overcome such constriction regarding their sexuality, later in his century hunger and eating became all the more shame and guilt ridden. In this way the late twentieth century mother functions as the conveyor and bastion of culture.

Brisman (2002), an interpersonal psychoanalyst who has revolutionized the treatment of eating disorders by focusing not only on the symptom itself, but also on the impact of such a focus on the therapeutic dyad, thus notes the very absence of desire in the back and forth between patient and analyst. She vivifies ways that analyst's measured words constrict, rather than reveal need in relation. Brisman (p. 339) puts the goal in the consulting room as "just the recognition of the desire itself." After sharing a clinical vignette, she ends, "It didn't matter why the patient and I were both wanting. It just mattered that we were."

The goal, then, is a less rigidly gendered, bifurcated consciousness. Anorexic women suffer amidst this elusive, unrealized promise—to be full bodied subjects in relation. Such interaction requires two subjects, hungry for each other in albeit asymmetrical ways, as that which actually feeds, or fails to nourish the process.

Psychoanalytic process has indeed changed in response to the post modern deconstruction of the analyst's "interpretation" as but his inevitable, culturally and privately driven participation in a powerfully intractable symptom. As Zerbe (2009) points out in her book, *Integrated Treatment of Eating Disorders,* recidivism rates for sufferers will remain high until psychoanalytically oriented clinicians become responsive not only to patient's unconscious conflicts represented in destructive habits with food, but also to their many developmental needs. Zerbe makes herself an active participant in this conversation, even supplying food for the abstaining patient as she becomes reacquainted with her hunger. However, like Brisman before her, Zerbe remains sensitive to the transference-countertransference issues that may result from such activity. The plot then thickens, but now there is more than one version of the narratives.

In 1995, at The William Alanson White Institute in New York, Jean Petrucelli and the late Catherine Stuart established the first center for Eating Disorders in a psychoanalytic setting, revolutionary for its focus on so called manifest content—or symptomatology—rather than exclusively upon latent, or symbolic interpretation of "meaning." Here principles of interpersonal psychoanalysis are integrated with many other treatment modalities. Candidates and graduates work alongside nutritionists, internists, psychopharmacologists and other professionals as they acknowledge, soothe, set limits, uncover, co-construct, and empower selves in relation.

References

Benjamin, J. (1988). *The bonds of love: Psychoanalysis, feminism, and the problem of domination.* New York: Pantheon.

Bloom, C., Gitter, S., Kogel, L., & Zaphiropoulos, L. (1994). *Eating problems. A feminist psychoanalytic treatment model.* New York: Basic Books.

Brisman, J. (2002). Wanting. *Contemp. Psychoanal., 38*: 329–343.

Bruch, H. (1972). *Eating disorders. Obesity, anorexia nervosa and the person within.* New York: Basic Books.

Brumberg, J. J. (1988). *Fasting girls. The history of anorexia nervosa.* New York: Vintage Books.

Butler, J. (1990). *Gender trouble: Feminism and the subversion of identity.* New York: Routledge.

Chodorow, N. J. (1994). *Femininities, masculinities, sexualities.* Lexington, KY: The University of Kentucky Press.

Chodorow, N. J. (2004). The American independent tradition. *Psychoanal. Dial., 14*: 207–232.

Chodorow, N. J. (2005). Gender on the modern-postmodern and classical-relational divide: Untangling history and epistemology. *J. Amer. Psychoanal. Assn., 53*: 1097–1118.

Dimen, M. (1995). The third step: Freud, the feminists, and postmodernism. *Am. J. Psychoanal., 55,* 303–319.

Dinnerstein, D. (1976). *The mermaid and the minotaur.* New York: Harper & Row.

Fairbairn, W. D. (1963). Synopsis of an object-relations theory of the personality. *Int. J. Psycho-Anal., 44*: 224–225.

Freud, S. (1923). The ego and the id. *The Standard Edition of the Complete Psychological Works of Sigmund Freud,* Volume XIX (1923–1925): The ego and the id and other works, 1–66.

Freud, S. (1915). *Observations on transference-love* (Further Recommendations on the Technique of Psycho-Analysis III). *The Standard Edition of the Complete Psychological Works of Sigmund Freud,* Volume XII (1911–1913): The case of Schreber, papers on technique and other works, 157–171.

Hanisch, C. (2012). The personal is political: the original feminist theory paper, www.carolhanisch.org/CHwritings/PIP.html

Harris, A. (1991). Gender as contradiction. *Psychoanal. Dial., 1,* 197–224.

Harris, A. (2005). Gender in linear and nonlinear history. *J. Amer. Psychoanal. Assn., 53,* 1079–1095.

Hatch-Bruch, J. (1996). *Unlocking the golden cage: An intimate biography of Hilde Bruch.* Carlsbad, CA: Gurze Books.

Levenson, E. A. (1979). *The fallacy of understanding.* New York: Basic Books.

Kurzweil, E. (1998). *The Freudians. A comparative perspective.* New Brunswick, NJ and London: Transaction Publishers.

Miller, J. B. (1976). *Toward a new psychology of women.* Boston: Beacon

Moulton, R. (1972). *Psychoanalytic reflections on women's liberation. Contemp. Psychoanal., 8*: 197–223.

Sands, C. (2003). *The subjugation of the body in eating disorders: A particularly female solution. Psychoanalytic Psychology, 20*: 103–116.

Sours, J. A. (1980). *Starving to death in a sea of objects. The anorexia nervosa syndrome,* New York: Aronson.

Spitzack, C. (1990). *Confessing excess: Women and the politics of body reduction.* Albany, New York: SUNY press.

Zerbe, C. (2008). *Integrated treatment of eating disorders.* New York: Norton.

INDEX

Note: 'f' after a page number indicates a figure.

Gangestad, S. 179
Gangestad, W. 179
Garofallou, L. (BODI) 302–7
Garver-Apgar, C. E. 179
gender development 59–60, 125
gender identity 59–73; clinical
  implications of 68; development of
  59–60; eating disorders and 60–3; self
  and relational experience dimension of
  63–7
gender identity disorder (GID) 61–2
general processes 294–7
Gentile, J. 124
gift giving: anorexia nervosa patients
  and 133–40; humanness aspect of
  134; overview 133–5; psychoanalytic
  position about 134; Tina vignette 135–9
Gimlin, D. 105, 109
Girls Will Be Girls vignette 68–72
Glover, E. G. 133, 134
going-on-being 106, 302
Goldberg, A. 250
Goldberg, B. 134
Goldner, V. 61, 104
Goleman, D. 294–5
gone wrongs 111
Gorden, K. (" 'Body and Soul': Eating
  Disorders in the Orthodox Jewish
  Population") 186–201
Gorkin, M. 249
Gottlieb, C. D. (" 'Come Together':
  Blending CBT/DBT and Interpersonal
  Psychotherapy in the Treatment of
  Eating Disorders") 269–82
Green, M. R. 248
Greene, B. 234
Greenfield, S. 37
Grief, D. 32

Halsted, E. 130, 282; " 'Stretched to the
  Limit': Body Image in the Reflexive
  Mind" 79–90
Hamilton, A. (" 'Sweet Thing': Racially
  Charged Transferences and Desire in
  the Interpersonal Treatment of a Black
  American Woman With Binge-Eating
  Disorder-Who Needs Chocolate Cake
  When You Can Have Chocolate Men?")
  231–42
Hanisch, C. 319
hippocampus, neural pathways in 37–8
historical trauma 46, 109

holes in Swiss cheese 208, 209–10, 217
Holocaust trauma 191–4
" 'Hooked on a Feeling': Emotions
  That Facilitate the Movement From
  Compulsion to Choice—Three
  Bodies. . . . Patient, Analyst, and
  Supervisor" (Buechler) 257–66
hormonal body 172, 173–4, 177, 183
hormonal cycle see cyclic hormonal cycle
hormones and sexuality 178–80
Horney, K. 174
Howard, J. C. (" 'Spitting Out the
  Demons': The Perils of Giving and
  Receiving for the Anorexic Patient")
  133–40
Howell, E. F. 108, 113, 164
humanness 134
hunger compulsion 39, 45, 47, 189, 193–4,
  258

" 'I Can See Clearly Now the Rain
  Has Gone': The Role of the Body
  in Forecasting the Future" (Ogden)
  92–101
identificatory love 65–6
implicit relational knowing 93–4
indwelling 303
I-ness 59
information-processing 40
Inge-Barry, L. 87
insula 295–8
Integrated Treatment of Eating Disorders
  (Zerbe) 321
integrative thinking 14
intergenerational transmission of
  embodiment 302–7
Internal Language Enhancement (ILE)
  288–300; emotional processing
  pathways 294–7; explained 288–90;
  frontal lobe development and 293–4;
  language development process 293;
  maternal care function and 291–3;
  program 297–8; protocol 299–300;
  right/left hemisphere communication
  and 293; risk factors 290–1; trigger
  material, nature of 298–9
International Journal of Eating Disorders
  182
interpersonal dream analysis 248
interpersonal field 152, 221
interpersonal neurobiology 36–40
interpersonal treatment 15, 48, 149, 152

religion 187, 199, 278, 281
restructuring 275–6
right hemisphere neural pathways 41–2
Rosman, B. L. 147
Rubenstein, B. 175

Sacred Therapy (Frankel) 266
safe surprises 45–6, 101
Samstag, N. 32, 54
Sands, S. 62, 198
Schnall, S. 98
Schoen, S. 32, 54, 130; "'You're the One
  That I Want': Appetite, Agency, and the
  Gendered Self " 59–74
Schore, A. N. 37, 40–1, 43, 93
secondary emotional reactions 275
Sedgwick, E. 63
selective inattention 26, 173
self-confrontation 262, 264
self-cure 36
self dimension, of gender identity 63–7
self-disclosure 116, 249, 250–1, 264, 265
self-identity development in Jewish
  adolescence 194, 195
self-image: menopause and 177–8; women
  and 106–7
self-object function 17–8
self-reflexivity 80
self-regulation 44–5
self-states 16, 99–100; cyclicity and
  175–6; defined 172; multiplicity of
  164–5
separation-individuation processes 64
sex drive: menopause and 177–8;
  treatment approach to reactivate 181
sexuality, hormones and 178–80
Shafran, R. 271
shidduchim 190–1
Siegel, A. 89
Siegel, D. 39, 96, 295; attachment 40–1
Slavin, J. H. 122, 130
Sliva, V. (BODI) 302–7
somatic narrative 93, 98, 101
Sperry, Roger 96
"'Spitting Out the Demons': The Perils of
  Giving and Receiving for the Anorexic
  Patient" (Howard) 133–40
Spitzack, C. 320
splitting 105–6; of mind and body 107–8
standing in the spaces 234–5
Stein, H. 134
Stern, D. 47

Still Face experiments (Tronick) 94–5
Still Practicing (Buechler) 260
"'Stretched to the Limit': Body Image in
  the Reflexive Mind" (Halsted) 79–90
Strober, M. 148
structural family therapy 147
Stuart, C. 321
subject-as-object distinction 127
subjective experience 42, 59, 64, 126,
  129
successful treatment, understanding of 15
Sullivan, H. S. 8, 14, 32, 174, 317–8;
  detailed inquiry 21, 22–3, 25, 26, 209;
  early epoch 159; juvenile epoch 157–8;
  preadolescence epoch 158
supervisory sessions, patient treatment
  257–66; absent body presence 260–1;
  concerns of 258–60; overview 257–8;
  shame of clinician and 263–6; theories
  and 262–3
surgical cultures, women and 104–17;
  culturally mandated scripts 108–10;
  mind and body, splitting of 107–8;
  overview 104–5; self-image 106–7;
  splitting 105–6; vignettes 110–7
*Surviving an Eating Disorder: Strategies
  for Family and Friends* (Siegel,
  Brisman, & Weinshel) 147
"'Sweet Thing': Racially Charged
  Transferences and Desire in the
  Interpersonal Treatment of a Black
  American Woman With Binge-Eating
  Disorder-Who Needs Chocolate Cake
  When You Can Have Chocolate Men?"
  (Hamilton) 231–42
symptomatology 121, 150, 198, 321
symptom-focused approaches to treatment
  18–9
symptom focused dynamic psychotherapy
  270
symptoms of eating disorders 14, 16

Tauber, E. S. 248
team approach 19
technological influences on treatment 18
Telch, C. F. 275
terrible twos 294
texting, food journaling and 31
"'The Circle (Cycle) Game': Ovarian
  Hormones, Self-States, and Appetites"
  (Kolod) 172–84
theory of mind 299

" 'These Boots *Aren't* Made for Walking, but That's Just What They'll Do': The Use of the Detailed Inquiry in the Treatment of Obesity" (Tintner) 207–18
Thompson, C. 319
Thornhill, R. 179
Tinder 105
Tintner, J. (" 'These Boots *Aren't* Made for Walking, but That's Just What They'll Do': The Use of the Detailed Inquiry in the Treatment of Obesity") 207–18
Todd, M. E. 94
Tortora, S. (BODI) 302–7
trauma/dissociation model 164
treatment of eating disorders: activities 275; affect 44–5; attachment 40–4; blending CBT/DBT and interpersonal 269–82; clinical relational moments 45–7; cognitive restructuring 275–6; contracting 26–30; cultural influences on 18; data, gathering in initial phase of treatment 21–2; detailed inquiry 22–6; family therapy 145–53; food journaling 31; food metaphors and metaphors as food 22; integrative thinking 14; interpersonal neurobiology 15, 36–40; meaning-centered long-term 18; mindfulness 274–5; obesity and detailed inquiry 217–8; pharmacological approaches in 283–5; psychoanalytically 14; relational treatment 15; self-monitoring via journals 274; self-regulation 44–5; successful, understanding 15; symptom-focused approaches 18–9; team approach 19; technological influences on 18; texting 31; uniqueness in 17–8
Tronick, E. Z. 93, 94–5, 97, 99
Tublin, S. 74

Under the Skin (Lemma) 115
uniqueness in treatment 17–8

vignettes: Alyx: Can I Have This Dance? 47–9; Carla: Witnessing a 'Kentucky Flying' Chicken 38–40; The Cat's in the Cradle: Attachment and Development 41–4; cosmetic cultures 110–7; Girls Will Be Girls 68–72; Kate 245–7, 251–6; Liza: What's Eating You? 49–52; Starving Soul of Lucy 20; Susie, binge eating 219–20, 222–9

Wachtel, P. L. 25
Walls, G. 130
Warner, H. 134
Watson, R. I., Jr. 248
Weinberger-Litman, S. 197
West, C. 235–6
" 'What's Going On, What's Going On?': An Interpersonal Approach to Family Therapy With the Eating-Disordered Patient" (Brisman) 145–53
William Alanson White Institute, Eating Disorders, Compulsions & Addictions Service at 8, 183, 321
Wilner, W. 253
Winnicott, D. W. 72, 116, 303; "going-on-being" 106
Wiser, S. 275
Wolfe, S. 61
women's liberation movement 319

" 'You're the One That I Want': Appetite, Agency, and the Gendered Self" (Schoen) 59–74
Yurgelun-Todd, D. 163–4

Zerbe, K. 32, 135, 321
Zwann, R. A. 98

Made in the USA
San Bernardino, CA
16 February 2016